CW00531170

Romanticism has often been associated with the mode of lyric, or otherwise confined within mainstream genres. As a result, we have neglected the sheer diversity and generic hybridity of a literature that ranged from the Gothic novel to the national tale, from monthly periodicals to fictionalized autobiography. In this new volume some of the leading scholars of the period explore the ways in which the Romantics developed genre from a taxonomical given into a cultural category, so as to make it the scene of an ongoing struggle between fixed norms and new initiatives. Focusing on non-canonical writers (such as Thelwall, Godwin, and the novelists of the 1790s), or placing authors such as Wordsworth and Byron in a non-canonical context, these essays explore the psychic and social politics of genre from a variety of theoretical perspectives, while the introduction looks at how genre itself was rethought by Romantic criticism.

ROMANTICISM, HISTORY, AND THE POSSIBILITIES OF GENRE

ROMANTICISM, HISTORY, AND THE POSSIBILITIES OF GENRE

Re-forming literature 1789–1837

EDITED BY

TILOTTAMA RAJAN

AND

JULIA M. WRIGHT

CAMBRIDGE
UNIVERSITY PRESS

PUBLISHED BY THE PRESS SYNDICATE OF THE UNIVERSITY OF CAMBRIDGE
The Pitt Building, Trumpington Street, Cambridge CB2 1RP, United Kingdom

CAMBRIDGE UNIVERSITY PRESS
The Edinburgh Building, Cambridge CB2 2RU, United Kingdom
40 West 20th Street, New York, NY 10011–4211, USA
10 Stamford Road, Oakleigh, Melbourne 3166, Australia

First published 1998

Printed in the United Kingdom at the University Press, Cambridge

Typeset in Baskerville 11/12½ pt [CE]

A catalogue record for this book is available from the British Library

Library of Congress cataloguing in publication data
Romanticism, history, and the possibilities of genre: re-forming literature
1789–1837 / ed. Tilottama Rajan and Julia M. Wright.
p.   cm.
Includes bibliographical references and index.
Contents: Godwin and the genre reformers / John Klancher – Radical print
culture in periodical form / Kevin Gilmartin – History, trauma, and the limits of the
liberal imagination / Gary Handwerk – Writing on the border / Ina Ferris – Genres
from life in Wordsworth's art / Don Bialostosky – A voice in the representation /
Judith Thompson – I am ill fitted / Julia M. Wright – Frankenstein as neo-Gothic /
Jerrold E. Hogle – Autonarration and genotext in Mary Hays' Memoirs of
Emma Courtney / Tilottama Rajan – The science of herself / Mary Jacobus – The
failures of romanticism / Jerome McGann.
ISBN 0 521 58192 3 (hardback)
1. English literature – 19th century – History and criticism.
2. Literature and history – Great Britain – History – 19th century.
3. Romanticism – Great Britain.   4. Literary form.
I. Rajan, Tilottama.   II. Wright, Julia M.
PR457.R459   1998
820.9'145 – dc21   97–6879 CIP

ISBN 0 521 58192 3 hardback

Contents

Notes on contributors

DON BIALOSTOSKY is Professor and Head of the English Department at Penn State University. His essay here develops further the Bakhtinian reading of Wordsworth's poetry he has argued for in *Making Tales: The Poetics of Wordsworth's Narrative Experiments* (Chicago University Press, 1984) and *Wordsworth, Dialogics and the Practice of Criticism* (Cambridge University Press, 1992) and the rhetorical reading he has developed in these books and, with Laurence Needham and others, in *Rhetorical Traditions and British Romantic Literature* (Indiana University Press, 1995).

INA FERRIS is Professor of English at the University of Ottawa. Her publications include *The Achievement of Literary Authority: Gender, History, and the Waverley Novels* (Cornell University Press, 1991) and various articles on nineteenth-century narrative. She is currently working on a book-length study of gender and the national tale in the early Romantic period.

KEVIN GILMARTIN is an Assistant Professor of Literature at the California Institute of Technology. He is the author of *Print Politics: The Press and Radical Opposition in Early Nineteenth-Century England* (Cambridge University Press, 1996), and of articles on English radical culture in the Romantic period.

GARY HANDWERK is Associate Professor in the Department of English and Comparative Literature at the University of Washington. He is author of *Irony and Ethics in Narrative* (Yale University Press, 1984) and essays on Joyce, Meredith, Lacan, F. Schlegel, Beckett, Disraeli, and Godwin, co-editor of *The Scope of Words* (Peter Lang, 1991), and translator of the forthcoming initial volume of Nietzsche's *Human, All Too Human* in the Stanford Press edition of the Complete Works of Nietzsche.

JERROLD E. HOGLE is Professor of English and University Distinguished Professor at the University of Arizona. Winner of numerous teaching awards and Guggenheim and Mellon fellowships for research, he has published extensively on Romantic poetry, most notably in *Shelley's Process* (Oxford University Press, 1988), and on Romantic and Gothic fiction. He is also the current President of the International Gothic Association.

MARY JACOBUS is Anderson Professor of English at Cornell University. Her books include *Tradition and Experiment in Wordsworth's Lyrical Ballads (1798)* (Oxford University Press, 1976), *Romanticism, Writing, and Sexual Difference: Essays on The Prelude* (Oxford University Press, 1989), and two books of feminist criticism, *Reading Woman* (Columbia University Press, 1986) and *First Things: The Maternal Imaginary in Literature, Art, and Psychoanalysis* (Routledge, 1995). She is the editor of *Women Writing and Writing about Women* (Croom Helm, 1979) and coeditor, with Sally Shuttleworth, of *Body/Politics: Women and the Representations of Science* (Routledge, 1989).

JON KLANCHER teaches at Boston University and is currently working on the disciplinary formations contributing to the history of British Romanticism. He is author of *The Making of English Reading Audiences 1790–1832* (University of Wisconsin Press, 1987), essays in Romanticism and cultural history, and advisory editor to World Wide Web humanities projects.

JEROME MCGANN is the John Stewart Bryan Professor of English, University of Virginia. He recently published *Poetics of Sensibility: A Revolution in Literary Style* (Clarendon Press, 1996).

TILOTTAMA RAJAN is Professor of English and Director of the Center for Theory at the University of Western Ontario, and has also taught at Queen's and the University of Wisconsin-Madison. She is the author of *Dark Interpreter: The Discourse of Romanticism* (Cornell University Press, 1980) and *The Supplement of Reading: Figures of Understanding in Romantic Theory and Practice* (Cornell University Press, 1990), and has coedited (with David Clark) *Intersections: Nineteenth-Century Philosophy and Contemporary Theory* (SUNY Press, 1995). She is currently working on Romantic narrative, and also on a study of the relationship between phenomenology and deconstruction in French theory of the sixties and early seventies.

JUDITH THOMPSON is Assistant Professor of English at Dalhousie University. She has published several articles on John Thelwall, is currently finishing an edition of his *The Peripatetic*, and is working on a book on Thelwall's intertextual relationship with Coleridge and Wordsworth.

JULIA M. WRIGHT is Assistant Professor of English at the University of Waterloo. She has published essays on a number of subjects, including Blake, Peacock, Fielding, and Carroll, and is currently working on a study of Irish literature of the Romantic period.

Acknowledgments

The stimulus for this volume came from the inaugural conference of the North American Society for the Study of Romanticism (NASSR) on "Romanticism and the Ideologies of Genre," held at the University of Western Ontario in August 1993. Although a majority of the papers in this volume were not actually presented there, all but one of our contributors participated in the conference, and we would accordingly like to express our appreciation to the organizing committee of the conference which, in an indirect way, helped to make this volume possible. Shannon Hartling and Joel Faflak have been of invaluable help in the preparation and checking of the manuscript, and our thanks also go to them, as well as to the University of Waterloo, which helped with funds for this purpose through a general grant provided by the Social Sciences and Humanities Research Council of Canada. Finally we would like to express our gratitude to Josie Dixon, who has encouraged this project from its inception and offered invaluable advice on all aspects of the manuscript from the technical to the substantive.

We are grateful to the trustees of Boston University for permission to reprint Tilottama Rajan's "Autonarration and Genotext in Mary Hays' *Memoirs of Emma Courtney*" which first appeared in a slightly longer version in *Studies in Romanticism*, 32:2 (1993), 149–76. Parts of Jerome McGann's "The Failures of Romanticism" have already appeared in chapter 15 of his recent book, *The Poetics of Sensibility: A Revolution in Literary Style* (Oxford: Clarendon Press, 1996), hereby acknowledged. Jon Klancher's "Godwin and the Genre Reformers: On Necessity and Contingency in Romantic Narrative Theory" is a considerably changed and refocused version of his article "Godwin and the Republican Romance: Genre, Politics and Contingency in Cultural History" (*Modern Language Quarterly*, 56 [1995], 145–65).

Finally Judith Thompson's "'A Voice in the Representation': John Thelwall and the Enfranchisement of Literature" is also a considerably revised and expanded version of her paper "John Thelwall and the Politics of Genre 1793/1993," which appeared in a special conference issue of *The Wordsworth Circle*, 25: 1 (1994), 21–25.

Introduction

Tilottama Rajan and Julia M. Wright

Genres are often seen prescriptively as a means of interpellating the subject into existing norms and hierarchies. Tzvetan Todorov, however, may well be closer to articulating the essential fluidity of the category when he argues that genres often originate as speech acts, though not all speech acts are immediately institutionalized as genres. If genres are confined to "the classes of texts that have been historically perceived as such,"[1] their classification is inevitably bound to the ideology of a society that chooses to encode only certain forms as genres. On the other hand the fact that there are uncategorized speech acts with the potential to become genres leaves a space for individual or collective intervention in existing system(s) of genre which must therefore be considered highly unstable. This situation is further complicated because the discursive and metadiscursive existence of genres do not necessarily coincide: a genre may have existed in the early nineteenth century but may not have been named until recently. Both in literary practice and in our discussions of it, genre is thus the site of a constant renegotiation between fixed canons and historical pressures, systems and individuals.

The essays collected here focus on genre as the privileged locus for a revaluation of cultural values, both because Romantic literature is characterized by its generic experimentation, and because the aesthetics of the long Romantic period correspondingly edges towards what seem "modern" questions about genre, its historicity, the very viability of the category, and the viability of the hierarchies by which generic law is maintained. In the Renaissance generic options also proliferate as thematic criteria replace the formal and technical differentials used by the Aristotelian tradition, but these genres (of which Scaliger lists over a hundred)[2] are arrayed in synchronic rather than diachronic fashion. Romantic critics, however, show a new awareness of the historicity and even the cultural specificity of genres. Thus Peacock postulates four ages of poetry, in the last of which, the age of bronze, poetry itself becomes obsolete at the hands of prose. Shelley famously counters in *The Defense of Poetry* by insisting on the transhistorical nature of a "Poetry" that differs from narrative and drama in not being subject to material contingency, but it is clear that his refusal to historicize genre is itself a historical response to a new generic economy. Like Peacock, Victor Hugo in the "Preface" to *Cromwell* periodizes literature, identifying the lyric, epic, and dramatic forms with the primitive, ancient, and modern epochs respectively.[3] Clara Reeve (and later Friedrich Schelling) recognize that genres which are culturally exhausted die or are displaced into other genres, as in the survival of epic and romance through the novel.[4] Sometimes these histories are deterministic in matching periods to genres and modes, as in the case of Peacock and Hugo. Alternatively, when they see genre as a scene of cultural competition (as Reeve does in mapping the struggle between novel and romance), they tend to harness ideology for the purposes of education rather than to critique it.[5] Nevertheless the emphasis of these critics on historicity is the condition of possibility for what it stops short of: namely an analysis of genres in terms of their specifically ideological investments, and of ideology itself as chosen and capable of modification rather than as historically predestined.

We shall return to the specific ways in which issues of culture and canonicity are played out even in the relatively conservative "histories" described above. But it is important to recognize that the Romantics (particularly in Germany) do not restrict themselves to seeing genres as determinate and singular categories monolithically identified with certain time-spans. Thus Hegel's *Aesthetics* likewise constructs a grand narrative in which a succession of *Gestalten* or modes (the Symbolic or Oriental, the Classical, and the Romantic) is seemingly matched to a series of art-forms (architecture, sculpture, and poetry/painting/music). But Hegel also sees each art-form as passing through its various modes, thus creating a system of permutations that recognizes style or mode as a cultural category, while deploying it as an analytic tool as well as a historical determinant. Nor does everyone follow Hugo in using "history" to maintain a restricted economy organized around what Alastair Fowler calls the "central" genres of lyric, drama, and epic, with "extended literature" relegated to an uncertain periphery.[6] Goethe has indeed been seen as the father of a canonically "Romantic" system confined to the central genres, which he normalizes as the three "natural" forms of poetry,[7] and this transcendental classification is also assumed by Shelley, who discusses only poetry, "story," and drama. But Friedrich Schlegel's famous distinction between natural and invented poetry (*Natur-* and *Kunstpoesie*) locates these natural forms only in classical literature, while identifying "romantic" or "modern" literature with the invention of a variety of new genres. Although Schlegel initially uses his distinction to dismiss extended literature as *"interessant"* or trendy, he increasingly comes to valorize modern variety, and on closer inspection even finds this variety in classical literature. In effect he realizes that the distinction between *natural* and *invented* is metadiscursive: that it describes a difference between classical and Romantic *theories* of genre, rather than privileging the central genres because they came first.[8] Schlegel thus stands on the verge of a radical redefinition of genre, and raises an issue crucial to the essay by Jon Klancher with which this volume begins: namely the question of whether it is not only genres themselves, but also the way we systematize them, that is profoundly historical.

Schlegel's provocative statement that "every poem [is] a genre for itself" is not meant to render the term useless, especially given his insistence that we desperately "lack" a theory of genre. Instead he means to question not the usefulness of classifying but the "rigid purity" of the "classical" genres. According to Schlegel nothing is so insignificant that it cannot "contribute something to the definition of some species," and the "species" he mentions thus include everything from travel writings and Dutch paintings to sighs and kisses.[9] This new inclusiveness responds to the emphasis on original genius by William Duff and Edward Young,[10] and to a literary experimentation in which England was as prolific as Germany was rich in theory. It also takes up the expansion of the literary economy begun more empirically (and cautiously) by eighteenth-century critics who recovered marginal or antiquarian genres such as the ballad (in the case of Thomas Percy) or subcanonical genres such as romance (in the case of Richard Hurd and Clara Reeve).[11] But that Schlegel's examples include cultural as well as literary phenomena reflects another aspect of Romantic theory: namely its search for alternative vocabularies to the purely literary category of genre (Bakhtin's "chronotope" being a contemporary example). In the aesthetic theory of the long Romantic period, "mode" and "mood" thus come to be as important as genre. These cognates, in turn, refigure the category of genre itself, unravelling the distinction between central genres and extended literature.

Modes are often thought of as adjectival derivatives of genre, so that "elegy" names a genre while "elegiac" desribes a mode that occurs across genres.[12] But the equivalent term in German Romantic aesthetics, though also thematic rather than formal, refers to a much broader category: whether it be Hegel's *Gestalt* – the "shape" assumed by a certain form of cultural consciousness – or Schiller's *Empfindungsweise* – meaning mode of experience, or sensibility. Thus conceived, "mode" radicalizes "genre" in two ways. To begin with, when Schiller distinguishes the terms in *Naive and Sentimental Poetry* by defining mode phenomenologically,[13] he also changes the way we approach genre, as an expression of (cultural) consciousness rather than a purely formal category. Secondly, the adjectival definition is inherently conservative in tying mode to a parental *literary* genre, such that the mode of pastoral can occur only when the (sub)genre of eclogue is already in place. But the modes discussed by Romantic theorists do not necessarily have antecedent genres. They can include forms of cultural sensibility such as Schiller's "sentimental," artistic styles such as the grotesque, or tropes that have been expanded into forms of experience, such as Kierkegaard's "irony." This looser usage persists in our own references to the "mode" of print. If modes are a mechanism for bringing new material into culture, they differ from subgenres because what they add is not restricted to what has been encoded as literature. By expanding literature to engage it with other areas of experience, modes also expand the range of genre, defined more narrowly as a "kind" with specific formal features. For the relationship between mode and genre is fluid, particularly where the mode generates the genre as a transposition into literature of changes occurring at the level of social life – as in the epistolary novel, discussed in two of the essays here.

Another cognate to genre is "mood" or *Stimmung*, traces of which exist in earlier theory, but which is first named and legitimized only in the Romantic period.[14] Kant's *Critique of Judgment* is exemplary in this respect, in that it approaches the sublime and the beautiful as others might approach romance and epic. What is significant in Kant is not the mood he analyzes, but the fact that he deems worthy of discussion what Jean-François Lyotard describes as a pre-conceptual "representation" that exceeds what we can grasp in a "form."[15] Though the moods that concern us may be different, the recovery of melancholy as aesthetically significant material (discussed in Mary Jacobus' essay) has been invisibly helped by the Romantic emphasis on the feelings as having their own value. Like mode, mood therefore exerts a reciprocal pressure on the conservatism of genre. Not only does it make affect part of generic analysis, but by recognizing that affect may have "genres" that need to be named, it concedes that there are forms of subjectivity that fail to find expression in "genre" and for which new genres need to be found.

The essays gathered here explore with reference to Romantic texts the expansion, and at times questioning, of the category "genre" discussed so far in Romantic theory and criticism. With two exceptions they deal with non-canonical writers such as John Thelwall and Mary Hays or sub-canonical ones such as William Godwin and Mary Wollstonecraft, because the relative lack of criticism on them and thus of preconceptions about them makes it easier to locate their distinctiveness in the ways they extended genre. But it may be that our own reading of the six canonical authors (all poets) has normalized their work so as to fit it into the central genres, thereby protecting a notion of "literature" that was theoretically instituted in the Romantic period,[16] even as it was being questioned in the "unwritten poetics" produced by the writers themselves. Thus we can ask if Wordsworth has been read in certain ways (first approvingly and then critically) because his work has been represented by the mode of lyric, and whether a change in the generic lenses through which we see his texts might not shift the current figuration of his corpus as transcendentally idealistic.[17] Don Bialostosky's essay is precisely such an attempt to defamiliarize Wordsworth by reading the *Lyrical Ballads* not as a homogenization of differences within the central mode of lyric, but as an experiment with extended genres that forces us to rethink how we ourselves classify speech acts.

The essays in this volume share a further assumption. In a curious return to the matching of periods with genres characteristic of some Romantic criticism, modern critics often identify Romanticism with the mode (if not the genre) of lyric, thus allowing us to critique the transcendentalism of the "Romantic ideology."[18] Our contributors, however, start from a sense that many Romantic writers are between cultures and ideologies, and thus between genres. This mobility can be reflected in the way individual texts move amongst genres, as Judith Thompson argues with reference to Thelwall's miscellany *The Peripatetic*, or work "aslant" of them, as Ina Ferris suggests with reference to the national tale, which cuts across a historical novel that more hegemonically represents the public sphere. Sometimes, as in the essay by Jerome McGann, it is reflected in the way a genre circulates between different users, so as to become the means by which cultural norms are not only encoded but also rethought.

Rather than attributing fixed social or political identities to genres, we might therefore think of them as forms with a "sedimented content" and history. As Fredric Jameson suggests, they carry "a host of distinct . . . messages – some of them objectified survivals from older modes of cultural production, some anticipatory."[19] Genres are "shifters," to adapt a term used by Emile Benveniste in connection with personal pronouns: like the pronoun "I," which is an existing grammatical position available to new tenants, they produce the subject in a shifting conjunction of past usage(s) with present appropriation.[20] Conceiving of genres as shifters would mean that they are not so much fixed "positions" in the socioliterary system as "transpositions."[21] At the same time, they would also be points of entry into this system, "discursive marker[s] through which [the subject] assumes linguistic identity," and thus forms that determine identity but also provide "the possibility of subjectivity" for both individuals and groups.[22]

Conceiving genres as a mobile category returns us to the question with which we began: that of the relationship between genre and history, and of whether the inscription of genre in literary history marks an attempt to radicalize or to codify genre. Eighteenth-century and Romantic attempts to produce conservative narratives of cultural evolution used genre to plot stages in that progress, rendering genre culturally determined rather than culturally determining. From John Aikin's *Essays on Song-Writing* (1770) and Thomas Warton's *History of English Poetry* (1774), both reprinted throughout the Romantic period, to William Hazlitt's *Select Poets of Great Britain* (1825) and Robert Southey's *Select Works of the British Poets* (1831), a flurry of anthologies was produced during the period, each seeking to outline a national tradition that would plot the evolution of literature to its current civilized state. Warton's Preface characterizes a chronological arrangement as an innovation in the genre of anthologies that is required to sustain the narrativization of cultural history as evolutionary, "to pursue the progress of our national poetry, from a rude origin and obscure beginnings, to its perfection in a polished age."[23] In Southey's anthology, a genealogy of genres is produced, as Southey historicizes genre by anchoring each form's entrance into English letters to a historical origin while representing the form itself as transcendental: Surrey, Southey writes, "was the first English poet who wrote metrically; and the first who used blank verse" and Sackville "was joint author of our first regular tragedy,"[24] historicizing use rather than invention. Organizing the corpus of English literature into a tradition of national literary explorers, discovering the genres of modern letters, supported the aims of the hegemony by validating the present culture as the epitome of civilization and providing a heritage in support of a national identity that was, as Marilyn Butler puts it, "comforting."[25] But this project is fraught with unexamined tensions which emerge in the literary histories' attempts to appear inclusive and comprehensive while validating the genres of the elite. Thus Southey must anxiously protect elitist genres from non-elite authors in his prefatory essay, "Lives and Works of our Uneducated Poets" (1831), by calling attention to cases of generic failure rather than success.

We see the same anxiety when Hazlitt nervously identifies the Lake Poets' innovations with political anarchism, even associating the declining use of capitals with the decapitations of the French Revolution:

There was a mighty ferment in the heads of statesmen and poets, kings and people . . . Nothing that was established was to be tolerated . . . [C]apital letters were no more allowed in print, than letters-patent of nobility were allowed in real life; kings and queens were dethroned from their rank and station in legitimate tragedy or epic poetry, as they were decapitated elsewhere.[26]

By putting so many cultural eggs in one basket by codifying and formalizing the associative links that tie authors to genres, literature to national culture, and the English canon to international relations, however, conservative histories thus prove vulnerable to the "contingency" that Jon Klancher (in our first essay) associates with their opponents. The writers discussed by our contributors reject the inertial model of generic force, in which genres function as predetermined evidence of progress along a predestined cultural evolutionary narrative, and invert conservative causality to suggest that cultural intervention can alter social evolution. Their project, however, develops from the cracks in the conservative unfolding of the category "history" – from the presence within this very tradition of something that works against, aslant, or underneath it, evading its closure and so subverting its totalizing claims.

The essays in this collection are concerned with the location of the firm place upon which to ground the generic lever that will move the world, and are arranged according to their subjects' sense of this location. The first group assumes that change must occur in the public sphere, as writers pry open the very category of "history," so as to explore the sometimes unpredictable relationships between subjects and the forces that affect them. The second group addresses the contesting discourses that exist in the social sphere, and thinks the (im)possibility of change in terms of the (im)permeability of the borders between them. In the final section the focus is shifted from the broad sweep of history and the heterogeneity of the social to examine and challenge the production of the private sphere. Genre thus emerges as a cultural tool rather than a formal category, a powerful instrument for social change. At the same time the outcome of generic reform is far from certain: the very arrangement of the sections is supplementary and marks the permeability of each sphere to the questions raised from within other spheres of experience.

The essays in the first section, "Genre, History, and the Public Sphere," focus on attempts to pry open sociopolitical paradigms through generic reform that offers a challenge to the model of history as progress propounded by Burke and other conservatives of the day. In "Godwin and the Genre Reformers: On Necessity and Contingency in Romantic Narrative Theory," Klancher discusses Godwin's enabling of such a challenge through his advocacy of contingency in a historiographical model which posits that minor changes in context have serious effects on the course of history. In this context, the kind of historical romance supported by Godwin enacts contingency by putting history and romance, the now-opposed genres of literary discourse, in unresolveable competition with undeterminable effects, "pursuing investigative historical-generic practices that might work against the self-assurance of modernity by excavating the 'materials' of possible histories that might have been made – or might yet be made" (34–35) and emphasizing individual agency rather than a national manifest destiny. Godwin's concern with the broader definition of literature also reminds us that our own notion of "literature" is a postromantic construction, itself shaped by historical contingency.

It is the broader idea of literature that is the focus of Kevin Gilmartin's essay, "Radical Print Culture in Periodical Form." In the radical periodicals of the later Romantic period, Gilmartin finds another subversive model in which the contingency of history is not based upon the gritty detail (the "grain of sand") but upon a larger sense of crisis, even apocalyptic crisis, in the ongoing struggle between the hegemony and the radical press. His essay details the ways in which generic distinctions often emerged explicitly in legislation, forcing a constant renegotiation of generic form in a far more confrontational climate as small periodicals struggled with the full force of the increasingly oppressive law. In order to retain their public efficacy, radical periodicals had to take full advantage of technological advances to be responsive to their changing subject matter, the shifting political landscape, and the minefield of government censorship, but their very responsiveness made them well-suited to the ideological disarray of the time. Topical rather than theoretical, dynamic rather than stable, and interventional rather than aloofly representational, this generic sensitive plant posed a "protean threat" (43) to the hegemony that was bound up in the prevailing sense of political crisis.

This struggle for dominance and the power to silence are likewise addressed in Gary Handwerk's essay. But there the struggle takes place within the historical subject, and society's sense of crisis is replaced with that subject's psychological trauma. With ideology, the substructure of any "law-governed" notion of history, on one side, and psychology on the other, Godwin represents the subject of history as trapped between irreconcilable, and mutually unintelligible, positions. Focusing on *St. Leon* and *Mandeville*, Handwerk explores the ways in which the novels "amplify and complicate Godwin's own understanding of history" (67), locating them on the crux between the Enlightenment and Romanticism, and between history and the historical subject. In this project, the novel functions as a form of non-institutional history that can also engage psychological barriers to the sweeping march of progress envisioned in Godwin's own *Political Justice*. This counter-movement is embodied through repetition rather than linearity, identifying epochs and anticipating the recurrence of certain kinds of historical events in a way that marks the incursion of other forces into the stream of history. Despite an optimistic claim in *Political Justice* for the power of fiction to effect psychic change, Handwerk argues, Godwin's novels remain fundamentally pessimistic and unable to envision a synthesis between the rational and the Romantic, or history and the subject. The tension between subject and history remains unresolved, leaving an unintegrated hybrid with visible, and vulnerable, grafts.

In Ferris' discussion of Lady Morgan's national tale, the power of the concept of progressive history is acknowledged but then complicated by the proliferation of such histories, as multiple, interpenetrating narratives unsettle coherence in ways that recall Handwerk's analysis of Godwin. Lady Morgan, Ferris notes, "perceived her writing as a public act," as a performative intervention in the public sphere that was predicated upon a "liberal belief in public opinion" (88) and validated through her disavowal of politics in favor of a patriotism founded upon the extension of familial affection to its national correlate. In Morgan's strategy, the competition between linear and non-linear time is gendered while remaining roughly commensurate with the Enlightenment/Romantic tension addressed by Klancher and Handwerk. Linear time is thus identified with the "rational male patriot" (91) of Morgan's later novels, *The O'Briens and the O'Flahertys* and *Florence Macarthy*, and his assumptions are unsettled by a female figure who occupies a non-linear temporality, a form of the "women's time" described by Julia Kristeva that is "diagonal," meeting linear history "aslant" (94), and acting in ways that often mirror Morgan's own interventions in the course of hegemonic history. Ferris' essay offers a different perspective on the efficacy of linear histories: instead of being powerfully constraining, they are self-limiting, and so vulnerable to the kind of disruptive temporality and the generic excess that unite both Morgan's heroines and the radical periodicals.

As the essays in the first section suggest, to reform the genre of historical narrative by replacing continuity with disruption, evolution with revolution, and predestination with contingency, is not only to challenge the coherent narratives which served conservative interests but to raise the question of change. Godwin, Morgan, and the writers and editors of the radical press sought to alter the sociopolitical domain by using genre as a form of cultural intervention. They sought to change the very shape of history writing by drawing on new modes such as periodicals and travel-writing to hybridize the more conventional genres of historiography and the historical novel. The dynamic effect of new cultural modes on the inertia of genre is likewise the subject of several essays in the second section, "Genre and Society," which extend the possibilities for change from the public sphere of history into the more diversified sphere of the social.

Drawing on Bakhtin's discussion of "speech genres," Bialostosky raises the question of whether genre can any longer be restricted to the literary kinds. In Wordsworth's experiment with genre in the *Lyrical Ballads*, he argues, genre becomes a transpositional space in which art and life rewrite each other, and in which readers must reflect on what they are doing when they read poems within particular literary frames. Conspicuous in his refusal to include such frames in the 1798 edition, Wordsworth anticipates Bakhtin's project of expanding discourse to include the genres of everyday life. He introduces an array of heterogeneous and sometimes paradoxical genres, including anecdotes, epitaphs not attached to a tomb, and artless sob stories told artfully. Correspondingly he also constitutes the social as a hybrid and distinctly unHabermasian consensus by breaking it up into various intersecting subspheres, including the public way as a sphere of communication, the extended family, and the literary. As interesting as Wordsworth's anticipation of Bakhtin is the way Bialostosky uses Wordsworth to *extend* Bakhtin. For Bakhtin sees speech genres as specific to certain spheres and thus makes them agents of class(ification), aiming ultimately at a taxonomy (though not a hierarchy) of speech genres. But Bialostosky makes them agents of destratification by exploring the hybrid nature of the term "speech genre" as a category that transfers life and art into each other. In effect speech genres collapse the project of genre as taxonomy, by returning the literary to the primary flux of the social. As important, since the "social" for Wordsworth is the everyday, the new forms that arise from life and its interactions are strictly temporary, thus encouraging us to reconceive genre itself as a purely local and "contingent" category.

While Wordsworth's experiment is epistemologically radical, it is his contemporary John Thelwall who develops the (de)stratification of genres in a more specifically political direction. In her essay, Judith Thompson addresses the implications of "generic transformation as a social act" (122) by examining the play of "intergeneric conversation" in Thelwall's polyvocal work, *The Peripatetic*. The reflection on the ideological investments of genre that arises from that mixing of generic forms and perspectives facilitates the emergence of a more democratized discursive field. The elitism implicit in the term "high Romanticism" is confounded by Thelwall's deconstruction of the socio-literary architecture behind that familiar phrase to make possible its reconstruction along different taxonomical principles, generating a more democratic system of polyvocal circulation rather than a hierarchical structure founded upon class distinctions of all types that segregates and censors. Addressing Thelwall's political writings, particularly *The Rights of Nature* (the author's contribution to the Burke-Paine debate), Thompson notes that his support for a more equitable distribution of economic power – as labor and property – is linked to his support for a similar liberalization of the distribution of intellectual labor and property, a project that emerges in *The Peripatetic* as an attempt to generate a "cooperative information economy" (128). By aligning the arbitrary with global codes and the natural with local subjects, Thelwall creates a public forum in which these personal expressions jostle against each other without being resolved into a codifiable pattern – a dynamic generic heterogeneity that surfaces with more positive consequences than in a contemporary text, Eliza Fenwick's *Secrecy*, discussed in the next essay by Julia Wright.

In Wright's essay, the "intergeneric conversation" discussed by Thompson does not create a liberating explosion of democratically empowered voices but marks the divisions implicit in the definition of democracy as polyvocal. These divisions are not only economic, but cultural and generically constituted as well as generically reflected. Romantic, gothic, libertinist, and didactic genres are deployed in Fenwick's novel not to empower marginalized voices, but to mark their marginalization. The common generic field of the letter – outside of the category of literature, whether broadly or narrowly defined, because of its informal, private, and feminine status – is submerged in the battle that is played upon it, the battle to control literary taxonomies that, by exclusion, demarcate stable essentials such as "truth," "morality," and the distribution of power within society. Lord Filmar, in an anticipation of Byron and Byronic irony, offers self-reflexivity as a way of undoing the self-assuredness that allows the others to wrap themselves up in their generic perspective and presume to try to impose it on others. In Filmar, the writing subject is exposed not as an individual member of a particular class or cultural group, but as the locus of disparate and irreconcilable cultural threads, the heterogeneous and hybrid product of a complex sociocultural space that must remain polyvocal and irreconcilably segregated. The social collapses into multiple competing discourses concealed within the liberal mode of the epistle which seems to promise interiority and consensus, so that the only solution is to internalize diversity through irony.

In the final essay of this section, Jerrold Hogle further explores this fragmentation through a psychoanalysis of capitalism as it is (dis)figured in the Gothic from Walpole to Mary Shelley. As Hogle has argued elsewhere, Gothic's link to capital is apparent in the architectural mode of the neo-Gothic and the social tendencies it houses.[27] Inaugurating the genre by transplanting into literature the faked conglomeration of styles used in his own estate-house, Walpole creates a form that is both a trope for how capitalism functions and a vehicle of its de/regeneration. In the present essay, Hogle sees the neo-Gothic castle as encrypting traces of various contemporary social texts: mercantile, scientific, and most importantly patriarchal. Concealing its desires within forms and characters left over from the past, it also houses them behind the façade of a fake unity. Its conglomeration of discourses thus parallels the structure of capital as a form that accumulates rather than uses productive forces. But the neo-Gothic is not just a mirror of capitalist production, it is also the trauma created by the latter's legitimation crisis. On the one hand it reflects a society whose authority, like Walpole's castle, comes from counterfeiting the new as the old. On the other hand, as it develops from Walpole to Mary Shelley, it increasingly becomes the psychic abject created by such fakery: a genre haunted by the ghosts of its own past, by guilt, monstrosity, and violence. The neo-Gothic thus seems to dismember the very project of generic reform already questioned by Handwerk, particularly since as "abject" it is betwixt and between in a traumatic way, and not in the fruitfully hybrid way discussed in the essays on Morgan and Thelwall. In this sense Hogle's argument has certain affinities with Handwerk's, but with one major difference: whereas Handwerk sees history as stopped by trauma, Hogle historicizes trauma, locating *Frankenstein* within a *history* of its genre and thus placing it within the political unconscious as a compulsive repetition that is also a traumatized rereading of the neo-Gothic.

The essays in the second section still assume that the social sphere can be a place for generic renegotiation. But there may also be a history beyond hi(story) and society: a history that does not get written, as Hans Kellner suggests.[28] In recovering for critical narrative a region of experience that resists being *posited*, the contributors to the final section on "Genre, Gender, and the Private Sphere" locate a *negativity* in excess of generic self-fashionings. It is no accident that the term "negativity" assumes philosophical prominence in the nineteenth century in the work of Hegel and (more darkly) the late Schelling. While "negation" remains predicative in rejecting an existing position so as to affirm itself through op(position), "negativity" is more radically and restlessly a movement between trans-positions none of which express the subject,[29] a remainder that resists being economized within positions that are adopted only as a difference from what they are not. Whether this radical negativity can be brought into some productive relationship with progressive history is the question Hegel leaves for the theorists on whom our final three contributors (as well as Hogle) draw. Georges Bataille, Baudrillard, and Kristeva all wrestle with the problem of an "unusable" negativity. For our contributors this negativity surfaces in the personal sphere, and calls into question the very economy of genre, considered as what Claudio Guillen calls "a problem-solving" mechanism that matches "form" and "matter," through a "symbolic resolution"[30] of the tensions between social codes and historical or psychic materiality.

In her essay on *Memoirs of Emma Courtney*, Tilottama Rajan discusses how Mary Hays displaces her life into her fiction in order to interrogate social and literary convention from the vantage-point of her own failed romance with William Frend. What Rajan describes as "autonarration" functions as a double negative in which the author's life is fictionalized, both to defamiliarize the social texts by which it has been written, and to make us speculate on how this life could be written otherwise, but through narratives whose imaginary resolution would still involve socially coded misrepresentations of the subject. Autonarration is not fiction, since its genesis in the life of a real person lends urgency to its attempt to *affect* change. But it is not autobiography, since it puts under erasure the notion that the subject can tell her own story. Instead Rajan defines it as an "intergenre" across which the reader senses what cannot quite be represented in the existing genres of life or art. Rajan's view of the relation between genre and subjectivity can thus be contrasted with that of Ferris, who is also concerned with a transpositional and contingent subject for whom discourses are shifters. But while Morgan's heroine *is* the position she occupies for the moment, Emma Courtney emerges more negatively as the difference between positions she cannot comfortably occupy.

Whereas Rajan defines in autonarration a *mode* that transfers affect into textuality, Mary Jacobus takes up the challenge posed by *mood* to genre. Jacobus' starting-point is the manual of female education as an encoding of liberal and rationalist values. But she deals with this genre only at the point of its transposition into "the fictionalized scene of female enlightenment" (248), through a series of novels that force one to encounter public discourse on the ground of the personal. Significantly the resistance to enlightenment is not formalized in an oppositional genre but emerges in a melancholia that conveys an unhappiness with the way things are, crystallized around the loss of the mother. But whether affect (like trauma in Handwerk's essay) stalls generic reform is a question with which the essay continues to affect us. On the one hand, although from a writer's viewpoint moods are "abjects" or waste material that she does not know how to integrate, by tracing the circulation of melancholy through a number of texts the *critic* puts it to epistemic use. Jacobus thus constructs melancholy as an ante(i)-discourse facilitating the emergence of new forms of feminine subjectivity. On the other hand by locating "resistance" in mood rather than generic strategy, she also knots its political potential back into its psychoanalytic implications.

The question of a mood that produces and unsettles generic reform returns in our final essay on the elegy, which deals not only with the literal experience of loss but also with what is lost by genre from literary history. Drawing on Bataille's distinction between "restricted" and "general" economies, Jerome McGann outlines two forms of elegy: a Wordsworthian form that repays psychic loss with spiritual gain, and a Shelleyan form whose loss is absolute. This opposition between "restricted" and "ecstatic" modes of the genre elegy is in turn displaced by a difference between "Romantic" and "sentimental" modes, represented by Byron and the women writers Smith and Hemans who provoke and more bleakly respond to his high Romanticism. That McGann's project involves "re-forming" our sense of elegy by drawing women writers into the Romantic canon is obvious. But as the essay traces the circulation of elegy through its mutually self-contesting modes, it also affects us with a *mood* of loss that cuts across its more programmatic attempt to construct new taxonomies that reform genre through gender. In specific terms, McGann is powerfully aware of what is "lost" by a new historicism that replaces Byron with Hemans. But more generally, there is the question of what is left out by the economy of criticism: what is lost when we deal with loss by classifying it in the genres and modes that constitute our own literary capital. The essay thus provides an appropriate coda for the volume, in that its story about Romantic literature implies a story about the ideologies of a criticism that must answer to its own contingency.

NOTES

1 Tzvetan Todorov, *Genres in Discourse*, trans. Catherine Porter (Cambridge: Cambridge University Press, 1990), 19, 21, 17. Todorov points out that the process that leads from speech act to genre is not always direct, and sometimes involves transformations or amplifications, as in the development of "telling" into the novel.

2 Alastair Fowler, *Kinds of Literature: An Introduction to the Theory of Genres and Modes* (Cambridge, Mass.: Harvard University Press, 1982), 26. On Renaissance genre theory more generally, including Scaliger, see Rosalie Colie, *The Resources of Kind: Genre-Theory in the Renaissance* (Berkeley and Los Angeles: University of California Press, 1976).

3 Thomas Love Peacock, *The Four Ages of Poetry* (1820) and Percy Bysshe Shelley, *A Defence of Poetry* (1823) in *A Defence of Poetry and The Four Ages of Poetry*, ed. John E. Jordan (Indianapolis: Bobbs-Merrill, 1965); Victor Hugo, "Preface" to *Cromwell* (1825; rpt. Paris: Garnier Flammarion, 1968).

4 Clara Reeve, *The Progress of Romance through Times, Countries, and Manners* (1785; rpt. New York: Garland, 1970). Reeve says "the modern Novel sprung up" out of the "ruins" of romance (I: 7, 110, 127). Schelling discusses the transformation of epic through romance into the novel in his 1800–04 lectures later printed as *The Philosophy of Art* (1859), trans. Douglas W. Stott (Minneapolis: University of Minnesota Press, 1989), 230–37.

5 Reeve sees the novel and romance as bearers of very different value systems (*Progress of Romance*, I: 111, II: 78). Although she is concerned with the moral assessment of texts with a view to their influence on children and other vulnerable groups, the very fact that she cannot construct an ethical opposition between the two genres and tries to recuperate both (II: 86) marks an incipient awareness of ideology, introduced under the

cover of *paideia*, or maintaining the moral hierarchies embedded in a "curriculum" of genres.

6 Fowler, *Kinds of Literature*, 17.

7 Cyrus Hamlin, "The Origins of a Philosophical Genre Theory in German Romanticism," *European Romantic Review* 5 (1994): 13.

8 For further discussion of Schlegel, see Tilottama Rajan, "Theories of Genre in Romanticism," in *The Cambridge History of Romantic Criticism*, ed. Ernst Behler and Marshall Brown (Cambridge: Cambridge University Press, forthcoming).

9 Friedrich Schlegel, *Philosophical Fragments*, trans. Peter Firchow (Minneapolis: University of Minnesota Press, 1991), 8, 27; *Literary Notebooks 1797–1801* (Toronto: University of Toronto Press, 1957), 72, 116; *Dialogue on Poetry and Literary Aphorisms*, trans. Ernst Behler and Roman Struc (University Park: Pennsylvania State University Press, 1968), 76.

10 William Duff, *An Essay on Original Genius* (1767; rpt. New York: Garland, 1970); Edward Young, *Conjectures on Original Composition* (1759; rpt. New York: Garland, 1970).

11 Thomas Percy, *Reliques of Ancient English Poetry*, ed. J. V. Prichard, 2 vols. (New York: Thomas Cromwell, 1876), 1: viii, x; Richard Hurd, *Letters on Chivalry and Romance* (1762; rpt. New York: Garland, 1971).

12 Northrop Frye, "Theory of Modes," *Anatomy of Criticism: Four Essays* (Princeton: Princeton University Press, 1957); Fowler, *Kinds of Literature*, 106. Though the word "mode" was not used until later, the adjectival use of generic terms was common in the Renaissance, as in "pastoral drama," "heroic drama," etc.

13 Friedrich von Schiller, *Naive and Sentimental Poetry*, in *Naive and Sentimental Poetry and On The Sublime*, trans. Julius A. Elias (New York: Frederick Ungar, 1966), 125.

14 For further discussion of mood, see Stanley Corngold, *The Fate of the Self: German Writers and French Theory* (New York: Columbia University Press, 1986), 206–15; "Nietzsche's Moods," *Studies in Romanticism* 29 (1990): 72.

15 Jean-François Lyotard, *Lessons on the Analytic of the Sublime*, trans. Elizabeth Rottenberg (Stanford: Stanford University Press, 1994), 31–32, 53.

16 For instance, despite the prose forms that proliferated during the period and the interrogation of the distinction between prose and verse in such works as Wordsworth's Preface to the *Lyrical Ballads*, Coleridge's *Biographia Literaria*, Shelley's *Defence of Poetry*, and Byron's *English Bards and Scotch Reviewers*, anthologists from Aikin, Percy, and Warton to Southey and Hazlitt focused exclusively on verse forms.

17 See James Chandler, *Wordsworth's Second Nature: A Study of the Poetry and Politics* (Chicago: University of Chicago Press, 1984); Marjorie Levinson, *Wordsworth's Great Period Poems: Four Essays* (Cambridge: Cambridge University Press, 1986); Alan Liu, *Wordsworth, the Sense of History* (Stanford: Stanford University Press, 1989); Richard Bourke, *Romantic*

Discourse and Political Modernity: Wordsworth, the Intellectual and Cultural Critique (New York: St. Martin's Press, 1993); Thomas Pfau, *Wordsworth's Profession* (Stanford: Stanford University Press, forthcoming).

18 On the lyricization of the Romantics, see Tilottama Rajan, "Romanticism and the Death of Lyric Consciousness," in *Lyric Poetry: Beyond New Criticism*, ed. Chaviva Hosek and Patricia Parker (Ithaca: Cornell University Press, 1985), 194–207. Neil Fraistat discusses the lyricization of Shelley in "Illegitimate Shelley: Radical Piracy and the Textual Edition as Cultural Performance," *PMLA* 109 (1994): 409–23; the same issue is taken up from the perspective of gender by Mary Favret in "Mary Shelley's Sympathy and Irony: The Editor and her Corpus," in *The Other Mary Shelley: Beyond Frankenstein*, ed. Audrey A. Fisch et al. (New York: Oxford University Press, 1993), 17–38.

19 Frederic Jameson, *The Political Unconscious: Narrative as a Socially Symbolic Act* (Ithaca: Cornell University Press, 1981), 99.

20 Emile Benveniste, *Problems in General Linguistics*, trans. Mary Elizabeth Meek (Coral Gables: University of Miami Press, 1971), 219.

21 The term is used by Julia Kristeva, though not in the context of genre (*Revolution in Poetic Language*, trans. Margaret Waller [New York: Columbia University Press, 1984], 59–60).

22 Benveniste, *Problems in General Linguistics* 224–27; Kaja Silverman, *The Subject of Semiotics* (New York: Oxford University Press, 1983), 200.

23 Thomas Warton, *History of English Poetry*, 4 vols. (London: Dodsley et al., 1774; London: Johnson Reprint Corp., 1968), ii. On this subject, see Julia M. Wright, "'The Order of Time': Nationalism and Literary Anthologies, 1774–1831," *Papers on Language and Literature*, forthcoming.

24 Robert Southey, *Select Works of the British Poets from Chaucer to Jonson* (London: Longman, 1831), 127, 131.

25 Marilyn Butler, *Literature as a Heritage, or, Reading Other Ways* (Cambridge: Cambridge University Press, 1988), 5.

26 William Hazlitt, *Lectures on the English Poets* (1818; rpt. Toronto: Oxford University Press, 1952), 247.

27 Jerrold E. Hogle, "The Ghost of the Counterfeit in the Genesis of the Gothic," in *Gothick Origins and Innovations*, ed. Allan Lloyd Smith and Victor Sage (Amsterdam: Rodopi, 1994), 23–33.

28 Hans Kellner, *Language and Historical Representation: Getting the Story Crooked* (Madison: University of Wisconsin Press, 1989), 26–54.

29 See Kristeva, *Revolution in Poetic Language*, 109–114.

30 Claudio Guillen, *Literature as System: Essays Toward the Theory of Literary History* (Princeton: Princeton University Press, 1971), 386; Jameson, *Political Unconscious*, 78–82.

Genre, history, and the public sphere

Godwin and the genre reformers: on necessity and contingency in romantic narrative theory

Jon Klancher

The aim of this essay is to investigate Godwin's movement from the genre of political and moral philosophy, in the *Enquiry into Political Justice* (1793), to the genre of cultural inquiry and criticism in *The Enquirer* (1797). Intellectual historians often narrate this trajectory as Godwin's shift from rationalism to empiricism or skepticism, radicalism to liberalism, or Enlightenment assuredness to Romantic ironism. Instead I will grasp Godwin's shift between genres in light of a wider late eighteenth-century crisis of the expansive early modern or Enlightenment category of "literature" – the spacious universe of educated genres ranging from the scientific and the historiographic to the poetic and the critical. It was within that crisis that Godwin sounded his great theme of "necessity." "Few engines can be more powerful," he wrote in 1793,

than literature . . . Literature has reconciled the whole thinking world respecting the great principles of the system of the universe, and extirpated upon this subject the dreams of romance and the dogmas of superstition . . . [Today] the race of speculative reasoners in favor of despotism, are almost extinct.[1]

Yet dreams and genres of romance were being widely revived throughout the late eighteenth century, often naively, sometimes in the sophisticated conservative accents of a Burke or a Scott. One romance dream would be Godwin's own.

In January 1797 he drafted an essay in narrative genre theory, "Of History and Romance," for a projected second volume of the *Enquirer*, though the draft remained unpublished until 1988. Here Godwin tried to negate the emerging conservative monopoly on the themes of "romance" by harnessing the genre to politically progressive rather than reactionary ends in history. "The writer of romance," he argued in paradoxical fashion, "is to be considered as the writer of real history; while he who was formerly called the historian, must be contented to step down into the place of his rival, with this disadvantage, that *he* is a romance writer, without the arduous, the enthusiastic, and the sublime licence of imagination."[2] Thus "Of History and Romance" may appear today as the first of those British Romantic critical programs that promoted literary genre-reform as a means to induce greater ideological or social change in history. I refer to the genre-reforming agendas of Baillie, Wordsworth, Coleridge, or Shelley, all sharing in one political sense or another the ambition of transforming a received poetic, dramatic, or narrative genre to produce, as Shelley put it, "the seeds at once of its own and of social renovation."[3] Literary history has traditionally dated British Romantic genre-reform to the imperious "I" of Wordsworth's 1800 "Preface," the modern author who claims to redirect the social institution of genre by centering the new subject-position of a reforming and ultimately self-transcendentalizing poet. But Godwin's 1797 essay offers evidence for the social origins of Romantic generic reform in the unheralded collectivities of 1790s argument and dissent.

Like the *Enquirer* as a whole, "Of History and Romance" was written at a time when the progressive sector of England's public sphere was about to collapse, and the machinery of the publications industry that had been central to it was being taken over by a new generation of "speculative defenders of despotism."[4] *The Enquirer* registered the crisis by seeking to reshape a progressive English intelligentsia by literary, educational, and canon-reorganizing means. Godwin's 1797 preface on method describes a critical stance engaged in "colloquial discussion[s]" with a dense social network of discussants. As filtered through the *Enquirer*, these "discussions" emerge as various "hints," ideas tested in debate, possibilities of thought tossed into the air, "not as *dicta*, but as the materials of thinking" (my italics).[5] In such ways *The Enquirer* translated a vanishing culture of critical discourse into the printed chapters of a book whose formal organization is marked by intensely serious conversational stops and starts.

Yet, if "Of History and Romance" makes the genre-reforming moves that would become characteristic of British Romantic criticism, Godwin also provocatively complicated the reflexive effort to transform genre in order to change history. To see why, I want to use Godwin's genre-shifting texts of the 1780s and 90s as a guide to the late eighteenth century's political crisis of the Enlightened category of literature and its imaginary social basis, the "republic of letters" – a universe of genres now felt to be contingent upon a greater historical process which no available discourse had yet come to comprehend.

I

Few observers of the eighteenth-century republic of letters, from Pierre Bayle to Oliver Goldsmith, missed the fact that its idealized intellectual community in the service of reason contradicted its quotidian reality, a fiercely competitive sphere of aspiring intellectuals and professional one-uppers struggling for position.[6] As a *parvenu* Dissenter working his way through the commercial hothouse of Grub Street, Godwin introduced himself to the British publications industry in 1783 by writing *The Herald of Literature*, a parody of the eighteenth-century literary reviews and thus of nearly all the current literary genres of the time, from historiography and political discourse to poetry, drama, and reviewing as such. Here Godwin presented reviews of books he claimed were forthcoming from well-known authors by inventing lengthy "quoted" passages from such non-existent works as volumes III and IV of William Robertson's *History of America*, volumes VI through VII of Edward Gibbon's *Decline and Fall of the Roman Empire*, a novel *Louisa* by Frances Burney, a Pope-like poem on fiction and criticism by William Hayley called "An Essay on Novel," and two imagined political tracts by Thomas Paine and Edmund Burke. *The Herald* mimed the Enlightenment literary review so persuasively as to mislead modern Godwin scholars into accepting these texts as authentic reviews of actual works.[7]

Insiders of the eighteenth-century reviewing business, knowing better, greeted the *Herald of Literature* as a canny piece of culture-industry oneupmanship. But its greater significance was that the Enlightenment literary reviews had claimed to be, as Derek Roper puts it, "installments in a continuous encyclopedia, recording the advance of knowledge in every field of human enterprise."[8] By imagining himself as a reviewer, Godwin was able to invent a simulacrum of this Enlightened category of literature as learned discourse. He made visible its internal relations between truth and fiction, history and novel, style and author, by fictionalizing long "quoted" passages of putative historiography and then setting them

alongside such passages as those "quoted" likewise from the imagined Frances Burney novel. The effect was to blur the literary reviews'
careful discrimination of generic boundaries. To William Hayley's
celebrated actual poem published four years earlier, "Essay on
History," Godwin matched the virtual poem "An Essay on Novel," a
generic shift in which he transformed verse on the history of history-
writing into a prospectus for what in 1784 was as yet unwritten
anywhere – a history of the novel, from the epics of Homer to the
"modern French writers of fictitious history" and the English novelists as well (288). What was "heralded" about the Enlightenment
category of literature was the unacknowledged instability of its
greater architecture of discursive and poetic genres.

From this perspective, Godwin's *Herald* amounted to a 115–page
quotation of "literature" as such; that is, the dominant category of
literature as locally materialized in the print devices of the literary
review. What literary history has taken to be the chief limitation and
defect of eighteenth-century reviewing – the reviewer's seeming
deference to long quoted passages of the book under review –
Godwin displayed as a revealing trope: quotation as a power of
invention, definition, and consecration. He exposed the book
reviewer as a text-producer whose productivity was dissimulated by
his guise of mere textual commentator. The *Critical* and *Monthly*
reviews had postured like magistrates "judging" an independently
existing "literature" that in fact, it would now seem, they were
constituting themselves in the universe of texts "under review."[9]
Like Pierre Menard in the Borges fable, Godwin never needed
actually to write the faked works he attributed to Hayley, Robertson,
Burney, or Gibbon – he needed only to "quote" from and comment
upon them in order to produce the reflexive effects of *The Herald of
Literature*. To draw Gibbon's unfinished historical narrative through
the looking glass of a carefully authenticated historiographic fiction
– only volumes one through three of the *Decline and Fall* had been
published by 1784 – was, in one important sense, to replicate the
older narrative conceit according to which novels entered the world
appearing as "true histories."[10] What belonged to the prehistory of
the modern novel, however, would now reappear in the printed
medium of the literary review as the eighteenth-century publishers
had constructed it. More technically, Godwin inverted the convention by which thick black ribbons of quotation marks on the left
margins of the eighteenth-century review attested to a world of

books and genres existing as an order outside the review itself. Glimpsed through such "quotation" was the mobile, historically contingent relation between the various genres, on the one hand, and the supervising category of "literature" on the other.

Or, to borrow an apt term from Bakhtin, Godwin's *Herald* performed the "novelization" of the Enlightenment category of literature.[11] By suggesting how this category of literature itself might be unexpectedly readable as a fictive world, the virtual reviewer of *The Herald of Literature* momentarily became the master artificer of that array of genres upon which the Enlightenment category of literature had depended in the commercial print culture of the eighteenth century. Without quite intending it, Godwin's parody exposed the way the literary review had always been working as a materialized, visible registration of what is never fully representable – that is, the *form* of the prevailing category or canon of literature, founded on a hierarchy of genres, rather than any particular writers or texts which may belong to it.[12] The printed form of the eighteenth-century review – as reproduced and burlesqued with exhausting exactness in *The Herald of Literature* – might be said to herald instead the *un*doing of "literature" as the Enlightened category of the modern discourses of knowledge.

The professed aim of Godwin's parody was to charge the *Monthly* and *Critical* reviews with promoting the eighteenth-century category of "literature" at the expense of the "ancient republic of letters." Thus in the *Herald* we read a peculiar version of the struggle between virtue and commerce documented throughout the eighteenth century by J. G. A. Pocock and his followers.[13] *Monthly* and *Critical* reviewers of the mid-eighteenth century had introduced the modernized modes of learning called "literature" to commercial print culture, becoming the chief exchange medium of both scholarly and commercial writing. But if the "ancient republic of letters" were now being eclipsed by the reigning commercial empire of the literary reviews, the older republic's "virtue" might be made "virtual" – a power of fictional interference with the new commercial order's monopoly upon the discourses of knowledge which the moderns call "literature." At the same time, Godwin's 1783 experiment revealed how the commercial media of modern learning might themselves have destabilizing, genre-shifting effects upon the authority of the very category they were so successful in promoting to reading audiences, namely, literature as the modern discourses of truth. In this way, Godwin confronted the two most important narrative developments of the later eighteenth century: what recent cultural historians have called the quantitative rise or culture-industrial "takeoff" of the British novel between 1770 and 1800, on the one hand; and the power of that new and imposing legitimation of commercial modernity, Scottish "philosophical history" on the other.[14] As a metacommentary on that process, the contingent effects of *The Herald of Literature* belong to a preoccupation in Godwin's work to be deepened and complicated in his more searching texts of the 1790s. In Godwin's career, the parodist was the earliest form of the cultural enquirer.

Despite its parodic mode, Godwin's *Herald* belongs to a historical process we do not usually associate with the Swifts and Fieldings of early-modern parodic literary effects. I refer to the rise of Dissenting intellectuals to editorships of Britain's leading reviews by 1791 – the *Monthly*, the *Critical*, the *Analytical*, and the *English* – and the Joseph Johnson circle's renascence of virtue within radical politics in the 1790s. When reviewing became "analytical," it was to begin redefining the commercial "republic of letters" in the republican terms of the English Civil War and to change the potential scope of the British publications business itself.[15] Such revamped reviews were motors in the "engine" of literature to which Godwin appealed in the first edition of *Political Justice* in 1793. But Godwin's confidence in that engine seemed to disappear from the next two editions of *Political Justice* in 1796 and 1798. What British audiences began reading instead was the polemical reply by T. J. Mathias in his work of Malthusian poetics, *The Pursuits of Literature*. "Literature," Mathias retorted, "whether well or ill-conducted, is the great engine by which all *civilized* States must ultimately be supported or overthrown." Anti-Jacobin conservatives, not radical intellectuals, were producing this starkly instrumentalized conception of literature as an engine of legitimation by the mid-1790s, and with great effect: Mathias's *Pursuits* would become the most widely read manual of British literary population-politics at the turn of the century (published in sixteen editions by 1812).[16] Its popularity coincided with the insurgent rise of the journal that bears an antithetical relation to Godwin's *Herald of Literature*, the more crudely and effectively parodic *Anti-Jacobin Review*.

Meanwhile, Godwin began to write of the circumstantial, the unforeseen, and the accidental in his revisions and new productions of 1795 to 1798. Rather than cite the Enlightenment category of "literature," with its axioms of internal necessity, Godwin began to relate peculiar, contingent eventualities of literary history, such as what might have happened if Shakespeare's mother had met "some hideous object" on her way to giving birth. Tracing Shakespeare to contingent origins was odd but not entirely trivial; careers and intellectual projects might also be apprehended as "produced by circumstances so minute and subtle as in few instances to have been made the subject of history."[17] Such imaginings could provoke visions of a chaos of possible histories within the larger necessitarian framework of *Political Justice*. Increasingly fascinated by contingent possibilities, Godwin punctuated his writings of 1796–97 with the what-if scenarios of possible histories. He began imagining the past as a cascade of consequences stemming from little moments occurring other than history decrees that they did. To become fascinated by the contingent was also to imagine that, in some unforeseen way, "everything is connected in the universe," since "every one of these incidents, when it occurred, grew out of a series of incidents that had previously taken place" (193). For authority, Godwin appealed to science. "Natural philosophers," he wrote, argue that "a single grain of sand more or less in the structure of the earth would have produced an infinite variation in its history." The notion of "necessity," as it will under intense historical pressure, began to produce in Godwin's revisions of *Political Justice* – and most fully in his project of cultural inquiry and criticism, *The Enquirer* – the complex and chaotic actions of the "contingent."

II

For us, the notion of contingency increasingly answers to a crisis of historicity in moral philosophy, political theory, literature, and the natural sciences alike – contexts I will want to invoke for Godwin's moment as well. Among the historical logics Godwin himself investigated in the 1790s – "necessity," "probability," "possibility" – there was no precise conceptual equivalent for what we currently refer to as "contingency" among a wide range of intellectual discourses – in anti-foundational moral philosophy, in post-Marxist rethinking of historical necessity, in revisionary Darwinist evolutionism, or even in the extraordinary postulates of a "radical contingency" in earth's history by comparative planetology or astrogeology.[18] Both like and unlike these postmodern articulations of the contingent, Godwin would seek in the concept a means to reconcile his own intellectual and social uncertainty about what is entailed by the skeptical or relative on the one hand, the actual or material on the other.

I want to locate Godwin's turn from the political theory of 1793 to cultural criticism and narrative concerns in 1797–98 between these senses of the "contingent." Central to the problem of contingency is the question of whether it is an epistemological or an ontological category – whether it designates how things actually happened (or might have happened), or whether it defines the horizon of limits of what we know.[19] One Romantic idealist solution to this question is well put by Hegel's provocative materialist interpreter Slavoj Zizek: "Contingency does express the incompleteness of our knowledge, *but this incompleteness also ontologically defines the object of knowledge itself* . . . [T]he object itself is not yet ontologically 'realized,' fully actual."[20] There were, of course, other solutions to legacies of empiricism, skepticism, and mutating genres of knowledge bred by the Enlightenment category of "literature."[21]

In *The Enquirer* Godwin renounced the theoretical ambition of *Political Justice* – the task of philosophical totalization that by 1797 he was calling "incommensurate to our powers" – in order now to pursue local "investigations" into "education, manners, and literature," which demanded questioning the method, the motive, and the reflexive position of the cultural inquirer himself. Many of these essays entailed re-educating the educators; or, in the hermeneutic context recently explored by Tilottama Rajan, of comprehending the complexity of authorial intentions and textual "tendencies" entailed by the construction and reception of meaning in history.[22] Yet none of the *Enquirer*'s published essays spoke to the Enlightenment category of literature with quite the polemical and methodological self-consciousness of the essay "Of History and Romance." This essay was an attempt to rethink the genre of historiography as an enquiry into the private, secretive, and politically formative moments of individual lives. The dominant mode of British historiography by 1790 was no longer the same progressive empiricist historiography of the Moderns who had waged their victorious quarrel with the Ancients by compiling tomes of antiquary offering empirical "evidence of the senses."[23] Rather it was the newer law-governed, universal or "philosophical" history-writing which had made prosperous and well-nigh canonical the figures of Hume, Robertson, and Gibbon in the genre Hume had called "the most popular kind of writing of any" in Britain.[24] The power of such historiography had been to grasp the emerging, differentiated spheres of a complex modernity as the unanticipated outcome of an inexorable historical process, periodized in the four great stages that culminate in commercial society. Its power was also, as Meinecke remarked, to shake history "violently" out of its comforting remoteness by "plunging it into the present," thereby ensuring that interpretive struggles about the historical past would henceforth "always go hand in hand with all the controversies about the shape of things to come."[25]

It was on both counts that Godwin opened his challenge in "Of History and Romance": to dispute philosophical history's ideological presentism that projected pasts and futures from the settlement of 1689, and to raise those alternative possibilities of making history that he would call "the depths of futurity." It begins as a critique of the Scottish historians' sweeping narratives of how modernity assumed its inevitable shape. The older testimony of antiquities had largely disappeared into the philosophical historians' effort to steer readers away from annals and sources, permitting whole continents of context, by the magic of abridgment, to vanish into the abstract national geographies of the universal historians' narrative machine. Their method was the "collation and comparison of successive ages"; their product was the autobiography of British nationhood – a collective or "mass" subject called England (in Hume's case) in which "individualities" on the one hand, and the particularities of such conjunctures as the English Civil War on the other, were equally abstracted away. But the armature of their method was the ineluctable logic of "probability," the "dull repetition" of a "general history" in which Hume, Robertson, and implicitly Burke connive to "furnish us precedents in abundance, . . . show us how that which happened in one country has been repeated in another . . . that what has occurred in the annals of mankind, may under similar circumstances be produced again" (362). Hume's intolerable credo – that "history teaches us nothing new or strange" – had made it scarcely conceivable how history could ever tell the moderns what they did not already know.[26] Universal history's cancellation of possible, unrealized futures prohibits us, Godwin urged, from conceiving "what it is of which social man is *capable*" (363, my italics), and sentences us to the institutional order of modernity, where we "dance in fetters," "blight[ed] . . . in every grander and more ample development of the soul" (365).

Against the probabilizing powers of Scottish conjectural history, Godwin promotes a new historiography focused on agents, motives, and actions. This biographically focused historicism would shift from the abstract subject of the emergent nation to the individual subjects whose public and private acts connive to produce "things as they are." It would carry out an investigative agenda designed to follow the agents of history off the public stage and into their closets, to re-examine the "public man" as a private "friend and father of a family," to perform close readings of his works and letters, and suspicious hermeneutics of his public orations and private behaviors (364). It would set aside enlightened abstraction by grasping the "materials" and "motives," "minute and near," through which history is made. It would replace the ideological trope of probability with the anticipatory figure of "possibility":

It is thus, and thus only, that we should be enabled to add, to the knowledge of the past, a sagacity that can penetrate into the depths of futurity. We shall not only understand those events as they arise which are no better than old incidents under new names, but shall judge truly of such conjunctures and combinations, their sources and effects, as, though they have never yet occurred, are within the capacities of our nature. (363)

But any reader must ask: what sort of historian could grasp "conjunctures and combinations" yet to occur, with all their "sources and effects"?

Had it been revised, "Of History and Romance" might have clarified the central tension it displays between the investigative empirical historian "ever on the watch for further and further particulars," and the ghostly historian whom Godwin regressively conjures up from a world of discredited knowledge. Improbably, he selects the ancient historian who had been vanquished by the moderns – Sallust, Livy, Plutarch – as a prototype of intellectual agency, capable of linking the past to unrealized futures, that is otherwise unavailable to the Humean or Burkean moderns groaning under the institutional weight of "prejudices and precedents." Though downclassed by the moderns as a kind of fabulist, the ancient historian may still serve pragmatically, if not referentially, to produce "a genuine praxis upon the nature of man" (367), a kind of *licentia historica* for imagining possible pasts and futures as something other than probabilistic versions of the world ratified by 1688 and the imposing narratives of philosophical history. Reanimating the ancient historian encourages Godwin to press skepticism toward history to the limit. The moderns' accusation that the ancients fabricated their histories can be reversed against the moderns themselves: "All history bears too near a resemblance to fable . . . Dismiss me from the falsehood and impossibility of history, and deliver me over to the reality of romance" (373, 371).[27] Such a conclusion – which Godwin will ultimately resist – would follow the logic of self-consciousness to the point of imputing a superior knowledge to the romancer who knows the true motives of his historical characters because he has invented them, as opposed to the hapless historian who must perpetually mistake the motives of historical characters whose inner lives he has been unable to grasp.

But the more emotional and allegorical reason to invoke the ancient historians is that "whatever they undertake they undertake with a full and undivided soul . . . and do not lose themselves in dark, inexplicable windings." They were not, that is, the skeptical, sophistical, dark imaginers that Godwin himself has become, brooding in the year of the Gagging Acts over a darkening cloud of reaction, the thinning circles of radical intellectuals, and modernity's betrayal of high purposes. The ancient historians provoke an imaginative resource to wield against the dark "windings" which afflict the progressive's public sphere that now appears, in late 1796, increasingly incapable of its own repair.

It makes sense, then, that Godwin's far regions of "romance" were not those of Burke's immemorial English antiquity or aristocratic idealism but rather the Roman republic and the age of Cromwell. So conceived, the historical romance would imaginatively reopen that possibility in English history – the moment of 1642 – which the Scottish historians, and most notoriously Hume in *The History of England* (1763), had been anxious to close. One of Godwin's later, more pessimistic historical novels would return to the Revolution scenarios of the mid-seventeeth century to investigate the failures of the revolution that finally produced 1689 rather than the possible worlds of republican imagining.[28] Likewise, his most extended work of political history, *History of the Commonwealth of England* (1824 28), would open reconstructively with the epigraph, "To attend to the neglected, to remember the forgotten."[29]

In 1797 the deeper subtext of the essay "Of History and Romance" was the unavailability to modern Britain of its own revolutionary moment except as what might be fictionally reconstructed and investigated by the historiographer capable of grasping the multitudinous "conjunctures and combinations" of historical possibility, or what the English revolutionary moment might now look like if narrated by the historical romancer, whose "express stamp of invention" opens investigation of past revolutionary failures and of possible conjunctures of thought and action yet to be made. The republican romance would thereby refute the necessity of British history as the universal historians had narrated it, the better to locate the unrealized futures that proliferated from the mid-seventeenth century. It is in this unfamiliar sense – as the regenerator of a historical narrative interrupted by the fate of the 1642 revolution – that Godwin ventures to call "the writer of romance . . . the writer of *real* history." To propose the genre of "historical romance" as the ideological alternative to the unacknowledged fictions of universal history was to claim that, through its reflexive awareness of its own fictional status, the novel was empowered to confer upon its authors and readers the constructive "sagacity" to imagine particular futures as well as pasts – to negate the Burkean monopoly on "romance" by reclaiming a reflexive fictionality for politically progressive ends in history.

The conviction Godwin brings to these passages – echoed elsewhere in *The Enquirer* – makes it all the more puzzling why he would retract his proposal for the sagacious historical romance in the final paragraphs of "Of History and Romance." Unexpectedly Godwin ceases to promote the project of literary genre-reform I have just outlined and abruptly forestalls it, as though his own argument for narrative genre-transformation were itself be read as a "fiction," a thought experiment in both the possibility and the difficulty of changing genres in order to change history. What he had written about the project of philosophical totalization at the beginning of the *Enquirer* – that it is "incommensurate to our powers" – must now be said of the reflexive romancer as well: "To write romance is a task too great for the powers of man . . . [for it] requires a sagacity scarcely less than divine" (372). Nearly two decades before *Waverley,* Godwin glimpses and declines – at least in theory – the spectral return of a divine placeholder or surreptitious theologian in the powerful act of authorship that makes things happen in the parallel universe of the British historical novel.[30]

Godwin's self-reversal at essay's end may be its most provocative as well as honest moment. Against the powerful act of knowing authorship he earlier attributed to the historical romancer, Godwin now invokes the language of yet another eighteenth-century narrative genre, natural history. Though it echoes the appeal to contingency we have read in the 1798 revision of *Political Justice*, it refers in the present context to what narrative genres can master and to what eludes them: "Naturalists tell us that a single grain of sand more or less on the surface of the earth, would have altered its motion, and in process of ages, have diversified its events" (372). What escapes the empirical historian are contingencies of psychology or "motive"; what eludes the form-giving historial romancer are the incalculable consequences of "action" (372). If the most historical thing about a narrative genre, romance or historiography, is what escapes it, then the peculiar incapacities of the various narrative genres are what best define them *as* genres in the wider representational field.

Hence, when he invokes the contingent as a means of locating the historicity of narrative genres, Godwin neither returns to the generic hierarchy of the Enlightenment category of literature (where historiography outranks novels and romances) – nor provides the first Romantic rationale for fictional narrative's greater symbolic truth of history. Instead, he turns both the empirical historian and the romance-writer into competitors in the now highly destabilized universe of modern narrative genres. The resulting vision of epistemological and political struggle between genres foretells not merely the evolutionary march of traditional literary history's account of genres in time, but something more like what Franco Moretti has recently proposed as a "Darwinian history of literature, where forms fight one another, are selected by their context, evolve, and disappear like natural species."[31]

The projects of Romantic genre-reform pursued by Baillie, Wordsworth, Coleridge, Shelley, and others sought to transform the ideologies of modernity by reforming genres and their effects; Godwin's alone accounted for the incalculability of those effects. The parody of 1783 and the rough-draft narrative speculations of 1797 both worked against the abstracting drive of Romantic genre reform by refusing the Romantic distinction between the merely "contingent, historical" genres and the "essential," "necessary" greater modes of the poetic, dramatic, and narrative. Baillie's reformed "drama" in *A Series of Plays* (1798), Wordsworth's "lyricized" ballads, Coleridge's philosophized "poetry," Shelley's trans-generic, regenerative "poet" contributed to modern thinking about genres the priority of generic necessity against the contingent formation and reformation of movable, actual genres in history. As Claudio Guillen first showed, that distinction has molded all modern genre theory and still remains to be fully grasped.[32] The reflexive shaping powers of the greater Romantic genre-reforms (where nothing can be "left out"), should thus be qualified by what I would call "Godwin's reflex," his abrupt response at the end of "Of History and Romance" to the awareness of an "outside" – signified by earth history's errant "grains of sand" – that cannot be made self-conscious or be incorporated into the narrative that would explain it. This reflex can be called "materialist" not because it finally grasps "real history" but because it grasps the escape of the real in even the most self-conscious narrative ambition. On this view, the contingent is less the polite, antifoundational gesture of the sort we read in Rorty's "postmodern liberal conversation" than the harder thing referred to in Zizek's remark that "there is always something of an 'encounter with the Real' in contingency, something of the violent emergence of an unheard-of-entity that defies the limits of the established field of what one holds for 'possible.' "[33]

As a sociohistorical rather than an epistemological category, the question of contingency locates where the observer stands, how the observer is situated, with whom he or she shares discussion. As a social effect of the breakup of the radical "republic of letters," Godwin's themes of contingency named a precariously lived social location whose members had willfully isolated themselves from a popular audience and were estranged in kind by the new cultural conservatives. The hoped-for knowledge of *The Enquirer* could be read in that sense as a far-from-complete attempt to render a "situated knowledge" at the end of the eighteenth century.[34] Perhaps the key word of *The Enquirer* is "materials": genres become "materials" for use rather than determinate logics. If there could be no available narrative solution to the ideological effects of modernity's self-justifying "philosophical history," the struggle between historical genres (including the novel) had to become the context for pursuing investigative, historical-generic practices that might work against the self-assurance of modernity by excavating the "materials" of possible histories that might have been made – or might yet be made. At a time of recovering "non-canonical texts" and generic experiments or dead-ends of the late eighteenth century, we have a more vivid sense now of genres as such historical materials than as stable classifications or determinate logics. The logic of normative genres as "institutions" contrasts with the contingent historicity of "genres" as materials that lie, sometimes urgently, ready to hand.

NOTES

1 William Godwin, *An Enquiry Concerning Political Justice* (1793), ed. Jonathan Wordsworth, facs. edn. (New York: Woodstock, 1992), 20.

2 William Godwin, "Of History and Romance," appendix IV of *Things as They Are: or, The Adventures of Caleb Williams,* ed. Maurice Hindle (New York: Penguin, 1988), 372. All subsequent page references will refer to the convenient Hindle text. The essay has subsequently appeared as "Essay on History and Romance," in *Political and Philosophical Writings of William Godwin,* ed. Mark Philp (London: William Pickering, 1993), V: 290–301.

3 Percy Bysshe Shelley, "Defense of Poetry," in *Shelley's Poetry and Prose: Authoritative Texts, Criticism,* ed. Donald H. Reiman and Sharon B. Powers (New York: Norton, 1977), 493.

4 Mark Philp, "The Decline of Radicalism," in *Godwin's Political Justice* (London: Duckworth, 1986), 214–30.

5 William Godwin, *The Enquirer: Essays in Literature, Education, and Society* (London, 1797), vii. As Philp suggests, "Godwin wrote as if a republic of virtue was possible because he lived in a community which attempted to realize the basic principles of such a republic," *Godwin's Political Justice,* 216; see also Philp's mapping of these communities and their memberships, 231–52.

6 Lorraine Daston, "The Ideal and Reality of the Republic of Letters in the Enlightenment," *Science in Context* 4 (1991): 367–86.

7 William Godwin, "The Herald of Literature" (1783), rpt. in *Four Early Pamphlets by William Godwin,* ed. Burton Pollin (Gainesville: Scholar's Facsimiles, 1966), 205–319. The text also appears, in a modernized form without the original typographical features I refer to below, in Philp, ed., *Political and Philosophical Writings of William Godwin* (London: Pickering, 1993), V: 23–71. On the reception of *The Herald*, see William St. Clair, *The Godwins and the Shelleys* (Baltimore: Johns Hopkins University Press, 1989), 22; Burton Pollin, "Introduction" to *Four Early Pamphlets,* xiv.

8 Derek Roper, *Reviewing before the "Edinburgh," 1788–1802* (London: Methuen, 1978), 36. On reviews from the eighteenth century through the 1820s, see also Marilyn Butler, "Culture's Medium: The Role of the

Review," in *The Cambridge Companion to British Romanticism*, ed. Stuart Curran (Cambridge: Cambridge University Press, 1993), 120–47.

9 On the judiciary powers of the reviews, see also Frank Donoghue, *The Fame Machine: Book Reviewing and Eighteenth-Century Literary Careers* (Stanford: Stanford University Press, 1996), 16–55.

10 Cf. Lennard Davis, *Factual Fictions* (New York: Columbia University Press, 1983); Michael McKeon, *The Origins of the English Novel, 1600–1740* (Baltimore: Johns Hopkins University Press, 1987).

11 "The novel parodies other genres (precisely in their role as genres); it exposes the conventionality of their forms and their language," Mikhail Bakhtin, "Epic and Novel" in *The Dialogic Imagination*, ed. Michael Holquist (Austin: University of Texas Press, 1981), 13.

12 The "canonical form," John Guillory argues, belongs to an architecture of genres and is transmitted by a specialized language ("general literariness") which accords with the social and cultural institutions of its dissemination (usually, schools). See *Cultural Capital: The Problem of Literary Canon-Formation* (Chicago: University of Chicago Press, 1993), esp. 29–38.

13 J. G. A. Pocock, *Virtue, Commerce, and History* (New York: Cambridge University Press, 1985).

14 On the "takeoff" of the novel, see James Raven, *Judging New Wealth: Popular Publishing and Responses to Commerce in England, 1750–1800* (Oxford: Clarendon Press, 1992); Clifford Siskin, "Eighteenth-Century Periodicals and the Romantic Rise of the Novel," *Studies in the Novel* (1994): 21–40. With a fourfold increase in novelistic production between 1750 and 1800, the literary reviews crowded their pages with both the promotion and the critique of popular novelistic culture. Raven estimates a rise from about twenty new British novel titles in 1749 – when the *Monthly Review* began appearing – to ninety plus new titles by 1788 and afterward, *Judging New Wealth*, 31–41.

15 Roper, *Reviewing before the "Edinburgh"*, 178–79.

16 Thomas James Mathias, *The Pursuits of Literature*, 14th edn. (London, 1808), 244. On Mathias's impact, see Joseph Sheldon Mabbett, *Thomas James Mathias and the Pursuits of Literature* (Switzerland: University of Fribourg, 1973).

17 William Godwin, *Enquiry Concerning Political Justice* (1798), ed. Isaac Kramnick (Baltimore: Penguin, 1976), 192; further references appear in the text.

18 Comparative planetology: Herbert Shaw, *Craters, Cosmos, and Chronicles: A New Theory of the Earth* (Stanford: Stanford University Press, 1994); paleontology: Stephen J. Gould, *Wonderful Life: The Burgess Shale and the Nature of History* (New York: Norton, 1989); political philosophy: Slavoj Zizek, *Tarrying with the Negative* (New York: Verso, 1991); moral philosophy: Richard Rorty, *Contingency, Irony, and Solidarity* (Cambridge: Cambridge University Press, 1989).

19 A good discussion appears in Susan Oyama, "The Accidental Chordate: Contingency in Developmental Systems," *South Atlantic Quarterly* 94 (1995): 509–26.

20 Zizek, *Tarrying with the Negative*, 153–54.

21 On early eighteenth-century questions of contingency and fiction, see the useful discussion of Lois Chaber, " 'This Intricate Labyrinth': Order and Contingency in Eighteenth-Century Fictions," *Studies in Voltaire and the Eighteenth Century* 212 (1992): 185–209.

22 William Godwin, preface to *The Enquirer: Reflections on Education, Manners, and Literature* (London, 1797), v–viii; Tilottama Rajan, "Wollstonecraft and Godwin: Reading the Secrets of the Political Novel," in *The Supplement of Reading: Figures of Understanding in Romantic Theory and Practice* (Ithaca: Cornell University Press, 1990), 168–69.

23 McKeon, *Origins of the English Novel*, 43. For an extended account, see Joseph Levine, *The Battle of the Books: History and Literature in the Augustan Age* (Ithaca: Cornell University Press, 1991), 267– 412.

24 On the popularity of universal history, see Roy Porter, *Gibbon* (New York: St. Martin's Press, 1988), 15–41; David Wooton, "David Hume, 'the historian,' " in *The Cambridge Companion to Hume* (Cambridge: Cambridge University Press, 1993), 281.

25 Friedrich Meinecke, *Historism*, trans. J. E. Anderson (1959; rpt. New York: Herder and Herder, 1972), 62.

26 David Hume, *Enquiry Concerning Human Understanding*, ed. Eric Steinberg (Indianapolis: Hackett, 1977), 54–55.

27 These arguments are revived from early eighteenth-century debates explored by McKeon, *Origins of the English Novel*, 47–65.

28 Pamela Clemit usefully reads *Mandeville: A Tale of the Seventeenth Century in England* (1817) in relation to Godwin's lengthy meditations on the English Revolution, in *The Godwinian Novel: The Rational Fictions of Godwin, Brockden Brown, Mary Shelley* (Oxford: Clarendon Press, 1993), 70–104.

29 William Godwin, *History of the Commonwealth of England* (London, 1824–28); the best commentary I have read on these matters is John Morrow, "Republicanism and Public Virtue: William Godwin's *History of the Commonwealth of England*," *The Historical Journal* 34 (1991): 645– 64.

30 In practice, Godwin himself, from *St. Leon* (1799) to *Cloudesley* (1830), would repeatedly occupy the authorial subject-position of the nineteenth-century novelist he more critically anticipates in "Of History and Romance." On the "Godwinian novel's" contribution to "novelistic modes of social control," see Jerome Christensen, *Lord Byron's Strength: Romantic Writing and Commercial Society* (Baltimore: Johns Hopkins University Press, 1993), 286–87.

31 Franco Moretti, "The Moment of Truth," and "On Literary Evolution," in *Signs Taken for Wonders* (New York: Verso, 1989), 251, 262–78.

32 Claudio Guillen, "On the Uses of Genre," in *Literature as a System*

(Princeton: Princeton University Press, 1971), 115–19. See also, on the Romantic construction of the "essential" modes, Gerard Genette, *The Architext: An Introduction*, trans. Jane E. Lewin (Berkeley: University of California Press, 1992).

33 Slavoj Zizek, *For They Know Not What They Do: Enjoyment as a Political Factor* (New York: Verso, 1991), 195–96. See also Judith Butler's trenchant critique of Zizek's own tendency to subordinate contingency to the Lacanian "Law" and thereby to "evacuate contingency of the contingent," in *Bodies That Matter* (New York: Routledge, 1994), 146–61. More generally in this paragraph, I am indebted to an unpublished paper on materialism and method by Marjorie Levinson.

34 I refer to Donna Haraway, "Situated Knowledges: the Science Question in Feminism and the Privilege of Partial Perspective," in *Simians, Cyborgs, and Women: The Reinvention of Nature* (New York: Routledge, 1991), 188, but also to the wider question of radicalism, feminism, and popular politics in the late 1790s that needs to be explored in such terms.

CHAPTER 2

Radical print culture in periodical form

Kevin Gilmartin

The period of British history that literary scholars have long associated with the second generation of romantic poetry also marked a distinct phase, and even a revival and recovery of strength, for a less exalted cultural sphere, the popular radical movement for parliamentary reform.[1] The defeat of Napoleon released some of the pressure towards ideological conformity that had built up over the course of the wars with Revolutionary France, and ushered in a period of economic dislocation that helped galvanize popular radical protest throughout the 1810s and early 1820s. While the struggles of the 1790s were not forgotten, and while the continued activity of figures like Daniel Isaac Eaton and Major Cartwright helped to link political protest in the first three decades of the nineteenth century with a broader radical tradition, a new generation of leaders and new strategies had clearly emerged. That individuals like William Cobbett, Henry "Orator" Hunt, Richard Carlile, and John Wade often shared little more than a hatred of what they termed the "system" of political and financial corruption, and that they clashed among themselves as often as they cooperated, only served to increase the energy and vitality of early nineteenth-century radical protest.

Throughout this period, the weekly newspaper or pamphlet of political argument and comment was the most important print organ of radical protest. While this periodical form had significant eighteenth-century antecedents, including the *North Briton* and the *Anti-Jacobin*,[2] William Cobbett took the first step in its nineteenth-century development with the founding of his (not yet radical) *Political Register* in 1802; the weekly format was then taken up by John and Leigh Hunt in their 1808 *Examiner*, and reinvented by Cobbett in November 1816 when he supplemented his stamped *Register*, priced at a shilling halfpenny (four pence of that going for tax), with a cheaper unstamped weekly that could legally print no news, but contained the lead essay of the more expensive paper. This appeared first on a single open sheet, then more permanently as an octavo pamphlet, subject only to the pamphlet tax of three shillings per edition.[3] For some months the "Two-Penny Trash," as it came to be known, achieved unprecedented sales in the tens of thousands per week, as compared with one or two thousand for the stamped *Register*. For the celebrated first number, his address "To the Journeymen and Labourers of England, Wales, Scotland, and Ireland," Cobbett claimed sales of 200,000 within two months (*CPR* 32 [1817]: 551).[4] With some variation in price, content, and physical appearance, the weekly format was widely imitated, and notable instances included T. J. Wooler's *Black Dwarf* (1817–24), William Hone's *Reformist Register* (1817), William Sherwin's *Weekly Political Register* (1817–19), John Wade's *Gorgon* (1818–19), John Hunt's *Yellow Dwarf* (1818), Richard Carlile's *Republican* (1819–26), the *Medusa* (1819), the *Cap of Liberty* (1819), and the *White Hat* (1819). Throughout the late 1810s, the threat of radical influence became inextricably linked with the regular appearance of "the SATURDAY'S lie."[5] Robert Southey, an equally acute and hostile observer of reform politics, traced popular unrest directly to what he called "the weekly epistles of the apostles of sedition": "It is the weekly paper which finds its way to the pot-house in town, and the ale-house in the country, inflaming the turbulent temper of the manufacturer, and disturbing the quiet attachment of the peasant to those institutions under which he and his father have dwelt in peace."[6]

These papers were as decisive an intervention in the history of print as in the history of politics or class consciousness. As G. A. Cranfield has written, where the daily newspaper in this period "was primarily a commercial concern, financed by advertisements, and not as yet venturing on extended political comment," the radical weekly "contained few or no advertisements" and was produced by "a single individual, virtually unassisted": "Here was a new type of journalism. The whole emphasis was on the 'editorial' essay, with its spirited attacks on domestic affairs and its proposed remedies for the desperate plight of the economically oppressed. It was a type of journalism which struck home as none had done since the days of Tom Paine."[7] Despite this pattern of individual production and strong editorial voice, the radical weekly was by no means the product of Cobbett's genius, nor the genius of any other radical writer or editor. Cobbett acknowledged the intertextual determinants of his experiment when he suggested that it was a reaction to a scheme in the *Courier* newspaper for "the *circulating of little, cheap publications* in populous towns" (*CPR* 31 [1816]: 612), and when he compared his unstamped paper to "Mrs. Hannah Moore's *Village Politics*" (*CPR* 32 [1817]: 353).[8] The cheap *Register* was a calculated response to existing press restrictions and, as such, was an intervention rather than an invention, the "one way which these Argus-eyed laws have left us to circulate our observations in a cheap form" (*CPR* 31 [1816]: 522). Like most aspects of radical thought and action, the radical weekly was deeply engaged and richly overdetermined. Its formal development must be understood in relation to the linked histories of press restriction, print technology, the economics of publishing, radical rhetoric and organization, and popular reading habits.

Cranfield's allusion to Paine suggests one important approach to the form. E. P. Thompson has proposed that, after the English reaction to the French Revolution, "English Jacobin" organization and a Painite discourse of natural rights were replaced by a more "pugnacious piecemeal" reform movement:

The term "radicalism" suggests both a breadth and an imprecision in the movement. The Jacobins of the 1790s were clearly identified by their allegiance to the *Rights of Man* and to certain forms of open organisation. "Radicalism" came to include very diverse tendencies as the 19th century advanced. In 1807 it suggests as much about the courage and tone of the movement as it does about any doctrine. It suggested intransigent opposition to the Government; contempt for the weakness of the Whigs; opposition to restrictions upon political liberties; open exposure of corruption and the "Pitt system"; and general support for parliamentary reform.[9]

While Thompson may overplay the ideological coherence of the previous period, early nineteenth-century radicalism had certainly become more defensive and resistant than positive or programmatic, more concerned with immediate strategy than with the abstract principles that had often guided English Jacobinism. Its characteristic print form, I would suggest, was the flexible and responsive weekly periodical rather than the programmatic volume or pamphlet, epitomized for the previous generation by Paine's *Rights of Man*. Even Richard Carlile, in many respects a staunch republican ideologue, maintained his flexibility by refusing allegiance to a

sacred text: "I have never made [Paine's] writing my Bible or Divine
Revelation . . . I have no idol; but am free to follow that line of
conduct and those opinions which shall promise the greatest amount
of public good" (*R* 10 [1824]: 392).

The radical weekly was the effective print vehicle for this "free"
and often eclectic "line of conduct." Like the movement itself, these
newspapers were contentious and heterodox, committed in the
absence of clear ideological landmarks to opposition and resistance.
"We hate the present infernal system of corruption and injustice,"
Wade announced in the first number of the *Gorgon*, "and our sole
object is to effect either its reform or overthrow."[10] The phrase
"reform or overthrow," of course, spanned a broad political spec-
trum and begged key ideological and tactical questions, but *negative*
engagement was itself the main principle that bound the radical
reform movement together. In keeping with this opportunism and
flexibility, a weekly interval seems to have provided the movement
with a fit interval of production, appearing often enough to preserve
the close relationship with readers and events that a popular movement required,[11] without demanding outlays in labor and capital
beyond the reach of an individual. Economic and technological
considerations were paramount. As Thompson suggests, the years
between 1816 and 1820 "were, above all, years in which popular
Radicalism took its style from the hand-press and the weekly
periodical. This means of propaganda was in its fullest egalitarian
phase. Steam-printing had scarcely made headway (commencing
with *The Times* in 1814), and the plebeian Radical group had as easy
access to the hand-press as Church or King."[12] Repressive conditions enhanced this technological minimalism. Under siege from a
legal campaign led by the Society for the Suppression of Vice,
Carlile reflected on the tactical advantage of a "kind of business"
that "might be said to be renewed every week": "We can begin any
where with half an hour's preparation, and laugh at the Vice Society
. . . If one web be destroyed, a few hours' work will spin another
stronger and better than before" (*R* 4 [1820]: 293).

The radical weekly was as versatile in its format as in its mode of
production. Built around a lead "editorial" essay, often signed and
invested with the personal authority of the editor, these newspapers
sometimes contained little else, and therefore served in effect as a
weekly political pamphlet. If it seems perverse then to treat the form
as a kind of newspaper, it is important to see how it emerged as a

hybrid out of legal struggles over "news" content. Modeled on stamped papers like the *Political Register* and the *Examiner*, which contained news and were (strictly speaking) "weekly newspapers," the unstamped weekly pamphlet took advantage of a legal loophole that exempted periodicals containing nothing more than commentary on the news from taxes meant to keep political information out of the hands of the poor. The legal distinction between news and commentary was obscure, and unstamped papers managed to incorporate news, in part through extracts from and critical commentary on respectable daily newspapers. When radical weeklies did extend beyond the essay format, sometimes in more expensive stamped versions, and sometimes in formal accommodations precipitated by subsequent changes in the law, they assimilated an impressive range of heterogeneous material: foreign and domestic news, market prices, reprints from books and pamphlets, transcriptions of radical meetings or trials, reports of parliamentary debates, letters to and from correspondents, commentary on other newspapers and periodicals, lists of subscribers to radical causes, domestic and agricultural instruction, poetry, reviews, satirical pieces, and so on. This heterogeneity complemented the flexible, even unstable character of a format that was constantly reacting to a concerted legal campaign against its very existence. As Cobbett put it, whenever a new legal restriction "checked" a "former channel" of radical expression, editors improvised until their work "broke out" in "a new manner" (*CPR* 39 [1821]: 1,003–04). Over the course of the three decades of its existence, the *Political Register* appeared under a number of formats and titles; it also spawned several books, some important serial compilations, an American *Register* designed in part for matter too dangerous for English publication, and a short-lived daily paper called *Cobbett's Evening Post*. Wooler summed up the protean threat of the radical weekly newspaper when he introduced his alter ego, the alien and stunted Black Dwarf, as a figure "secure from his invisibility, and dangerous from his power of division, (for like the polypus, he can divide and redivide himself, and each division remain a perfect animal)": "Neither the throne, nor the altar, will be sanctuary against his intrusion."[13]

Radical weekly newspapers were also worldly and combative, a formal expression of the engaged character of radical discourse. Efforts to incorporate news content through commentary on daily newspapers established a dialogic structure of argument. Readers were encouraged to get involved too, by contributing letters and essays, conducting controversies of their own, and joining the improvisational networks through which news was gathered and distributed. Although radical editors developed their own strategies for negotiating their relationship with "the public" and "opinion," such concepts were treated pragmatically, as a mode of rhetorical empowerment and an anticipation of a constituency, without the deep suspicion that often characterized the contemporary reflections of Wordsworth and Coleridge.[14] In radical hands, the periodical remained an engaged form, the appropriate medium of a movement that tended to avoid abstract theorizing, and instead used "the current situation and events to support [its] arguments for the necessity of political change."[15] The appearance of a spate of radical weeklies immediately after the Peterloo Massacre in 1819 confirmed the form's intimate relation with the course of political events. The new papers typically set out from a sense of imminent crisis: "At an epoch the most eventful that ever occurred in the annals of British history"; "The affairs of this country have now evidently reached an important crisis"; "The times have an awful aspect."[16]

In the ringing opening sentences of his retrospective address to the first volume of the *Republican*, Carlile vividly mapped the critical intersection of history and politics in periodical form, *and* in the life of an imprisoned editor:

At the expiration of the year, at the expiration of that shadow of liberty we have lately possessed, and at the close of the first volume of this work, I feel an inclination, as well as a duty, to address a few words to you out of the usual way. This work, under its present title, was commenced at a critical period; at that moment when the troops were ordered to draw their swords on the people. It was at this critical period, that the Editor of this work pledged himself not to shrink from duty, because there was danger; but where there was danger, there to take his stand . . . He was at liberty when writing that short address; the next week he dated the first number of this work from a prison, and now he feels no shame in saying, that it is from a prison, and under a confinement of the strictest nature, that it is likely to be continued. The trial of the Editor occasioned some little embarrassment in attending to this work; his removal from London has added to that embarrassment: some little deviations have occurred from the proposed mode of proceeding, but the Editor hopes that a candid allowance will be made for this; and finding himself again composed and settled, to resume the second volume with the pristine vigour of the first, if a publisher can be found under the existing state of things . . . He is fully aware of the aspect of the times: but unless they are met by a boldness equivalent to martyrdom on the part of writers and publishers, the press will become that destructive engine in England which it has proved to be in other countries. (*R* 1 [1819]: vii–viii)

From the "critical period" of its inception, the *Republican* and its editor proceeded through a series of difficult events that linked the fortunes of a periodical form with the fortunes of a political move-ment. A preliminary "liberty" yielded quickly to Carlile's prosecu-tion for blasphemous libel, which forced "some little deviations" in the *Republican*; these included the movement of his bookselling operations, changes in his publisher, and his own inability to write for the paper when the courtroom demanded his full attention. Now that he was "again composed and settled," Carlile could promise the rehabilitation of his work in a second volume, but his subscription to the address indicated the irony of his stable situation: "Dorchester Gaol, Dec 30, 1819." Despite the dream of returning to an original condition of liberty and "pristine vigour," there was no escaping confinement and "deviation." Like other radical weeklies, the *Repub-lican* was from the outset a form in crisis, scarred and limited by the repressive conditions under which it was produced, and eager to propagate the sense of extremity that had penetrated its own periodical rhythms. Its career was a case study in periodical discontinuity. A journeyman tinsmith become hawker of radical periodicals, Carlile inherited *Sherwin's Political Register*, itself the successor of an earlier *Republican*, when Sherwin feared to proceed in the repressive climate of late 1819, and immediately restored the paper's original title; working substantially from prison, he then brought his *Republican* through a number of significant disruptions, including complete suspension for the year 1821, as dozens of his shop-hands, hawkers, and publishers were arrested and imprisoned. All the while, he supplemented his trademark journal with a number of more specialized periodical projects, including the *Deist* (1819–20), the *Moralist* (1823), and the *Newgate Monthly Magazine* (1824–26). If there was no getting beyond crisis and disruption, Carlile could at least try to insure that he and his work were not always its victims. The *Republican* may have shared the fragmentary characteristics that Marjorie Levinson has described in some romantic poetry, but it did not deploy that fragmentation as a sign of "artlessness," nor as a means of withdrawing "from aggressive textual determination . . . into a more refined mode of creative existence."[17] The fragmenta-

tion of radical print forms was a consequence of their furious sense
of purpose, and their combative interactions with power. When
Carlile insisted that "the aspect of the times" be "met by a boldness
equivalent to martyrdom on the part of writers and publishers," he
announced his intention to represent and intervene in a rapidly
unfolding crisis – to make the *Republican*, as he elsewhere put it, "a
journal worthy of the times" (*R* 5 [1822]: 2). Repressive conditions
demanded equally vigorous print forms and political personalities.

Political periodicals, with their strong presumption of immediate
reference to the world, are by definition serially linked with an
unfolding pattern of events. The radical weekly newspaper was
remarkable not because it was time-bound, but rather because its
temporal structure was so disrupted and discontinuous. Michael
Warner has written suggestively about the "normative routinization
of print discourse" inscribed in such early projects of the bourgeois
public sphere as *The Spectator* and *Cato's Letters*, which "incorporate
their ongoing – even routine – appearance in print as an assumption
about political legitimacy. For Addison and Steele, and even more
for Trenchard and Gordon, political publication is far from being a
deviation from social order produced by crisis." By the early nineteenth century, regular periodical expectations were fully established
among middle-class readers, and the division of the political press
between the two parties completed its integration into the stable
political life of the nation. This routine was challenged by a radical
reform movement that belittled the difference between the two
parties, and cultivated an ominous new class of political readers.
Persistent legal harassment combined with a sense of political
extremity to deprive the early nineteenth-century radical weekly of
what Warner calls "continuous, normal, normative publication."[18]
These periodicals can be defined as an ongoing but never routine or
reassuring set of deviations motivated by crisis; they preferred to
display rather than conceal their disruption, and became forms in
crisis, a visible and legible sign of political upheaval. Where political
periodicals had long structured time by breaking it into "predictable
segments," which were then recuperated in "the comforting framework of journalistic stereotypes,"[19] the radical press sought to
discomfort and challenge its readers by exposing the frightening
instability of events in the latter days of a corrupt system. The
forgotten hubris of the first *Spectator*'s advertisement, "To be Continued every Day,"[20] was suddenly recollected by a set of periodicals

that faced imminent suppression, and made their very appearance a defiant political gesture. Quotidian periodical conventions were a useful counterpoint to the more strenuous rhythms of radical print culture. Annual prefaces became a lively forum in which to reflect back on a journal's survival through repression and political unrest: "The *Examiner* closes its third volume under circumstances precisely similar to those at the conclusion of the two preceding years, – an increase of readers and a Prosecution by the ATTORNEY GENERAL."[21] Cobbett launched the Ninth Volume of the *Political Register* with a stunning Jeremiad, under the tedious newspaper heading, "Summary of Politics": "Will nothing, oh, people of England, short of destruction itself, convince you that you are on the road to destruction?" (*CPR* 9 [1806]: 1). Elaborate narratives of the trial or imprisonment of an editor followed missed or late articles or numbers; changes in title and format were accompanied by detailed accounts of new laws and new strategies of evasion, under such ominous headings as "Future Publication of the Black Dwarf" (*BD* 3 [1819]: 853). The survival of a paper through constant mutation became in every sense its plot. Even where this plot assumed a certain continuity, as in Wooler's linked series "Prosecution of the Editor," "Trial of the Editor," and "Liberation of the Editor" (*BD* 1 [1817]: 261, 305, 353), narrative suspense hinged on a threat to the very capacity to narrate. These and countless other editorial markers of discontinuity reinforced an atmosphere of crisis, and helped the radical movement challenge both traditionalist and progressive conceptions of historical experience. History became a field of combat, strewn with gaps and obstructions, and liable to rupture at any moment under the accumulated pressure of political corruption and economic injustice.

Never simply a consequence of government harassment, periodical interruption in this period operated within a complex dialectic that linked opportunistic reform strategies and reactive government policies. Radical editors alternately sought and avoided continuous production, and the state by turns enforced and prevented it. Wholly regular periodicals were from a radical perspective an imperfect vehicle with which to track a political sphere that was by turns dense and diffuse, lurching towards catastrophe, but somehow always pulling back from the brink. The radical weekly spanned the entire era of protest that extended from the Luddite riots of 1811 to the Queen Caroline affair and beyond, but episodes of acute unrest witnessed a proliferation of papers, and were punctuated too by spates of occasional pamphleteering. Shortly before he suspended the *Republican* in 1821, Carlile expressed his resistance to periodical routine: "I do not expect to publish at regular periods, I shall write only when I feel an inclination, and have a subject to proceed upon. Above all things I dislike writing by measure" (*R* 4 [1820]: 621–22). Occasional pamphlets consumed his energies during the year in which the *Republican* did not appear.[22] Regular appearance could also be experienced as an oppressive discipline, imposed by a government that made periodical order a prerequisite to control. As Castlereagh argued in a House of Commons debate over the Newspaper Stamp Duties Bill, "it might be necessary that the periods of publication should be required to be uniform" if "the channels of mischief" were to be stopped.[23] The law that was soon adopted did monitor periodical forms in part by defining their period of appearance.

Distasteful as Castlereagh's "uniform" regimen might seem to a versatile editor like Carlile, "writing by measure" was the only way to sustain a regular audience, an important consideration for a movement that relied on the press for matters of political organization.[24] Consistent appearance also challenged a political elite that had learned to fear the habit of radical reading. Conservative argument often figured the radical threat in terms of regular consumption and ingestion. An 1818 *Blackwood's* article expressed horror at the ease with which "Jacobinical journalists" managed "to hit the taste of the vulgar" through "the daily, the weekly, [and] the monthly press":

The lie that we read with a shudder to-day, is repeated to-morrow and to-morrow, for weeks, for months, and for years, till the eye and the mind learn to glance over it with unconcern. Newspapers are not studied, they are simply read. Their contents are swallowed by us when our bodies and our minds are in a state of listlessness and inaction . . . Men give themselves up gradually to their incessant and irritating influence, because they cannot always resist.[25]

Effective distribution networks extended this periodical saturation through space as well as time, until "the public mind" was "saturated with the odious poison": "In the manufacturing districts they had been circulated by every possible contrivance; every town was overflowed by them; in every village they were almost innumerable, and scarcely a cottage had escaped the perseverance of the agents of mischief."[26] The conservative nightmare of periodical hegemony helps explain the sometimes erratic logic of repression in this period. Even where prison terms, fines, and confiscations did not succeed in destroying a paper, they might interrupt what Lord Ellenborough called the "continual stream of falsehood and malignity," and prevent the radical attitude from becoming habitual.[27]

If "Jacobinical journalists" dominated the weekly press, daily newspapers remained the print incarnation of the status quo. In parliamentary debates over the Six Acts, government and opposition members alike singled out the "reputable" and "respectable" daily papers as "defenders of social order" and "efficient allies" of the state.[28] The "transparency of dailiness," as Richard Terdiman has termed it, promised an uninterrupted pattern of expectation and reception, and sure victory in the struggle for periodical dominance.[29] The daily newspaper became an object of envious speculation among leading radical publicists. Where Wooler's decision in 1824 to scale the *Black Dwarf* back to monthly production signalled its gradual demise, radical moves towards greater frequency were grasped as the empowering periodical register of a quickening crisis. While others were busy setting up weeklies in the year 1819, Cobbett supplemented his weekly assault on the system with a new daily paper, *Cobbett's Evening Post*. His Prospectus treated the project as a strategic intervention in the politics of periodicity:

Another strong motive to this undertaking, is the pressing necessity of *speedily noticing what passes in Parliament*, of which I think myself able to give a little better account than is given by the lazy and selfish wretches whose stupid comments now disgrace the daily press. Never was there a time so full of events as the present. *The fate of England* will probably depend upon what the Parliament shall do, during this very Session. To wait a week, in order to be able to observe what passes in Parliament, at such a crisis, is to neglect the means of doing a great part of the good that I think myself able to do. "Sufficient unto *the day* is the evil thereof." (*CPR* 35 [1819–20]: 510–11)

This notion of a "sufficient" medium suggests a formal realism for newspaper discourse, articulated along the axis of periodical frequency: times "so full of events as the present" required a swift and capacious print vehicle. The *Evening Post* left Cobbett with the problem of what to do with his less nimble weekly paper. He briefly considered monthly publication, but perhaps sensing that the new project would not take, soon committed himself to the *Register*'s original weekly format, in terms that confirmed a division of periodical labor but reversed its priority. *"Speedily noticing"* events, it seemed, meant superficially affecting them: "It is on the *Register* I rely for producing *lasting conviction* and *final success*. The Register proceeds against the fortress of Corruption by regular and steady approaches: the Evening Post acts as a *skirmisher* to keep off the assassin-like assailants, who have hitherto annoyed the main body on its march."[30]

As it turned out, the *Evening Post* survived less than a year, and did not play a pivotal role in reform politics. The "overwhelmingly commercial pressures" shaping the development of the daily news-paper press in this period were a major factor in its relatively peripheral role in reform politics.[31] The cost and scale of a daily grew steadily from the end of the eighteenth century through the early nineteenth century, and advertising expanding commensu-rately, until "by 1820 advertisements, not subscription sales, furn-ished the largest part of the revenue of daily papers."[32] While the *Times* led the way into this more commercially and capitally intensive era of newspaper production, the demographics of a radical reading audience consigned the unstamped weekly to the stable "egalitarian phase" of the hand press.[33] *Cobbett's Evening Post* set out promisingly with more than a page (five columns) of reasonably diverse adver-tising, but by the second number this commercial space was cut in half, and within a few weeks it shrunk to a single column; later numbers often contained just a few notices for radical publications, or no advertisements at all. In this same period, readers of "respect-able" dailies like the *Times, Courier,* and *Morning Chronicle* were greeted by an entire first page of commercial advertising, and a final page of paid notices for auctions and places; even a more roguish, ultra-conservative daily like John Stoddart's *New Times* managed to secure a full page of commercial advertising.[34] The *Evening Post* turned out to be a costly failure. Its main promotional function was to secure subscribers to Cobbett's bid for a parliamentary seat at Coventry, confirming his restriction to a circuit of political rather than commercial interests.[35]

Radical publicists did their best to incorporate daily expression into the weekly format, through extensive commentary on the daily press, and through rhetorical devices that mimicked more frequent appearance when events seemed to require it. During the trial of Queen Caroline, Carlile perceived a sharp increase in the density of political time, similar to the shift that motivated Cobbett's *Evening Post.* "It is difficult to say much on this business," he wrote, "every day becomes an age, and the news of yesterday is lost sight of by the more important intelligence of to-day" (*R* 4 [1820]: 255). The *Republican* went on to provide a more sensitive register of this uncertain world by resorting to a diary mode: "Friday morning, Oct. 13th. – The Queen's advocates have now beaten down every tittle of evidence that has been given against her" (*R* 4 [1820]: 226). Or more intimately still, in a public letter to the Queen: "P.S. Dec. 13th. It was not my intention to have divided this letter, but . . . we have come to a still more important epoch in your life, and one which appears calculated to lead to some sudden and important change" (*R* 4 [1820]: 545–46). At a moment when the imprisoned Carlile was increasingly frustrated by his isolation from London politics, this vivid postscript served to knit reader, writer, and Queen together in the close atmosphere of crisis. Theological dispute, it is worth noting, proceeded in the *Republican* at its regular weekly pace, unaffected by the shifting density of political time. Carlile grew painfully aware that economic and political upheaval did not necessarily touch upon matters of Christian faith.

The historian Jeremy Popkin has observed that reading old newspapers reminds us "that history is something that people make without knowing how it will come out."[36] This sense of contingency became in radical hands a polemical weapon. In "Napoleon's Return," a virtuoso performance that still evokes a sense of dramatic uncertainty, Cobbett provided a vivid, present-tense account of the French leader's escape from Elba in 1815. "It is now *Tuesday noon,*" the article began, "The next newspapers may inform me, that Napoleon is *at Paris,* or, that he *is dead*" (*CPR* 27 [1815]: 358). Using ellipses to mark subsequent interruptions in the arrival of news, Cobbett continued to track the course of events: ". . . . . . It is now *Wednesday* afternoon, and we are told, that Napoleon was at AUTUN on Thursday, in spite of all the forces in his front and in his rear"; ". . . . . . *Thursday* afternoon. The great question is decided. Napoleon has entered Paris without a single shot being fired, except in the way of rejoicing, or the least opposition shewn to his resumption of all his former power and dignity" (366). Throughout the article, he pitted his own sense of Napoleon's "triumph" against the hostile expectations of the "legitimate" English and French press. "All that is said about the loyalty of the people of France, about the zeal and fidelity of the French soldiers, about the numerous corps which surround Napoleon: these may all be true, and they may all be false as the hearts of those who publish them" (358). "Napoleon's Return" was a daring contest, staged on the field of periodical writing, between Cobbett's own contempt for a post-Napoleonic settlement in Europe, and the official view that the French people were glad to be rid of their deposed emperor.

Looking back from a late twentieth-century perspective, it may be hard to associate newspapers, even in their radical manifestation, with the kind of disruptive effects I have described. In an incisive account of the French mass daily, Richard Terdiman has described the modern newspaper as the sign of a "dominant discourse self-confidently bodied forth." This dominance, which seems "to *go without saying*," can be traced to the form's relentless display of sheer, undifferentiated content: "The newspaper is built by addition of discrete, theoretically disconnected elements which juxtapose themselves only in response to the abstract requirements of 'layout' – thus of a disposition of space whose logic, ultimately, is commercial." Current skepticism about the newspaper press is mediated in part by romantic assumptions about the stupefying rather than energizing impact of mass print culture, so it is appropriate that Terdiman pits newspaper "layout" against romantic "canons of text structure and coherence": "The newspaper can be understood as the first culturally influential *anti-organicist* mode of modern discursive construction. Its form *denies form*."[37] This daunting cultural formation was just beginning to emerge in early nineteenth-century Britain. The *Times* again led the way with innovations in typography and layout that facilitated inconsecutive (and inattentive) reading of heterogeneous material, distancing newspapers from their antecedents in more continuous news books and pamphlets.[38] Radical publicists actively resisted this emerging tendency for print news to be "organized *as disorganization*" and as "consumer commodity,"[39] without resorting to the organicist theories of their romantic contemporaries. Cobbett treated his unstamped *Registers* as "Little Books" to be bound in volumes and preserved (*CPR* 32 [1817]: 364). He joined other radical editors in producing lead essays that gathered several issues under one rubric, demanded sustained attention, and served as the formal expression of a radical belief that everything was connected, that a single system of oppression extended from rotten boroughs and legitimate monarchy to paper money, bible societies, savings banks, and tea drinking. The organizational logic of radical print culture was oppositional rather than commercial. "All my designs, wishes, and thoughts," Cobbett wrote, "have this one great object in view: *the overthrow of the ruffian Borough-mongers*" (*CPR* 35 [1819–20]: 8).

Cobbett's "one great object" did not generate the internal textual coherence associated with aesthetic forms, in part because an oppositional imperative extended outward from the printed text to politics and the law, and to calculations about circulation and readership. Radical discourse presented itself as having been shaped and misshaped *from without*, not organically structured from within. The frank attention paid to extrinsic circumstances and material conditions was partly a consequence of the limited scale of radical print culture. Far from idealizing itself as original creation or imaginative expression, the radical weekly reflected on everything from print technology and methods of distribution to typographical errors and the relentless pressure of periodical deadlines. For political purposes, legal harassment was the chief limit on the development of the form. As Carlile's 1820 Address "To the Readers of the *Republican*" insisted, "deviations . . . in the pages of the *Republican*" could be traced to the "deviations . . . in my situation" (*R* 4 [1820]: 615), brought about by prosecution and imprisonment. If this recourse from the page to an extrinsic "situation" suggests Terdiman's "anti-organicist" impulse, it is important to insist that the radical weekly was less concerned to "deny form" than to insist that form was being denied to it. Jerome McGann provides a useful counterpoint in his account of Byron's *Don Juan*, a nearly contemporary serial improvisation in print. Like Byron, radical editors tended to "convert the whole (i.e., the human world) into a series," and to thematize formal contingency, but unlike Byron, they struggled with strict legal regulations on form, and did not imagine that they were abdicating prevenient control in favor of "accidents, trivia, the unexpected, 'mere' possibilities." Where the character Don Juan embodied a print "experiment" in "informality," the radical weekly was a print experience of deformation, embodied in the character of the Black Dwarf.[40] Just as Wooler's protean alter ego occupied the social and political space mapped by oppression ("neither the throne, nor the altar, will be sanctuary against his intrusion"), so papers like the *Black Dwarf* exercised their subversive mobility in a print space mapped by the government. The pleasures of accident

that McGann finds so appealing in Byron would have deflected
attention from a painful conspiratorial design. While respectable
daily newspapers of the same period tended to allow their densely
printed pages to pass as an unremarked consequence of restrictive
taxation,[41] the radical press reflected obsessively on its own deformation. Even trivial shifts in format, content, title, and price could
be traced to changing political and economic conditions, and to the
government's sustained campaign against the very existence of the
unstamped weekly format.

The ability to work through repression, and especially imprisonment, became a litmus test for the viability of radical protest in print.
Though atypical in the period of its appearance, the *Newgate Monthly
Magazine* was in this sense paradigmatic. Edited and written from
Newgate by a group of Carlile's imprisoned shop-hands, it opened
with an apologetic glance at its own circumscribed condition: "In
the perusal of the following pages, the reader must not expect to find
a display of literary excellence. He is requested to consider the
circumstances under which the work was commenced, and to make
the consequent allowances" (*NM* 1 [1824–25]: v). The inescapable
sign of the title, "Newgate," hovered over the production and
reception of the magazine, but its impact was not entirely negative,
since prison called attention to injustices that demanded reform.
The differential hermeneutic ("make the consequent allowances")
required by the *Newgate Monthly* forced the reader to attend to
repressive conditions: to read was to acknowledge power. An
imprisoned magazine found a way to exceed its formal limitations by
circulating the restricted conditions under which it was produced. In
an appropriate irony, the magazine ceased production when its
editorial collective was released from prison:

In judging of the work it must be remembered that but for the religious
prosecutions, the individuals who have conducted it would in all probability, never have intruded themselves upon the public . . . We stop here,
not only because we have effected all we desired, but to go further would
be inconvenient to ourselves. Before twelve more numbers could be
published we may be very widely dispersed. (*NM* 2 [1825–26]: 529–30)

Men like William Campion, a Lancaster shoemaker, and Richard
Hassell, a Dorset farm laborer, had found an oppositional voice in
the discursive spaces opened up by a legal machinery meant to
silence them. Or as Hassell himself put it, with almost painful

immediacy, "the hand which describes these lines, but for persecution for opinions, might, and most probably would, have guided a plough" (*NM* 1 [1824–25]: vi). While the *Newgate Monthly* was an exceptional case, most of the leading radical writers and editors at some point worked from prison, and the effort to effect resistance from within a corrupt system was among the fundamental problems of radical discourse.

Under the pressure of its own literal and figurative imprisonment, the radical weekly became a crucible of political conflict. Denied the regular patterns of production and circulation that would allow it to "go without saying," these newspapers spoke through every feature, even those normally filtered out by a reader's unconscious screen of periodical expectations. Writers and editors prominently subscribed articles from prison and from exile. Wooler introduced the ironic claim that his prison cell had become the perfect classroom for a radical autodidact into the *Black Dwarf*'s legally required notice of publication, and then moved the notice from its usual place at the end of each number to the masthead: "Edited, Printed, and Published by T. J. Wooler, late of 81, Bishopsgate Without, and 85, Bartholemew Close; and now of Ellenborough College, Surrey" (*BD* 1 [1817]: 225–26, 240).[42] In 1822, Carlile raised the specter of French Republicanism by first dating his articles from the Spanish Revolution, and then moving on to more elaborate polemical formulations: "Nov. 3, Year 3, of the Spanish Revolution, and last, or last but one, of the Holy Alliance," "Nov. 12, Year 3, of the Spanish Revolution, which the Despots at Verona cannot revolve or digest. It will choke them," "Feb. 23, Year 1823 of the last of the Gods."[43] Meanwhile, the legally required date at the top of the *Republican* continued to register what Benedict Anderson has termed the "steady onward clocking of homogeneous, empty time."[44] By preserving the ordinary calendar, yet infusing secondary appearances of the date with his own sense of an ironic radical apocalypse, the atheist Carlile managed to lodge an explosive tension within the confines of periodical form: he invoked all the energy and authority of Christian eschatology in order to break its stranglehold upon history and upon human experience.

If this kind of formal satire seems like an editorial fantasy, and a distraction from the real business of political resistance, it is important to see that the struggle between print protest and state repression had long been played out at the level of form. From the outset,

the English state had controlled printed news through strict defini-
tions of its formal and material dimensions.[45] Cobbett merely
continued a longstanding contest over form when he reprinted the
lead essay of the *Register* in a manner that fell just outside the letter of
the law. The government responded with the Newspaper Stamp
Duties Act of 1819, which regulated everything from the price of a
newspaper and the interval of its appearance to the size of a sheet of
newsprint.[46] The upshot of the Act was to confine the radical weekly
to just two formats, an unstamped edition double the previous size
and priced at six pence, or a stamped edition entitled to free postage
but costing seven pence or more. Neither option served the needs of
radical editors and readers, and a cheap press did not really recover
until the law was widely ignored in the 1830s.[47] The formal impact
of the new legislation was immediately evident to radical readers.
The Cap of Liberty tried to adjust by merging with the *Medusa*:

> We . . . shall not pay the smallest attention to the late Acts of Parliament,
> which have been enacted in direct opposition to the spirit of the
> Constitution. We mean to say, that we shall pay no attention to them, as far
> as regards the spirit of this publication, which will be kept up with the same
> undeviating adherence to truth as heretofore . . . To effect this object, with
> the least possible increase of price to our readers, matters have been
> arranged so as to unite the MEDUSA with the CAP OF LIBERTY, which when
> together will form two sheets, for sixpence, that being the lowest sum which
> Lord Castlereagh will allow any thing political to make its appearance
> without a stamp.[48]

Despite the defiant tone, neither title survived the first month of the
new year. Other radical periodicals struggled with similar expedi-
ents. After the last of his cheap *Registers* appeared in January 1820,
Cobbett enlarged the paper to fit the new six-penny format, and a
year later supplemented this version with a stamped edition. Old
articles were sometimes reprinted to fill extra space, and in 1821 "a
leaf of Advertisements" was added to meet the expenses in paper
demanded by "the *Six-Acts Parliament*" (*CPR* 38 [1821]: 596–97).
Wooler also acknowledged "a difficulty in finding *valuable* materials
for the space required to be filled," and in 1824 announced that he
would scale his paper back to monthly publication (*BD* 12 [1824]:
403). Denied the protean mobility that had once allowed it to
"divide and redivide," the unwieldy *Black Dwarf* was defunct within
a year.

If the Six Acts helped engineer the demise of the radical weekly newspaper, the period of their introduction was a high water mark in the critical engagement between print protest and state repression. In parliament, advocates of the new restrictions named for the record the papers that "had done the most mischief," and warned of an emerging "despotism of the press" that could only be put down by an equally vigorous campaign of state repression.[49] If the law determined the form of the radical press, the radical press determined the form of the law. The preamble to the Newspaper Stamp Duties Act acknowledged this dialectic of legislation and transgression: "Whereas pamphlets and printed papers containing observations upon public events and occurrences, tending to excite hatred and contempt of the government and constitution . . . have lately been published in great numbers, and at very small prices; . . . it is expedient that the same should be restrained."[50] In a widely reprinted 1820 speech to his constituents at Liverpool, Canning put the most elegant construction on the Six Acts as the last word in a complex political dialogue:

And, Gentlemen, what was the character of those measures? – The best eulogy of them I take to be this: it may be said of them, as has been said of some of the most consummate productions of literary art, that though no man beforehand had exactly anticipated the scope and the details of them, there is no man who, when they were laid before him, did not discover that they were precisely such as he would himself have suggested. So faithfully adapted to the case which they were framed to meet, so correctly adjusted to the degree and nature of the mischief which they were intended to control, that while we all feel that they have done their work, I think none will say there has been any thing in them of excess or supererogation.[51]

The language of aesthetics was alone sensitive enough to convey the perfect fitness of the "measures" to the conditions "they were framed to meet." If the Six Acts limited a radical response, they were not the last word in the dialogue. Cobbett continued to search for gaps in the web of repression. "*Inspired*" to find that the Six Acts allowed "for the free circulation of pamphlets on religion," he began "preaching in print" in his *Monthly Religious Tracts* (1821–22). Not to be outdone, he met Canning's aesthetics of repression with an evangelical theology of radical protest in print: "The nation has to thank *Six-Acts* for this publication. The spirit was in motion: it was working within: and, feeling itself checked, in its former channel, by Six-Acts, it broke out in this new manner" (*CPR* 39 [1821]: 560, 1,003–04).

While the political and polemical saturation of these newspapers directs attention to particular features, it is important to see that they were at the same time remarkably ambitious, even totalizing, in their scope. Radical editors resisted a contemporary tendency to parcel out matters of culture, commerce, politics, and entertainment in distinct intervals and forms. From its inception, Cobbett promised that the *Political Register* would "at once embrace every rational object of a news-paper, a magazine, and a review."[52] Wooler had similar ambitions, and though politics soon dominated the *Black Dwarf*, he promised that a "New Series" prepared in 1823 would restore his "original intention" and "embrace every interesting topic of general information."[53] To some degree, the limited economic resources of radical print culture prevented any more elaborate articulation of periodical modes; the prohibition on news in the first phase of the cheap weekly, and the extra paper required for the six-penny format after the Six Acts, further directed these papers towards the function of a miscellany or review. However, synthetic forms had a critical point as well, allowing editors to comprehend the massive form of corruption. Carlile knew that radical reform appealed to more readers than religious freethought, but he defended his practice of introducing "theological subjects or disputes in an alleged political publication" on the grounds that "the corruptions of the legislature" were "so deeply rooted in, and so ardently supported by the Church" (*R* 1 [1819]: xiv).[54] The disparate materials of the radical editor were forged in the crucible formed by an oppressive system and a radical countersystem: every issue took its appropriate place in a hierarchy of vice and virtue that extended upward to parliamentary corruption and radical reform. This urge to assimilate everything to "system" has often been criticized, but there can be no doubt that a principal appeal of popular radicalism was its bold proposition, in the face of the increasing complexity and fragmentation of human experience, that everything was connected.

A comprehensive structure also registered the movement's powerfully utopian impulses. By combining periodical modes, radical publicists struggled to complete print forms that were damaged and deformed from the outset. In this desire to recover some lost wholeness, the radical weekly presents its most romantic face, and betrays the reform movement's nostalgic and even reactionary premises. By combining in their own persons professional functions (writing, editing, printing, publishing) that were increasingly divided at the higher levels of print culture,[55] radical editors attempted in Blakean fashion to reverse the socially and psychically divisive consequences of modernity and corruption. The highest radical aim in print was a book of the world that contained everything the radical citizen could require. The last vestige of Cobbett's doomed effort to attract commercial advertising in the *Political Register* was a remarkable notice for "The Cobbett-Library" that buried evidence of his isolation from wider markets under an absolute faith in the sufficiency of his work: "When I am asked what books a young man or young woman ought to read, I always answer, Let him or her read *all* the books that I have written."[56] Carlile offered a similar account of his own work, in an intriguing comparison between himself and a poet whose "genius" he recognized and sometimes pirated:

If a young man, fairly in search of knowledge, were to sit down and read carefully through every line that Lord Byron has written, he would find that he had scarcely added any thing to his former stock of knowledge; but if that same young man, unacquainted with the works of Thomas Paine or any other Republican writer, were to read through the ten volumes of "The Republican," with all their literary defects, with all their "clod-like" sentences, with all their misprints and mistakes, he would find, that he had gained a store of the most important knowledge. (*R* 11 [1825]: 164)

Here, the fantastic hubris of print sufficiency met a frank acknowledgment of the imperfect condition of any radical library. Carlile excused even as he celebrated the modest art of political editing: the "misprints and mistakes" scattered through the *Republican* did not interfere with its primary purpose, to offer the reader a capacious "stock" of radicalizing "knowledge." Where the poet of *Don Juan* was able to recuperate contrived "literary defects" as the comic register of a liberated attitude toward the world, the "clod-like" impairments of Carlile's work remained just that, an intractable sign of the repressive conditions under which the *Republican* had been produced.

The synthetic energy of radical argument and radical form was a further challenge to prevailing trends. Suspended as it was between the daily newspaper and the monthly magazine, the radical weekly seemed unusually systematic from the one perspective, and dangerously chaotic from the other. Writing for the *Edinburgh Review* during the revival of the unstamped press in the 1830s, J. R. McCulloch preached a whiggish policy of combatting the radical editor's "omnivorous system" through a reduction of the newspaper taxes that brought such a system into being. The article wove a dense web of social, economic, and textual hierarchies, and seemed unembarrassed about deploying periodical forms as instruments of social control:

The unjust stigma that now attaches to low-priced papers would be removed; and men of talent and principle would find it equally advantageous to write in them, as in those sold at a higher price. Were such an alteration made, we venture to predict that the present twopenny papers, than which nothing can be conceived more utterly worthless, would very soon be superseded by others of a totally different character; so that in this way the change would be in the highest degree beneficial. It would also, we apprehend, introduce into newspaper compiling, that division of labour, or rather of subjects, which is found in every thing else. Instead of having all sorts of matters crammed into the same journal, every different topic of considerable interest would be separately treated in a low-priced journal, appropriated to it only, and conducted by persons fully conversant with its principles and details.

The same "division of labour" and "subjects" that radical editors refused became in McCulloch's view a way of regularizing periodical discourse, encouraging psychic and social discipline, and assimilating "the lowest ranks and orders of the people" into the orderly "regimen" of a new century.[57] Radical editors, soon to be superseded by McCulloch's program, escaped his reified vision of expert ascendancy and audience fragmentation because they rejected its political corollary, the theory of specific interest representation. The radical press pitted a single popular interest against the interests of corruption, and served the mixed and comprehensive audience that resulted with an "omnivorous system" of periodical production. "All we desire," Carlile modestly announced during the era of repression that led up to McCulloch's market solution, "is to have our publications read by all" (R 9 [1824]: 709).

NOTES

1 I am grateful to the participants in the 1993 NASSR conference in London, Ontario for their very helpful response to this paper.
2 See William Wickwar, *The Struggle for the Freedom of the Press, 1819–1832* (London: George Allen and Unwin, 1928), 51–52.
3 *Cobbett's Weekly Political Register* 31 (1816): 520, 737; hereafter abbreviated as *CPR*, and included in the text. Other radical periodicals will be abbreviated in the text and notes as follows: *BD* for *Black Dwarf*; *NM* for *Newgate Monthly Magazine*; and *R* for *Republican*.

4 The story of the phenomenal impact of the cheap *Register* has been told many times, usually following Cobbett's own detailed account. See Wickwar, *Struggle for the Freedom of the Press*, 49–55; George Spater, *William Cobbett: The Poor Man's Friend*, 2 vols. (Cambridge: Cambridge University Press, 1982), II: 347–49; Richard Altick, *The English Common Reader: A Social History of the Mass Reading Public, 1800–1900* (Chicago: University of Chicago Press, 1957), 324–28; G. A. Cranfield, *The Press and Society, From Caxton to Northcliffe* (London: Longman, 1978), 92–108; Joel H. Wiener, *The War of the Unstamped: The Movement to Repeal the British Newspaper Tax, 1830–1836* (Ithaca: Cornell University Press, 1969), 3–6; and Arthur Aspinall, *Politics and the Press, c. 1780–1850* (London: Home and Van Thal, 1949), 29–32, 57–60.

5 *Anti-Cobbett* 1 (1817): 95–96.

6 Robert Southey, *Essays, Moral and Political*, 2 vols. (London: John Murray, 1832), I: 120, 132–33.

7 Cranfield, *Press and Society*, 90–91.

8 See R. K. Webb, *The British Working Class Reader, 1790–1848* (London: George Allen and Unwin, 1955), 49–50.

9 E. P. Thompson, *The Making of the English Working Class* (New York: Vintage Books, 1966), 459, 466.

10 *Gorgon*, no. 1 (1818): 8.

11 See Wiener, *War of the Unstamped*, 5.

12 Thompson, *Making of the English Working Class*, 674.

13 *BD* 1 (1817): title page.

14 See for example Wordsworth's well known distinction between "the People" and "the Public," in his "Essay, Supplementary to the Preface," in *William Wordsworth: Selected Prose*, ed. John O. Hayden (Harmondsworth: Penguin, 1988), 411–13. For Coleridge on "the reading public," see *The Statesman's Manual*, in *The Collected Works of Samuel Taylor Coleridge*, vol. 6, ed. R. J. White (Princeton: Princeton University Press, 1972), 36–38.

15 J. Ann Hone, *For the Cause of Truth: Radicalism in London, 1796–1821* (Oxford: Clarendon Press, 1982), 326.

16 *London Alfred*, no. 1 (1819): 1; *White Hat* 1 (1819): 1; and *Briton*, no. 1 (1819): 2.

17 Marjorie Levinson, *The Romantic Fragment Poem: A Critique of a Form* (Chapel Hill: University of North Carolina Press, 1986), 209–10, 214.

18 Michael Warner, *The Letters of the Republic: Publication and the Public Sphere in Eighteenth-Century America* (Cambridge, Mass.: Harvard University Press, 1990), 65–66.

19 Jeremy Popkin, *News and Politics in the Age of Revolution* (Ithaca: Cornell University Press, 1989), 7. See also Lennard Davis, *Factual Fictions: The Origins of the English Novel* (New York: Columbia University Press, 1983), 73–74.

20 Warner, *Letters of the Republic*, 65

21 "Postscript for the Year 1810," *Examiner* (1810), no pagination.

22 See Wickwar, *Struggle for the Freedom of the Press*, 212.

23 *Parliamentary Debates* (London: T. C. Hansard), 41 (1819–20): 1,176.

24 For regular readership and periodical production, see Margaret Beetham, "Towards a Theory of the Periodical as a Publishing Genre," in *Investigating Victorian Journalism*, ed. Laurel Brake, Aled Jones, and Lionel Madden (New York: St. Martin's Press, 1990), 28. For radical readership as organization, see Thompson, *Making of the English Working Class*, 494; Raymond Williams, *Cobbett* (Oxford: Oxford University Press, 1963), 16; and Geoff Eley, "Re-Thinking the Political: Social History and Political Culture in 18th and 19th Century Britain," *Archiv für Sozialgeschichte* 21 (1981): 449.

25 *Blackwood's* 4 (1818–19): 354–56.

26 *Parliamentary Debates* 35 (1817): 554.

27 *Parliamentary Debates* 41 (1819–20): 1,591.

28 *Parliamentary Debates* 41 (1819–20): 539–42, 1,538–41, 1,546.

29 Richard Terdiman, *Discourse/Counter-Discourse: The Theory and Practice of Symbolic Resistance in Nineteenth-Century France* (Ithaca: Cornell University Press, 1985), 121.

30 *Cobbett's Evening Post*, no. 5 (February 3, 1820).

31 Jeremy Black, "The Eighteenth Century British Press," in *Encyclopedia of the British Press*, ed. Dennis Griffiths (London: Macmillan, 1992), 15.

32 Marcus Wood, *Radical Satire and Print Culture, 1790–1822* (Oxford: Clarendon Press, 1994), 187.

33 For the shifting commercial conditions of the newspaper press in the late eighteenth and early nineteenth centuries, see Black, "The Eighteenth Century British Press," 13–15; Ian Christie, "British Newspapers in the Later Georgian Age," in *Myth and Reality in Late-Eighteenth-Century British Politics* (Berkeley: University of California Press, 1970), 319–23; Raymond Williams, "The Press and Popular Culture: An Historical Perspective," in *Newspaper History from the Seventeenth Century to the Present Day*, ed. George Boyce, James Curran, and Pauline Wingate (London: Constable, 1978), 46–48; and James Curran, "Press History," in James Curran and Jane Seaton, *Power Without Responsibility: The Press and Broadcasting in Britain* (London: Methuen, 1985), 7–9, 11–12.

34 In *Victorian News and Newspapers* (Oxford: Clarendon Press, 1985), 16, Lucy Brown has estimated that by the Victorian period a newspaper was financially secure if half of its space was devoted to advertising.

35 Cranfield, *Press and Society*, 109.

36 Popkin, *News and Politics*, xi.

37 Terdiman, *Discourse/Counter-Discourse*, 117–18, 122.

38 See Stanley Morison, *The English Newspaper* (Cambridge: Cambridge University Press, 1932), 184–85.

39 Terdiman, *Discourse/Counter-Discourse*, 120, 127.

40 Jerome McGann, *"Don Juan" in Context* (Chicago: University of Chicago Press, 1976), 103, 107–09, 115–17.

41 Morison, *English Newspaper*, 185, 206; see also Wood, *Radical Satire and Print Culture*, 186–87.

42 For the radical use of the prison as a school, see Iain McCalman, *Radical Underworld: Prophets, Revolutionaries and Pornographers in London, 1795–1840* (Cambridge: Cambridge University Press, 1988), 191.

43 For these and other instances, including some in letters from readers, see *R* 6 (1822): 605, 737, 751, 769, 801, and *R* 7 (1823): 321.

44 Benedict Anderson, *Imagined Communities: Reflections on the Origin and Spread of Nationalism* (London: Verso, 1983), 37.

45 Davis, *Factual Fictions*, 95–97.

46 See *Parliamentary Debates* 41 (1819–20): 1,678–80.

47 For the later revival of cheap publication in illegal form, see Wiener, *War of the Unstamped*; and Patricia Hollis, *The Pauper Press: A Study in Working-Class Radicalism of the 1830s* (Oxford: Oxford University Press, 1970).

48 *Cap of Liberty* 1 (1819): 275–76; for related announcements, see *Medusa* 1 (1819): 359, 369–71.

49 *Parliamentary Debates* 41 (1819–20): 1,677–78.

50 *Parliamentary Debates* 41 (1819–20): 396, 577–78, 1,505, 1,545.

51 George Canning, *Speech of the Right Hon. George Canning, to his Constituents at Liverpool, On Saturday, March 18th, 1820, at the Celebration of His Fourth Election* (London: John Murray, 1820), 10.

52 Advertisement, *CPR* 1 (1802), no pagination.

53 "New Series of the Black Dwarf," *BD* 11 (1823), no pagination.

54 For Carlile's efforts to negotiate religion and politics, see James Epstein, *Radical Expression: Political Language, Ritual, and Symbol in England* (New York: Oxford University Press, 1994), 104–07, 126–27; and Robert Hole, *Pulpits, Politics and Public Order in England, 1760–1832* (Cambridge: Cambridge University Press, 1989), 206–13.

55 For Cobbett as "self-publishing periodical essayist," see Jon Klancher, *The Making of English Reading Audiences, 1790–1832* (Madison: University of Wisconsin Press, 1987), 48.

56 The advertisement appears in many of Cobbett's published works; I quote from the third edition of *A Year's Residence in the United States of America* (London: n.p., 1828).

57 *Edinburgh Review* 53 (1831): 436–37.

CHAPTER 3

History, trauma, and the limits of the liberal imagination: William Godwin's historical fiction

Gary Handwerk

Men make their own history, but they do not make it just as they please; they do not make it under circumstances chosen by themselves, but under circumstances directly found, given, and transmitted from the past. The tradition of all the dead generations weighs like a nightmare on the brain of the living.

Karl Marx, "The Eighteenth Brumaire"

The determination of mind, in consequence of which the child contracts some of his earliest propensities . . . is produced by circumstances so minute and subtle, as in few instances to have been made the subject of history.

William Godwin, *Political Justice*

I

It is a curious fact of literary history that the historical novel should be the genre whose definition and status have been most indissolubly connected to the output of one individual author. Whatever we make of the historical novel, we can scarcely avoid making it begin with Scott, and whatever we make of Scott, our image of him will crucially predetermine our definition of the historical novel and, by extension, our understanding of Romantic historical consciousness in general. There is, to be sure, a certain aptness in the way that the purveyor of monumental historical fictions himself acquired monumental status in literary history, through a combination of astute marketing, unmatched popularity as a writer of fiction, and a critical self-consciousness rare among British novelists of the period. Scott's greatness, as Virginia Woolf wryly noted, had become so secure that it could even persist past the time of his real influence upon English literature.[1]

Yet our sense of the historical novel has begun to shift in ways that might ultimately displace Scott from his solitary centrality. We have moved past the historical moment when Georg Lukács could seem paradigmatic in his critical view of Scott as the sole originator and ideal exemplar of historical fiction – not so much because of his skill in rendering the past, but because of the self-conscious way that his representations of the past were made part of the process of constructing a distinctively modern historical consciousness. Lukács's perspective, shaped as it was by his own debt to Marxist historiography, saw in Scott a novelistic equivalent to Hegel, an essential and revolutionary step forward in European literary history.[2] Yet that confident portrayal of the larger historical picture is precisely what, for postmodern skepticism, signals Lukács's subjection to his own historical moment and its rather touching nineteenth-century faith in metanarratives. Lukács's view of Scott faces a further, more empirical challenge from the contextualizing scholarship of such recent critics as Marilyn Butler, Gary Kelly, and Ina Ferris, whose work has both broadened and loosened our definition of historical fiction.[3] They and others have altered our sense of what texts might count as historical fiction and of how complex the connections of the historical novel to more general issues of history and historiography during the Romantic period really are. Conceiving history less homogeneously, we can suddenly see all sorts of historical fictions appearing alongside Scott.

Yet Lukács's discussion remains a valuable touchstone for defining the problems raised by historical fiction and his analysis of how Scott's texts were constructed remains in many respects unsurpassed. Lukács was exceptionally clear, for instance, in distinguishing between novelistic uses of history that were merely ornamental and those that were fully and self-consciously historical. His discussion of character thus praises Scott for the "specifically historical" portrayal of his characters, that is, for the "derivation of the individuality of characters from the historical peculiarity of their age" (19). Scott's characters not only reflect their era, but give form to its most typical and essential features. "Scott's greatness lies in his capacity to give living human embodiment to historical-social types" (35), that is, to give an allegorical resonance to individual figures. Yet this strategy does not in itself make fiction fully historical, since such realist particularity could serve a merely documentary or antiquarian function.

Though Lukács does not do so explicitly, one might therefore argue that Scott's distinctiveness and originality derive more from the way that he handles plot and connects events. In contrast to his eighteenth-century predecessors, Scott had "a clear understanding of history as a process, of history as the concrete precondition of the present" (21), two elements that are essentially linked for Lukács. Scott realizes the first through his focus upon periods of change, moments when one phase of history is giving way to another. Furthermore, Scott underscores the contemporary relevance of the past by choosing events that lie just a few generations in the past, at the borders of personal memory, but readily retrievable as the events that gave rise to present circumstances. His narrative method thus transforms realist conventions by explicitly presenting the particulars on which they typically focus as conditional, relative, subject to change.

Lukács also notes that Scott's novels operate between two modes of consciousness, that of the characters and that of the reader. A historical understanding of the events in the plot is made available to the reader without being realized within the narrative by those characters who are caught up in the actual events.[4] Their limited historical consciousness leaves them to rely upon transhistorical ethical criteria in making their decisions, as if they were still operating within the parameters of cultural conventions that Scott was already leaving behind. They remain, for Lukács, subject to a historical mystification that the reader is induced to look beyond.

Scott was, however, not the only writer of this period to grapple with the problems of historical fiction, nor was his version of historical consciousness the only one available. His solutions, while distinctive, need not be seen as wholly definitive for his era or for Romantic thought in general. Presuming that to be the case may provide us with a certain theoretical neatness, but it keeps us from recognizing important differences in the ways that history and subjectivity were conceived during the Romantic period. Turning our attention and Lukács's model toward other writers makes it easier, in fact, to recognize the complexity of our own debt to our Romantic past. The historical fiction of William Godwin provides an apt, if somewhat neglected, starting point for these questions, despite the fact that most critics locate him within the Enlightenment tradition rather than a Romantic one. For Godwin holds a pivotal place between these two perspectives and thus provides a useful vantage point on emerging Romantic ideas of history – as his strong appeal for so many Romantic writers helps to confirm.

II

William Godwin gave many of his novels a particularized historical setting, but the most self-consciously historical among them are *St. Leon* (1799) and *Mandeville* (1817). These fictional texts amplify and complicate Godwin's own understanding of history, continuing a task that had already been part of the philosophical project of *Political Justice*. Yet as his novels explore the subtle dependence of individuals upon tradition and history, they cast doubt upon the optimistic foundation of Godwin's philosophy, his insistence that there are no inherent obstacles to rational behavior and that it should be relatively easy to persuade individuals to act in accordance with reason. At the same time, they raise its aspirations to a level of historical sophistication that belies those critics who find Godwin's ethical claims naive. In ways that extend but also displace *Political Justice*, these novels give shape to the tension in Godwin's own thought between Enlightenment liberalism and an emergent Romantic mentality.[5]

Godwin's explicit comments on history tend to have a distinctly eighteenth-century cast, both in their sense of historical process and in their view of historiography. *Political Justice* presumes that history is essentially and irreversibly progressive, its shape linear and evolutionary. "Intellect has a perpetual tendency to proceed. It cannot be held back, but by a power that counteracts its genuine tendency, through every moment of its existence."[6] The past, then, is the record of a struggle between prejudices (modes of reasoning that have outlived their validity and utility) and reason, or in more explicitly political terms, between government and a rationality embodied in the individual's mind, for "government by its very nature counteracts the improvement of individual intellect" (I: viii). Any genuine use of reason thus fosters humanity's inherent momentum toward a standard of perfection in personal and social conduct.[7]

The all-sufficient motor for this intellectual progress is rational discussion. "Sound reasoning and truth, when adequately communicated, must always be victorious over error" (I: 96), for "It is the property of truth to spread" (I: 98). When the political and social barriers to the free dissemination of ideas have been removed, a process that Godwin labels the euthanasia of government, progress toward truth and justice will be uninterrupted. For, "if there be such a thing as truth, it must infallibly be struck out by the collision of mind with mind" (III: 240). For Godwin, the translation of individual rationality into social change seems effortless, as if there were an invisible hand of ethics directing human affairs. Hence, as its critics have repeatedly noted, *Political Justice* shows a striking unconcern with any political mechanism by which its utopian ideals might be reached.

This text takes as its fundamental historical principle the conviction that change is good, both innate in human beings and essential for their well-being. "Incessant change, everlasting innovation, seem dictated by the true interests of mankind" (I: 245). Hence tradition, especially as it gets embodied in political forms, creates a fundamental obstacle to progress. "Institutions calculated to give perpetuity to any particular mode of thinking, or condition of existence, are pernicious" (I: xxvi) – and all institutions, in Godwin's view, tend to be so constituted. Reason, however, allows us to step outside history and to negate or reshape historical circumstances. Though we can doubtless learn from the past, we clearly do not *need* to do so in order to dismantle unnecessary governmental activities and social prejudices.

Godwin's explicit statements on historiography in *The Enquirer* (1797) do nonetheless have a strikingly modern effect at times, due to their genuine skepticism about the accessibility of historical truth. Godwin argues there that "History is in reality a tissue of fables. There is no reason to believe that any one page in any one history extant, exhibits the unmixed truth. The story is disfigured by the vanity of the actors, the interested misrepresentations of the spectators, and the fictions, probable or improbable, with which every historian is instigated to piece out his imperfect tale."[8] An unpublished essay from this period even reverses the epistemological priority of history over fiction due to the greater consistency and depth that a novelist can give to his characters' psychology. "The writer of romance then is to be considered as the writer of real history; while he who was formerly called the historian, must be contented to step down into the place of his rival, with this disadvantage, that he is a romance writer, without the ardour, the enthusiasm, and the sublime licence of imagination, that belong to that species of composition."[9]

Yet Godwin's general sense of the relevance of historiography remains quite traditional, an instance of the attitude that Reinhart Koselleck has termed *historia magister vitae*.[10] He blurs the line between fiction and history because the same ethical purposes and standards can be applied to both. History has value for him insofar as it provides an array of exemplary models, embodiments of ethical ideals that are themselves really transhistorical. "There are characters in history that may almost be said to be worth an eternal study. They are epitomes of the world, of its best and most elevated features, purified from their grossness" ("Of History," 364). The purpose of historiography, like fiction, is to spark identification with and emulation of its heroic figures ("Of History," 362).

Godwin's fairly conventional views on these matters make it less surprising that his historical novels do not fit neatly into Lukács's definition of the new genre. On the one hand, his characters are distinctly historical; Godwin always insists that character must be understood as a function of circumstances. But Godwin tends to depict his past as parallel to the present rather than, in Lukács's sense, prior to it in a causal way. St. Leon's own reflections are typical in this regard, as when he signals a historical analogy between the Inquisition and contemporary England. "Two centuries perhaps after Philip the Second shall be gathered to his ancestors (he died in 1598), men shall learn over again to persecute each other for conscience sake."[11] While clearly political in intent, such comments blur the distinctions between different historical times and see the past bearing on the present in an unproblematic, unmediated way.

Yet Godwin's fictional treatment of historicity moves beyond his explicit theorizing in ways that a perspective oriented toward Lukács and Scott might well overlook, because Godwin reflects a variant of Romantic thought quite different from the one that Scott represents. The fictional form allows Godwin to extend his analysis in *Political Justice* of how, "[Government] insinuates itself into our personal dispositions, and insensibly communicates its own spirit to our private transactions" (1: 4). Working in the mode of historical fiction, Godwin comes to appreciate the more specifically historical dimensions of this relation between politics and psychology, while raising an issue largely absent within Scott's narratives, how historical consciousness affects the subject's identity and whether its effects enhance or inhibit that subject's power as an agent of historical (or even personal) change.

Second, Godwin's plots take their fundamental shape from a typically Romantic perception of historical process, one that stresses the recursive nature of historical causality. It was in part the political circumstances of his own era that brought Godwin to acknowledge the power of repetition within history. *St. Leon* was written immediately after Mary Wollstonecraft's death and Godwin's publication of his memoir of her life, hence at a time when anti-Jacobin attacks on him had become virulently personal. *Mandeville* was written in the period after the fall of Napoleon, likewise a time of increasing political reaction. So history presented for Godwin a rather different problem than it did for Scott. Godwin's practical concern in his fiction is less with historical progress than with historical stasis, with explaining the apparent possibility of significant breaks in the forward momentum that *Political Justice* had largely taken for granted.

Indeed, Godwin's fiction is almost obsessively repetitive in structure, his characters almost compulsively resistant to change. It rejects the Enlightenment assumption that the past can simply be left behind, yet it also resists assimilation into a dialectical model where the past can easily be sublimated into the present. Instead, Godwin's texts take seriously the questions of why the past can "weigh like a nightmare" upon the present, why we always tend to read the present in terms of the past, and how those anachronistic interpretations circumscribe our capacities for acting in and upon the present. His fiction suggests that the recursive insistence of history has its origin in traumas that seem to lie beyond what the liberal imagination can conceive or alter, in psychic complexes whose irreducibility arises from their intricate interweaving of personal and ideological affect.[12]

III

History enters Godwin's fiction, as it does for much narrative in this period, through the side-door of the Gothic. *St. Leon* is the tale of a sixteenth-century French nobleman who, having gambled away his fortune and having been reduced to an impoverished vulnerability, accepts two gifts from a dying stranger – the formulas for the elixir of life and the alchemical creation of gold. The one condition on his acceptance, absolute silence concerning his powers, ultimately estranges him from his family and frustrates his attempts to re-establish his family position or to engage in political philanthropy. His quest to alter both his personal state and more general political circumstances leads him across the face of Europe, brings him into direct contact with all the prevailing political orders, and culminates in his involvement in the struggle between Christians and Turks for control of Hungary.

Critical reception of this novel was mixed and often perplexed, a not surprising result since its Gothic trappings and picaresque structure can make it hard to discern a coherent narrative purpose behind the text. Its mingling of philosophical and narrative elements, its multiple plots and diverse generic modes, can give an impression of stylistic unevenness or lack of authorial control. Recent critics have consequently tended to emphasize the more readily ascertainable biographical or allegorical elements of the text, taking St. Leon's wife as a representation of Mary Wollstonecraft, seeing the text as indicative of Godwin's shift from the pure rationalism of *Political Justice* to a more Romantic stress on the power of emotion, or reading the novel as a further broadside from an increasingly isolated Jacobin philosopher against the power of social prejudices.[13] Such connections are instructive, indeed essential, in dealing with all of Godwin's novels, yet their emphasis on external interpretive elements can cause us to leave aside the puzzling intellectual and narrative complexity of this text, a text that merits much closer critical analysis than it has yet received.

St. Leon fills a dual role as character in the novel. He is, in Lukács's sense, a representative product of his age, embodying its chivalric and feudal values to perfection. Godwin deftly traces those traits to his childhood, when he was groomed by his mother as the bearer of familial honor, a substitute for his heroically fallen father. Yet he is also a critic of his age; the subsequent events of his life, starting with his military initiation at the siege of Pavia, give him an intellectual detachment from prevalent values that makes him historically self-conscious. Such aspects of St. Leon's character as his isolation, his impetuosity, and his melancholy made him an attractive figure to Godwin's Romantic readers (not only Byron and Shelley, but even Coleridge). At the same time, he clearly embodies certain liberal and progressive values, above all in his capacity to rationally rise above the prejudices of his age. His pact with the stranger gives St. Leon every advantage for promoting social change, bestowing upon him both infinite time and limitless money. The elixir of life might even be seen as the ideal Enlightenment drug, for (in theory) it allows St. Leon to accumulate enough personal experiences and precedents to make truly informed, rational choices. It grants him as an individual the wisdom ascribed by the Enlightenment to historical progress as a whole. In addition, his wealth makes him (again, in theory) essentially independent of social or governmental constraint on his freedom of action.

St. Leon does indeed turn against many of the prevalent social values. He exposes the blindness in the chivalric love of distinction, both the ease with which it degenerates into pointless competitiveness such as gambling and the harsher form it takes in sustaining the national, religious, and ethnic separatisms on which feudal allegiances were based. Yet St. Leon's efforts to bring about change, or even to live apart from social prejudices, all fail, thus raising a crucial interpretive problem present in all of Godwin's fiction. Why does Godwin focus so insistently upon the power of institutional mechanisms to recuperate individual resistance? Most critics, reading *St. Leon* in light of *Caleb Williams*, see Godwin simply continuing his critique of entrenched political interests, diagnosing a problem for which *Political Justice* provides the implicit cure. Yet Godwin seems most interested here in how St. Leon himself impedes his own reformist efforts, how he internalizes and perpetuates the ideology that he consciously rejects. To consider why this occurs, we have to turn our attention to the larger narrative structures of the text.

St. Leon's plot takes its essential pattern from liberal historical optimism, the expectation that one could at any time make a new beginning in life relatively independent of exterior circumstances. St. Leon is an indefatigable planner, ceaselessly striving to control his destiny and to enhance his independent status as a basis for social or political engagement. Yet the actual course of events is marked by an inescapable, unassimilable trauma. The key event for this text occurs after St. Leon and his family, at his wife's urging, have retreated to a pastoral life in Switzerland. Just when he has begun to feel satisfied with their circumstances, a hailstorm devastates their crops and leaves them without resources. The family's pastoral independence proves a weakness, for the local authorities refuse to assist outsiders and foreigners. Driven into ever-worsening circumstances, St. Leon observes his family on the brink of starvation. "No change of circumstances, no inundation of wealth, has had the power to obliterate from my recollection what I then saw . . . Haunted, as I perpetually was, by images of the plague of famine, nothing appeared to be so valuable as wealth; nothing so desirable as to be placed at the utmost possible distance from want" (103).

Despite his emphasis on the power of these events, St. Leon does not himself call them back to the reader's attention as the text proceeds. Yet just as they determine his decision to accept the stranger's gifts despite the condition of secrecy, they can also be seen behind virtually every subsequent decision he makes.[14] They shape, for instance, his liberal antipathy toward all institutional authority, leading him at all times to try to position himself outside whatever governmental system he encounters. They prompt him to align himself with other outsiders, as in his fatal alliance with Bethlem Gabor. In certain circumstances, St. Leon's stance has a heroic aspect, as when he argues at length against every justification for the Spanish Inquisition, yet the primary effect of his liberal individualism is to circumscribe his power as an agent of change.

St. Leon's textual amnesia, though, has a functional role in calling our attention to the deeper patterns of repetition within the text, ones that are even less under St. Leon's conscious control. His failure to recall and work through his trauma, by measuring it against each new set of circumstances, produces an unconscious displacement of his desire, subjecting him to a symptomatic blindness in his self-perception and a symptomatic repetition of his fate. His failures in each new phase of his life are tragic from his perspective, yet almost comically predictable for the reader. He makes similar mistakes time after time and ends each stage of his life in one prison or another, symbolically entrapped by forces that seem unalterable.

The final scenes of the novel, those that take place in Hungary, can nonetheless give us some clues to the logic that governs this narrative pattern. St. Leon's final aspiration is his most philanthropic one; rejuvenated by his elixir and adopting an assumed name, he attempts to use his resources to restore Hungary's war-ravaged economy. Though he hopes to be perceived as a neutral figure above the ongoing civil war, he is eventually forced to bribe the Turkish bashaw to gain protection for his storehouses. Trying to regain his independent position, St. Leon aligns himself with Bethlem Gabor, a Hungarian mercenary who is one of Godwin's most remarkable Gothic villains. Gabor's family had been slaugh-

tered by marauders during his absence as a soldier, leaving him
with an implacable hatred for which the present ideological
divisions provide an outlet. Despite knowing his history, St. Leon
remains blind to the depth of Gabor's misanthropy and thus to how
deeply Hungary has been scarred by the war. Gabor wants nothing
more than that the war should continue and therefore despises all
of St. Leon's schemes, a hatred that St. Leon's rationalism can
neither perceive nor accommodate.

St. Leon's blindness toward Gabor, however, anticipates his blindness toward himself and toward his own complicity with his era.
Rescued from Gabor's (inevitable) prison by his own son, St. Leon
adopts a more limited aim: to further the career of a son who, thanks
to his father's changed appearance, recognizes him neither as his
father nor as the Chatillon who has been trying to rebuild Hungary.
That son ironically embodies the very chivalric values that St. Leon
has come to oppose and to which he rightly attributes his own
failures. The son's intolerance for the Turks and their allies and his
contempt for humanitarian schemes to end the war mirror the
ideological prejudices that St. Leon has been trying to overcome.
His judgment of his father's projects, which the latter had seen only
in the light of disinterested benevolence, reveals the depth of their
ideological differences. "To the eternal disgrace of the nation that
gave him birth, [Chatillon, i.e., St. Leon] had joined the Turkish
standard, and, by exertions difficult to be comprehended, had
rescued the infidels from famine at a time when, but from his
inauspicious interference, Buda, and perhaps every strong town in
Hungary, were on the point of falling into the hands of the
Christians" (352).

St. Leon befriends his son and in so doing comes to see the
ideological aspects of his own "philanthropy." Yet even though he
perceives how his son has become an extreme manifestation of
chivalric values, St. Leon cannot help himself from being attracted
once again by their power. "Though I could not entirely enter into
this sentiment of his, and indeed regarded it as an infatuation and
delusion, I did not the less admire the grandeur of soul with which
this heroic fable inspired him" (361). He ultimately succeeds in
aiding his son, but only by revealing his assumed identity and
casting himself as a scapegoat whom the son can villainize, thus
reinforcing that son's ideological intransigence. He saves his son
from his own isolation only by reconfirming him as a version of his

own younger self; his most private act of penance is also his most resonantly political one. Yet St. Leon remains blind to this historical repetition, never aware of his own inconsistency in promoting a feudal ideology.

The desire for security and invulnerability that stems from St. Leon's trauma, transferred here on to his son, provides the channel through which the chivalric prejudices of his era flood back into his mind, erasing the critical distance from them that he thought he had established. To be sure, *St. Leon* remains on one level a liberal critique of institutional power fully consistent with *Political Justice*. At the same time, however, it provides a Romantically skeptical assessment of the power of any individual to free his mind or his actions from the ideological fetters of his age. Godwin invokes the power of historical repetition to provide a tough-minded demonstration of how deeply embedded ideological pressures are within the psyche and how insistently they re-emerge. Ideological stasis thus proves as much a psychological as an institutional problem, frustrating St. Leon's reformist endeavors at every turn because he fails to acknowledge his complicity with his age. His final retreat into a world of private values and aspirations, as if they were independent of ideological traces, is the most symptomatic gesture of all. As he strives to aid his son, the domestic affections that had charged the starvation scene so intensely for him succeed in overriding his critical, historical insight.

IV

Mandeville is a decidedly paradoxical text, on the one hand more narrowly focused on the psyche of its titular character than was *St. Leon*, on the other hand more explicitly concerned with the nature of history and historical consciousness. Set in the period of the English civil wars, it takes the obsessively self-centered aspirations and reflections of a solitary Presbyterian orphan for its subject matter, tracking the repeated frustrations that eventually lead him into madness. More explicitly than in *St. Leon*, repetition becomes the explicit organizing principle of the text, as Godwin traces the effects of Mandeville's historically conditioned trauma in the recurrent patterns of his mind and his behavior. Godwin created in Mandeville a remarkable picture of madness from within, not as pure irrationality, but as a paranoia normalized and justified by its ideological encoding within contemporary Presbyterianism.[15] His demonstration of how hard it can be for truth, even when clearly perceived, to penetrate the mind puts enormous pressure on many of the assumptions in *Political Justice*. For if the ideological disease that afflicts Mandeville cannot be cured, what prospects are there for overcoming historical stasis?

Mandeville himself is quite consciously aware of those patterns, so that historical repetition becomes a theme within the novel itself. Yet that awareness gives him no power to control or change his psychological propensities; instead, the repetitions simply get absorbed into the structure of Calvinist predestination that dominates his mental outlook. Godwin's text demonstrates with brutal clarity how Mandeville's sense of absolute subjection to history leads inevitably to insanity. Although in important respects he sees himself more clearly than did St. Leon, that vision is in no way liberating, its rationality too partial and intermittent to be effective.

Mandeville takes its entire plot and structure from an original, inerasable trauma. The text opens with Mandeville's memories of the Irish revolt of 1641, focusing on the slaughter of English and Anglo-Irish civilians by Catholic militia forces. As a three-year-old child, he witnessed the plundering, neglect, and eventual murder of hundreds of captives during their march toward imprisonment – victims of Catholic vengeance for long-standing grievances, but victims as well of the reciprocal brutality with which the British were attempting to put down the rebellion. Mandeville's own parents die during the revolt, though his Catholic nurse manages to save him by claiming him as her own child.

Mandeville escapes, but with this vision of history forever etched in his mind. "I saw, I say, in my dreams, whether by night or by day, a perpetual succession of flight, and pursuit, and anguish, and murder. I saw the agonising and deploring countenances of the Protestants, and the brutal and infuriated features of the triumphant Papist."[16] These "memories," however, are as much social as personal in nature, as much the products of cultural prejudice as of his own experience, as Mandeville himself sees. "All this of course came mixed up to my recollection, with incidents that I had never seen, but which had not failed to be circumstantially related to me. It would indeed have been difficult for me to have made a separation of the two; what I had heard, had been so fully detailed to me, and had made such an impression upon my juvenile fancy, that it stood out not less distinctly pictured to my thoughts, than if I had actually seen it" (44).

What the retelling of these events by others inevitably adds, however, is an ideological supplement. Godwin uses these historical events to analyze the complex way that ideological and psychological factors intersect in the structure of trauma. Tracing this original event through the other "minute and subtle" circumstances of Mandeville's upbringing, he illustrates how trauma focuses affect, producing an intensification and immobilization of emotional energy around a certain definitive moment. That affective intensity keeps the moment permanently alive for Mandeville, without him being able to process the event on an intellectual level. Precisely because it remains unprocessed, however, the trauma remains available for ideological determination of its meaning from without.

Mandeville's impressions are given their ideological shape by his tutor, a Presbyterian of the most uncompromising sort who constructs for him a neat Manichean world. "This was all the world to me. I had hardly a notion of any more than two species of creatures on the earth, – the persecutor and his victim, the Papist and the Protestant, and they were to my thoughts like two great classes of animal nature, the one, the law of whose being it was to devour, while it was the unfortunate destiny of the other to be mangled and torn to pieces by him" (44–45). Mandeville adapts himself with fanatic zeal to his role, driven by both character and circumstances to play the victimized martyr. Godwin depicts the idea of predestination not as an independent, external force, but as a force at work within the mind itself, a function of character. As Mandeville notes, by the end of his childhood, "My fate was determined, and my character was fixed" (76). At the same time that he is wholly filled by Presbyterian ideology, though, he lacks any sense of solidarity with or practical opportunities for interaction with a Presbyterian community. Presbyterianism represents for him exclusion and isolation, a radicalized Protestant interiority that places him beyond the reach of rational discourse.

His relation to his own trauma, however, remains complex. On the one hand, he is obsessively aware of it; it dominates his consciousness far more than St. Leon's starving family preyed on his mind. On the other hand, it remains repressed, its absence figured in the lack of eloquence that haunts Mandeville throughout the text and cuts him off from others. Mandeville's ideological prejudices have their first public enactment when he goes away to boarding school, where the schoolboys play out the attitudes of their elders. Falsely accused of possessing illicit republican literature, Mandeville accepts the blame and the consequent public humiliation – partly to shield the real culprit, but perhaps more because it lets him play the part of the martyred Protestant. "There appeared to me . . . a sort of lordly delight in standing the scorns and reproaches of my companions, when all the time in my own reflections I smiled contemptuously at their error, and rose serene above the clouds in which their misconstructions sought to envelop me" (103). The reality of public disgrace, however, proves far harder to bear and sears into Mandeville's mind his role as ideological victim.

The original trauma increasingly gets displaced onto one particular schoolmate, Clifford, who provides a mirror image that defines Mandeville's identity. His antipathy for Clifford begins as mere envy at the latter's popularity and success, but acquires a force that remains mysterious for Mandeville because it plays out so perfectly his own political unconscious, a force that he endeavors to explain in essentialized, ahistorical terms. "As, in the world of human creatures, there exist certain mysterious sympathies and analogies . . . so, I was firmly persuaded, there are antipathies, and properties interchangeably irreconcilable and destructive to each other, that fit one human being to be the source of another's misery. Beyond doubt I had found this true opposition and interdestructiveness in Clifford" (141). Godwin's text makes it quite evident that this hatred involves a displacement of Mandeville's primary trauma, when Mandeville points out how Clifford's name becomes more unspeakable than even his parents' deaths. "But I never mentioned Clifford . . . I could speak of my father and mother: but that not without the greatest difficulty, and with a feeling as if I was somehow violating a secret, which it was the most flagitious of crimes to violate . . . [I]f I could have given vent to the various emotions he had excited within me, I should have become a different man" (132–33). To perfect this oppositional scenario, Clifford obligingly converts to Catholicism at a key moment of the text. The subsequent plot traces their intertwined fates and establishes a rigorously repetitive structure. At every turn of events, the same ideological oppositions recur, the same behavior results, the same outcome ensues – defeat and frustration for Mandeville. "He crossed me at every turn, and darkened me in all my lights . . .

That he did this without the smallest tincture of malice, aggravated my grievance" (309).

Two external forces nonetheless have some effect on Mandeville, in the positive form of his sister and the negative form of a malicious former schoolmate, Mallison, and the latter's uncle. Mandeville's sister represents a liberal rationalism that confronts its own limits in dealing with historical trauma. Henrietta is an ideal figure with whom Mandeville has an idealized relation, the one figure whom he recognizes as like himself. "I seemed now for the first time to associate with a being, with whom I felt an affinity, and whom I recognized as of the same species as myself" (63). Raised apart from him, her pastoral upbringing seems to have erased any signs of trauma in her, and her presence seems likewise to have the power to erase its effects upon him, extending so far as to make him see Clifford more justly and objectively (290–91).

Yet she remains unable to resolve or dispel Mandeville's trauma; her influence remains a function of her person and vanishes in her absence. Godwin describes her influence in an extremely instructive way, for it suggests that reason itself, as embodied in her, operates along subconscious channels and is itself an instrument of power that can dispossess rather than validate the self. "She cast down all the intrenchments and bastions which my wilful passions had set up for my ruin, and entered with triumphant wheels the fortress of my heart . . . The soul of Mandeville seemed to have left me, and the soul of Henrietta to have entered my bosom in its stead" (158–59). That possible transference, though, marks the limit of her powers as well. When she (inevitably) comes to be attracted by and engaged to Clifford, Mandeville sees her as one more symbol of his trauma, a hapless victim to be saved at all costs from her insidious and incomprehensible seduction to the Catholic cause.[17]

Like Henrietta, the text's villains are hard to place in any specific historical terms. Mallison and Holloway conspire to become Mandeville's guardians and confidants, destroy his sanity, and gain control over his estate. Though Hobbesian rationalists of a certain sort, their roles have more of the ahistorical flavor of melodrama (with perhaps a dash of Shakespeare) than any distinctive historical resonance. Hence their interactions with Mandeville are difficult to read historically, seeming at best to provide one additional instance of how Mandeville's trauma keeps him from acting on the basis of his clear insight into the motives of others.

The insistence with which Godwin traces the repetitions, now genuinely insane, of Mandeville's fate seems more grimly despairing than even *St. Leon*. The climactic scenes of the novel follow Mandeville's descent into full paranoia, wholly narcissistic on the one hand, yet fueled by its affinities to the general ideological paranoia of his era. Mandeville's final madness involves a full erasure of historical consciousness, an entrapment within an eternal, unvarying present. His mind blurs past and present, seeing repetition everywhere and equating Henrietta and Clifford with their historical types, the Duke of Savoy and his queen (316). He attempts to re-enact the terms of his childhood trauma and to rescue his sister, on her way to her marriage, from what he views as her abduction and imprisonment. History repeats itself as tragedy for Mandeville, as farce for the reader, and Mandeville escapes from the contest with only a more visible symbol of his obsession. "The sword of my enemy had given a perpetual grimace, a sort of preternatural and unvarying distorted smile, or deadly grin, to my countenance . . . [N]ow I bore Clifford and his injuries perpetually about with me" (325).

V

In what precise sense, then, can we appropriately term Godwin's fictions historical? First, by explicitly deriving character from cir-cumstance, the novels clearly sustain the explanatory framework of *Political Justice*. Their portraits of St. Leon's chivalric values and Mandeville's Presbyterianism particularize and historicize the more abstract insistence of Godwin's philosophical work upon the social determination of character. More importantly, the novels demon-strate in much greater detail how prejudices persist by grafting themselves on to personal traumas and encoding those traumas as part of a larger historical text. As government fixes prejudices by political force, so traumas do the same with psychic force, and in ways less susceptible to a pleasant euthanasia. These later novels thus cast additional light on the psychological dynamics behind Caleb Williams's incapacitating guilt.[18]

Yet the novels also reflect back upon *Political Justice* in unsettling ways, for they confront the ambivalent nature of historical conscious-ness, at once a necessary supplement to reason and a reminder of its limits. Godwin's narratives remain poised between their liberal, enlightened aspirations and a Romantic historical sensibility that seems to undercut the force of Godwin's social criticism. Skeptically critical of the value of the past, they remain fully cognizant of its subtle and pervasive power, even in those individuals and at those moments that may seem most free of it. Committed to the individual subject as an agent of change, they remain alert to the forces that immobilize that subject from without and within. Anticipating one of the characteristic concerns of Romantic historicity, they acknowledge the recursiveness of history as a problem that may set limits on any progressive vision. For they take the persistence of the past seriously, as a problem at once psychological and ideological, one that cannot be fictionalized away.

In this sense, they confront the Lukácsian paradigm (and much modern historical consciousness) directly, because they see the moments of historical upheaval that they depict as moments when things may *not* in fact be changing, *not* moving forward, perhaps not even moving at all. Godwin's novels might (somewhat surprisingly) be seen to anticipate the interpretive strategy that Marx deploys in "The Eighteenth Brumaire." Their sense for the ironic persistence of the past denies the straightforward linearity of historical causality and the singleness of any historical "moment," thus creating a space for more complex models of historical process. Because every historical moment is marked by repetition and set in multiple, asynchronic relations with what precedes it, its place within any sequential narrative becomes highly unstable, its meaning much more elusive.

With Godwin's political values still oriented toward Enlightenment liberalism, the recognition of historical repetition comes perilously close to being tragic. Both St. Leon and Mandeville are strikingly insightful about the patterns and processes that entrap them, yet never able to find the place from which they could change the world around them or even their own responses to it; the mood of malaise that characterizes most of Godwin's fiction arises from their realization of this. This incapacity may mark the limits of Godwin's liberal imagination in its inability to conceive recursiveness except as traumatic repetition and thus to assimilate its own Romantic insight. Valorizing individual judgment and ethical freedom, imagining them carried forward as part of an unstoppable tide of reason in history, it finds itself at a loss when confronted by the recurrence of the past – of its roles, its prejudices, its patterns – a state of mind whose contemporary parallels are all too evident.

As critic, one might respond to this analysis by contending that Godwin would ultimately have us read past the ending and take the apparent pessimism of the narratives themselves as a provocation rather than an endpoint.[19] Their function might therefore be termed diagnostic rather than prescriptive, their answers necessarily indeterminate. Yet Godwin's own comments on fiction suggest that he thought it ought to do more, that it should direct the critical energies it arouses. "When the mind shakes off the fetters of prescription and prejudice, when it boldly takes a flight into the world unknown, and employs itself in search of those grand and interesting principles which shall tend to impart to every reader the glow of enthusiasm, it is at such moments that the enquiring and philosophical reader may expect to be presented with the materials and rude sketches of intellectual improvement" (*Political Justice*, III: 270).

So the most telling mark of history in Godwin's fiction may be its inability to displace itself from its own time, to move beyond the uneasy interstice between rationalism and Romanticism, to envisage a positive synthesis for them and thus to shake off the fetters of Godwin's own psychological and political traumas. Their power and significance as historical fictions rest on their embrace of that paradox, on their steady truth to what Godwin saw around himself, and on their refusal to invent consoling fictions or metanarrational solaces of any kind.

And yet we, from a different vantage point, might still be tempted to ask how historically specific Godwin's dilemma is; that is to say, whether his inability to assimilate the insights of Romantic historicity into his liberal imagination were peculiar to him or to his era, or are instead somehow endemic to liberalism generally. The perspective of history suggests that Godwin's failure to blend these traditions may indeed be symptomatic. Liberalism and Romanticism had already in his lifetime begun to drift further and further apart, the former prey to recurrent waves of an unselfconscious progressivist optimism, the latter trapped within one or another nostalgic vision of the past.[20] Two centuries later, Godwin's question remains as open for us as it was for him: how might the liberal imagination come to acknowledge the reality of repetition and, rather than denying its force or lamenting its futility, seek to invest it with some positive value in the political economy of the psyche?

NOTES

1 "We must avow ourselves either much behind the times or much ahead of them in rating the Scottish novels, however the game of placing may be played, among the permanently great, which are none the less great because they have ceased to influence the living," *The Essays of Virginia Woolf*, vol. III, ed. Andrew McNeillie (New York: Harcourt Brace Jovanovich, 1988), 301. The language of Avrom Fleishman in *The English Historical Novel* (Baltimore: Johns Hopkins University Press, 1965) is typical in measuring Scott's stature. "At this point there occurs one of the greatest cultural phenomena of this or any other age, a phenomenon that goes by the name of Sir Walter Scott," 23.

2 Georg Lukács, *The Historical Novel*, trans. Hannah and Stanley Mitchell (London: Merlin Press, 1962), 39–40. Further references appear in parenthesis in the text.

3 See in particular, Marilyn Butler, *Jane Austen and the War of Ideas* (Oxford: Clarendon Press, 1975); Gary Kelly, *English Fiction of the Romantic Period: 1789–1830* (New York: Longman, 1989); and Ina Ferris, *The Achievement of Literary Authority: Gender, History, and the Waverley Novels* (Ithaca: Cornell University Press, 1991).

4 Lukács's comments on the difference between Scott's heroes and world-historical individuals highlight this distinction (*Historical Novel*, 43–44).

5 See Mark Philp's perceptive discussion of the revisions in *Political Justice*, in chapters 6, 7, and 9 of *Godwin's Political Justice* (Ithaca: Cornell University Press, 1986); and also Don Locke's study, *A Fantasy of Reason: The Life and Thought of William Godwin* (Boston: Routledge and Kegan Paul, 1980).

6 William Godwin, *Enquiry Concerning Political Justice and Its Influence on Morals and Happiness*, ed. F. E. L. Priestley (Toronto: University of Toronto Press, 1946), II: 535. All quotations from volumes I and II of *Political Justice* come from the 1798 third edition; quotations from volume III are from the original 1793 edition.

7 Perfectibility for Godwin implies not that we will ever reach perfection, but that we can continually move closer to what remains a single, fixed standard (I: 93; I: 240). Philp's analysis of this aspect of Godwin's philosophy as a form of perfectionism is extremely helpful, highlighting what ought to be seen as an important point of connection between the British tradition and German Romantic ideas of *Bildung* (see *Godwin's Political Justice*, especially 81–89). For a more general overview of the idea of perfectibility in this period, see Ernst Behler, "The Idea of Infinite Perfectibility and its Impact Upon the Concept of Literature in European Romanticism," in *Sensus Communis: Contemporary Trends in Comparative Literature*, ed. Peter Boerner, Janos Riesz, Bernhard Scholz (Tübingen: Günter Narr, 1986), 295–304.

8 William Godwin, "Of Posthumous Fame," in *The Enquirer: Reflections on*

Education, Manners, and Literature (London: G. G. and J. Robinson, 1797), 288–89.

9 William Godwin, "Of History and Romance," reel 5 of the Duke University microfilm copy of Godwin's papers in the Abinger Collection, reprinted in Maurice Hindle's edition of *Caleb Williams* (New York: Penguin Books, 1988), 372.

10 Reinhart Koselleck, *Futures Past: On the Semantics of Historical Time*, trans. Keith Tribe (Cambridge, Mass.: Harvard University Press, 1985), 21–38. Koselleck traces this topos from Cicero through the nineteenth century.

11 William Godwin, *St. Leon* (London: William Pickering, 1992), 275. Further references appear in parenthesis in the text.

12 Trauma is, I would argue, one of the two characteristic patterns of historicity for Romanticism, the other being nostalgia, both prefigured in the structural patterns of Rousseau's *Confessions*.

13 See, for instance, Peter Marshall, *William Godwin* (New Haven: Yale University Press, 1984), 205–10; Pamela Clemit, *The Godwinian Novel: The Rational Fictions of Godwin, Brockden Brown, Mary Shelley* (Oxford: Clarendon Press, 1993), 90–91; and the introductory remarks by Marilyn Butler and Mark Philp to the *Collected Novels and Memoirs of William Godwin* (London: William Pickering, 1992), 1: 30–33. Even B. J. Tysdahl, generally Godwin's most tolerant commentator, seems to grow exasperated at times with Godwin in his analysis of this text, *William Godwin as Novelist* (London: Athlone, 1981).

14 This element of secrecy is perhaps the most difficult detail of this text to read allegorically. While it serves one textual purpose in isolating St. Leon even from his wife, it remains clearly inconsistent with a reading of St. Leon as Jacobin philosopher, for whom sincerity and dissemination of truth should be paramount values.

15 Tysdahl has an excellent analysis of this dimension of the text and is particularly insightful on the narrational consequences of having a madman as first-person narrator (*William Godwin as Novelist*, 134–43). His suggestion (135–36, 142–43) that certain apparent defects of description (hence implicitly of characterization and of other textual features as well) in the text must be understood as a consequence of Godwin portraying everything through Mandeville's eyes makes a crucially important interpretive point.

16 William Godwin, *Mandeville* (London: William Pickering, 1992), 44. Further references appear in parenthesis in the text.

17 Like most of the secondary characters in this novel, Henrietta seems more a type than an individual. Yet with Godwin, it always proves immensely difficult to discern just what such a character is a type *of*. Henrietta's relation to Mandeville, with its hints of incestuous attraction, is a key issue for future criticism of this text to examine.

18 I have examined the intersection of psychology and ideology in *Caleb*

Williams in more detail in "Of Caleb's Guilt and Godwin's Truth: Ideology and Ethics in *Caleb Williams*," *ELH* 60 (1993): 939–60.

19 Tilottama Rajan's reading of the hermeneutic dimensions of Wollstonecraft's and Godwin's fiction is an ingenious and rigorously argued version of this critical move; the same strategy is also adopted by the editors of the Pickering Godwin edition. See Rajan, "Wollstonecraft and Godwin: Reading the Secrets of the Political Novel," *Studies in Romanticism* 27 (1988): 221–51, and volume 1 of the *Collected Novels and Memoirs*, especially 42–44.

20 Though Stanley Rosen, for one, sees both being similar in crucial respects as responses to a shared Enlightenment aporia that proves incapable of reconciling history and freedom. See *Hermeneutics as Politics: Against Theory* (New York: Oxford University Press, 1987).

CHAPTER 4

Writing on the border: the national tale, female writing, and the public sphere

Ina Ferris

> I never could draw a perpendicular line in my life.
> See now my pencil *will* go into a curve or an angle.
>
> Glorvina in *The Wild Irish Girl*

When it came to review Lady Morgan's last Irish national tale, *The O'Briens and the O'Flahertys*, in 1827, the *New Monthly Magazine* opened with a mock complaint. The reviewer, casting himself as a harried professional reader longing for books with "a decided and single character," declared that in Morgan's text he encountered a heterogeneity of discourses and moods apparently formed to "puzzle and confound" his critical desire. "It is too tricksome and rapid for our art," he lamented, "and will not be constrained by mastery."[1] This mock-lament nicely points to the way in which the genre of the national tale, inaugurated by Morgan with the publication in 1806 of *The Wild Irish Girl*, is premised on a certain elusiveness that confounds the discourse of the public sphere in which, nevertheless, it places itself. "Elusiveness" may seem an odd term for so heavily didactic a fiction as *The Wild Irish Girl* and so flamboyant and public a figure as Lady Morgan herself (born Sydney Owenson), who was widely known – and often vilified in the reviews – for her passionate partisanship of Irish and liberal causes and for the extravagance of her writings.[2] But her theatricality functioned in large part parodically and polemically as a form of cover or critique, allowing intervention in areas generally outside the feminine sphere and enabling her to write herself as an author in the public realm. Anticipating Nancy K. Miller's point about feminist intervention as the "ironic manipulation of the semiotics of performance and production," Morgan shrewdly exploited the motif of excess linked to romance and to women by the cultural discourse of her time so as to open up certain possibilities of narration and agency that challenged, if they did not dislodge, that same discourse.[3] More precisely, her national tale – a generic innovation strangely neglected by feminist literary history – functions as a genre that operates *aslant* the domestic and the private. Informed by a liberal belief in the public sphere, it operates self-consciously on the very border of the literary and the political, rewriting the trope of the public sphere in the process; and it defines as central to the fable of the subjected nation a form of female authority neither identical with nor opposed to the domestic authority rooted in home and family.[4]

I

It was primarily through domestic-pedagogical modes that women entered the literary public sphere in significant numbers in the late eighteenth century, and by the turn of the nineteenth their writing was primarily defined as part of a cultural pragmatics aimed at shaping the reading practices of new entrants into the culture of literacy: women, children, servants, and so forth. By contrast, Morgan's national tale was directed at the male and adult "articulate classes,"[5] and its agitated narrative, casting itself in a polemical-performative (as opposed to domestic-pedagogical) mode, eschewed formal decorum and propriety to throw itself onto a terrain of contention. "The quiet, prudent Miss Edgeworth shunned Irish politics," commented Julia Kavanagh in 1863, "but fearless Lady Morgan rushed into them, and into politics of every sort as well."[6] Morgan's national tale, that is, operated in deliberately controversial terms from the outset, highlighting rather than eliding the political. And it did so at some risk to its literary status, as witnessed by a statement in the *Athenaeum* in the year of Morgan's death: "In her youthful time Lady Morgan was less a woman of the pen than a patriot and a partizan. Her books were battles."[7] With their peculiarly aggressive form of gentry nationalism and liberal politics,[8] Morgan's writings aroused contention and debate in the reviews, while at least one of her books, *Italy* (1821), prompted even more dramatic response: it led to her being proscribed by the King of Sardinia, the Emperor of Austria, and the Pope. Morgan herself plunged with some relish into the controversies she occasioned, caricaturing her critics in her novels, answering them in prefaces, issuing testy pamphlets, and so on. What all this underlines is the degree to which she perceived her writing as a public act, an intervention in and performance for the public domain in which the stake was public opinion.

The liberal belief in public opinion was central to Morgan, shaping her pragmatic sense of genre and language. Linguistic and narrative meaning for her was generally less a matter of signification (meaning *that*) than effect (meaning *to*), a distinction neatly captured by a brief exchange early in her 1818 novel *Florence Macarthy.* In this scene, a newcomer to Dublin (who turns out to be an Anglo-Irish absentee) notices that the statue of King William is being decorated with orange and blue ribbons. He turns to his Irish guide:

> "What does it mean," demanded Mr. —.
> "What does it mane? why it manes to vex the papists sore,
>   your honor, shure that's the ascendency [*sic*], Sir."[9]

Words and gestures that mean-to-vex operate in an active, dialogic space, and Morgan's own writing moved in such a space, informed by a strong sense of itself as always aimed at the forum of public opinion. Thus the Advertisement to *Florence Macarthy* opens by noting, "The Irish have been accused of making an ostentatious display of their injuries, and of clanking their chains to excite compassion." The Irish, Morgan responds, have been right to do so: "The appeal to public opinion belongs to the age in which we live; and it is the certainty of its ultimate success, not the abject hopelessness of its repetition, which has excited this affectation of disgust."[10] Over and over again, she makes the standard liberal case for the power of opinion over the power of force, the openness of publicity against the sinister secrecies of the state. The preface to *The O'Briens and O'Flahertys* underlines that the novel (dealing with the period of the 1798 rising) charts an "epoch of transition between the ancient despotism of brute force, and the dawning reign of public opinion." And its hero (like most Morgan heroes) is an enlightened patriot steeped in the civic discourse of Locke and Rousseau.

That hero is Murrough O'Brien, son of Terence O'Brien, now Lord Aranmore. The father has had a complicated and bitter history: as the product of an illicit union between an O'Brien and an O'Flaherty (long-standing rival families in the west), he witnessed his abandoned mother's anguish and anger, and he was early left an outcast orphan, wandering the bleak landscape of Connemara. Through a series of events, he moved from this alienated status in the Gaelic periphery to a successful career as lawyer and politician in the corrupt Dublin of the Ascendancy, and now in the 1790s he has turned into a tormented and demented figure, obsessed with Gaelic myths and intent on restoring "ancient ould Ireland."[11] Hating not only the Ascendancy but also Henry Grattan's liberal Protestant Nation and the radical United Irishmen, Terence O'Brien plans a reactionary revolution in which his son will play a prominent role. But Murrough O'Brien, student at Trinity College, has embraced the liberal politics of Grattan, and his patriotism is of a more moderate and modern order. However, the complicated politics of post-Revolutionary Ireland enmesh him in various confrontations with government authority. He is expelled from the university, and initiated into the United Irishmen by the charismatic Lord Walter Fitzwalter (a fictional portrait of Lord Edward Fitzgerald), though he remains at a distance from the failed rebellion of 1798 that ensues. In the course of the novel O'Brien moves across Ireland, and he is frequently arrested and as frequently rescued, usually by the unknown female figure who proves to be the novel's heroine (of whom more later). His journey reveals a country crossed with tangled loyalties and darkened by violence, betrayal, and suffering. His father dies, the family mansion in Dublin literally collapses, and near the end of the novel he finds himself accused of murder. Rescued from prison and death in Ireland one final time, Murrough O'Brien goes into exile in Paris, serving as an officer in Napoleon's army and holding on to those liberal principles defeated in Ireland – and now threatened in Napoleonic France as well.

Enlightened patriot and exemplary theorist of the public sphere, Murrough O'Brien is explicitly identified by Morgan with the favored liberal causes of the day: Greece, Poland, Ireland, and – most important – France, whose revolution established for Europe the modern sense of the nation as the sovereign "people" in whom rests all legitimacy. For O'Brien (as for many of his historical prototypes) the French Revolution was a crucial sign; he describes it at one point as "a brand from the altar of American independence – an event that terminated the struggle between kings, and began the contest between governments and nations" (*O'B*, 66). Operating within what Lyotard calls the master narrative of emancipation, O'Brien claims that a new political day has dawned precisely because "learning and opinion" are no longer the monopoly of the few. In the enlightened present, he contends, the power of the nation-as-state is counteracted by the power of the nation-as-public, and literacy is the key: "the education which the public gives itself absorbs and neutralizes the instruction prepared for it by governments and hierarchies, whenever the results of both do not coincide" (*O'B*, 367). At no moment, perhaps, is his exemplary status as precisely *public* hero more clear than when he balks at the idea of joining the United Irishmen because of the secrecy of the organization: "It was in no secret association . . . that the great principle of American Independence originated. It was the free and bold explosion of public opinion, which, in giving birth to the French Revolution, worked openly, and in the face of day" (*O'B*, 298).

In the end, the hero does join the United Irishmen, in part because (as Lord Fitzwalter puts it) "wretched Ireland has no public opinion, no public to express an opinion" (*O'B*, 298). Implicitly, therefore, O'Brien recognizes that the universal narrative of emancipation does not apply evenly across time and space, that it bumps up against (even as it bumps out) local tales that do not fit. To be Irish – even privileged Irish – is in some way to be excluded from the modern form of power represented by the public sphere. And to be an Irishwoman – even an Anglo-Irishwoman – is to be doubly excluded. But Morgan shrewdly plays the card of gender to authorize her own open participation in the matter of the nation: she confirms the standard lines of demarcation, so eluding charges of transgression, but she takes advantage of the logic of the public sphere to make a place for herself within it. Repeatedly her prefaces anticipate and deflect charges of what she refers to in the preface to *The O'Briens and the O'Flahertys* as "unfeminine presumption in 'meddling with politics'." The same preface cites in defence the biblical precedents of Esther and Judith, claiming that "love of country is of no sex. It was by female patriotism that the Jews attacked their tyrants" (*O'B*, xv). Like the actions of Esther and Judith, Morgan's own writing participates in the acceptably feminine and literary work of "patriotism," and does not infringe on the masculine and nonliterary work of the "political." "Politics can never be a woman's science;" she agreed, "but patriotism must naturally be a woman's sentiment."[12] Deploying a standard line of the period, Morgan locates the "naturalness" of this sentiment for women in its domestic and local roots: domestic affections expand into "sentiments of national affection."[13] Patriotism thus simply extends the domain of the domestic, underscoring Jürgen Habermas's point about the dependence of the liberal public sphere on forms of subjectivity forged in the private, intimate sphere of the conjugal family.[14]

The key point, however, is that the distinction between patriotism and politics, never firm, is further blurred by the trope of the public sphere, an unstable trope in that it posits a symmetrical space but in fact divides into asymmetric spheres. In theory, that is, the public sphere was one, open as a whole to all literate persons by virtue of the literacy that enabled them to communicate, in the words of Habermas, as "human beings pure and simple." But complex exclusions and stratifications were always at work; literate women, for instance, had a certain (limited) entry into the literary sphere, but no entry into the political. Since liberal ideology held that there was only one sphere, however, the borders between the literary and the political were fuzzy, opening up (even as they closed down) a certain room for manoeuvre for women writers like Morgan who sought to move out of (but not repudiate) the domestic genres. Morgan could thus adhere to the official, gendered distinction between patriotism and politics, positioning her narrative safely inside the literary, but at the same time she could slide it toward the political, for the boundary of demarcation (like the concept of patriotism itself) looked both ways.[15]

But even as Morgan's narrative authorizes itself on the public stage by foregrounding the trope of the public sphere, it problematizes the entire trope through an image of female agency that "confounds" (to use one of Morgan's own favorite terms) its authority. The enlightened, rational male patriot exemplified in figures like Murrough O'Brien or General Fitzwalter of *Florence Macarthy* typically finds his perceptions and principles disconcerted by an enigmatic woman, who moves in and out of his purview and who is linked to different temporalities and different principles, while she joins with him in embracing a liberal politics. Enlightened patriotism, grounded in texts and in the example of the French Revolution, works deductively from assumptions about liberty and universal rights as it seeks to realize a civic ideal of the nation. Murrough O'Brien, for example, is inspired by its centripetal and rational model of the nation-as-project to enlist in the task of unifying the disparate nation and of harnessing into coherent action the disjunctive energies of the crowd that haunts the novel. His model of the nation (like the public sphere itself) depends on the rational temporality of linear time: the time of modern history. From his liberal constitutional reading of the French Revolution, he has derived a historical *series* into which he and like-minded others seek to enter Ireland. But the drive for modern nationhood is blocked with the defeat of 1798, and Murrough O'Brien himself must literally go underground and travel into the hinterland, where he encounters another Irish nation, attached to temporalities outside the cursive flow of history and the rational structures of the law.

He encounters in the hinterland the archaic time of the nation-people, but this is not the pure time of origin or authenticity that makes visible the nation, as was the case in Morgan's first national tale where the symbolic heroine, Glorvina, gathered Irishness into herself, revealing to the English hero "the pure national, natural character of an Irishwoman."[16] Where *The Wild Irish Girl* moved directly to an origin, dissolving nation into nature, later tales like *Florence Macarthy* and *The O'Briens and the O'Flahertys* provide no centre or "heart" of the nation from which to tell its story. Instead they operate disjunctively in that "double-time" of the nation to which Homi Bhabha has recently drawn attention,[17] interrogating notions of identity and substance, and writing the nation as shadowy and mobile – a persistence (or perhaps resistance?) through time but not an identity. The changed nature of the heroine – who continues to represent the Irish motherland – makes this especially clear.

In the hinterland, Murrough O'Brien finally encounters face-to-face the mysterious female protector who, in various guises, has repeatedly effected his rescue both earlier in his life on the Continent and more recently in Ireland. She turns out to be his cousin, Beavoin O'Flaherty, an uncloistered nun who runs an abbey, and a figure whose actions and eventual romance with O'Brien replay earlier events in the long and complicated history of their two families. She thus evokes repetitive and recursive temporalities that counter the cumulative temporality of modernity, but the hybrid Beavoin (she is half-Italian and half-Irish) does not exist in any one temporality. A modern cosmopolitan, she is also an Irish native with roots in Gaelic female culture; a nun in an ancient patriarchal institution, she uses its resources to teach modern liberal ideas to local girls. Operating in a chronotope outside the chronotopes of either social everyday time or the consequential linear time of history, Beavoin O'Flaherty evidences a striking power of mobility and metamorphosis. She moves about Europe and Ireland apparently at will, continually assumes different names and different disguises, and shifts easily among various discourses. Suggestively, her first appearances in the novel are accompanied by motifs of masquerade and carnival, and in general she confirms Julia Kavanagh's point about the waywardness of the Morgan heroine: "They have many attractions – beauty, wit, generosity, fervour – but a spirit of mischief and intrigue, an aversion to the straight ways of life, mark them all save Glorvina."[18] For most of the narrative, in fact, Beavoin refuses to reveal her identity to the hero whom she protects, bewildering him with her shifting shapes and confounding him with her sardonic wit – she operates, that is, well outside the openness and publicity of the public sphere.

In her potent mix of religion, sex, politics, and play, Beavoin O'Flaherty represents the highly eroticized nationalism characteristic of the later Morgan. Morgan's fictions as a whole, of course, depend on an implication of the sexual and the political. As J. Leerssen has pointed out, the nationalist project of her very first national tale depends on its treating the tropes of exoticism and eroticism as isomorphic structures.[19] But the "natural" allure of the blushing Rousseauian heroine of *The Wild Irish Girl* gives way in the later novels to the ironic and worldly play of figures like Beavoin O'Flaherty. Here is no pastoral, harp-playing Glorvina, firmly rooted in place and embodying the "pure national, natural character" (*WIG*, 56), but a peculiarly atopic, hybrid figure marked by narrative mobility and intermittence. As she darts in and out of the narrative, Beavoin O'Flaherty does not coalesce into a locatable, coherent subject; indeed, she begins to take on some of the disconcerting characteristics of the anonymous and volatile crowd that shadows both urban and rural settings of *The O'Briens and the O'Flahertys*. This crowd – lighting forbidden bonfires, harassing the Dublin oligarchy, attending mass in underground caves, cheering the Irish Volunteers – also swirls in and out of the novel, changing shape and mood, itself a fluid and inchoate sign. Like the crowd, the heroine is linked to an archaic temporality, to the underground, and to an unformedness that releases an unpredictable, often phantasmagoric, energy.

Through figures like Beavoin O'Flaherty, Morgan rewrites what Kristeva has called "women's time": that specially gendered archaic temporality marked by repetition and immobility, which stands in problematic relationship to the linear time of history, that is, to time as project, as departure and arrival.[20] Women's time, as Kristeva notes, acutely poses the question of female agency and subjectivity in history, for it threatens the kind of inertness exemplified in a figure like Glorvina, immobilized in repetition and symbolization. But hybrid heroines like Beavoin O'Flaherty or Florence Macarthy harness women's time, make it tell in history by transforming it (to paraphrase Kristeva) into the time of the diagonal. The diagonal neither collapses into nor remains outside but connects with the line of history – meets it aslant.

Mediating this transformation for Beavoin are images of women's historical agency to which she turns for sanction of her activities as patriot, abbess, protector, educator, and so forth.[21] Her study in the abbey displays portraits of "the *mothers* of the church" and of "saintly women of all ages" (*O'B*, 498). Three are singled out for narrative attention: the sixteenth-century Spanish writer and mystic St. Teresa, who founded and reformed religious houses all over Europe; the fifteenth-century Italian saint Catherine of Siena, who mediated in the great papal schism and corresponded extensively with the powerful men of her time; and the eighteenth-century French patroness and writer Alexandrine de Tencin, who broke her religious vows, took a series of lovers, and founded an important salon in Paris. All three women turned their role in the religious sphere toward public action and public discourse, and their prominence in Beavoin O'Flaherty's study underscores that for her (and for her author) the assumption of female agency does not mean moving out of women's time but involves activating it to take advantage of the special kind of mobility that it offers. It means, further, harnessing the power of history and its institutions by appropriating it to her own ends. "I wield the power and influence they have given me," Beavoin O'Flaherty says of her Jesuit teachers, "for purposes directly opposed to their intentions" (*O'B*, 521). In the epilogue to the novel, the heroine (now out of the nunnery and into marriage with her cousin) runs a salon in Napoleon's Paris frequented by those who oppose Napoleon's restoration (under new signs) of the old order. Soon, it is rumored, she will be ordered to leave the city. At the moment of narrative closure, then, Beavoin O'Flaherty continues to circulate, moving into the public sphere only to disappear, and operating always at an angle, on the diagonal.

II

Rather like its heroines, Morgan's own narrative draws on opposing temporalities and lives several lives, undermining the assumption of a stable point of vantage.[22] With its sprawling, web-like structure and abrupt shifts among different modes, *The O'Briens and the O'Flahertys* itself is a striking example, well meriting the *New Monthly Magazine*'s description of it as a "splendid phantasmagoria" (*NMM*, 498). As it generates its complex representation of revolution and repetition, the narrative line is repeatedly broken and tangled by the play of multiple genres – letters, annals, essays, Gothic romance, the carnivalesque, and several others. But this late novel is simply the culmination of a "mongrel heterogeneity" (the phrase is J. Leerssen's) characteristic of Morgan's national tale from the very outset. As Leerssen notes, *The Wild Irish Girl* assumes the appearance of "an unblended accumulation of superimposed discursive sediments," most obviously in the literal splitting of the text itself into two parallel texts.[23] An upper text takes the form of an epistolary narrative written by the English hero, recounting his journey into Ireland; and a lower text of extensive footnotes supplements, in the authorial mode, the case for Irish culture being made by the main narrative.[24] Furthermore, each text is itself composed of heterogeneous elements. In the upper narrative, for example, gentlemanly antiquarian genres intersect with the Jacobin novel of sensibility, the nonfictional discourse of travel writing with the deliberate artifice of sentimental comedy. The passage between genres is both constant and awkward, neither a smooth integration nor a clear demarcation; and the unevenness of the narrative is reinforced by a heavily allusive prose filled with multilingual citations. Italian, Latin, French, and Gaelic surface repeatedly, along with several varieties of English.

Similar generic jostlings and heteroglossic textures inform the subtext, where Morgan quotes from a range of works in a variety of genres (e.g., historical, elegaic, satiric, political, biographical). Even more dramatically than the main text, the footnotes perform their authorizing function in several languages and in a variety of tones. Learned figures like "Dr. Percy" and "Dr. Campbell" appear alongside informal sources like the peasant "Hugh Dugan" or "the author's father." Bits of Latin stand next to Irish English; Italian Renaissance poets beside Edmund Burke. The author herself, meanwhile, is an insistent personal presence, recounting anecdotes and recalling memories of her experiences in rural Ireland in a voice that is openly female, as opposed to the "genderless" voice often assumed by rational women writers of the period like Maria Edgeworth or Mary Wollstonecraft. This authorial voice, passionate in its nationalist commitment, crosses with the voice of the heroine, which speaks and sings within the main text as the sign of the Irish nation. The gap between the two texts, then, turns out to be less a barrier than a border crossing, as genres migrate back and forth and spill over into one another.[25]

If, however, the discursive surface of Morgan's text in *The Wild Irish Girl* resists homogeneity in an almost obsessive way, in thematic terms the narrative is almost equally obsessive in its unifying drive, for all its energies are drawn to the same point: the vindication of Gaelic culture as the origin of the nation, the repository of the true "ancient Irish" character. Later tales sharply modify this centripetal vision. The unifying power of the nostalgic Gaelic chronotope dissolves, and the Irish nation now "appears" in different locations and among different groups, an internally stratified and dispersed category. In *The O'Briens and the O'Flahertys*, for instance, Dublin itself uncovers several different kinds of Irishness, while the countryside proves to contain, not a pure Gaelic core, but various layers with different histories. So descendants of the "old English" (the Norman Catholic layer of Ireland's history) mingle with Gaelic Catholics (both gentry and peasantry) through intermarriage and shared suffering, even as they remain a distinct group. Such complicated entanglements yield a density of time, language, and history that Morgan increasingly begins to signal through what might be called an "infolding" (rather than simple juxtaposition or parallelism) of genres and discourses. Her later narratives may assume a smoother, more conventional look than *The Wild Irish Girl* with its sharply separated texts, but they contain within themselves narrative cuts and folds that point to a heightened sense of the Irish nation as a synchronicity of different (often hidden) temporalities. They thus confirm Katie Trumpener's point that the national tale after *Waverley* challenges the model of history informing the newly powerful genre of the historical novel, which finally privileges (though with a certain difficulty) a progressivist linear model of historical process. Refusing the impersonality and narrative distance of the historical novel (what Trumpener calls its "aesthetiquarianism"), the later national tale reads history with a present-tense sense of urgency, and fractures the wholeness of national-historical time.[26]

More specifically, Morgan adapts the gothic technique of embedded texts to convey the ways in which one kind of time contains, often unexpectedly, other kinds of time, and one language several meanings. Her second national tale, *O'Donnel* (1814), initiates this practice, including early in the narrative an interpolated text of a historical figure, Red Hugh O'Donnell, rebel ancestor of the (fictional) titular hero of the novel. Placed in a highly resonant scene, the interpolation is triggered by a suggestive interplay between a contemporary, upper-class English tourist, Lady Singleton, and an Irish servant, M'Rory. Lady Singleton and her party have been touring Ireland in search of the picturesque and the sublime, and one dark night they find themselves stranded in a region where the militant White Boys are said to be operating. They take shelter in the cabin of the absent Roderick O'Donnel (impoverished and dispossessed descendant of the chiefs of Tyrconnel), where Lady Singleton glances with some apprehension at a large sword hanging over the chimney-piece. At this point, M'Rory (who has already demonstrated his ability to gull the tourists while pretending to be obliging), identifies the marks on the blade as blood, and boasts of "the great O'Donnel, my lady, who bate the English troops fairly out the province." Was this lately? asks the lady, and M'Rory asserts that indeed it was.[27] The exchange that ensues plays off M'Rory's sense of "lately" (he is referring to the end of the sixteenth century) against Lady Singleton's sense, which is informed by anxiety about the very recent White Boy raids. A comic moment, its linguistic doubleness nevertheless generates a hermeneutic instability that opens up a gap, and in this gap appears the interpolated text titled "O'Donnel the Red; or The Chiefs of Tirconnel. A Fragment." This text, not one fragment but a set of fragments, tells a story of injustice, rebellion, and murder in the final days of the Gaelic order.[28] Lady Singleton reads it aloud to pass the time while awaiting the appearance of their reluctant host, after which the regular chapters resume.

This dark, alternative history of Ireland, which (briefly) intrudes into the contemporary comedy of touristic manners, is precisely a kind of fragment within the dominant narrative of the nation. As fragment, this history can be readily dismissed or, as Lady Singleton demonstrates, incorporated as simply a diversion. But its interpolation also testifies to the simultaneous circulation within the nation of unassimilable kinds of memory and desire. In the hands of a M'Rory (who literally gives the text to Lady Singleton) the fragment can serve to disconcert and unsettle the colonial story, while in the fugitive hands of White Boys this text of the past finds a material echo and re-enactment. In the context of an Irish national tale, therefore, the gothic swerve of interpolation takes on a particular political edge. Morgan's point is not so much that local speech and local chronicle represent a "real" Ireland. Certainly, she clearly privileges local speech over colonial text, as the extended critique of Edmund Spenser's *View of the Present State of Ireland* in the first chapter of *Florence Macarthy* serves to indicate. But the interpolations work more directly to move into the foreground a sense of the layered density of cultural processes and historical time that contests homogenizing narratives of the nation.[29] Such narrative moments generally do not so much overturn as cut across the tropes authorizing, on the one hand, English colonial history and, on the other, French-Scottish enlightenment history. Rational tropes of linear history, like the public sphere, remain in place but are marked by the simultaneous working of murkier and less stable temporalities.

The striking interpolation of the Annals of St Grellan into *The O'Briens and the O'Flahertys* (vol. 2, chap. 6) offers a telling instance. At one point in the narrative, Murrough O'Brien finds a volume of annals in the deserted and decaying house of his bankrupt, Gaelic-obsessed father, and he sits down to read them. This annalistic history of Ireland, which begins before the proverbial flood, is focused through the region in which the O'Briens and the O'Flahertys have long played out their rivalry ("greate strife and hurly-burly between the O'Flahertys and the O'Briens," *O'B*, 230). The annals thus assemble local, familial, and national histories, and entries of varying lengths appear on a range of topics: invasions, oysters, prophecies, transportations, frogs, lawsuits, abductions, and so on. Even more dramatically than the embedded fragments of Red Hugh O'Donnell, the Annals of St Grellan draw attention to the unevenness of history and of writing. The text read by O'Brien is a copy of the original, which was smuggled out of Ireland to the Vatican when the Elizabethan governor Sir George Carew ordered the destruction of all Irish manuscripts in the area. The actual volume, bound in rich Roman binding of white vellum, stands out as an incongruity in the crumbling Dublin mansion, but it proves to be very much connected to its site. The volume contains unfinished drawings of some of the family relics, drawings that are clearly still in process. These underscore the open-endedness of the annalistic genre, the ongoingness that distinguishes it from standard historiography. Unlike standard historiography, annals are an assemblage rather than a configuration of events, a compilation rather than a narration. The characteristic tense of the genre is the present ("The saintes multiplie exceedingly," *O'B*, 221), and this leaves the annals always open to addition. Authorship is then necessarily multiple, as different scribes make their entries over different periods of time. In the case of the Annals of St Grellan, even the modern volume containing the annalistic text is very much a composite production: it is illuminated (it will turn out) by Beavoin O'Flaherty, translated by the Abbot Malachi O'Flaherty, and annotated by the elder O'Brien who (like Morgan herself in *The Wild Irish Girl*) mingles quotations from authorities with comments of his own. One layer of the text gives way to another layer, while the annalistic entries themselves follow the discontinuous and asymmetric style of the genre.

Where the fragments on Red Hugh O'Donnell functioned as a cut in the narrative line, underlining history as rupture, the Annals are folded *into* the main narrative. Narrative attention keeps shifting from annalistic entries to the response of Murrough O'Brien, so layering the texts into each other through the representation of their reading. Such shifting exposes a certain fluidity of time and consciousness that threatens the clarity of the line of modern history and the coherence of modern subjectivity. O'Brien is a modern subject ("an epitome of the regenerated age to which he belonged," *O'B*, 212), but his immersion in the unstable matrix of Irish temporalities has made him a peculiarly conflicted subject: his mind may belong to the enlightenment, but his "prejudices and sentiments" have been unconsciously formed by his father's obsession with the Gaelic past, while his "memory and imagination" have been profoundly shaped by the tales and sufferings of his Irish foster-mother, the uncanny Mor ny Brien (*O'B*, 212). His reading of the annals enacts this splitting and confusion. On the one hand, he reads at the distance of precisely modern rationality, finding in the annals "sanguinary absurdities, and confused and barbarous details of the wars of his ancestors" (*O'B*, 220– 21). Condescending and fascinated by turns, O'Brien reads the past as an exotic text with which his own modern self has little to do. At the same time, however, he experiences moments of identification, of weird recognition, that betray his rational sense of time, place, and identity. Such moments move into the foreground a stranger temporality, one that places the present inside the past and the past inside the present.

Two such moments of temporal merging are of particular interest. In the first instance, O'Brien encounters in the annals the name

"Beavoin O'Flaherty," a name he does not consciously know but one that seems "familiar to his memory" and somehow linked to his infancy on the isles of Arran with Mor ny Brien. He repeats the name aloud, and the sound resonates "as the echo of sounds known, and half forgotten" (O'B, 222). It echoes not simply because (as he will later learn) O'Brien did in fact meet Beavoin in childhood but for less empirical reasons as well: an earlier Murrough O'Brien was involved in an ill-fated romance with an earlier Beavoin O'Flaherty, and their eighteenth-century namesakes will now play out that romance to a rather happier end. O'Brien, of course, knows nothing of this, but the original story of Murrough and Beavoin does stir in him a sense of history as re-enactment. He notes how the lives of his grandmother and aunt, for instance, have replayed parts of the old story, and in his reading of the annals he increasingly encounters time as repetitive loop.[30] In the second instance, the memory of a certain death leads to another kind of blurring of temporal boundaries. Reading the final entry of the annals, O'Brien is brought to tears by the account of the brutal extermination during the reign of William of Orange of the outlaw Irish figures known as "rapparees." The report of their executions stirs his memory of the death of his foster-brother, Shane, who had been tried and executed seven years previously. Ashamed of his "womanish sensibility," O'Brien stops reading only to catch sight of a drawing representing "the rapparee or wild Irishman," which he recognizes as a portrait of the very foster-brother he has been remembering (O'B, 243–44). At this point – in a classic gothic moment – the dead Shane himself materializes "on the threshold of the door" (O'B, 245). Inevitably, the narrative goes on to naturalize the apparition, as it does the echo of Beavoin O'Flaherty's name, but such doubling places within modern Dublin an archaic power, a literal return from the dead. Folded into rational temporality, it suggests, are nonrational temporalities that cannot be untangled from it.

Through techniques of generic infolding like interpolation, Morgan attempts to suggest something of the stereoscopic depth of the nation's time. And it is as the figure peculiarly suited to operate in such a heterogeneous temporality that the hybrid and mobile heroine achieves her narrative centrality. Moving easily among temporal zones and cultural strata, she herself can be seen as the characterological embodiment of generic infolding. With her different names and different roles, she participates in several genres, activating different modes of discourse and action as the situation requires. Herein lies the key to her special power as national heroine, as a resonant scene near the end of *Florence Macarthy* helps to illustrate.

Of Spanish-Irish parentage, Florence Macarthy is another of Morgan's hybrids, and she plays at least three distinct roles in the novel (including one in a disguise impenetrable to the reader). She has several names, the most prominent being Lady Clancare, a title that signals her link to metropolitan and colonial genres like the fashionable tale and the comedy of manners, genres that include the national tale (she herself writes Irish novels). But she is also the Bhan Tierna, and as such she is linked to the traditional, rural genres of Gaelic Ireland, familiar with Irish language and lore. In the final volume this figure marries General Fitzwalter (Marquis of Dunore), and immediately thereafter soldiers appear to arrest Fitzwalter on a charge of murder. The crowd of local peasants escorting the bridal couple immediately forms a protective phalanx around them, flinging stones and turf at the military. Both General Fitzwalter and the officiating priest O'Sullivan try to calm the crowd but to no avail. As the soldiers prepare to fire, "the voice and interference of Lady Clancare produced an effect, as unexpected as singular." The key to her effect is a change in language and in genre: "She addressed them in Irish; but it was evident neither in command nor in supplication. Whatever she said produced bursts of laughter and applause; every eye, flashing humour and derision, were [sic] turned on the constables and their satellites." Their anger dissipated and exchanged for contempt, the crowd pulls back and proceeds "in regular order" (*FM*, IV: 235–36). A certain nostalgic feudalism surfaces here, as so often in the closural moments of Irish national tales (including those of the resolutely modern Maria Edgeworth). At the same time, however, the scene pivots on the collapse of the masculine institutions on which feudalism depends. As the discourses of military, ecclesiastical, and aristocratic authority fail, a female voice intervenes, drawing on local tradition and on unofficial, notably comic, genres. This voice moves around official discourse, addressing the crowd "neither in command nor in supplication," and the intervention itself, significantly, lies outside representation. It remains a moment of narrative opacity, connecting with official discourse and moving into representation only in its effect – a paradigmatic instance of the oblique angle of action and discourse characteristic of the Morgan heroine.

Such a scene, highlighting the way in which the cultural power of the heroine derives from her ability to move among languages and genres, gains further resonance from Florence Macarthy's own status as writer of national tales. A metropolitan celebrity, she has produced a series of Irish novels directed at the English market, and she suffers a certain anxiety as a result: "With Ireland in my heart, and epitomizing something of her humour and her sufferings in my own character and story, I *do* trade upon the materials she furnishes me; and turning my patriotism into pounds, shilling and pence, endeavour, at the same moment, to serve her and support myself" (*FM*, III: 265). The national tale, that is, is defined not only by the "mongrel heterogeneity" of discourses referred to by Leerssen in his discussion of *The Wild Irish Girl* but by an inevitable ethical ambiguity in its "trading" in national wrongs and "selling" of patriotism for personal gain. Suggestively, what underwrites this doubleness for the heroine, translating her writing from private commerce and personal exploitation into public good, is a specifically female activity. As she works at a spinning wheel in her impoverished rural holding, Florence Macarthy finds in spinning the sign of a gendered heritage outside class and generation: "our grandmothers of the highest rank in Ireland were all spinners," she declares (*FM*, III: 264). She then conflates spinning and writing in metaphoric interchange: "Meantime my wheel, like my brain, runs round. I spin my story and my flax together; draw out a chapter and an hank in the same moment; and frequently break off the *thread* of my reel and of my *narration* under the influence of the same association" (*FM*, III: 265). Such a moment seeks to effect the transformation of text into tradition, to link the modern, literate heroine and the nation she writes with the rural and oral rhythms of the preliterate community. In one sense, of course, it represents standard modern nation-building, as Ernest Gellner points out in his analysis of the way in which the literate elites, who typically forge the nation, validate it through appeal to a preliterate "folk."[31] But Morgan's fractured narrative and its hybrid heroines place pressure on the modernist model. In particular, femininity, rather than erasing discontinuities and contradictions, moves them into the foreground, while the "imagined community" produced by narratives like *Florence Macarthy* emerges as an unstable construct held together in marginal, clandestine spaces and through incoherent acts.

To read Morgan's national tale in this way is to read it as postmodern in Lyotard's sense of the postmodern as an energy of interrogation and excess that shadows modernity from the outset (as within and not after modernity).[32] Morgan's fiction, that is, signs itself as modern precisely because the postmodern erupts within it. And the postmodern typically erupts in her fiction through the encounter of femininity, the public sphere, and the unformed nation, an encounter that marks femininity as a destabilizing but productive excess, and constructs woman as national author by placing her in oblique relation to the linear flow of both writing and history. "Rapid and tricksome," as the *New Monthly* reviewer found it (*NMM*, 497), Morgan's national tale deploys for the female writer a mode of intervention in and interrogation of the public sphere, taking as its task the formation of the colonial nation, that project of early romanticism whose haunted and potent life resonates into our own day.

NOTES

1 *New Monthly Magazine* 20 (December 1827): 497 (hereafter cited as *NMM*).

2 On the characterization of Morgan in the reviews, see Ina Ferris, *The Achievement of Literary Authority: Gender, History, and the Waverley Novels* (Ithaca: Cornell University Press, 1991), 45– 52. For a recent account of Morgan's life and career, see Mary Campbell, *Lady Morgan: The Life and Times of Sydney Owenson* (London: Pandora, 1988). See also Tom Dunne, "'Fiction as the Best History of Nations': Lady Morgan's Irish Novels," in *The Writer as Witness: Literature as Historical Evidence*, ed. Tom Dunne (Cork: Cork University Press, 1987), 133–59; and Ann H. Jones, *Ideas and Innovations: Best Sellers of Jane Austen's Age* (New York: AMS Press, 1986).

3 Nancy Miller, "Changing the Subject: Authorship, Writing, and the Reader," in *Feminist Studies/Critical Studies*, ed. Teresa de Lauretis (Bloomington: Indiana University Press, 1986), 116. Tom Dunne suggests that Morgan's theatricality "partly masked a serious political purpose" in his "Haunted by History: Irish Romantic Writing 1800–50," in *Romanticism in National Context*, ed. Roy Porter and Mikuláš Teich (Cambridge: Cambridge University Press, 1988), 73. More recently, Terry Eagleton underlines that the way in which Morgan "converted her domestic life into a public stage" points to her significant (and under-recognized) troubling of the boundary between the domestic and the political. See his *Heathcliff and the Great Hunger: Studies in Irish Culture* (London: Verso, 1995), 184.

4 Insofar as the national tale has entered into critical discourse, its relationship to domestic and realist genres of the period has been the

subject of some debate. Gary Kelly places the genre among those romantic genres confirming the socio-political centrality of the bourgeois family, as in his "Revolutionary and Romantic Feminism: Women, Writing, and Cultural Revolution," in *Revolution and English Romanticism: Politics and Rhetoric*, ed. Keith Hanley and Raman Selden (London: Hemel Hempstead, 1990), 107–30. So does Nicola Watson, who notes the genre's tendency to found national identity on the domestic trope. See her *Revolution and the Form of the British Novel 1790–1825: Intercepted Letters, Interrupted Seductions* (Oxford: Clarendon Press, 1994), chap. 3. By contrast, Katie Trumpener (in the most extensive discussion of the genre to date) foregrounds a resistant and subversive power that challenges the domestication of history and the premises of realism in her "National Character, Nationalist Plots: National Tale and Historical Novel in the Age of *Waverley*, 1806–1830," *ELH* 60 (1993): 685–731. Trumpener notes the convergence of feminist and nationalist concerns in Morgan, as do Colin B. Atkinson and Jo Atkinson in "Sydney Owenson, Lady Morgan: Irish Patriot and First Professional Woman Writer," *Éire-Ireland* 15 (1980): 60–90.

5 I take this useful phrase from Walter E. Houghton, "Periodical Literature and the Articulate Classes," in *The Victorian Periodical Press: Samplings and Soundings*, ed. Joanne Shattock and Michael Wolff (Leicester: Leicester University Press, 1982), 3–28.

6 Julia Kavanagh, *English Women of Letters*, 2 vols. (London, 1863), 1: 350–51. On Edgeworth as national novelist, see Marilyn Butler's fine Introduction to *Castle Rackrent and Ennui* (Harmondsworth: Penguin, 1992), 1–54. Edgeworth's is generally a more domestic accentuation of the genre than that of Morgan; even so, as Butler points out, the female characters in Edgeworth's Irish tales take on a public and political resonance they do not have in her novels of English manners (50).

7 Review of Lady Morgan, *Passages from My Autobiography*, *Athenaeum* (January 15 1859): 73.

8 On the gentry nationalism of late eighteenth-century Ireland, see R. F. Foster, *Modern Ireland 1600–1972* (Harmondsworth: Penguin, 1988), 247–58. Morgan's admired Grattan offers an exemplary instance. The gentry nationalism of the Anglo-Irish of this period is structurally analogous to the creole nationalism Benedict Anderson sees as shaping modern nationalism in general. See his *Imagined Communities: Reflections on the Origin and Spread of Nationalism*, rev. edn. (London: Verso, 1991).

9 Lady Morgan, *Florence Macarthy: An Irish Tale*, 4 vols. (London, 1818), 1: 53 (hereafter cited as *FM*).

10 The Advertisement is actually signed by her husband, Charles Morgan, but the sentiments correspond to those in Lady Morgan's writings.

11 Lady Morgan, *The O'Briens and O'Flahertys* (1827; rpt. London: Pandora, 1988), 32 (hereafter cited as *O'B*).

12 Lady Morgan, Preface, *Patriotic Sketches of Ireland* (London, 1807), x.

13 On the way in which the figure of domesticity underwrote the "national" in women's writing of the period, see Gary Kelly, *Women, Writing, and Revolution 1790–1827* (Oxford: Clarendon Press, 1993), chap. 5; and Anne K. Mellor, *Romanticism and Gender* (New York and London: Routledge, 1993), chap. 4.

14 See his classic *The Structural Transformation of the Public Sphere*, trans. Thomas Burger (Cambridge, Mass.: MIT Press, 1989).

15 For many of her reviewers, her national tales did not maintain the distinction firmly enough, mingling politics and patriotism a little too freely in their representations. The *Westminster Review*, for instance, chided Morgan for her introduction of "a lecture on liberty apropos of lace-flounces, or a discussion of the various forms of government on occasion of a dirty walk in Back-lane, Dublin," [F. D. Maurice?], "National Tales of Ireland," *Westminster Review*, 9 (April 1828): 424. Even the generally sympathetic *New Monthly Magazine* (in the review of *O'Briens and O'Flahertys* cited earlier) found that "her politics are sometimes introduced a little more prominently than the severest patriotism can require," *NMM* 20 (December 1827): 505.

16 Lady Morgan, *The Wild Irish Girl* (1806; rpt. London: Pandora, 1986), 56 (hereafter cited as *WIG*).

17 Homi K. Bhabha "DissemiNation: Time, Narrative, and the Margins of the Modern Nation," in *Nation and Narration*, ed. Homi K. Bhabha (London: Routledge, 1990). Bhabha's specific interest is in the construction of the "people" in the double narrative modalities of pedagogy (the people as prior "objects" of representation) and performance (the people as "subjects" of a signifying process). "In the production of the nation as narration," he argues, "there is a split between the continuist, accumulative temporality of the pedagogical, and the repetitious, recursive strategy of the performative" (279).

18 Kavanagh, *English Women of Letters*, II: 342. As the epigraph to this paper suggests, however, even Glorvina herself has some difficulty with very straight lines.

19 J. Leerssen, "How *The Wild Irish Girl* Made Ireland Romantic," *Dutch Quarterly Review of Anglo-American Letters* 18 (1988): 209–27.

20 Julia Kristeva, "Women's Time" (1979), in *The Kristeva Reader*, ed. Toril Moi (New York: Columbia University Press, 1986), 188–216.

21 Morgan was much interested in the question of female agency in history, producing in later life a two-volume narrative recounting the very early history of western women, *Woman and Her Master* (1840; rpt. Westport: Hyperion Press, 1976).

22 Deidre Lynch has argued that the project of romantic women writers like Morgan was to destabilize standard categories and boundaries, and she identifies the mobile heroine as central to this project, in "Nationalizing Women and Domesticating Fiction: Edmund Burke and the Genres of Englishness," *Wordsworth Circle* 25 (Winter 1994): 45–49.

23 Leerssen, "How *The Wild Irish Girl* Made Ireland Romantic," 211.

24 *The Wild Irish Girl* thus exemplifies what Gary Kelly calls the "footnote novel," a type of fiction developed by women writers in the Revolutionary aftermath "to practise learned discourses and engage in political issues conventionally closed to them," *Women, Writing, and Revolution 1790–1827*, 133.

25 Jeanne Moskal reads the textual splitting of *The Wild Irish Girl* in more clearly gendered terms in her "Gender, Nationality, and Textual Authority in Lady Morgan's Travel Books," in *Romantic Women Writers: Voices and Countervoices*, ed. Paula R. Feldman and Theresa M. Kelley (Hanover and London: University Press of New England, 1995), 171–93.

26 Trumpener, "National Character, Nationalist Plots," 709–10.

27 Lady Morgan, *O'Donnel: A National Tale* (1814; rpt. New York: Garland, 1979), 86.

28 For a decade at the very end of the sixteenth century, Hugh Roe O'Donnell (who spent several years of his youth imprisoned in Dublin Castle) waged war against the English. He was defeated in 1601, a defeat that completed the Tudor conquest of Ireland. Morgan had originally planned to make this O'Donnell the subject of her novel, but abandoned the plan when she realized that his story was too bitter for her liberal purposes. As she put it in her Preface to the first edition, "when I fondly thought to send forth a dove bearing the olive of peace I found I was on the point of flinging an arrow winged with discord," *O'Donnel: A National Tale* (London, 1814), xiii. The embedded text is thus the trace of this earlier, discordant story.

29 Morgan's narrative practice thus recalls both Lyotard's influential argument about the role of local narratives in contesting the grand metanarratives of a culture and Bakhtin's equally influential model of the dialogic processes of the novel, which resist the monologic drive of the official sphere. For a cogent analysis linking these two thinkers as theorists of narrative, see David Carroll, "Narrative, Heterogeneity, and the Question of the Political: Bakhtin and Lyotard," in *The Aims of Representation: Subject/Text/History*, ed. Murray Krieger (New York: Columbia University Press, 1987).

30 Cf. Katie Trumpener's point that the narrative processes of *The O'Briens and the O'Flahertys* as a whole suggest that "the Irish people are caught in a repetitive historical loop of gothic proportions," "National Character, Nationalist Plots," 711.

31 Ernest Gellner, *Nations and Nationalism* (Ithaca: Cornell University Press, 1983).

32 For a feminist take on Lyotard that usefully applies his understanding of the postmodern to certain nineteenth-century novels, including those of Walter Scott, see Diane Elam, *Romancing the Postmodern* (London: Routledge, 1992).

Genre and society

CHAPTER 5

Genres from life in Wordsworth's art: 'Lyrical Ballads' 1798

Don Bialostosky

Debate over Wordsworth's poetic adaptation in *Lyrical Ballads* of "the language of conversation in the middle and lower classes of society"[1] disappeared in the deconstructive moment of recent criticism but has returned in the materialist and historicist inquiries that have succeeded it. Preoccupied with allegories of reading and writing that featured language in general as a counterspirit or a mortal material, deconstruction did not worry about the poet's *choice* of one language among others. The choice seemed trivial compared to the fatality of the poet's finding himself in language at all. Historicist and materialist criticism, interested in reading poetic discourse in its social and political situations, has turned away from deconstruction's Sunday sermons on the mortal linguistic dilemmas suggested by Wordsworth's texts to examine the weekday affiliations their language bespeaks.

Not surprisingly, some of these materialist inquiries have turned to Mikhail Bakhtin's theories of discourse to describe and explain Wordsworth's theories and practices, since Bakhtin provides a model of language attuned to the ideological interrelations among literary and other social spheres of communication. David Simpson, for example, has recently resorted to Bakhtin's distinction between discourse in prose and discourse in poetry to suggest an explanation for

the absence of true "heteroglossia" from Wordsworth's avowed language of the ordinary person in a state of vivid sensation. In Wordsworth's poems, the exchanges between the educated speaker and the much-lampooned vagrants, bedlamites, and yeomen he encounters are transcribed in a decorous, subbiblical diction ("With something of a lofty utterance drest") that has always divided its readers according as they attribute different identities to ordinary language. They find the poet's reported speech to be either fraudulently euphemistic, and hence a concession to bourgeois taste, or plausibly dignified, and hence a reflection of the inherent respectability of working or homeless people. Clearly, one is here deciding for a politics rather than validating any factual evidence about what such people could not have said around 1800 . . .[2]

Simpson suggests that Wordsworth follows the practice of Bakhtin's poets rather than his prose writers in regularizing the language of his middle- and lower-class subjects toward a unifying, centralizing, hegemonic common language, but his judgment of Wordsworth's practice and the notion of language upon which that judgment is based do more to reproduce Coleridge's criticism of Wordsworth's poetry than to inaugurate a Bakhtinian inquiry into it. Simpson seems to expect that a "true heteroglossia" would be reflected exclusively in a choice of words actually used by speakers of the class Wordsworth represents in his poems, that his speakers would have "demographic credibility" (164) by having representative middle- and lower-class dialects. This was the standard on which Coleridge insisted, that the language of rustics would show up in the choice of words or order of words characteristic of rustics, and finding little of such characteristic dialect, he could declare, as Simpson does, that Wordsworth in fact failed to produce the language he declared he wished to produce and worked instead on producing a common language shaped to a large degree by familiarity with the Bible. Simpson's Bakhtinian vocabulary here makes a Coleridgean point, demonstrating already that choice of words alone does not provide a reliable index of the source or ideological import of an utterance.

Even in the essay from which Simpson draws, however, Bakhtin insists upon a distinction between a literal selection of the words used by a class of speakers, an imitation of their dialect, and an adoption of their linguistic point of view, their verbal-ideological view of the world. "Language is stratified," he writes, "not only into linguistic dialects in the strict sense of the word (according to formal linguistic markers, especially phonetic), but also – and for us this is the essential point – into languages that are socio-ideological: languages of groups, "professional," and "generic" languages, languages of generations and so forth.[3] He adds that "social stratification is also and primarily determined by differences between forms used to convey meaning and between the expressive planes of various belief systems – that is, stratification expresses itself in typical differences in ways used to conceptualize and accentuate elements of language, and stratification may not violate the abstractly linguistic dialectological unity of the shared literary language" (290). Further, he insists that "the referential and expressive – that is, intentional factors [are] the force that stratifies and differentiates the common literary language, and not the linguistic markers (lexical coloration, semantic overtones, etc.) of generic languages, professional jargons, and so forth – markers that are, so to speak, the sclerotic deposits of an intentional process . . . These external markers, linguistically observable and fixable, cannot in themselves be understood and studied without understanding the specific conceptualization they have been given by intention" (292). Finally, in artistic representations of language, social language

becomes the object of re-processing, reformulation, and artistic transformation that is free and oriented toward art: typical aspects of language are selected as characteristic of or symbolically crucial to the language. Departures from empirical reality of the represented language may under these circumstances be highly significant, not only in the sense of their being biased choices or exaggerations of certain aspects peculiar to a given language, but even in the sense that they are a free creation of new elements – which, while true to the spirit of the given language, are utterly foreign to the actual language's given evidence. (336–37)

I have documented Bakhtin's departure from Simpson's and Coleridge's empirical linguistic criteria for understanding the imitation and adoption of another's language in literature because I believe that the resort to Bakhtin to rethink this question of Wordsworth's poetry and poetics will only be fruitful, as Simpson hopes it will be (165), if we appreciate Bakhtin's radical departure from the notions of language that have previously been brought to the question. If we are to follow Bakhtin into a reconsideration of this question, we will need to learn to recognize that "languages" in his sense are distinguished not only or necessarily by differences in their characteristic vocabularies, syntaxes, or styles in the narrow sense but by the beliefs and evaluations they typically produce, by the contexts in which they are typically used, and by the shapes of utterance in which they typically occur.

Bakhtin synthesizes these several typifications of language in his notion of genre. The stratification of languages he describes in "Discourse in the Novel" is

accomplished first of all by the specific organisms called *genres*. Certain features of language (lexicological, semantic, syntactic) will knit together with the intentional aim, and with the overall accentual system inherent in one or another genre: oratorical, publicistic, newspaper and journalistic genres, the genres of low literature (penny dreadfuls, for instance), or, finally, the various genres of high literature. Certain features of language take on the specific flavor of a given genre: they knit together with specific points of view, specific approaches, forms of thinking, nuances and accents characteristic of the given genre. ("Discourse in the Novel," 289)

He develops this point more precisely in his essay devoted to "The Problem of Speech Genres":

Language is realized in the form of individual concrete utterances (oral and written) by participants in various areas of human activity. These utterances reflect the specific conditions and goals of each such area not only through their content (thematic) and linguistic style, that is, the selection of the lexical, phraseological, and grammatical resources of the language, but above all through their compositional structure. All three of these aspects – thematic content, style, and compositional structure – are inseparably linked to the *whole* of the utterance and are equally determined by the specific nature of the particular sphere of communication. Each separate utterance is individual, of course, but each sphere in which language is used develops its own *relatively stable types* of these utterances. These we may call *speech genres*.[4]

Style, the choice and arrangement of words, Bakhtin goes on to add, is not an independent criterion that differentiates one social language from another; it is "inseparably linked to particular thematic unities and – what is especially important – to particular compositional unities: to particular types of construction of the whole, types of its completion, and types of relations between the speaker and other participants in speech communication (listeners or readers, partners, the other's speech, and so forth). Style enters as one element into the generic unity of the utterance" (64).

To imitate a language in these terms would be not simply to imitate the words and order of words of a dialect or style but to imitate utterances that participate in genres that belong to spheres of communication that involve relations among participants, whose roles entail functions and statuses and ideologies, or views of the world. To imitate or adopt a language in these terms is to take on the role of a participant in a sphere of communication, to speak or write in the genres that bespeak that participation, and to see the world and other participants, as it were, through the eyes of those genres. Though a certain style may be one of the characteristic features of a genre, it may in some spheres be a more variable feature than the discursive function, the role of the speaker, the attitude toward content and listener, and the compositional structure the genre entails.

In some genres of the literary sphere of communication generic requirements of style are prominent; in others the development of an individual style is uppermost; in still others style is subordinate to functions of emplotment or argument. At different times and in different genres, the literary sphere entails different roles and relations among its participants, or, as Wordsworth puts it in the Preface, different "formal engagement[s]" that the writer will "gratify certain known habits of association" of the reader (*Lyrical Ballads*, 43). As both Wordsworth and Bakhtin recognize, this sphere of communication has a tendency to close itself off from other spheres of communication and the genres that operate in them, but as Wordsworth claims and Bakhtin makes clear, the literary sphere of communication is a secondary one that draws upon and trans- forms for its distinctive purposes the genres of primary, everyday communication. Bakhtin's account of literary genres as secondary genres declares:

Secondary (complex) speech genres – novels, dramas, all kinds of scientific research, major genres of commentary, and so forth – arise in more complex and comparatively highly developed and organized cultural communication (primarily written) that is artistic, scientific, sociopolitical, and so on. During the process of their formation, they absorb and digest various primary (simple) genres that have taken form in unmediated speech communion. These primary genres are altered and assume a special character when they enter into complex ones. They lose their immediate relation to actual reality and to the real utterances of others. For example, rejoinders of everyday dialogue or letters found in a novel retain their form and their everyday significance only on the plane of the novel's content. They enter into actual reality only in the novel as a whole, that is, as a literary artistic event and not as everyday life. ("Speech Genres," 62)

Despite the tendency of literary communication to consider its own genres in isolation from the genres in everyday communication they have absorbed and digested, it is always reasonable in these terms to ask what primary, nonliterary genres have gone into the making of a secondary literary genre and what "special character" those primary genres have taken on in their new setting. It is even more reasonable to ask these questions of the work of an author who could be said to have set out to foreground the primary genres from which literary language derives, thereby altering both the roles of participants in literary communication and the relation of literary to everyday language. It might be worthwhile then to ask how we would read the *Lyrical Ballads* if we were looking not for "demographic credibility" in transcribing the style of "men in low and rustic life" or of "the middle and lower classes of society" (*Lyrical Ballads*, 245, 9) but for imitation of the speech genres characteristic of those people and that society. What types of everyday utterances from what everyday spheres of communication does Wordsworth imitate and adopt in his poems and how are those genres of utterance transformed by their appropriation into the literary-artistic sphere of communication? What social relations, values, and ideologies are implied by those genres, and how are those relations, values, and ideologies modified by their incorporation into the secondary artistic context of individual poems and the larger collection of poems?

A survey of Wordsworth's contributions to the 1798 *Lyrical Ballads* informed by these questions may provide a suggestive starting place for this inquiry (see Table 1). I will try in each case to give an everyday characterization of the type of utterance enacted or imitated in the poem, noting its departures from expected norms for that type of utterance as well. It is worth remembering, as we survey the list of genres here named that, as John E. Jordan notes, "Not only does Wordsworth in *Lyrical Ballads* refuse the common generic tag of 'tale,' but he is exceedingly and uncommonly chary of any genre designations in the 1798 edition."[5] Wordsworth, in effect, invites his reader to engage in the exercise of naming we are about to undertake or at least to recognize the types of utterance his poems embody.

Table 1 *Speech genres in Wordsworth's 1798 Lyrical Ballads*

Title of Poem	Type of Utterance
"Lines left upon a Seat in a Yew-Tree which stands near the Lake of Esthwaite"	An epitaph not attached to a tomb
"The Female Vagrant"	An "artless" sob-story artfully retold
"Goody Blake and Harry Gill"	A strange but true tale for the farmer's almanac
"Lines written at a small distance from my House, and sent by my little Boy to the Person to whom they addressed"	A brother's invitation to his sister to come outside and play

"Simon Lee, the old Huntsman"	A confused description of a colorful character that doesn't lead where its narrator expects we expect it to lead but to an exhortation to the reader and a personal anecdote
"Anecdote for Fathers"	A "kids say the darndest things" anecdote, but almost addressed to the kid
"We are seven"	A "what can you expect a kid to understand" anecdote addressed to another adult
"Lines written in early spring"	A five-paragraph essay in six stanzas on the theme "what man has made of man"
"The Thorn"	An overheated direction to a sight-seer deflected into lurid speculations about a neighbor the speaker has never talked to
"The last of the Flock"	An artless sob story artfully retold – two of a kind!
"The Mad Mother"	A crazy homeless lady's raving to her baby
"The Idiot Boy"	A comic narrative poem that turns upon an idiot's defamiliarizing utterance
"Lines written near Richmond, upon the Thames, at Evening"	A poet's meditation on reality and illusion and the miserable life of another poet
"Expostulation and Reply"	A narrative of an expostulation and reply
"The Tables Turned; an Evening Scene, on the same subject"	An exuberant rejoinder
"Old Man travelling"	A description of a striking figure that leads to a personal anecdote
"The Complaint of a forsaken Indian Woman"	An imagined complaint of an Indian woman left to die by her tribe
"The Convict"	A fanciful sketch of a convict in the context of a meditation on the impermanence of joy that leads to a sympathetic apostrophe to its hero
"Lines written a few miles above Tintern Abbey"	An eloquent protestation of continuing love, or alternately an eloquent testimony to unremitting faith in nature that appeals to the speaker's sister to bear witness to his feelings

Of the nineteen poems I have described here, two explicitly situate their speakers in the sphere of literary communication by identifying them as poets – "Lines written near Richmond, upon the Thames" and "The Idiot Boy" – an odd couple published right next to each other in the text. "Simon Lee" addresses a reader with literary expectations and so implicitly joins the poems in this group. The titles, as Jordan long ago reminded us, do not identify any tales, sonnets, odes, or other literary genres. "Anecdote," "Complaint," "Expostulation," "Reply," and the not very informative "Lines" are the closest we come to generic designations, and none of them names an exclusively literary genre.

One poem, "Goody Blake and Harry Gill," is addressed to a professional group, "ye farmers all," though the topic of the poem is not professional but moral and psychological, a human interest story that might also be a lesson for people who have property to protect.

The largest group includes utterances that address strangers or report speeches addressed to strangers, usually travellers or people encountered on travels. Together they identify the public way as a sphere of communication with its own genres. "Lines left upon a Seat in a Yew-Tree" are to be imagined as left there for the stranger passing by to find and feel addressed by. The female vagrant tells her tale to whoever retells it, the sort of thing we could hear on skid road from a complete stranger. The speaker in "We are seven" reports in the comfort of his family a discomfiting conversation he has had with a child he has no relation to. The narrator of "The Thorn" presses his impressions of and directions for seeing the remarkable tree on an auditor who knows neither him nor Martha Ray; here the listener is the tourist, though the speaker doesn't seem to belong to the community he reports on either. The speaker of "The last of the Flock" has encountered and questioned a stranger on the road, though the stranger is no vagrant. "Old Man travelling" reports the same sort of exchange. "The Convict" sketches and apostrophizes a stranger, but not on the road. The encounter seems to be in fancy rather than in fact and so may belong as much among the utterances that imply a poetic speaker. "Tintern Abbey" is occasioned by an experience on the road, but it is addressed partly to nature, partly to the speaker's sister, and the place is a familiar one, though not home.

A smaller number of utterances are addressed to or report exchanges with friends or family members – the Wordsworth Circle as sphere of communication. The "Lines written at a small distance from my House" belong to the domestic sphere. The "Anecdote for Fathers" grows out of and is spoken within a father's relation to his

son, and "We are seven" in the 1798 edition is addressed to a
fictional brother. "Expostulation and Reply" and "The Tables
Turned" report and imitate exchanges with a friend. The speaker of
"Tintern Abbey" appeals to his sister as a witness of his feelings but
not in a domestic setting. It is interesting that all these poems are
argumentative, marking the domestic sphere as one in which giving
and receiving reasons, not just taking assent for granted, is the
generic norm. Even the chaste sibling *carpe diem* sends reasons to the
sister to abandon her work for a day in the sun, and "We are seven"
tells its story of an unsuccessful argument to win its point with a
more amenable listener. "Anecdote for Fathers" grows out of an
inappropriate and misleading request for a reason. I would therefore
associate the argumentative "Lines written in early spring" with this
group, though it is not addressed to a specified listener and might
appeal beyond the circle of family and friends for the confirmation
of any reasonable being who can appreciate its reasons to lament
"what man has made of man."

The two monologues of abandoned women, "The Mad Mother"
and "The Complaint of a forsaken Indian Woman," identify a
sphere of uncommunicating communication that marks their
speakers as beyond the pale of normal social relations but still
involved in their own minds with others who have abandoned them.
The mad mother speaks of her relations to the man who has left her
to the uncomprehending infant he has left her with, and the dying
Indian woman complains to those who have left her behind.

"Tintern Abbey," which has aspects of both traveler's discourse
and sibling speech, may ultimately make the most sense as addressed
to the Wye itself and through it to Nature, placing it in a quasi-
religious sphere of communication addressed to quasi-divine beings
in the genre of testimony of faith with overtones of the amatory
genre of lover's proof of his fidelity while he was away from his
beloved. Its relations to several different spheres of communication
and its suggestion of multiple primary speech genres mark it as
probably the most complex secondary reworking of primary genres
and help to account for its being undoubtedly the most provocative
of multiple interpretations.

Except for "The Idiot Boy," whose poet-narrator narrates from a
privileged, though non-omniscient, perspective only available in
literature, "Lines written near Richmond," whose poet-speaker
meditates as a poet on the delusions, fantasies, and sorrows of poets,

and perhaps "The Convict," whose speaker mysteriously "repairs" to the convict's cell and apostrophizes him, none of the utterances depicted in the poems I have enumerated depends for its initial intelligibility on any interest or device peculiar to poets. Even where poetic genres hover in the background to provide special pleasures to a sophisticated reader who can see the lines sent to the speaker's sister as an odd *carpe diem*, or "Tintern Abbey" as a variation on the ode, or "Old Man travelling" as a modified dream vision, or "Anecdote for Fathers" as a Theocritean pastoral,[6] speech genres from the spheres of everyday communication provide alternate models for initially recognizing the utterances the poems represent, even if those initial recognitions usually lead to questions that provoke further interest and inquiry.[7]

Even if all the poems imitated unproblematic instances of primary speech genres, however, their metrical setting and their very presentation as poems in a collection would mark all of them as secondary poetic utterances, and none of them functions immediately and simply in the primary sphere of communication from which it is taken. In this secondary literary sphere of communication, it is out of order to say, as Dr. Burney did of "The last of the Flock," that "the author . . . ought not to have suffered this poor peasant to part with the last of his flock" (*Lyrical Ballads*, 322), though it is in order to wonder what pleasurable interest the poet invites the reader to take in a report of such a painful case. The representation of these utterances in verse makes a claim for their interest as especially revealing or affecting utterances worthy of sustained attention. As Wordsworth puts it in his Preface, their presentation in verse is a sign of "purpose" and a promise of "pleasure" and a producer of "dissimilitude" from "the language really spoken by men" sufficient to the purposes of poetic pleasure (*Lyrical Ballads*, 246, 272, 254). These poems allow readers to enter them on familiar everyday discursive terms only to compel those readers to wonder what such utterances are doing in verse and to contemplate and construe the diverse communicative situations they represent as not as familiar as they seemed. Even the two poems that invoke a poet's reader, "Simon Lee" and "The Idiot Boy," do so to call attention to and disappoint literary generic expectations and raise the question of how they are to be taken, not to elicit familiar literary responses. Wordsworth declares in the Preface that these disappointments should in the end provoke the reader to enjoy a greater and a better pleasure than literary communication usually produces.

Each poem is ideological in the sense that the utterance it presents takes for granted certain attitudes toward its subject and listener shaped by the genre it participates in. The epitaphic "Lines left upon a Seat," for example, speaks with epitaphic confidence in its values and an unproblematic understanding of the meaning of the completed life of its hero and presumes to teach the meaning of that life to passersby. The privileged position of knowing the outcome of a whole life and being authorized to teach its meaning to all comers belongs to the genre of epitaph and distinguishes this poem from the many less certain and authoritative poems that fill the collection. Among them the anecdotal "We are seven," for example, appeals to a sympathetic listener to confirm the speaker's insistent judgment of an encounter in which his fundamental values have been challenged by an interlocutor whom he hopes to discredit in narrating his exchange with her. Simpson draws an interesting characterization of the genre of anecdote from Isaac D'Israeli that marks this genre's distance from the authoritative epitaph: "'A skillful writer of anecdotes, gratifies by suffering us to make something that looks like a discovery of our own; he gives a certain activity to the mind, and reflections appear to arise from ourselves. He throws seeds, and we see those flowers start up, which we believe to be of our own creation.' "[8] It is important to note that this description applies from the point of view of the poet-maker of this anecdote but not from that of its speaker, who seeks not to reveal his insecurities but to put them to rest by winning his brother Jim's agreement to his judgment of the child.

If any narrator of a lyrical ballad seems deliberately to frame an anecdote to put his readers in the position D'Israeli describes it is the narrator of "Simon Lee" who sets a problem, exhorts his readers to address it, and tells an anecdote that he realizes tells more of a tale than he can or will tell directly. The readers of that poem can follow his instructions to think about the anecdote, though the instructions do not tell them what to think. The readers of other poems addressed to "travellers" or the speaker's "dear brother Jim" or his "good friend Matthew" or the unnamed auditor of "The Thorn" cannot simply take up the subject positions addressed by the poems and participate unproblematically in the ideologies those positions entail. Since the listeners of the poems are hailed as, among other things, farmers, brothers, sisters, friends, and traveling strangers, as well as readers, the actual readers of the poem must question their interpellation by the poems or at least experience that interpellation as confusing. Careful readers, readers who are willing to take the invitation to close and thoughtful reading implied by the poetic presentation of these utterances, must reflect upon the values the utterances depend upon, consider their speakers' and listeners' varying relations to them, and ponder the ideologies of their varying genres. Even readers less eager to learn and less willing to forgo their habits of being "pleased in that particular way in which [they] have been accustomed to be pleased" (*Lyrical Ballads*, 272) are likely, as Wordsworth knew, to be disoriented and disappointed rather than duped into reproducing the poems' unspoken values.

At the risk of producing such disappointment, Wordsworth could be said in Bakhtin's terms to have conducted in *Lyrical Ballads* of 1798 an experiment to test whether the metrical representation of primary discourse genres from ordinary life could cultivate a pleasurable critical responsiveness to those everyday genres and to the poetic genres that derive from them. Experimenting not so much with the vocabulary and syntax but with the evaluative stances and discursive actions of primary speech genres, he employed the resources of verse to provoke his readers not just to enjoy the habitual pleasures of familiar generic transactions but to take satisfaction in glimpsing the ways in which everyday and poetic genres define relations among their participants and shape their responses to the world and to one another.

Though a favorite target for our own demystifying critiques of his supposed authoritarian gestures, he is a pioneer in cultivating through poetry the prosaic modern critical consciousness that is not confined, like Bakhtin's image of the poet, within the limits of its own language but can, like Bakhtin's prose writer, turn that language into "an object to be perceived, reflected upon or related to" ("Discourse in the Novel," 286). We might, with Bakhtin's help, see Wordsworth's turn to "the language of conversation in the middle and lower classes of society" or "the language of men in low and rustic life" not as the discovery of an alternative poetic or a common language with which to replace the degraded "language of poets," though the Preface sometimes sounds as if these are his aims. Rather those languages function as an *other* language from the perspective of which he can make "the language of poets," the language of his chosen profession, audible *as a language among other languages.* Like Bakhtin's prose writer, he "attempts to talk about even his *own* language in an alien language . . . ; he often measures his own world by alien linguistic standards" ("Discourse in the Novel," 287), and he cultivates in his readers the discomfiting if interesting habit of learning to hear both his and their own languages among others. In doing so he helps his readers to turn against him the critical capacities he turned against himself.

NOTES

1 Advertisement to *Lyrical Ballads and a Few Other Poems*, 1798, in *Words-worth and Coleridge, Lyrical Ballads*, ed. R. L. Brett and A. R. Jones (London: Methuen, 1963), 9. Further quotation from this edition of *Lyrical Ballads* will be noted parenthetically.
2 David Simpson, "Public Virtues, Private Vices: Reading Between the Lines of Wordsworth's 'Anecdote for Fathers,'" in *Subject to History: Ideology, Class, Gender*, ed. David Simpson (Ithaca: Cornell University Press, 1991), 164.
3 M. M. Bakhtin, "Discourse in the Novel," in *The Dialogic Imagination*, ed. Michael Holquist, trans. Caryl Emerson and Michael Holquist (Austin: University of Texas Press, 1981), 271–72. Henceforth referred to par-enthetically as "Discourse in the Novel."
4 M. M. Bakhtin, "The Problem of Speech Genres," in *Speech Genres and Other Late Essays*, ed. Caryl Emerson and Michael Holquist, trans. Vern W. McGee (Austin: University of Texas Press, 1986), 60. Henceforth referred to parenthetically as "Speech Genres."
5 John E. Jordan, *Why the Lyrical Ballads?* (Berkeley: University of California Press, 1976), 144.
6 For this last observation, see Stuart Curran, *Poetic Form and British Romanticism* (New York: Oxford University Press, 1986), 100.
7 A survey of the 1800 volume of *Lyrical Ballads* would yield quite a different profile of genres and spheres of communication. There are more explicitly poetic utterances, fewer imitations of encounters with strangers on the high road, and the domestic "Poems on the Naming of Places" are not argumentative. One of the problems in reading Wordsworth's Preface in relation to the poems it prefaces is the difference between the earlier volume that calls most for defence and the later one that first contains the Preface itself.
8 [Isaac D'Israeli], *A Dissertation on Anecdotes; by the Author of Curiosities of Literature* (London: Kearsley and Murray, 1793), 8, quoted in Simpson, *Subject to History*, 88–99.

CHAPTER 6

"A voice in the representation": John Thelwall and the enfranchisement of literature

Judith Thompson

With the rise of "new" literary history in the 1980s has come a resurgence in and reconceptualizing of genre studies, derided by Derrideans as futile and irrelevant. Always more congenial to various forms of historicism than to formalisms constructive or deconstructive, genre criticism has nevertheless been marked by the same long-standing dichotomy between essentialist and historical, synchronic and diachronic theories that has marked literary criticism in general: between notions of genre as law and as process, as abstract system and as concrete manifestation, as structural ideal and as textual reality. Under the influence of new historicism, however, this field has been further problematized by the recognition that this dichotomy itself is historically determined, and that, like any other literary category, genre is deeply implicated in the means and conditions of its own production: it is neither a simple ahistorical hierarchy or norm, nor a development of hierarchies and norms through history, but is itself a form of, and a participant in, historical change through ideological struggle. Though their critical methodologies are very different, both Ralph Cohen and Frederic Jameson have argued that a fully historical understanding of generic transformation as a social act requires a theory of genre broad, dynamic, and "differential" or "dialogic" enough to acknowledge and account for the coexistence and interaction within any single text of several genres, or generic elements, and to attend to the social and aesthetic purposes for which these elements are grouped, defined, and redefined by authors and readers through time.[1] Under such a theory, any text appears not as a simple manifestation of or deviation from a norm, but as a complex web of sometimes concordant, sometimes contradictory generic messages, which the author selects, appropriates, reshapes, and recontextualizes, but which nevertheless retain traces of the contexts from which the author took them and the purposes for which they were used in the past. The object of the critic thus becomes to trace the dynamics of this generic interaction, to reveal the earlier ideological messages encoded in the present usage, and to account for the author's manipulations or translations of these messages. An example of this kind of critical endeavor is Alan Liu's *Wordsworth: The Sense of History*; the sheer size of this tome is testament to the difficulty of the application of a fully historicized and dialogic genre theory.[2]

The example of Romantic studies is an instructive one, for rigid models of genre break down precisely at such periods of literary transition, dislocation, or disruption, when "mixed genres" proliferate. The individual generic transformations and innovations of the Romantic period must be seen in the context of the broader and more profound social and ideological ferment of that era: the democratization and professionalization of the literary marketplace, agitation for constitutional and electoral reform, the struggle for women's rights, the rise of nationalism. At such a time, when all laws, systems, and hierarchies are under pressure, the true historical dynamics of genre – the processes by which and reasons for which generic laws, systems, and hierarchies are constructed and deconstructed – are revealed, and genre itself appears less like an orderly courtroom or hierarchical house of lords than an open-air political forum or speaker's corner in which competing voices engage in discussion, debate, and harangue.

Yet while the Romantic period might thus appear to offer fertile ground for the development and application of the kind of fully historicized, differential genre theory that Cohen and Jameson propose, the established "high" Romantic view of the literary text as a transcendent artifact, and of the Romantic writer as a privileged originator, has militated against this pursuit. More often, as Siskin has argued, Romantic studies have treated genre as they have history: when they have not altogether ignored it in favor of tales of transcendence and originality, they have imposed upon it a "sweet developmental narrative,"[3] treating single forms as "independent, organic entit[ies] evolving naturally toward greater sophistication . . . [e.g.] *the* Novel's rise or *the* Lyric's flowering."[4] Hence the complex and highly political process of negotiation, appropriation, and subversion by which Romantic writers engaged with their generic inheritance in an age which faced widespread challenges to all inherited institutions remains to be fully explored.

One of the most insistent voices in the scrum that presses outside the privileged chambers of high Romanticism is that of John Thelwall. Best known today as a political theorist and orator, defendant in the notorious treason trials of 1794, and "maker of the English working class,"[5] Thelwall was also an active poet, novelist, journalist, and editor. Yet his literary reputation has been slower to emerge from the shadows cast by the Romantic ideology.[6] Critics appear to have found his style too conventional, mannered, and hyperbolic to warrant serious attention,[7] and while some (notably Reiman) have acknowledged and praised his experimental use of form, none has noted the self-reflexive acuity and irony with which he manipulates stylistic and generic conventions, or the political purposes for which he does so. Instead, as with so many 1790s writers, Thelwall is valued simply as a precursor of greater Romantic achievements, as in Reiman's summary evaluation of him as a "pennant at the masthead . . . of a fleet of British poets, some of whom would successfully navigate the strange seas of thought that Thelwall but dimly perceived."[8]

I will argue, however, that Thelwall not only knew which way the wind was blowing but, like an observant stowaway or knowledgable mutineer, provided a set of alternate charts and logbooks for the high Romantic voyage. His own handling of style and genre, though perhaps flawed when judged by high Romantic standards of originality and organic unity, offers acute insight into the ideological stakes involved in the stylistic and formal choices and stances that helped to define high Romanticism. In particular, his 1793 text *The Peripatetic*, a quasi-novelistic medley of verse and prose, literature and journalism, politics and sentiment, satire and effusion, oratory and anecdote,[9] offers, by means of its politically self-conscious manipulation of style and form, a new way of reading Romantic genres in their complex interrelations with other genres, as ideological forms.[10] Profoundly committed to an ideal of free speech, open debate, and friendly conversation, Thelwall writes a text in which not only characters, but also genres interact, are questioned, challenged, undermined, and redefined. It is a text which a dialogic or differential genre theory can help to understand, and one which can contribute uniquely to the development of such a theory. For *The Peripatetic* amounts to an exercise in applied genre theory, which parallels and complements the explicit political theory developed in Thelwall's pamphlets and speeches of the 1790s. Highly conscious and critical of oppressive distinctions of birth, class, or "hereditary privilege and prejudice" which dominate his society, Thelwall is also acutely aware of the literary, discursive, and linguistic distinctions which reinscribe and reinforce those false social distinctions. Refusing to take the characteristic Romantic turn (later practised so skilfully by his friends and contemporaries Coleridge and Wordsworth) of separating the purely literary or aesthetic elements of texts from their ideologically charged contexts, Thelwall demands that his readers see and question the political implications of each genre that he invokes. At the same time he invites them to reconfigure each genre on the enlightened democratic principles which he espouses, thereby effecting an enfranchisement of literature analogous to the political enfranchisement sought by the members of the reform societies. Perceiving the "elite" literature of his time as an antiquated structure devoted to displaying, maintaining, and perpetuating the pleasure and power of the ruling classes, he deconstructs it, attempting to build out of its ruins a more truly democratic structure, in which "every one who has an interest" has "a voice also in the representation" (*Peripatetic*, 1: 146).

THELWALL AS REFORMER

A London silk-mercer's son, whose formal education was cut off when his father's death left the family almost destitute, John Thelwall, like so many reformers of the period, was largely self-educated: at his family's urging he had served apprentice to various occupations, among them tailoring and law, but his literary ambitions proved stronger than his business sense, and he had already been supporting himself and his family by his pen for three to four years when the French Revolution transformed him, like so many of his contemporaries, into a radical. During the early 1790s he became increasingly active in the debating and reform societies, and by 1793, when he was 29, he had risen to become a prominent lecturer and, according to E. P. Thompson, the leading theorist of the working-class London Corresponding Society.[11]

The publication of *The Peripatetic* coincides with this rise to public prominence, and marks the crossing of his political and literary interests and discourses. It is an earlier version of the debate with Edmund Burke over economic and intellectual inheritance, property, and freedom that would later take form in his political writings and speeches. But it is a more interesting one from a literary point of view because it registers the impact of this debate, so crucial to the origins and development of English Romanticism, in the broadest possible terms, exploring and dramatizing the emotional and imaginative contexts and contiguities of politics in a way that a work of philosophy or a pamphlet cannot.

The most direct articulation of the political principles which inform *The Peripatetic* is Thelwall's *The Rights of Nature* (1796), which, as its title suggests, is strongly influenced by Paine's *The Rights of Man* (1792), the text whose publication, in answer to Burke's *Reflections on the Revolution in France*, profoundly changed the nature of British political and intellectual life. Thelwall attacks Burke from the same democratic, enlightened rationalist position as Paine: where Burke locates authority and value in feudal tradition, hereditary institutions, and "natural" compacts which are binding upon successive generations, Thelwall valorizes individual merit and labor, common knowledge, and the "natural" rights of man, including the right to freedom of speech, the right to popular representation, and the right to reform or overthrow unjust or corrupt institutions and constitutions. Where Burke defines the country in terms of property, Thelwall regards the nation as the aggregate of its population, and, in a startling anticipation of socialist and communist theory which goes beyond Paine, defines property as labor.[12] The principle of unequal distribution of property through inheritance, which Burke praises, Thelwall scourges, linking it to a system which "multiplies the divisions and enmities of the human race, by splitting them into casts and factions – into 'classes, orders and distinctions,' different in their views, and hostile in their particular interests" (*Rights*, III: 473–74). In its place he advocates, if not complete equality of property and state distribution, at least a system of more "[g]eneral and impartial distribution" (*Rights*, IV: 483) governed by social rather than personal expediency, in which the laborer has a right to a share of production proportional to his contribution to it (*Rights*, III: 476–77).

What makes these political ideas interesting from a literary standpoint is the way Thelwall explicitly links his economic argument to issues of intellectual and discursive labor, property, inheritance, and distribution. Like Paine, he attacks Burke's inflated rhetoric as elitist and exclusionary, and appropriates the "plain solid Socratic" style to the excluded, who, he asserts, are fully capable of understanding political principles and recognizing Burke's "flimsy sophisms," and require only "practical fluency" to "render them most formidable antagonists to the whole college of aristocratical disclaimers" (*Rights*, 1: 399–400). In the late eighteenth century knowledge is no longer, as Burke asserts, an inherited tradition of established usage dressed in "learned metaphors and dashing periods" (*Rights*, 1: 399) available only to the top ten percent of the population, but is being diffused to a large and largely urban proportion of the remaining ninety percent, primarily through the workshops and factories which operate as a kind of credit union of ideas:

> . . . a sort of Socratic spirit will necessarily grow up, wherever large bodies of men assemble. Each brings, as it were, into the common bank his mite of information, and putting it to a sort of circulating usance, each contributor has the advantage of a large interest, without any diminution of capital.[13] (*Rights*, 1: 401)

Yet this burgeoning underground system for the "general and impartial distribution" of intellectual property is impeded both by direct government measures like taxes on the production and circulation of written material, and by the accumulation and mono-polization of knowledge which, Thelwall asserts, "cannot operate, to any beneficial purpose . . . till it becomes pretty generally diffused. Like all other things, good in themselves, it becomes, when perverted by monopoly, a source of evil: for *Knowledge is Power!* and as such, when monopolised, is an instrument of oppression" (*Rights*, IV: 486).

In short, then, Thelwall's work is an attempt to wrest the space of discussion away from the aristocratic monopoly, to enlarge and recenter that "narrow circle" to include the intelligent and informed masses that populate the reform societies. Such an attempt involves the subversion, appropriation, and reconfiguration not only and not primarily of the politico-philosophical discourse represented by works like *The Rights of Man* and *The Rights of Nature*, but also, and more importantly, of the literary discourses in which, as Klancher and Kelly have pointed out, the struggle to define, mediate, and contain "the competing values, visions and relations of self and society during the years 1789–1830" were carried out.[14]

It is for this reason that Thelwall's literary works, and especially *The Peripatetic*, are arguably more important than his political writings. A virtual compendium of early Romantic genres, high and low, quoting from and alluding to a wide variety of sources, literary

and extra-literary, *The Peripatetic* is designed not only (or not
primarily) to develop "practical fluency" in artisan readers, but to
muscle in on Burke's "aristocracy of thinkers and discoursers"
(*Rights*, 1: 399) by displaying both its mastery and mockery of their
codes and conventions, and seizing their intellectual property for
redistribution. As such it resembles the radical periodicals with
which Thelwall was closely allied.[15] Like Daniel Isaac Eaton's
Hogwash or Thomas Spence's *Pig's Meat*, it is a "salmagundy,"[16] a
"riotous"[17] mixture of incongruous styles and genres which is
characteristic of late eighteenth- and nineteenth-century radical
discourse, according to Klancher, who defines this mode as "*inter-
discourse*, a language of countermand and critique, a dialogue in the
most explicit sense . . . Radical writers quote, parody, compile,
ridicule in a politics of warring contexts."[18] Such strategies produce
a profoundly indeterminate and hence highly problematic text,
impossible to fit into existing generic hierarchies, except as a case of
deliberate subversion or "oppositional structuring."[19] Yet to read
The Peripatetic simply as confrontational and subversive in its use of
genre, neglecting its constructive revisionary aims and practices, is to
do it and its author an injustice. No mere "Luddite of language,"[20]
Thelwall dismantles and disorders in order to reconstruct and
reorder: softening the detached bombastic rhetoric of the pamphlet
wars, he exploits literary strategies in order to engage his readers
personally, and attempts to institute a method of writing and reading
that closely corresponds to the kind of Socratic interchange, or
cooperative information economy, that he outlines in *The Rights of
Nature*.

THE DISTINCTIONS OF *THE PERIPATETIC*

In his Preface to *The Peripatetic*, Thelwall acknowledges and defends
the "singularity" and "irregularity" of his work, asserting that his
"design" was to "unite the different advantages of the novel, the
sentimental journal and the miscellaneous collection of essays and
poetical effusions" (1: v–vi). One of these advantages, related to
Thelwall's project of cultural redistribution and rapprochement, is
"the prospect of more extensive circulation" (1: vi) afforded by the
novelistic framework he has chosen: the inclusion of a fictitious but
autobiographical narrator, Sylvanus Theophrastus, with whose
eccentric but engaging personal anecdotes readers of all classes may

identify; and the extension of the narrative of Belmour and Sophia throughout the three volumes, which allows him to interweave "the subject of our political abuses . . . with the scenes of distress so perpetually recurring to the feeling observer" (I: viii), exploiting the widespread popularity of the sentimental novel to criticize society in the "guise of 'mere' entertainment," in a manner characteristic of other Jacobin novelists such as Wollstonecraft and Holcroft.[21] But to place too great an emphasis upon such novelistic elements, as most commentators have done, is to underestimate the importance not only of the other individual genres represented in the text (epic, lyric, topographical poetry, anecdote, periodical essay, gothic and chivalric romance, letter, travel writing, history, children's literature) but of the crucial relationships between these genres – the inter-generic conversation – in which most of *The Peripatetic*'s originality and effectiveness lies. For among the irregularities of form which Thelwall acknowledges in his preface is the dismissal of "the arbitrary and usual distinctions of book and chapter" (I: iii) in favor of the "natural" divisions of Sterne, which, by appropriate titles, "rouse[ ] the attention to every change of the subject" (I: iii). What this means, in effect, is that the usual structural and generic markers for distinguishing, classifying, and evaluating forms of literature are absent; in their place the reader is asked to respond to the book in terms of its own "natural" divisions, its politico-sentimental poetical-prosaic episodes, which engage themselves with other episodes to create loose clusters of meaning which level the normal distinctions of stanza and chapter, poetry and the novel, the literary and the non-literary.

Levelling arbitrary distinctions, whether of genre, language, birth or class, and replacing them with more natural, rational or enter-taining distinctions of character, opinion, perspective, heart or intellect, is a fundamental part of Thelwall's program, both social and literary. From the beginning of the text, Thelwall attacks the oppressive nature and effects of social distinctions. In a poem addressed to the ancient Greek "immortal sages" to whom he looks as his peripatetic and philosophical ancestors, he celebrates the freedom of these spiritual giants of the past from the "tyrant badges of distinction" which cramp the "pigmy slaves" of the present (I: 9–10). In a series of oratorical poems which follow, he condemns the social abuses caused by Pride, Ambition, Tyranny, and other members of "false Distinction's pageant" (I: 31) (such as building thrones on trampled crowds, stealing Labour's honest earnings, and pressing Oppression's foot on the bowed necks of fallen races) and calls on Britons, like their American brothers, to throw off "the brazen yoke of loath'd distinctions" (1: 41). At the same time, however, he is aware of the extent to which these social codes are deeply ingrained not only in people's minds, but in their language. In one of the prose segments that separate the poems noted above, Thelwall's speaker and alter ego, Sylvanus Theophrastus, meets an old sailor who assumes that Sylvanus is a tradesman. When Sylvanus replies "you are mistaken," the sailor apologizes deferentially. Automatically a barrier of class is raised between them, an obstacle to that "freedom of conversation from which alone the human heart can be revealed; and those shades and distinctions of character that constitute the vast and entertaining variety of human nature can be developed" (1: 47). That barrier is caused not simply by the "slavish impress[ion] of . . . supposed distinctions" upon the sailor's mind, but by the inevitable inscription of them upon Sylvanus' own discourse: he acknowledges that "the little paltry vanity of arbitrary and ideal distinctions" may have given an "involuntary emphasis of triumph to my manner of making this brief reply" (1: 47). Hence he apologizes for his curtness, and while he cannot completely eliminate the false distinctions of class that come between himself and the sailor, does succeed in understanding something of his truly distinctive character and sentiments during the conversation which follows.

That Thelwall is attempting not only to cross social boundaries, but to interrogate and dismantle the discursive structures and literary conventions that support them, becomes clearer when we recognize the self-conscious artificiality with which he depicts both the sailor (a type character such as one might find in any sentimental tale or poem) and Sylvanus' encounter with him. Thelwall highlights this literary artifice by introducing the encounter with a comment which ironically draws attention to the narrative conventions whereby strangers who meet accidentally, say on a stage coach, immediately, "according to the courteous practice of knights and heroines of romance," seek to know one's "name, profession, place of abode, amours and singular exploits" (1: 45). That Sylvanus resists the sailor's leading questions may be taken as an attempt to bypass or get beyond such conventions, and the social codification that they inscribe. Sylvanus, Thelwall's freethinking spokesman, does not want to participate in a rigid class structure wherein he is defined by his job, clothes and place of origin rather than by his democratic "citizen-ship." Thelwall does not want to write a "sentimental journey" in which encounters between the middle-class "man of feeling" and his lower-class interlocutors and beneficiaries merely reinforce stereo-types and supply occasions for sentimental pathos or isolated acts of benevolence, while doing nothing to reduce social inequities or to address the underlying systemic causes of individual misfortune. Hence here, as throughout the book, he draws attention to the limitations of the sentimental framework he employs, broadly and comically exaggerating the excesses and improbabilities of plot and character in his "novel," and punctuating his narrative with episodes of social commentary and literary criticism in which he analyzes sentimental conventions in terms of his radical social philosophy.

For example, knowing that readers of sentimental tales might expect a meeting with an old sailor to focus on his modest bravery, simple piety, lonely frailty, or adventurous exploits, Thelwall men-tions some of these characteristics. But only briefly, and only to expose their philosophical deficiencies – for the real focus of the episode is on the way such stereotypes, both literary and non-literary, serve to sustain and promote a repressive ideology. In this case, both the sailor's "unlettered prejudices" (1: 52) in favor of a war-based naval economy, and the tacit acceptance of war implicit in the literary idealization of such veterans, reflect and indeed underwrite a system led by war-mongering profiteers, whom he goes on to attack pointedly at the end of the episode.

The old sailor episode is a good example of how Thelwall re-examines the distinctive characteristics of a literary genre – in this case sentimental typology – in the light of his radical philosophical principles, showing the link between literary and social codes and conventions (or prejudices and predecents, to use his terminology), and analyzing both as symptoms of the nation's malaise. In its idealization of conversation as a means of lowering social barriers, removing prejudices, and attacking codes and conventions, this episode offers a paradigm for the reform of literature as a space for such friendly converse and the free exchange of ideas.

INTERGENERIC INTERROGATIONS

While interpersonal conversations, discussions, and debates like the one with the old sailor provide much of the substance of *The*

Peripatetic, the real originality of the text lies in the complex interrelationships, conversations, and interrogations of genre that occur within and between episodes. A fine example of this is in the cluster that precedes the old sailor episode, which shares its concern with sentimental typology. Here Sylvanus meets a beggar: at once the classic test of democratic social principles; and an ideologically overdetermined "scene" common to several genres, literary and non-literary. In fact, in this cluster several such encounters are juxtaposed, nested within one another, and so too are several genres. Walking along the road, Sylvanus sees two "idle" and "ill-looking" fellows up ahead (1: 19–20), and is immediately frightened, as he remembers two earlier encounters: one in which he was violently mugged; and another in which, having refused charity to a rude and impudent professional cripple, he was threatened with the beggar's crutch. As he relates these encounters, Sylvanus' tone is anything but sentimental: his withering condemnation of professional beggary as a "vicious profession of indolence and hypocrisy" (1: 24) echoes a common eighteenth-century political genre – the anti-beggary pamphlet – and, insofar as it draws on Thelwall's own experience, also takes the shape of an autobiographical anecdote or personal testimonial.[22]

These encounters frame a third, in which Sylvanus is asked for charity by an unemployed laborer, upon whom he projects all the virulent antipathy generated by the two earlier encounters, and whom he consequently passes by, coldly and fearfully denying, not only charity, but any kind of human connection. Significantly, the laborer is carrying a hay fork, an emblematic "instrument of industry" which focuses not only the personal fears of Sylvanus (and Thelwall behind him), but the revolutionary anxieties of an entire generation only too aware, in the year of the Reign of Terror, of "how quickly . . . the sharp prongs of that implement [might] level the proud distinction between this *moving* and that *insensate* clay" (1: 26). That the haymaker does not, despite suffering under the "hard conditions of [a] society . . . prone to unequal distribution," take the opportunity to "abuse the peaceful steel" (1: 26), brings Sylvanus to recognize that his own suspicious, aggressively defensive attitudes are forms of prejudice which have "[ ]steeled" his bosom against the "gentle puncture of compassion" (1: 24). (The compound of fear, upper-class prejudice, aggression, and defensiveness is masterfully conveyed, generically, by the modulation of the steel metaphor into a romance key, as Thelwall sketches a ludicrous image of himself and the haymaker as a pair of armed knights meeting in battle). This realization brings about a literal turn, which is also a literary turn: "I turned instantly around, and my hand, sympathizing with the feelings of my heart, waited not for the cold approbation of Reason, but went immediately and instinctively to my pocket" (1: 26). Here we are back in the realm of the sentimental, with a stock gesture that evokes a whole tradition of poems and narratives in which Shaftesburian benevolence and sympathy are offered as gentle correctives to Hobbesian cynicism and self-interest. Obviously Thelwall intends his generic shift to function in a similar way, as a critique of and corrective to the narrow self-interest inscribed in both the anti-beggary pamphlet and the personal testimonial. Yet the critique goes more than one way. For, given the context in which it is placed, we cannot help but read this sentimental gesture (the "instinctive" motion of hand to pocket) ironically, as an act more likely motivated by fear and a desire for self-preservation, than by sympathy or a desire to assert equality with the sufferer. Thus what appears to a casual reader to be mere cliche, becomes, when seen in context, a critique of sentimental convention which reflects Thelwall's own uneasy awareness of the middle-class anxiety that underlies the popularity of this apparently humanistic, even democratic, literary genre. At the same time, one might argue, Sylvanus' conscious and self-critical recognition of the mixed motives and emotions with which he approaches the beggar also serves to reanimate the gesture, to lift it from the realm of cliche and to refocus attention on it as a symbol of thoughtful engagement between sentimentalist and sufferer, which breathes new life into an ideologically suspect literary form. Here as elsewhere, Thelwall's point is not simply to expose the inadequacies of a literary convention or tradition, but literally to re-form it. Recognizing that neither sentimental pathos, empirical pragmatism, nor pamphleteer's invective is an adequate response to the complex social and psychological reality of poverty and suffering, Thelwall sets them against one another, using each to interrogate the other in what becomes his signature technique in *The Peripatetic*.

Nor are these the only voices at play in Thelwall's intergeneric conversation. For the scene of charity I have been discussing here in the context of sentimental narrative is framed and punctuated by a series of poems in which the language and symbolism of sentimental and Romantic poetry are likewise interrogated and brought to bear on one another, and on the narrative that surrounds them. In one of these, Thelwall attacks the sentimental economy that creates suffering in order to satisfy the market for sympathy. Observing two bird-catchers, who supply that fashionable commodity and Romantic symbol of Nature's Harmony, Joy and Beauty, the skylark, to the Daughters of Albion, he laments, in exaggeratedly sentimental terms, the fate of the poor birds, cut off from their families and their freedom:

> Daughters of Albion's gay enlighten'd hour!
> Hail the sweet strains your captive warblers pour;
> . . .
>
> Nor ever think – that, for a sordid joy,
> Their hopes, their rights, affections ye destroy;
> Doom them the air's unbounded space to change,
> For the dull cage's loath'd, contracted range;
> There, every social throb condemn'd to mourn
> Which each sad summer bids in vain return.   (1: 35)

But his harshest satire is aimed, not at the violation of animal rights, but at parallel but much greater violations of human rights, specifically the evils of slavery and colonialism, which, he implies, are part of the same false sentimental economy, in which the few take pleasure in and profit from the imprisonment of the many. Mixing the richly artificial diction and imagery, and the satiric couplets of Pope's *The Rape of the Lock* (especially the coffee-drinking scene, with its veiled references to European imperialism), with the sensationalistic conventions of anti-slavery poems and narratives, Thelwall satirizes vain, superficial society belles who cultivate sentiment and benevolence while drinking tea sweetened with the blood and tears of the slaves who harvest the sugar:

> Each sweeten'd drop, yon porcelain cell contains,
> Was drawn, O horror! from some brother's veins;
> Or, wrought by chemic art, on terms too dear,
> Is but transmuted from some negro's tear,
> Which dropt, 'midst galling bonds, on foreign strand,
> His bride still answers from his native land! –
> Still turn indiff'rent from these *foreign* woes,
> Nor suffer griefs so distant to oppose
> The sickly taste, whose languid pulse to cheer
> *Two rifled worlds* must drop the bitter tear! –   (1: 35–36)

In his condemnation of their "polish'd arts refined," he has in mind not simply the social art of tea-drinking, but the literary art of sentimental poetry that testifies to the apparent sensibility that masks their actual monstrosity.

But of course Sylvanus is himself implicated in this same monstrosity by virtue of his own participation in the "polished art" of poetical effusion. It is no surprise, therefore, that he often turns his satire upon himself, constantly questioning and revising his literary motives and methods. For example, at the beginning of the cluster of episodes I have been discussing, Sylvanus himself has been addressing the lark, "Sweet attic warbler! poet of the skies!" (I: 16). But in the midst of a rather conventional celebration of Nature's bliss and rapture, he breaks off and questions his own Romantic discourse as, turning from the rhapsodic and religious to the didactic and socioscientific, he addresses another poem to the overtly non-poetic stork and pelican as better symbols of "the practical religion of the heart! and the glorious maxims of relative and social duty" (I: 17–18). Then, as his moral and poetical effusions are interrupted by the beggars just mentioned, he turns yet again, and, as if chastising himself for the abstraction and indulgence of poetry altogether, switches to prose.

Elsewhere too, poetry or elevated poetic diction is aligned with refinement, excess, inflation, and corruption, while prose is associated with simplicity, common sense, reason: the "plain solid Socratic" he lauds in *The Rights of Nature*. Yet this critique of poetry is by no means categorical, for just as often the emphasis is reversed, and poems are frequently used for the finale or climax of a narrative episode in order to emphasize, summarize or elevate the subject. In "A Digression for the Anatomists," for example, he poeticizes medical discourse in order to lay bare, even to the "elegant votary of the polite arts," "the laws of human oeconomy" (I: 161–62). Prose interrogates poetry, poetry supplements prose: the alternation between them ultimately is another aspect of the intergeneric conversation, the Socratic interchange of opinion and perspective that Thelwall aims at throughout *The Peripatetic*. Indeed a careful look at the interchange of poetry and prose, or song and philosophy in the lark/beggars cluster reveals that it reflects, expands, and participates in the alternative economy which Thelwall sets against the exploitative sentimental economy he scourges in the second lark poem. For the first lark poem, beneath its conventional Romantic rhapsodizing, contains an image of a cooperative economy based on the free exchange and diffusion of "lib'ral blessings," as the lark, who "pays the bounteous season, with its song, / For the kind boon her cheering smile bestows," becomes a model for the "sons of earth! who boast superior souls" to "give to other hearts the bliss ye feel" (1: 16). This is a paradigm for the role of the poet, or poetry, in the credit union of ideas.

It is in this highly developed analogy between Thelwall's analyses of genre and politics, that the value of *The Peripatetic* lies; yet it is this analogy that is so often missed by critics who pay insufficient attention to his dialogics of genre. Even a critic with a sophisticated understanding of the ideology of language, like Olivia Smith, misunderstands Thelwall's aims and achievement when she categorizes him among a group of bravely experimental but ultimately "awkward" and unsuccessful writers who are unable to "align their political beliefs with their writings."[23] She bases her evaluation upon a piece by Thelwall published in D. Isaac Eaton's periodical *Hogwash; or Politics for the People* under the title "A Debtor's Tale." This consists of a sentimental narrative in which a legal clerk goes to a debtor's house to collect money but is too tender-hearted to complete his task, followed by a piece of political oratory and satire aimed at an unjust legal system which feeds off the debtor's sufferings. According to Smith the inconsistencies between these two parts, both generic (one speaks to the "emotive heart," the other to the "political mind") and stylistic (the language of one, though adorned, is simple; the language of the other is "convoluted, multi-syllabic, and unclear"), are confusing and confirm Thelwall's failure to harmonize politics and literature.[24]

What Smith doesn't mention (though she does quote from *The Peripatetic* in her introduction to Thelwall) is that the debtor's tale is taken from *The Peripatetic*, where it forms part of a larger cluster of three episodes or divisions (with different titles). This cluster begins with an anecdote in which Sylvanus recalls "one of the earliest inspirations of [his] Muse" (1: 110) while on a walk during a "vernal shower." But before he relates the product of that inspiration he discusses the destination of the walk – the house of the debtor – and thus enters into the sentimental narrative and anti-legal harangue outlined above. He then returns to the poem referred to several pages earlier – which happens to be a sonnet to a lark in the manner of the *Elegiac Sonnets* of Charlotte Smith – and a discussion of sonnet form in general, in dialogue with his friend Ambulator, ensues. This cluster comprises at least six identifiable genres – loco-descriptive prose, autobiographical anecdote, sentimental narrative, literary criticism in dialogue form, political oratory, and sonnet – and the reader unaccustomed to reading these dialogically might easily find the switch from one to another confusing. Yet upon such reading it is evident that the parts are carefully related. For instance, the critical dialogue centers on Charlotte Smith's "glorious crime" of "burst[ing] the unnatural fetters of arbitrary authority, and exert[ing] the free-born energies of the soul" (1: 123) by rejecting the "affected" versification of the formal sonnet, which constrains those energies even as the "arbitrary authority" of the law has constrained the "free-born energies" of the poor in the preceding harangue. Furthermore, Charlotte Smith's well-known status as victim of the legal system, her harassed, dependent, vulnerable position as the wife of a debtor, reflects back on and enriches the images of the hospitable wife and "little blooming maiden" in the sentimental debtor's tale; while the way she simultaneously exploits and overcomes these oppressions by making them the stuff of her very popular poetry, freeing herself from subject status by writing herself as subject, underwrites Thelwall's own motives for using anecdotal and other autobiographical material. Finally, because Sylvanus' own sonnet is addressed to the lark (and he uses a similar bird image for himself and Smith as poets), this entire cluster is linked to the earlier cluster and to the critique of the interimplications between literature and the broader socio-economic system developed there. The debtor, the sentimental narrative which describes his situation, the sonnets produced by another debtor's wife, the lark addressed in those sonnets – all are imprisoned forms of human creative energy, expression and existence which have been implicated in and exploited by a repressive system of hierarchical distinctions, inherited laws, and arbitrary authority, from which they need to be liberated, repossessed by and redistributed to, the common reader.

It is precisely this rich and self-conscious analogy that Thelwall develops between his choice of genre and the political situation he describes with it, that Smith, with her focus on language, and on the debtor's tale in a limited generic context (the periodical) misses. Granted, as Smith argues, Thelwall does not often achieve an "intellectual vernacular," a thoughtful language of common people free from literary adornment or political rhetoric; nor does he often allow the poor to speak for themselves, free from sentimental

convention, as fully-individuated "politically knowledgable characters speaking an adequate language."[25] Yet in a sense his rich
dynamic complexity of genres serves the purpose that such language
and such characterization might in a more conventional novel,
constituting a highly effective mix of voices, an intellectually challenging and aesthetically pleasing experience of conversation and
debate.

<h2 style="text-align:center">REMAPPING THE TERRITORY</h2>

One of the means by which Thelwall contains and manages the
multivocal and generic eccentricities of his text is through its over-
arching topographical framework. As its title suggests, *The Peripatetic*
takes the form of a series of pedestrian excursions, and this allows
him to introduce digressions, interruptions, and juxtapositions ca-
sually and naturally. The scene of these excursions, the vicinity of
London, is far from random, however: the beaten track from which
Thelwall strays, but from which he nevertheless takes his bearings in
The Peripatetic, is the main axis of England's economic, historical, and
literary landscape. He follows the Thames, the main artery of
Britain's commercial empire, and the old Roman road from London
to Dover, which is also the route of Chaucer's Canterbury pilgrims,
leading back through the heartland of British society and literature.
He takes full advantage of this literal and metaphorical grid to
comment on national affairs, from the vanity and tyranny of imperial
ambition whether Roman, Norman, or British, to the instability of
commercial grandeur based on "public misery and oppression" (1:
177), to the hollowness of the poetic rhetoric that glorifies such
ambition and grandeur in conventional topographical poetry or
prose. But it is his deviance from the beaten track of topographical
discourse that defines his achievement in *The Peripatetic*. For while the
text imitates both topographical or loco-descriptive poetry and prose
tourist guides in its concern with scenic, historical, architectural, and
antiquarian details and descriptions, it subverts and reorients both
these genres by directing attention away from rich, landed interests,
towards the lowly structures of the common people.

Nowhere is Thelwall's reorientation of topographical poetry
clearer than in Sylvanus' visit to a suburb of London, Bermondsey.
Its churchyard, having "the least picturesque beauty to boast of any
one in the environs of London" (1: 125), offers nothing but "prospects

of disgust" (1: 126). The graveyard is bare, disorderly, resistant to poetic figuration: "not a yew tree spreads over them its funereal shade, nor a blade of grass, scarcely, mantles the dreary soil" (1: 125–26). Likewise Bermondsey itself, home to the "labourers and mechanics who administer to the luxuries of the gay metropolis" and who live in "miserable shelters" patched together within, beside or out of the "ruinous remains" of ancient stately buildings (1: 126), is a population and a place literally marginal, and apparently unassimilable to literature.

Yet Thelwall attempts to assimilate them in the following episodes, which are focused on the possibility of writing a "Bermondsey pastoral" despite the scorn of critics and their "slavish maxims" which "have forbidden a tongue to the necessities and attachments of the poor" (1: 134). Thelwall's interest in the marginal nature of Bermondsey – like England itself, caught halfway between rustic peace and urban sprawl, the ruins of the feudal past and the commercial energies of the present – is reflected in the form of the episode, in which pretty pastoral poems celebrating honest swains, homely sheds, and untainted zephyrs are interspersed with hard-edged satirical and sociological prose passages attacking the system of "improvement" and enclosure which forces peasants away from their cottages into dirty, crowded, and unhealthy urban slums.

Insofar as it attempts to give "tongue to the attachments . . . of the poor," this episode displays the same flaws that marked the debtor's tale: the laborers and mechanics do not appear as individuals, much less speak for themselves; and the style modulates between the poetic and the oratorical. Certainly Thelwall's Bermondsey pastoral does not compare with the detailed poetic realism of Crabbe's *Borough*, the documentary vehemence of Cobbett's *Rural Rides* or the powerful verbal and narrative simplicity of Wordsworth's *Lyrical Ballads*. Clearly Thelwall is interested less in the voices of the poor as individuals, more in the position that they hold, as a class, within the economic and literary order, a position that is symbolized in his text by the cottage and the space that it occupies, geographically, economically, and aesthetically. The real object of Thelwall's satirical pastoral is to assert the value and legitimacy of lower-class interests by attacking the system which denies them; and in particular, the canons of taste which banish, sanitize or demonize "wretched" or "common" objects and subjects in the name of aesthetic purity and moral ascendancy. Specifically, he decries the

levelling of cottages by gentlemen who rearrange their estates
according to the principles of sentimental and neoclassical aesthetics:
because their "tender feelings cannot endure the sight of . . .
wretchedness; and [they] find extermination less expensive than
relief" (1: 134–35); or because "nothing has any charms for [them]
but what reflects upon their habitations something like corresponding grandeur" (1: 137–38). To this exclusionary aesthetic, Thelwall opposes an ideal of aesthetic and political inclusiveness and
heterogeneity which parallels his own mixing of genres: a landscape
in which "humble thatch" and "stately pile," "rustic wicket" and
"Attic temple" (1: 129) stand side by side, enriching, beautifying, and
completing one another; a political system in which "every one who
has a interest" has "a voice also in the representation" (1: 146).

Thelwall's remapping of the literary and political landscape of
England is evident too in his subversion of the rhetoric and structure
of the prose tourist guide, a burgeoning genre catering to the
increased mobility of the growing middle-class in the eighteenth
century. These guides, like the topographical poems, characteristically present landscape – frequently the wide and varied prospect
seen from a hill, often a fine estate, country house, palace, or
historical landmark – as an emblem of the historical, cultural and
economic institutions, rituals, and values of society. Thelwall usually
begins, in the same fashion, by describing country seats, palaces,
castles, monasteries, and other fine buildings he passes on his
excursion, noting their noble histories, notable inhabitants, spacious
grounds, and magnificent architecture, and sometimes even borrow-
ing verbatim from his sources.[26] He does not show his true colors
until the end, when he reveals, not with conventional elegiac
nostalgia or Gothic melancholy, but with positively gleeful democratic irony, that they have now been reduced to ruins, or, better still,
converted into more worthwhile structures – schools, almshouses,
hospitals, farmhouses, or even barns. Such is the fate of the great
hall of King John's palace at Eltham, whose regal history and recent
lowly fate are described in an episode entitled "Shooter's Hill. –
Topographical Digressions." Thelwall begins by describing Eltham
itself, now a prosperous suburb of London

> Where the tame drudge of six successive days,
> His Sunday's coat and rural taste displays, –
> Demure to church, with wig of snow parades,
> The gaze of clowns and antiquated maids.   (1: 183)

But just as the "plodding cit's . . . snug retreat" is built "O'er Gothic splendour's fallen seat" (1: 182), so Thelwall reveals that the complacent power of the commercial class who live in Eltham is based on a long-standing tradition of tyranny and injustice, which he describes and denounces in the rest of the poem:

> Yes, here (where grinning Humour hies to seek
> Her *country gentleman of once a week,*)
> Once the proud tyrants of the groaning land
> Grasp'd the stern sceptre with ensanguin'd hand;
> . . .
>
> Ye rocky fragments of each ruin'd pile
> That guarded once the robber and his spoil!
> Ye, ye could tell (might heaven a voice afford)
> Full many a crime of many a savage lord,
> When thirst of blood, and violence were the same,
> And abject myriads trembled at a name,
> Or groan'd despis'd in slavery's falling chain
> A master's boundless riot to maintain.   (1: 183)

Thelwall's use of genre registers and reinforces his message: the complacency of the middle-class "cits" is reflected in the snug Popean end-stopped couplets, which gradually break down into run-on lines as the verse gathers Gothic steam to reveal the foundation of riot, slavery, and corruption upon which the modern commercial empire of Britain is built. Yet ultimately neither satiric wit nor Gothic gusto are adequate to Thelwall's republican purposes, for both are forms of linguistic inflation such as he has earlier attacked for glossing over and detaching the reader from plain, harsh socio-economic realities. Hence Thelwall breaks off and returns to prose in order to describe, more briefly and factually, the history of the palace, focusing on the waste, misery, and conflict that marked the reigns of each of its possessors, ending at last with the revelation that the great hall of the palace, where Edward IV once entertained 2,000 persons, "now, converted into a farmer's barn, affords an occasional banquet to rats and owls, and is the storehouse of the best wealth of the nation" (1: 186–87).

Thelwall's amusing account of architectural deconstruction and reconstruction is subversive not only of topographical prose and poetry but of all genres. Like the palace at Eltham (and all the other antiquated buildings which Thelwall describes throughout the text) literature, whether Gothic romance, mock-heroic satire, pastoral elegy or sentimental novel, has been a structure devoted to displaying, maintaining, and perpetuating the pleasure, power, and profligacy of the ruling classes. By mocking, interrogating, and subverting these and other genres, Thelwall strives for the literary equivalent of the palatial barn at Eltham: a structure devoted to the preservation of the "best wealth of the nation" (1: 187), the resources and labors of the class to which Thelwall himself belongs, enlightened artisans, laborers, shopkeepers, farmers, and journalists to whose intellectual and political interests and independence groups like the London Corresponding Society devoted their efforts. And in a sense *The Peripatetic* itself is like the palatial barn – a literary storehouse in which the remains of the traditional elite literatures of the past are bound together with miscellaneous bits and pieces of the low, marginal or non-literary discourses of the late eighteenth century to create a unique, dynamic, and truly revisionary text which attempts to democratize literary institutions so that all those who have an interest will have a voice too in the representation.

WHITHER *THE PERIPATETIC*?

Fascinating as it is to read, however, the fact remains that *The Peripatetic* has rested in almost total obscurity for 200 years, evidence enough that despite the eventual adoption by British society of many of Thelwall's political ideas, his parallel attempt to reform and open up literary institutions did not succeed, at least not by him or in the way he intended. A brief look at the obstacles it faced in circulation may help illuminate why.

In its own time, of course, the text's reception was obstructed by the growing backlash against political radicals, including several royal proclamations against seditious writings, and the seizure of all of Thelwall's writings upon his arrest. Thelwall's publisher refused to print the manuscript, forcing him to produce and sell it privately; it circulated among radicals but in the reactionary period that followed, its audience fell off, its opinions appeared at first dangerous and then dated, and its overt literary critique, like its political message, was discredited, disregarded, and finally displaced by the rise of Romanticism, exemplified by Coleridge and Wordsworth's dedication to the inviolability and autonomy of the domestic circle and the individual mind over the activist poetics of their early careers. In this respect, the text's fate parallels that of its author.

Fleeing political persecution in London, Thelwall visited Coleridge and Wordsworth in Dorset in 1797, and wanted to join them there, but he was rejected as too dangerous; he ended up in Wales, trying to farm for a living, in a state of intellectual insulation and alienation far more debilitating creatively than the relatively cozy retirement of the charmed circle at Alfoxden. One cannot help but wonder what might have happened had Thelwall been allowed to take up residence near the other poets, to maintain and strengthen his friendship with them, to add his experienced and critical voice to the lyrical dialogue of that year, and to make his own iconoclastic, socially committed contribution to the annus mirabilis that changed the shape of English literature. Idle speculation perhaps. Nevertheless it is possible to see in Coleridge and Wordsworth's rejection of Thelwall in 1797 not only, as Nicholas Roe has suggested, the germ of *their* later apostasy,[27] but a paradigm for the exclusion from the literary canon of writers like Thelwall, and texts like *The Peripatetic*, which do so much both to illuminate and to challenge the discursive and interpretive practices the Romantics bequeathed to the twentieth century.

What then does this neglected text of the 1790s offer to the scholar of genre and Romanticism in the 1990s? It offers, in the broadest sense, a vision of genres as inevitably ideological forms, incapable of being separated from the socio-political systems in which they are implicated in various complex ways, but capable, in the hands of a skilful and self-reflexive practitioner, of interrogating and critiquing both those systems and themselves. It reminds us that generic distinctions themselves are arbitrary and historical, and that the relationships between the poles of literary and non-literary, polite and vernacular, are more complex than the simple appropriation of the vernacular by polite society, or the categorical subversion of belles lettres by the masses. But most importantly, by positing an ideal of the text as an open space for Socratic interchange, it teaches us a new way of reading – deeply historical, pluralistic, aware of ideological resonances, but most of all willing ourselves to enter into conversation with the text, on all its levels.

Such a method of reading is, as Siskin suggests, a particularly salutary development for Romantic studies, and it is obviously to Romantic studies that *The Peripatetic* is most immediately relevant. To the Romantic scholar and teacher it offers, first of all, an indispensable and entertaining introductory handbook on the politicization of genre in the Romantic period, a text which will throw light upon the use of genre by any writers of the period, major or minor. More particularly, when *The Peripatetic* is read intertextually with canonical Romantic texts, it cannot fail to open them up in new ways. Let us take only one particularly apt example: that of Wordsworth, friend of Thelwall and reader of *The Peripatetic*. Certainly after reading Thelwall's multi-voiced, self-reflexive, ambiguous, market-conscious effusions and meditations on beggars, skylarks, cottages, etc., one must approach all those Wordsworthian figurative trademarks with a greater degree of irony; one is encouraged to return such figures as the Discharged Soldier and the Leech Gatherer to the sociopolitical context from which Wordsworth has so scrupulously removed them (in effect to notice, along with Dorothy Wordsworth, the price of leeches); and one is skeptical about any "universalizing imaginative idealizations"[28] which are constructed, by poets or critics, out of such encounters. At the same time the similarity between the digressive, miscellaneous, generically indeterminate structure of *The Peripatetic* and that of most of Wordsworth's major works suggests that those works may retain more traces of the strategies of radical discourse (and of Thelwall's own intergeneric influence) that Wordsworth absorbed in his Jacobin days than has heretofore been acknowledged. Certainly reading *The Prelude* in the light of *The Peripatetic* allows us to shift the focus away from the authoritative and hegemonic master-genres – lyric and epic – in whose terms the text has almost always been discussed, and instead to see its generic miscegenation and eccentricity, its plurality of self-questioning voices, as fundamental, representative, and ideologically meaningful. Such a democratization of reading, such an enfranchisement of literature, such a return to a Thelwallian understanding of literary history, would profoundly gratify the author of *The Peripatetic*, which ends comically with the resuscitation by the Humane Society of a body thought dead.

NOTES

1 See Fredric Jameson, *The Political Unconscious* (Ithaca: Cornell University Press, 1981), and Ralph Cohen, "History and Genre," *New Literary History* 17 (1986): 203–32. Jameson uses the term "differential" as a relational concept, in an Althusserian sense, to signify the structural difference yet interrelatedness of all elements in a text (or any social formation) (41). According to dialogical theory, as Jameson uses it, these

different elements reflect (or more properly echo) the utterances of social groups or classes (necessarily antagonistic in Jameson's Marxist analysis) whose ideological confrontation the text symbolically enacts (84–85). Like many critics I use the term dialogic in a more general, less Marxist sense, to suggest that individual generic elements represent both individual positions and group voices in a broader social dialogue which is not exclusively antagonistic or class-based. In that sense my position is closer to that of Cohen, who uses neither term, but who emphasizes the differences between individual members of a genre and the varying public aims and practices which genre serves through time (208–09). Resisting the essentialism of Jameson's assertion that ideology is immanent in genre (Jameson, 141), Cohen maintains that only individual texts, as generic members, can possess ideologies (209). Nevertheless both critics agree in proposing a regenerated, historicized, self-reflexive genre theory which would regard texts as sedimentary structures of heterogeneous elements and examine the interimplications between generic, ideological, and cultural change.

2 Alan Liu, *Wordsworth: The Sense of History* (Stanford: Stanford University Press, 1989). Liu's chapter on the contest of genres in Books 9–10 of *The Prelude* is exemplary of his exhaustive and exhausting practice of untangling generic threads in Wordsworthian texts and tracing their origins in contemporary cultural and aesthetic phenomena. Yet insofar as Liu reads Wordsworth's generic interrelationships in terms of a broader lyric master-narrative, in which Wordsworth ultimately denies or flees generic and historical otherness and multiplicity, "refashioning . . . unstable generic differentiation into the very signifier, the unconscious language, of selfhood" (361), he participates in the "lyric turn" which, as Clifford Siskin has argued, has dominated Romantic criticism in recent decades (see note 3).

3 Clifford Siskin, *The Historicity of Romantic Discourse* (New York: Oxford University Press, 1988), 8.

4 Ibid., 10.

5 The most influential figure in the resuscitation of Thelwall's political reputation in the twentieth century has been E. P. Thompson, in whose *The Making of The English Working Class* (London: Victor Gollancz, 1963; rpt. London: Penguin, 1980) Thelwall plays a prominent role. See also Carl B. Cone, *The English Jacobins* (New York: Charles Scribner's Sons, 1968).

6 Thelwall's literary works include six books of poetry (including miscellaneous dramas, verse romances, and essays) and a novel in three volumes. He was editor of *The Biographical and Imperial Magazine* from 1787–90 and owner and editor of *The Champion* newspaper from 1818–22, as well as contributing to many other periodicals. Garland reprinted a series of his major literary works in the 1970s, and the critical introductions to these provide virtually the only general criticism of his

work, apart from an unpublished thesis, an early twentieth-century biography, and brief mention of his work in studies of major Romantic writers by David Erdman, Nicholas Roe, Kenneth Johnston, Gary Kelly, and David Simpson.

7 Donald Reiman, for example, in his "Introduction" to Thelwall's *The Peripatetic* (1793; rpt. New York: Garland, 1978), 1: x, repeats Hazlitt's assertion that, in comparison to his oratory, Thelwall's writing is "flat" and "drab," and states that his poetry has little "intrinsic merit" (ix). See also Olivia Smith's comments, *The Politics of Language 1791–1810* (Oxford: Clarendon Press, 1986), 14–15 and note 23 below.

8 Reiman, "Introduction," 1: x.

9 Gary Kelly, in "The Limits of Genre and the Institution of Literature," in *Romantic Revolutions: Criticism and Theory*, ed. Kenneth R. Johnston et. al. (Bloomington: Indiana University Press, 1990), 166–70, uses the term "quasi-novel" to describe an unusual Romantic genre which mingled fact, fiction, and literariness, "questioning, challenging, or transgressing generic and discursive boundaries for political, philosophical, intellectual, satirical, or other reasons" (166), and discusses *The Peripatetic* as an example of this genre (167).

10 John Thelwall, *The Peripatetic*, 3 vols. (1793; rpt. New York: Garland, 1978). Future references to this text will be given parenthetically within the text, by volume and page number only.

11 Thompson, *Making of the English Working Class*, 134. Chief biographies of Thelwall are John Thelwall, "Prefatory Memoir," in *Poems Chiefly Written in Retirement* (1801; rpt. Oxford: Woodstock, 1989); Mrs. C. Thelwall, *The Life of John Thelwall* (London, 1837), 1: 1–39; Charles Cestre, *John Thelwall* (London: Swan Sonnenschein, 1906).

12 "Let the proprietor reflect upon the nature of his possession – let him reflect upon the genuine basis of property. What is it, after all, but human labour? And who is the proprietor of that labour? – Who, but the individual who labours?" John Thelwall, *The Rights of Nature, against the Usurpations of Establishments* in 4 letters (London, 1796); rpt. in Gregory Claeys, ed., *The Politics of English Jacobinism: Writings of John Thelwall* (University Park: Pennsylvania State University Press, 1995), 475. Further references to this text will be given parenthetically by page number.

13 On the democratization of knowledge and reading in the period, see David Vincent, *Bread, Knowledge and Freedom* (London: Methuen, 1981) and Jon Klancher, *The Making of English Reading Audiences 1790–1832* (Madison: University of Wisconsin Press, 1987), which deal with autobiography and periodical literature respectively.

14 Gary Kelly, *English Fiction of the Romantic Period 1789–1830* (London: Longman, 1989), 9. See also Kelly, "The Limits of Genre" and Klancher, *Making of English Reading Audiences*.

15 While the subversive, carnivalesque style of *The Peripatetic* has much in

common with the radical journals, its mixing of sentimental narrative and enlightenment philosophy links it more closely with English Jacobin novels like those of Holcroft (who was a literary mentor to Thelwall) and Godwin (whom he regarded as his philosophic father): See Cestre, *John Thelwall*, 131–39; and Kelly, *English Fiction*, 26–42. Godwin and Thelwall would later break over the latter's activism and populism, but *The Peripatetic*, with its literary and historical allusions, genial tone and elaborate ironies, seems more obviously addressed to educated, genteel readers than to the artisan classes whom Thelwall roused with fiery oratory in 1795–96. This may reflect Thelwall's intense anxiety about his lack of education and his literary reputation; his desire to overcome the former and not to alienate the audience which governed the latter. At the same time, however, the text contains enough explosive rhetoric, republican opinions, and attacks on aristocratic and bourgeois culture to serve as a clear index of his growing radicalism and populism in 1793.

16 Spence's *Pig's Meat*, published periodically between 1793 and 1796, was subtitled "A Salmagundy for Swine," picking up on the pig metaphor introduced by Burke, and adopted, satirically and defensively, by radical journalists of the 1790s. See Thompson, *Making of the English Working Class*, 176–78.

17 Klancher, *Making of English Reading Audiences*, 43.

18 Ibid.

19 Ibid., 35.

20 Ibid., 100.

21 Kelly, *English Fiction*, 11.

22 In her biography, Mrs. Thelwall tells the story of Thelwall's being assaulted and robbed in the same manner (*Life of John Thelwall*, 15).

23 Smith, *Politics of Language*, 87.

24 Ibid.

25 Ibid.

26 For example, his description at 1: 178–81 of the mansion of Sir Gregory Page in Blackheath, which was rapidly built, and just as rapidly fell into ruin, is lifted directly from the 1787 edition of a popular guidebook, *The Ambulator*. But unlike his source, which dwells on the magnificence of the mansion, Thelwall uses the house as an example of a kind of architectural inflation (paralleling his earlier attacks on economic and verbal inflation), as he traces how the value of the house decayed to the price of its materials.

27 Nicholas Roe, "Coleridge and John Thelwall: The Road to Nether Stowey," in *The Coleridge Connection: Essays in Honour of Thomas McFarland*, ed. Richard Gravil and Molly Lefebure (New York: St. Martin's, 1990), esp. 77–79, and *Wordsworth and Coleridge: the Radical Years* (Cambridge: Cambridge University Press, 1992), esp. 236–62. See also David Simpson, "Public Virtues, Private Vices: Reading Between the Lines of

Wordsworth's 'Anecdote for Fathers,'" in *Subject to History: Ideology, Class, Gender*, ed. David Simpson (Ithaca: Cornell University Press, 1991) for a Marxist-materialist analysis of the importance of the rejection of Thelwall in 1797 to Wordsworth.

28 Don Bialostosky, *Wordsworth, Dialogics and the Practice of Criticism* (Cambridge: Cambridge University Press, 1992), 150.

CHAPTER 7

"I am ill fitted": conflicts of genre in Eliza Fenwick's 'Secresy'

Julia M. Wright

In her only known novel, *Secresy; Or, The Ruin on the Rock* (1795), Eliza Fenwick uses the epistolary form to present an unresolved cacophony of social values, mores, and expectations that reflects the turmoil of the period. Fenwick's experience of the increasingly complex and conflicted world of the 1790s was extraordinary, even for the age. A non-aristocratic woman from Cornwall married to an Irish nationalist and member of the London Corresponding Society, John Fenwick, she was part of the Johnson Circle and a close friend, in particular, of Mary Wollstonecraft and Mary Hays as well as the Lambs. She had an unusual variety of jobs, including teacher, governess, translator, and author, and lived in Ireland, the West Indies, the United States, as well as various regions of England.[1] In London during the 1790s, she would have been close to the Revolution debate and the impeachment of Warren Hastings, proceedings which questioned the behavior of English "nabobs" in India and ended in the year of *Secresy*'s publication. Fenwick was thus exposed to the clash of cultures between regions of England, between England and its colonies, and between genders and classes, as well as the burgeoning public and intellectual debate about the issues raised by those differences. In *Secresy*, the rising conflict is dramatized through a series of letters in which the misogynist clashes with the feminist, the libertines with the romantics, and the nabobs with the radicals, as advocates of conflicting visions of society try to manipulate the course of events and of other characters. Throughout the letters of the novel, there is an insistent extradiegetic concern with genre as an articulation of and rubric for social relations – and that concern is, in part, insistent because of the clash of genres that corresponds to the clash of plots and cultural assumptions that leads to the novel's bleak conclusion.

DRAWING THE BATTLELINES IN THE GENERIC SAND

In the Introduction to *Nation and Narration*, Homi K. Bhabha examines the ways in which nations are produced through their narrativization, particularly in relation to the "problem of closure."[2] Bhabha is interested in the process by which nations are defined through the progress of a novelistic plot and disrupted through the subversions of formal closure. A linear narrative that has certain truth claims, as history or the realist novel, inserts the nation into an evolutionary progress in which improvement co-exists with the promise of destiny and inherent value is tied to potential. But this is just one genre, and one ideology. In his essay, "Social Space and the Genesis of 'Classes,'" Pierre Bourdieu extends the Marxist theory of classes that are united by real conditions to include textually posited classes:

On the basis of knowledge of the space of positions, one can carve out *classes* in the logical sense of the word, i.e. sets of agents who occupy similar positions and who, being placed in similar conditions and submitted to similar types of conditioning, have every chance of having similar dispositions of interests, and thus of producing similar practices and adopting similar stances.[3]

Such a "class on paper" produces "categories of perception of the social world [that] are essentially the product of the incorporation of the objective structures of the social space. Consequently, they incline agents to accept the social world as it is, to take it for granted, rather than to rebel against it."[4] Bourdieu thus offers a more general articulation of the mechanism which concerns Bhabha and one that applies to what I would term cultures rather than classes to emphasize their discursive rather than their material determination. While Bhabha's national narratives carve out the nation through a "process of hybridity, incorporating new 'people' in relation to the body politic,"[5] Bourdieu's sociological taxonomies carve out cultures through a process of differentiation that incorporates objective differences in relation to the social world through discursive modelling. Most pertinently, Bourdieu pays attention to the individual's acceptance of the paradigm because of its power to locate the individual: "The sense of one's place, as the sense of what one can or cannot 'allow oneself', implies a tacit acceptance of one's position, a sense of limits ('that's not meant for us') or – what amounts to the same thing – a sense of distances, to be marked and maintained, respected, and expected of others."[6] This drive to sustain the paper culture is at once political, because of its ability to affect the distribution of power in the social domain, and generic in the sense that Bhabha addresses because of the desire for the recognizable formal closure which ratifies that distribution. By the term, "formal closure," I mean to extend the narrative closure of Bhabha's discussion to include other elements of genre in the sense of completing the pattern rather than ending the line. The text's recognizability as a member of a literary class reinforces and validates its ideological containment of the culture which it describes, and which subscribes to it.

Fenwick's contemporary, Elizabeth Hands, outlines the threat of this dynamic in a pair of poems that reflect on the reaction to Hands' first volume, *The Death of Amnon* (1789). In "A Poem, On the Supposition of an Advertisement appearing in a Morning Paper, of the Publication of a Volume of Poems, by a Servant-Maid" (1789), Hands parodies the response of the served-maids. One lady remarks,

> If servants can tell
> How to write to their mothers, to say they are well,
> And read of a Sunday *The Duty of Man*,
> Which is more I believe than one half of them can;
> I think 'tis much *properer* they should rest there,
> Than be reaching at things so much out of their sphere.[7]

In the sequel, "A Poem, On the Supposition of the Book having been Published and Read" (1789), a Rector entones,

> 'This book,' says he (snift, snift), 'has, in the beginning' . . .
> 'Some pieces, I think, that are pretty correct:
> A style elevated you cannot expect
> To some of her equals they may be a treasure,
> And country lasses may read 'em with pleasure.
> That "Amnon", you can't call it poetry neither,
> You may style it prosaic, blank verse at the best.'[8]

The threat here is to a cultural segregation that enforces the segregation of social power: Hands has read their literature, written within their literary genres, and entered their world of print by publishing a volume that is advertised in their morning paper. Their anxiety did not only arise because she had gone too "much out of [her] sphere," but also because she had entered theirs, and her verse makes it clear that she knows it. Hands' subversion of existing codes must be understood in this reactionary context: the terms of battle for both

sides are the same, controlling literary genres to control social *gens*.
The form, the principles, and the audience of the text are inter-
dependent and mutually constitutive as, for instance, part of being an
aristocrat is belonging to aristocratic culture and part of that culture
is founded upon the assumption that the elite has a monopoly on the
more overtly stylized forms of literature. Hands' writings break that
monopoly and thus the cultural identity that it enforces.

In *Secresy*, Fenwick proliferates these textual classes. In a gothic
variation on the education plot, George Valmont tries to raise a
woman who embodies his misogynist assumptions and a man who
will share his misanthropy, so he educates his wards – his niece,
Sibella Valmont, and his unacknowledged son, Clement Montgomery – according to his strict, outmoded views. He then releases
Clement into society in the expectation that Clement will respond as
he had in his youth and acquire the same contempt for contemporary aristocratic culture. Caroline Ashburn plays the mentor to
Sibella, Valmont, Arthur Murden, and quite a few others, trying to
convert them to her rational, reformist code through letters that
often contain moral fables as well as advice. The romantic hero,
Arthur, plays various roles in various scenes and makes plans to
rescue Sibella from Valmont's castle while the ironic libertine Filmar
repeatedly plans to kidnap her so that he can marry her and acquire
her fortune. All of the plans go awry. Sibella learns to think, in part
because Valmont's attempt to isolate her from others was not entirely
successful, Clement, oppressed in the paternal castle, adores society,
Caroline is respected by many but heeded by few, Filmar remains
single and impoverished, and Arthur is left to play one last tragic
scene. In the tangle of marriage plots, Sibella believes that she is
married to Clement but does not realize that Valmont, while forcibly
separating the lovers for educational purposes, is plotting their
marriage so that his son can acquire the Valmont wealth through
her, Caroline wishes her to marry Arthur and so helps Arthur to
effect her escape from Valmont's castle, Filmar kidnaps her from
Arthur in order to marry her himself, and then quickly returns her to
Caroline after discovering that she is pregnant by Clement, who, at
the time of Sibella's arrival at Caroline's home, has just married
Caroline's mother. At the end of the novel's convoluted and involuted
plots, Sibella and her infant lie dead, Arthur has expired for love of
Sibella, Caroline, Filmar, and Valmont are apparently stricken with
remorse about their parts in the events that led to those deaths, and

readers searching for moral closure must make do with the slim pickings of a minor character's exposure as a "fallen woman." Fenwick uses a number of stock literary elements: the innocent, and orphaned, heroine is trapped in a forbidding castle by a wicked male relative; two women form an epistolary friendship in which confidences are shared and advice given by the elder; various rakes accumulate gambling debts and mistresses while reluctantly seeking useful marriages, in one instance through the heiress-abduction plot; a hero risks all to save his beloved from a villain; a virtuous woman educates those around her, encouraging them to follow her moral path; and the abandoned ingenue survives childbirth only long enough to be abandoned by her lover and see her infant's corpse.

But Fenwick interweaves these elements, forming a mosaic of the gothic, the romantic, the libertinist, and the didactic (of various ideological stripes) under the general generic rubric of the epistolary. Fenwick, however, does not mix genres. "Genres," as Jacques Derrida notes, "are not to be mixed," as they "play the role of order's principle."[9] Instead she grafts them together to articulate the complex cultural topography in which the various genres do not mingle, but collide to mark separations in cultural perspectives and the principles of order with which they are commensurate. In *Secresy*, genre is used explicitly to give a name to a derided culture, as it is in Hands' poems, as well as implicitly to express or validate the classifier's culture: in the former case, generic naming tends to mark an artificiality, a literary derivativeness that diverts the character who follows it from the proper course; in the latter case, generic expectations inform social expectations without ever being named as generic, submerging the source of the assumptions to imply that they are proper or natural. For Fenwick's characters, literary genres often offer a means by which the incomprehensible and the alien can be differentiated from the cultural codes that they accept and so securely bounded. Caroline, for instance, represents the passions that she cannot understand as "romantic" and a consequence of being "refined upon romance" (*S*, 188). Fenwick thus puts a different spin on the pattern which Bourdieu analyzes: genre does not only create a sense of place, but is used to put people in their place, and not just people such as Hands. By foregrounding the literariness of another's cultural perspective, Fenwick's characters imply not complete cultural integrity but a rift between nature and (artificial) culture that misdirects the individual, or produces a mask that conceals the proper self, indirectly validating the terms by which that "proper self" is codified by the would-be taxonomist. But the mixture of voices in her novel means that each classifier's perspective is coded as literary: no one voice stands above the rest, secure from critique, contradiction, or generic classification.

LITERARY MASKS: FITTING INTO PUBLIC CULTURES

The collapse between life and literature and its cognate concern with the blurriness of the line between public, literary masks and private, authentic selves emerges from Fenwick's primary source. Isobel Grundy traces Fenwick's debts to such writers as Mary Wollstonecraft, Jean-Jacques Rousseau, Samuel Richardson, and William Shakespeare, while Nicola Watson locates *Secresy* among other English Jacobin responses to Rousseau's novels.[10] But, in *Secresy*, Fenwick is, above all, indebted to the notorious work of a French reader of Richardson and Rousseau who was also, for a time, a member of the Jacobin party: Pierre-Ambroise Choderlos de Laclos' epistolary satire, *Les Liaisons Dangereuses; Ou Lettres* (1782).[11] Correspondences between the two novels are numerous and extensive.[12] Besides being epistolary in genre and satiric in mode, both novels trace, within an aristocratic setting, the fissure between public models and private actions through a plot that entails a series of seductions as elder mentors deliver flawed advice to their naive counterparts. Morals are conveyed through the same coded endings: a cloistered and naive woman is destroyed through her contact with a corrupt society, an honorable woman dies for love of the wrong man, and a dishonorable woman is exposed and disgraced by the publication of her letters. More to the point, both novels deal with attempts to fit an individual into the role defined by the cultural precepts of others and represent such deformations as ultimately tragic in their consequences because of their difference from a private, more innate, identity. In *Secresy*, Fenwick addresses both imposed and selected deformations, associating the former with the influence of education in shaping the subject to conform to the culture of the educator and the latter with the practice of assuming a persona to conform to the culture of someone that a character wishes to please. Characters who self-consciously shape themselves to fit their contexts tend to be the most aware of cultural differences, but even the naive Sibella and the moralist Caroline acknowledge it, one admitting to being "ignorant" "of the customs of [the other's] world" (*S*, 250) and the other complaining, "my habits would not so suddenly yield to your's [*sic*]" (*S*, 54).

Valmont's character is explicitly represented as the product of the family castle. Caroline writes, "Appearing to act, to speak, to look, according to some rule settled for the hour, I deemed his character too much assumed to be quickly understood. From the solemn pride which sat on his brow, I judged, however, that he was fitted for his castle, and his castle fitted for him" (*S*, 53). Having "received a stately kind of education within the castle walls" (*S*, 62) under the watchful eye of a father for whom "Every stone of the building" was "an idol" (*S*, 61), he went "to court, where he expected to find only his equals, and those equals alive to and exact in the observance of all that haughty decorum, which Mr. Valmont deemed indispensably necessary to the well being of social institutions" (*S*, 62). Discovering instead a "contaminating mixture" (*S*, 62), he retreated to his castle to become "quack-royal to the human race" (*S*, 207–08), or at least to his own Adam and Eve, Sibella and Clement. With expectations derived from his castle-formed education, expectations in which manners and social order are inextricably intertwined and class determines one's social circle and code of behavior, Sibella's uncle is unable to join a society constituted outside of his centuries-old castle and can only attempt to produce an alternative society along his ideological and cultural lines within the confines of that same castle, constructing cultural difference in Burkean fashion as the difference between "the well being of social institutions" and corrupt social decay. Unable to enter society himself, Valmont renders Sibella and Clement similarly incapable, though not in the ways that he expects. As Caroline notes, in one of Fenwick's tacit nods to Wollstonecraft, "How is he who has never reasoned [to] be enabled in his turn to train his offspring otherwise than he himself was trained?" (*S*, 349). But Valmont is not the only influence on his wards: they are also affected by the other inhabitants of the castle and, particularly in Sibella's case, the castle grounds as well as, like Valmont himself, the castle. Filmar compares his own horror of Valmont's Norman castle to Sibella's comfort with it: "What wonders will not education, custom, and habit accomplish! Miss Valmont, I dare say, feels no horror in listening to such sounds, nor tracing these murmuring galleries, lonely staircases, &c. I should not exist six months in this castle" (*S*, 228). Filmar's remarks strongly suggest that his own education in gothic literature has determined his own response to the building, but it is her reaction that he finds odd and so it is her reaction that he assumes must be artificial. Filmar thus joins Caroline in affirming the power of architecture and customs to shape identity: he even writes that the castle is so "admirably contrived to fix odd impressions on the mind" that, after "Another such night, in another such place," he could begin to see ghosts himself (*S*, 223).

In Sibella and others, Caroline sees an authentic self beneath the false exterior produced by such cultural conditioning. As she tells an acquaintance, "I do not want . . . to hear what every body says. I want, Lady Mary, to know your own sincere opinion" (*S*, 70). Introducing her plans for Sibella and Arthur to marry, Caroline writes, "You are both at present the victims of erroneous education, but your artificial refinements being so admirably checked in their growth, now I know not two people upon earth so calculated, so fitted for each other as Murden and Sibella" (*S*, 286).[13] Usually, however, fitting is represented as the consequence of masquerade rather than unveiling. It is the libertinist set that are most aware of the role-playing required by cultural expectations. Janetta Laundy, the mistress of Filmar and Clement whose compromising letters are exposed at the novel's end, thus complains, "In the unhappy and dependent situation which the misfortunes heaped upon my family have compelled me to seek, it is not the least of its afflicting circumstances that I am obliged to shape all of my actions to the will or opinions of those by whom I am surrounded" (*S*, 292). Clement, who, unlike Sibella, has periodically left the antiquated castle to visit modern London, is well-aware of the adjustments that he must make when he changes social contexts (contexts that he, like Filmar and Caroline, defines architecturally in relation to the castle):

Half an hour or so, I stood before the looking-glass, to find what face was fittest to carry to the castle. The glances that I have of late been used to, may do for the wood when Mr. Valmont is out of sight, but they will not suit the library. They speak of a promptitude for pleasure. I must hide them under my cloak, and borrow something, if I can, of Mr. Valmont's sallow hues. (*S*, 117)

Filmar, like Clement, can conform to cultural codes to which he does not subscribe, but he is far more self-reflexive about the internal rift that such conformity creates. While Clement shapes himself as circumstance requires to pursue the desire of the moment, Filmar repeatedly emphasizes the difference between the mask and the masquer to mock the deceptions of masquerade. His description of honor-bound posturing in a confrontation between Valmont and his father, Lord Elsings, in which both use the strongest language possible without risking a challenge to a duel, is typically colorful and ironic:

my father . . . was lighter than Gossamer. – And valiant too – talked big and bluff about honour, – and satisfaction – and could but just be prevailed on by my intreaties only to write the following pacific answer, in which, were he not a gentleman, the Earl of Elsings, and my honoured father, you or I might be bold enough to say – He tells a *falsehood, an absolute falsehood*. (*S*, 280)

Didst thou never, dear Walter, see two curs pop unexpectedly on one another within a yard and a half of a bone? – Er-er-rar – says one, softly setting down his lifted fore foot. – Er-er-rar, replies t'other; and each clapping his cowardly tail between his legs slinks backward a little way; then ventures to turn round, and scampers off like a hero. – If thou has wit to find the moral, thou mayst also apply it. (*S*, 281)

With his attention to the forms of writing and social interaction, Filmar avoids positive assertions of morality and propriety, marking only his isolation from various systems – from his uncommendable behavior to his want of boldness and his ironic analysis of his class's cultural codes – that he represents as false and self-deceptive.

Like the libertines of Laclos' novel, Filmar is aware of the influence of literature on such public masks. Laclos' Valmont, for instance, laments,

je ne puis rien faire qu'au hasard: aussi, depuis huit jours, je repasse inutilement tous les moyens connus, tous ceux des romans et de mes mémoires secrets; je n'en trouve aucun qui convienne, ni aux circonstances de l'aventure, ni au caractère de l'héroine. (*LD*, 252)

I can do nothing except at hazard: therefore, for a week, I have been uselessly going over all of the known means, all those in novels and in my secret memoirs; I have not found any which fit either the circumstances of the adventure, or the character of the heroine.

The masks and disguises of Laclos' novel are self-consciously constituted within a heavily coded social domain that is much indebted to literary models, so indebted that Valmont must consult his "memoirs" rather than his memory. Madame de Merteuil, the arch-plotter of the novel, is most aware of the literariness of such

codings. In a passage that recalls Clement's description of his
rehearsal before the mirror, she writes, "je lis un chapitre de *Sopha*,
une lettre d'*Héloïse* et deux contes de La Fontaine, pour recorder les
différents tons que je voulais prendre" (*LD*, 37) ("I read a chapter of
Sopha, a letter of *Héloïse* and two tales of La Fontaine, to practice the
different tones that I wished to take").[14] Filmar shows the same kind
of self-consciousness about his literary models. In a letter to his
correspondent, Walter Boyer, in which he narrates his first attempt
to abduct Sibella, he repeatedly reflects on the literariness of his
writing and experiences:

I grant you, this is all rattle (that is the manner not the matter, upon my
honor), and poor forced rattle too. (*S*, 216)

I am gone, in reputation I mean, to seek the earl, the baronet, and the
simple squire, but, in propria persona, returned to my chamber to tell you
a story – a story of stories. (*S*, 217)

My part in the plot will soon commence. – Be content, Walter, to trace it in
its several progressive steps toward the catastrophe. (*S*, 219)

To you, Walter, I give a sober straight forward history. (*S*, 220)

This gap between "in reputation" and "in propria persona," or "the
manner" and "the matter," marks the scission between true and
false representations, as it does in *Liaisons*: literary models are, it is
assumed, used to deceive, oneself as well as others, whether "a story
of stories" or a "history" that might not be "straight forward."

In a letter to Sibella, Caroline represents letter-writing (as always,
without irony) as a dangerous diversion from self-reflection that
leads to self-deception: "had you, instead of sitting down to detail
your reasons to me, enquired narrowly into the cause of your
sensations, you must have discovered that error was creeping in
upon you, and that your native frankness and stedfast [*sic*] sincerity
were making a vigorous effort to repel *secrecy*, that canker-worm of
virtue" (*S*, 139). Caroline must similarly suppress self-reflection to
write. In the final letter of the volume, in which she describes
Sibella's final hours to Filmar, she separates her emotional self from
her rational reading and writing self and places them in conflict:

I scarcely recollect the verbal message I sent in answer to your letter of
yesterday; for I was then under the dominion of feelings more powerful
than reason – yet not more powerful; it was that reason had yielded for a
time her place. I will fortify myself for the relation of the events of
yesterday, because I think it will do you a service. I am sure you are not

incorrigible; and one example of the consequences of error has often more power than a volume of precepts. (*S*, 351–52)

Earlier, Arthur had dealt with an emotional strain by writing to Caroline: "It is a relief . . . to write" (*S*, 320). But while Sibella, Caroline, and Arthur are not themselves when they write – though Caroline's remarks on Filmar's reform remind us that she believes that she can affect the identity of her readers through her writing – Filmar achieves the kind of self-reflection that Caroline encourages, though without her moral or rational certainties, through the irony of his writing. Instead of the conventional forms of closing letters, such as "Your humble servant," his father's choice (*S*, 280), or "thy ever faithful," the duplicitous choice of Janetta (*S*, 314), Filmar signs a letter to Boyer, "I . . . am as I am. / FILMAR" (*S*, 281), and to Janetta, "Thine, whilst I had love and money" (*S*, 289). Particularly when describing his heavily formalized interactions with his father, Filmar repeatedly attends to the irony behind Caroline's complaint, "people of a superior class must have superior forms" (*S*, 46). Filmar is the only letter-writer whose correspondent's letters do not appear in the novel, adding to the sense that his irony internalizes the tension that resonates inarticulably between the other characters. While the others turn away from contradiction and crisis by writing, Filmar turns contradiction and crisis into writing.

Clement, Filmar, Valmont, Caroline, and others acknowledge the self-deformation that is necessary to fit into a particular cultural niche constituted in the public domain, whether a medieval castle, the epistolary genre, or a narrative persona. Each deals with it in a different way, but the essential problem remains the same: different social contexts require different behaviors, behaviors codified in such cultural arenas as architecture, literature, and customs, and people must conform to those requirements to fit into the social sphere at hand. This self-deformation, however, results not from the super-imposition of culture onto nature, but from the conflict between the culture with which they identify and the one in which they must interact socially or textually. Raised on medieval notions of aristo-cratic behavior, Valmont is alienated from the modern aristocracy as surely as his system of education renders Sibella and Clement unfit to survive in it. Sibella's alienation from that society is so complete that she can even disparage weddings and represent them as a trivial custom: "The vow of the heart is of sacred dignity. Forms and ceremonies seem too trifling for its nature" (*S*, 250). Caroline is equally tenacious about her reformist principles, principles held after her own "reformation" (*S*, 50). Caroline claims that, as a child, she was shocked out of aristocratic complacency by a poor woman's negative representation of the rich, a representation that reversed Caroline's sense of her social place: "Her lesson had awakened in my mind a true sense of my situation" (*S*, 49). These characters locate themselves securely within different cultural paradigms that provide them with a sense of place and propriety, as described by Bourdieu. When Caroline is a haughty aristocrat, she plays the role to the hilt; and when she loses her certainty about her innate superiority, she works to earn it by "remedy[ing] the defects" (*S*, 50) of her earlier behavior within the context of the social view that shattered her aristocratic identification. But it is the tensions that result when individuals enter a public domain for which they have not been culturally trained, as when the young Caroline is shocked to discover that she is not universally admired, that constitute Fenwick's focus rather than the possibilities of any particular sphere that is coherent only insofar as it is represented as inviolate. That the characters "inhabit polarised fictional universes" testifies not to the "imaginative incoherence" of *Secresy*, as Terry Castle suggests,[15] but to Fenwick's dramatization of the deployment of generic expectations in social relations.

PLOTS AND COUNTER-PLOTS: FITTING OTHERS INTO A CULTURE OF ONE'S OWN

Like *Liaisons*, *Secresy* resists reduction to a single plot. As Susan K. Jackson has recently argued, the reduction of *Liaisons* to the machinations of "Merteuil and Valmont, the novel's own two 'masters' of deceit," is an extension of the discourse of mastery which pervades and surrounds the novel, "reducing their victims . . . to the status of more or less insipid secondary characters."[16] Similarly, to characterize *Secresy* as a novel about two women, Sibella and Caroline, or female education, is to narrow the novel to Valmont's brave new world and lose the larger context in which Sibella is only one of Caroline's epistolary students and Caroline is only one character interested in shaping Sibella's character.[17] Fenwick has much broader concerns that extend Wollstonecraft's interest in the duplicity that patriarchy requires of women to Laclos' interest in the conflict between public and private personae, a conflict played out in each of the many plots in the novels. The incommensurability of the letter-writers' varying sets of expectations means that each character is a point of dislocation for all of the others, an incongruity that must be accommodated through conversion or, as a last resort, dismissed through an alignment with an overtly literary stereotype. Filmar sums up the players with his usual flair: "Miss Ashburn is an angel, Mr. Murden a fine fellow, Mr. Valmont an ideot [*sic*], Sibella a saint, and Montgomery – a scoundrel" (*S*, 339). But while Sibella is "a saint" for Filmar, she is many other things to other characters and at other times: "A vision for the poet" (*S*, 264), "the adorable romantic girl" (*S*, 195), a "Miss" who "had not a right understanding" (*S*, 261), "Wood Nymph, Dryad, and Hymadriad" (*S*, 54), or a "Barbarous" "rival" (*S*, 317), she is inserted into the role appropriate for each letter-writer's script. The epistolary format of the novel allows Fenwick to interweave the writings of a range of writers, or plotters, and it is this clash of plots that produces the novel's cacophony and disallows the emergence of an authoritative voice.[18] In plots, counter-plots, and resistance to plots, character after character expects or tries to produce a particular narrative and finds that the others are too engaged in their own plots to follow another plotter's cues. Even Caroline, while condemning the plans of various figures, including Arthur and Valmont, plots Arthur and Sibella's marriage, various figures' education and reformation, her own escape from her corrupt mother, and the restoration of her family's colonially obtained wealth to those from whom it was extracted. As Filmar exults, just before the total collapse of Caroline's plans, "Henceforward be plot and strategem sanctified! for Miss Ashburn deigns to plot" (*S*, 329). While Laclos warns that even the consummate plotter can be out-plotted, Fenwick suggests that no plot can work while everyone is plotting according to different interests and expectations.

As each plotter tries to deal with actors who are reading from their own scripts, each purportedly public script is finally only a private one that intersects with a public domain that the author cannot control, direct, or re-write because it is too heterogeneous. Caroline articulates the problem for Arthur, while falling into the trap herself:

I would not unite you as you are to the Sibella Valmont whom you have loved with all the fervour the most impassioned language can describe, the erring Sibella while she sees neither spot nor stain in him with whom she has pledged herself in union ... You are but two beings in the great brotherhood of mankind, and what right have you to separate your benevolence from your fellow-creatures and make a world between you, when you cannot separate your wants also? – You must be dependent for your blessings on the great mass of mankind, as they in part depend on you. – When you can thus love, I would unite you to Sibella, who in her turn shall be roused from the present mistaken zeal of her affections. (S, 285)

This is an astonishing letter: Caroline claims the power to plan Sibella's and Arthur's separate transformations to accord with her value system and social vision as well as the power to "unite" them at the time of her own choosing, while condemning their own belief systems as erroneous and identifying Arthur's emotions with "impassioned *language*" rather than authentic feeling. But she only states baldly what most of Fenwick's characters would state less explicitly while identifying the central quandary of the novel: reconciling a private culture or "world" with "the great mass of mankind" may conform to the desire for closure which so much literature teaches, but the complexity and range of generic models which interact in the public sphere make such closure impossible. As Filmar laments when his own plans, or narrative expectations, are thwarted by their unforeseen interaction with other plots and characters, "How could I foresee that I should have to deal with a knavish sort of nameless something?" (S, 236).

The tensions between the various lovers, for instance, is implicated in the incompatibility of their "textual classes." The result when Arthur tries to court Sibella reveals Arthur's dependence on romantic and gothic models and their inappropriateness for a budding rationalist like Sibella who has not read such texts. Sibella describes the meeting to Caroline, a meeting that begins with Arthur's appearance in the disguise of an aging hermit, "descending from the Ruin on the Rock":

"Fair virgin, weep not! The spirits of the air gather round you; and form a band so sacred, that the malignant demons hover at a distance, hopeless of approach. Your guardian angel presides over this grove. Here, Mildew, Mischief, and Mischance, cannot harm you. Fair virgin weep not!" He paused, I said, "Who are you?"

"Once," he continued, "I was the hallowed tenant of yon ruined mansion; once, an inhabitant of earth, it was my lot to warn the guilty, and to soothe the mourner. Well may such tears as thine draw me back to earth. I come, the spirit of consolation. Fair virgin, why weepest thou?"

"I know," I said, "that the sleep of death is eternal. That the grave never gives back, to form and substance, the mouldering body; and it indeed matters little to me who or what you are, since I well know you cannot be what you seem."

I stepped down from the monument; and turned up the wood path, leading to the castle.

"Stay," cried he. "Do you doubt my supernatural mission?" (*S*, 101–02)

Since she has just stated that she does not believe in the supernatural, the answer is clearly "yes." Sibella has little patience with Arthur's attempt to play the part of her spectral protector, as her querulous, "Who are you?" suggests. She later recognizes the masquer's voice in the "mysterious and whimsical stile" of a letter that she receives (*S*, 180), identifying Arthur with a mode of writing rather than intentions or a spiritual state.[19] While Sibella debunks Arthur's romantic impulse, Arthur is befuddled by her failure to behave like the heroine of romance:

"I do not deem you worthy of enquiry," I said; "for you come with pretences of falsehood and guile, and those are coverings that virtue ever scorns."

"Fair philosopher," he exclaimed, "teach me how you preserve such vigour, such animation, where you have neither rivalship to sustain, nor admiration to excite? Are you secluded by injustice from the world? Or, do you willingly forsake its delights, to live the life of hopeless recollection? Say, does the beloved of your soul sleep in that monument?" (*S*, 103)

A friend of Sibella's confidante, Caroline, and the reluctant confidant of Sibella's lover, Clement, Arthur well knows by this point that Sibella is imprisoned by her uncle and loves a man who still breathes. He also knows by this point that the monks who inhabited the hermitage, now "the Ruin on the Rock," were not as holy as they purported to be – he reached the woods in which he meets Sibella by using their secret path across the moat, "the saintly contrivance of the starving monks" (*S*, 263) who had claimed to survive without food because of the power of their faith. But Arthur cannot stray from the terms of the romantic and gothic narratives in which he hopes to forge a bond with a woman he imagines as an ethereal figure from such genres – as Caroline remarks, he was "refined upon romance" (*S*, 188). He repeatedly acknowledges that this imagining is of a Procrustean kind, fitting Sibella to conform to his own preconceptions and fantasies. Arthur recounts the soliloquy that he claims he uttered after hearing Caroline list Sibella's virtues,

"Hast thou not a thousand and a thousand times, in thy waking and sleeping visions, described a being thus artless, thus feminine, yet firm, such an all-attractive daughter of wisdom? – Ay: but I had never *personified* her in Sibella Valmont" (*S,* 258–59; my emphasis). Sibella, for Arthur, is the embodiment of his fantasies: "And here let me pause, Miss Ashburn, to remark how strongly I discovered in her the mind I had pictured and panted to possess" (*S,* 265). Arthur even acknowledges the disparity between Sibella and his ideal, as well as his dismissal of that disparity: "I heard every interesting particular of her mind, manners, and seclusion. Her love of Clement Montgomery, was also remembered. To me, his love of her never bore any striking features; and, somehow, her's [*sic*] to him seldom intruded amidst my chimeras. Strange wishes arose – tremulous expectations" (*S,* 259), "flattering illusions wherewith fancy fed my flame" (*S,* 268).

But it is not only Sibella that Arthur inscribes into what he terms, "the romance of my scheme" (*S,* 261). He is his own leading player. He admits that he has assumed the character of a libertine while in society and gives different explanations for that masquerade to Clement and Caroline, both of whom have taken him at face value. To Clement, he writes,

Be assured I am neither your *soulless* marble, nor Seymour's *libertine.* At a boyish age from boyish vanity I aimed to be called a man of pleasure. It was easy to imitate the air and manners of such a man, and not less easy by such imitation alone to arrive at the contemptible fame among persons equally ready to encourage the practice and accuse the practitioner. I renounce the loathsome labours of the flatterer, the despicable renown of the libertine. (*S,* 135)

Arthur implicitly acknowledges that he is subject to the very misrecognition that appears in his own characterizations of Sibella, that he is being misrepresented by Clement as "*soulless* marble" and by Seymour as a "*libertine.*" But though he would "renounce" such identities and tells his would-be apprentice, Clement, "I am ill fitted to become your adviser" (*S,* 135), he does not claim another – he only announces his submission to Caroline's characterization. In a later letter to Caroline, his early attraction to a rakish role is left unexplained and her role in his reformation unacknowledged while he persists in refusing to identify his new "propria persona": "I adored your disdain of a character I equally disdained, while I contemptibly descended to wear it; and, though I could not instantly resolve to cast aside the unmerited fame of my licentiousness, yet you never moved or spoke, that I was not all eye and ear" (*S*, 258). To fit himself into his romantic scheme, he assumes another character, "fixing on [him]self the character of an eccentric whimsical solitary" (*S*, 261). After he discovers that Sibella has unofficially married, and consummated that marriage with, Clement – an act euphemistically termed a "contract" or "romantic contract" – he decides to assume yet another role:

although I feel an internal testimony that I cannot live without her, yet was she, and is to this moment, more effectually banished from my wishes by her contract with Montgomery, than she could have been by age, disease, or any possible deformity . . . The sweetly soothing promise of speedy dissolution . . . determined me to retire to a romantic and fit retreat for sorrow I once saw on the banks of the Danube. (*S*, 270)

A libertine in society, a romantic hero in the woods of the gothic castle, an eccentric aristocrat among the peasants with whom he lives while visiting his castle, and an abandoned lover who wishes only to die slowly in a romantic setting, Arthur fits his public face to his environment and his audience, even when it is "disdained" and self-consciously assumed:

Frequenting the resorts of dissipation from custom, labouring to compel my revolting senses to the gratification of pleasure, struggling to wear a character opposite to my inclination, seeking in public to seduce the attentions of women, from whose hours of private yielding I fled with disgust, effectually removed from society which would have taught me the importance of mental pursuits . . . I almost prayed for . . . something, any thing, that could interrupt the routine of sameness, that could make me cease to be as it were the mere automaton of habit. (*S*, 243)

Arthur's narrative fantasies determine the role that he plays. Rather than straining against other cultures' mores, he throws himself into the genre that will allow him to play a particular part that he finds attractive at the moment, with no trace of Filmar's ironic reflections. And he readily tries to manipulate others to fit into his narrative in order to further it, whether seducing women, praising Caroline as inspirational, or trying to convince Sibella that he is the ghost of a monk.

Locating character generically, however, makes identity contingent on narrative in a way that ultimately proves destructive: the unproductive interaction of various plots leads to a crisis of identity for each of the genre-crossed lovers, culminating in Sibella's death,

Arthur's madness and demise, and silence for the others. After Arthur realizes that Sibella has not only had sex with Clement, but become pregnant, he is unable to look at her. A visibly pregnant heroine cannot be written into his sort of narrative, and it unhinges him. As Caroline writes,

A romantic love of Miss Valmont sapped its [his life's] foundation, and his nights of watching amidst the chilling damps of the Ruin hastened the progress of its destruction. Sibella's unaccountable escape from him at a time when his high toned feelings were wrought upon, in a way that I cannot express, by the *alteration* in her person, drove him to madness. (*S*, 338)

Caroline, the moral rationalist, "cannot express" the romantic emotionalism of Arthur's response any more than Arthur can deal with a pregnant Sibella; it is a "nameless something," in Filmar's phrase. At the inn after the escape from Valmont castle, he cannot even look at Sibella and turns his back to her while he writes to Caroline: "It is a relief . . . to write – tho' any thing upon earth would be preferable to hearing – I mean, *seeing her*" (*S*, 320). Sibella is similarly disconcerted by her realization that Clement has failed to conform to her own "romantic" expectations. At the climactic moment of the main plot, Sibella – thinking that she is about to be reunited with Clement after escaping her uncle and soliciting the aid of her kidnapper, Filmar – bursts into the wedding breakfast of Clement and Caroline's mother. Caroline's attempts to avert catastrophe crystallize the means by which Fenwick's characters attempt to exert control:

Miss Ashburn endeavoured to retain Sibella in her embrace; and began hurryingly to enquire of her where she had been, and by what means she had got hither. But Miss Valmont knew nothing of the past. She was alive only to the present . . . *"Hear me! listen only to me!"* exclaimed Miss Ashburn. (*S*, 344–45; my emphasis)

"I can bear this no longer," cried Miss Ashburn. "Silence, Madam! – Sibella, dear Sibella, turn your eyes on me! Let not their pure rays beam on a wretch so worthless!" Devoured by emotions over which friendship has no controul, she was still deaf to Miss Ashburn. Still those pure eyes bent their gaze on Montgomery. (*S*, 346)

The novel's final "progressive steps toward the catastrophe," to use another of Filmar's phrases, follow from Caroline's inability to control events, to control the information available to Sibella, and to control the cultural paradigms and convictions through which she manages it as she had when Arthur was "all eye and ear" for her (*S*, 258). After the loss of Sibella to Filmar during the escape from the castle, Caroline's plot to disentangle Sibella from what she thinks is Valmont's plot is at the mercy of other characters' plots, from Clement's marriage to Arthur's despairing decline and Filmar's ill-timed arrival with Sibella.

Just as Arthur's plans cannot accommodate a rational heroine, let alone a pregnant one, Valmont's cannot manage a man who loves pleasure or a woman who loves to think, Sibella's cannot make allowances for duplicity, and Caroline's cannot anticipate the intrusion of the irrational into her rational plans or the more traditional use of the heiress-abduction plot by Filmar. The inability of their plots, and the expectations upon which they were built, to predict behavior and events suggests the inability of their cultural models to totalize the social domain, reinforcing the characters' anxieties about fitting into certain culturally defined societies rather than allowing them to resolve those tensions. Finally they are left with only one desperate strategy, to refuse to see or hear those who their views cannot accommodate, to control discourse through censorship or by taking narrative control through writing, and thus to make their alienation a separation: Valmont retires to his isolated castle and carefully limits the access of his wards to books and the outside world, Arthur turns his back to Sibella to write to Caroline, and Caroline demands that only she be allowed to speak. But the breach in a "class on paper" cannot be hermetically sealed, even by such textual deflections.

"TALKING ALGEBRA": PUBLIC CULTURE AND PRIVATE LANGUAGE

At issue here are negotiations between the private and the public, for these differences of perspective are the generic equivalents of Ludwig Wittgenstein's "private language":

Let us remember that there are certain criteria in a man's behaviour for the fact that he does not understand a word: that it means nothing to him, *that he can do nothing with it.* And criteria for his 'thinking he understands', attaching some meaning to the word, but not the right one. And, lastly, criteria for his understanding the word right . . . And sounds which no one else understands but which I '*appear to understand*' might be called "private language."[20]

"Genre" is a term that brackets a subset of the criteria to which Wittgenstein refers, telling us what to do with nightingales, the unusual syntax of verse, and the bleak landscapes of the gothic, indicating the semiotic context in which to place those signifiers. Fenwick, by splicing together the epistolary form with the more public genres of romance, gothic, education narratives, and libertinist novels, produces a generic tension that resonates throughout the novel. Against the shared comprehension of the letter's form strain codes and models that the letter-writers "appear to understand" but with which their readers "can do nothing." Arthur thus writes to Clement, "I know I am talking algebra to you, and if you take me for a companion, you must even be content to travel on in the dark" (*S*, 133). Clement later takes up the term to identify the genre of Arthur's discourse without decoding it: "His letters are algebra to me" (*S*, 191).

Formally, *Secresy* is entirely epistolary. Even the dedication is written as a letter, and no notes, or editor's preface, or indications of ellipses or marred manuscripts intrude upon this collection of letters as they do, for instance, in *Liaisons*. The insistent epistolarity of the novel and the letter-writers' references to narratives, tale-telling, style, and so forth sandwich the form of private social discourse, the letter, between the generically and culturally complex, public, coded sphere of that copious category of discourse, "literature." The gothic-inspired romantic writes to the educator and a libertine, the educator writes to the naive romantic, the libertine, and the gothic tyrant, the libertines promiscuously write to nearly everyone but particularly each other, and the ironic libertine writes about the genres and styles that he employs to a silent correspondent. It is upon these points of contact between incompatible types and cultures that the plot turns. All of the characters see continuities between their own perspectives and the world around them or expect those continuities to be forged – and turn away from evidence that those continuities do not exist – but cannot escape their cultural determination to find new continuities elsewhere or accept the limited range of their perspectives. The forms of other cultures remain the broad equivalent of private languages. But there is also a sub-generic private language here that is not subsumed within these discursively coded cultures but which strains against them.

In the dedication to *Secresy*, Fenwick addresses the distinction between a public declaration and a private letter:

What does the world care about either you or me? Nothing. But we care for each other, and I grasp at every opportunity of telling it. A letter, they may say, would do as well for that purpose as a dedication. I say no; for a letter is a sort of corruptible substance, and these volumes *may* be IMMORTAL . . . I desire then the world to let it pass; for, to tell them a truth – you have paid me for it beforehand. (*S*, 37)

In the dedication, the public and the private spheres mix, even as their separation is reinforced. It is addressed to "Eliza B — " and remains unsigned, publicly effacing the identities of those involved in its private communication. This apparent anonymity, however, extends only to the public, as the elision of the correspondents' names sustains the privacy of their epistolary communication but does not, as the dedication assumes, keep those names secret from the correspondents themselves. The public domain, moreover, is defined as the space through which such communications "pass" unheeded, distinct from and unconcerned with private exchanges such as the dedication and the feelings to which it refers. Yet the public is the implied reader of the final sentence, witnessing the author's authentication of the dedication as a token in a private economy that remains otherwise hidden from public view. Through the dedication, Fenwick characterizes the publication of epistolary communication as a means of rendering their contents "immortal," of sustaining their power to mark private affections, while depersonalizing those contents by maintaining the privacy of the correspondents. Fenwick thus addresses some of the vexed implications of a published letter's relationship to the divided domains of public and private, identifying the published letter as a public monument that marks, but, like a monolith, does not represent, an economy, form of relationship, and history that remains hidden from public view.[21] This, ultimately, is the locus of "secresy" in the novel: the private meanings that cannot be transposed, undeformed, to a public world with its own concerns and expectations.

This split between form and a sub-formal, private self is a source of some concern to Filmar. He is caught not between the castle and society but between aristocratic, libertinist, and quasi-romantic mores, the first valorizing honor and status, the second the pursuit of pleasure while ironically casting an eye on conservative social values, and the third private feeling. While Arthur claims to have adored Sibella before he even met her and Clement claims to love Sibella even as he has affairs with other women and declares his love for them too, Filmar openly describes his reluctance to meet with Sibella after the abduction: "What could I have said but what amounted to this: 'Miss Valmont, I ran away with you, because I wanted your estate, for want of a better. – As to yourself, I know nothing about you, therefore how can I care for you?'" (S, 341). To his own confidant, Filmar laments his abduction of Sibella, "I do not find, when carefully examined, that my own character and motives in this business possess much to recommend them" (S, 332), and again locates a scission between his actions in the world and his private epistolary expressions: "my thoughts, in gadding after the enterprize, possessed all the saucy gaiety which youth and untamed spirits could impart. Nay, when I began to write this letter, they wore their natural character" (S, 333). In telling Walter why he prefers Sibella to Mrs. Ashburn, Caroline's rich mother, a preference that Clement declares in reverse, he writes, "Your hint, dear knight, respecting Mrs. Ashburn, was not lost upon me; but, though I would not marry for aught but money, I should like to have a wife thrown into the bargain whom I could love now and then" (S, 299). Later, explaining his decision to return the abducted Sibella to her friends, Filmar praises Sibella as "a very lovely and adorable woman" (S, 339) that he "could love . . . dearly" (S, 340) were it not, he laments, "my name is Filmar, and as a Lord I am bound in duty to love and cherish no son but a son of my own begetting" (S, 340). Filmar identifies a "natural character" that is based upon private feeling and valorizes it while tracing the effects of social codes in constraining such naturalness. Filmar thus complains of the formality upon which his father insists, describing a cool altercation in which the Earl calls his son "Lord Filmar" and the son calls his father "my Lord": "Now, Walter, this man, the Earl of Elsings! a peer of the realm of Great Britain! had not courage to say to his own son – 'Dick, thou art a fool, and wilt be a beggar'" (S, 171). It is the only reference to Filmar's first name, and here appears to mark his father's inability to use it.[22] While other characters in the novel strain against externally imposed narratives, struggle to accommodate those in which they are trapped, or seek to impose their own on others, Filmar acknowledges his dual allegiances as well as the ethical dimensions of these tensions.

As in *Liaisons*, the rupture between public and private identities collapses in these letters with varying degrees of awareness on the part of the characters trying to construct their identities. Not only does the cultural and generic complexity of the novel prohibit closure, but the "romantic" desire for authentic, private feeling creates an undertow that compromises the stability of each cultural code. The novel's letter-writers are effectively silenced by the failure of those codes and the feelings that consequently erupt. Caroline thus cannot write when she grieves for Sibella and denies her assertion that feeling has overcome reason as soon as she makes it. Fenwick's novel has no single ending, but an uneasy amalgam of endings that never fully meet or evade the requirements of a genre: Sibella, still unmarried in the eyes of others if not herself, dies shortly after giving birth, but dies unrepentant; Arthur dies for love of her, but still unloved by her; Clement's deception, and paternity of Sibella's child, is exposed, but his wife willfully looks away and refuses to blame him; Filmar is chastened, but not publicly vilified; and Caroline's quest to return her family's colonially acquired riches remains as quixotically unfulfilled as her hopes for Arthur and Sibella. The tragedy of the novel is less Arthur's and Sibella's deaths than the crisis of faith in their own cultural expectations which all of the letter-writers experience. Arthur and Sibella only react to that crisis with more romantic drama than the others by dying rather than merely ceasing to write, but dying and not writing are two inflections of the same consequence of narrative failure. At the end of the novel, all of the characters are silenced by the shock of being unable to imagine how to continue the narratives of their lives in the face of a world that does not operate as they expect and is filled with figures who do not fit their models. To use Filmar's exasperated query, "How could they foresee that they would have to deal with a knavish sort of nameless something?"

In Charlotte Brontë's novel, *Jane Eyre*, the protagonists move through a range of social spheres. Rochester travels in Europe, the West Indies, and across England, while Jane lives in a great house, an impoverished school, Rochester's manor, the Rivers' home, and an industrial town. Happiness is found only at the end when both retreat from the world and cut off all non-familial communication. Brontë's resolution of the marriage plot reveals a pessimistic view of the public sphere, securing her protagonists safely in the domestic.

Fenwick, however, offers no hope of retreat. Caroline's lecture to Arthur condemns such solutions as anti-social, and no private space in the novel is represented as secure from incursions by the public domain and its codes. Even Valmont's well-fortified castle is routinely breached by Arthur and Filmar as it was, at the start, by the hypocritical monks. The novel, like Arthur, envisions no "animation" where there is "neither rivalship to sustain, nor admiration to excite" (*S*, 103). Filmar perhaps offers the only viable approach to the problem of a culturally heterogeneous public domain, namely a self-consciousness about the structure of cultural codings in which their investments, breaches, facades, and artificiality are mapped and distinguished from as-yet-uncodified personal feelings, a cultural map that allows movement across frontiers without the loss of a subcultural sense of identity and the stability it offers.

NOTES

1 I take the details on Fenwick's life from A. F. Wedd, "Introduction," *The Fate of the Fenwicks: Letters to Mary Hays (1798–1828)*, ed. A. F. Wedd (London: Methuen, 1927), ix–xvi; and Isobel Grundy, "Introduction," in *Secresy; or, The Ruin on the Rock* by Eliza Fenwick, ed. Isobel Grundy (Peterborough: Broadview Press, 1994), 7–20. All references to *Secresy* cite Grundy's edition (hereafter *S*) and will be included in the text.

2 Homi K. Bhabha, "Introduction," in *Nation and Narration*, ed. Homi K. Bhabha (New York: Routledge, 1990), 2.

3 Pierre Bourdieu, "Social Space and the Genesis of 'Classes,'" in *Language and Symbolic Power*, ed. John B. Thompson, trans. Gino Raymond and Matthew Adamson (Cambridge, Mass.: Harvard University Press, 1991), 231.

4 Bourdieu, "Social Space," 231, 234.

5 Bhabha, *Nation and Narration*, 4.

6 Bourdieu, "Social Space," 235.

7 Elizabeth Hands, "A Poem, On the Supposition of an Advertisement appearing in a Morning Paper, of the Publication of a Volume of Poems, by a Servant-Maid," in *Eighteenth-Century Women Poets: An Oxford Anthology*, ed. Roger Lonsdale (New York: Oxford University Press, 1989), 29– 34 (hereafter *ECWP*).

8 Hands, "A Poem, On the Supposition of the Book having been Published and Read," in *ECWP*, 96, 98–104.

9 Jacques Derrida, "The Law of Genre," trans. Avital Ronell, in *Acts of Literature*, ed. Derek Attridge (New York: Routledge, 1992), 223, 252.

10 Grundy, "Introduction," 29–30; and Nicola Watson, *Revolution and the Form of the British Novel, 1789– 1825* (Oxford: Clarendon Press, 1994), 40.

11 All references to Laclos' novel will be incorporated parenthetically into the text and are taken from Pierre Choderlos de Laclos, *Les Liaisons Dangereuses; ou Lettres* (Paris: Flamarion, 1981), hereafter *LD*. Translations from the novel are mine. Laclos mentions both Richardson and Rousseau: Madame de Merteuil tells Valmont early in the novel that she is reading Rousseau's *Héloïse* (*LD*, 37) and later writes to him praising the novel's authenticity (*LD*, 74); la Présidente de Tourvel reads Richardson's *Clarissa* to fortify her resistance to Valmont (*LD*, 245); and Valmont refers to both *Héloïse* and *Clarissa* when discussing Tourvel's predicament with Merteuil (*LD*, 252). No character is helped much by these epistolary conduct books – which is perhaps Laclos' point.

12 Fenwick acknowledges her debt in the names of her characters. As Watson notes, Fenwick's gothic tyrant, George Valmont, shares the surname of Laclos' exquisite libertine, the Vicomte de Valmont (*Revolution and the Form of the British Novel*, 41). But so does his niece, the innocent heroine, Sibella Valmont, and George's wife, "a votary of dissipation" (*S*, 64). Moreover, Chevalier Danceny's double in Fenwick's novel, Clement Montgomery, is nicknamed "Le Chevalier" (*S*, 189). This doubling is at the center of the novel. Sibella Valmont's relationship with Clement Montgomery begins with echoes of Cécile Volanges' relationship with the Chevalier Danceny, mutual romantic love between two relative innocents, and ends resonating with Présidente de Tourvel's relationship with Valmont, as Sibella dies abandoned by Clement, who has been exposed as a libertine. The shift occurs in Sibella's and Clement's different epistolary narrations of their night together: Sibella, like an English Tourvel, characterizes it as a consummation of a marriage that needs no legal or religious sanction because of its natural truth; Clement, like a novice Vicomte, characterizes it as a successful act of revenge against George Valmont.

13 Caroline and Arthur fail to convince Sibella, or anyone else, that the two are "so fitted for each other" but Caroline puts aside her own love for Arthur on the basis of her convictions and persists in her claim to the end. The lack of corroborating evidence almost demands an ironic reading of Caroline's assertions on the subject.

14 Merteuil also takes great care with her letter-writing, keenly aware of the letter's ability to convey a persona and affect the reader, and offers telling advice on the subject to Cécile (*LD*, 240).

15 Terry Castle, Review of *Secresy; Or, The Ruin on the Rock* by Eliza Fenwick, ed. by Isobel Grundy, *London Review of Books* (February 23, 1995): 18–19.

16 Susan K. Jackson, "In Search of a Female Voice: *Les Liaisons Dangereuses*," in *Writing the Female Voice: Essays on Epistolary Literature*, ed. Elizabeth C. Goldsmith (London: Pinter Publishers, 1989), 154.

17 This view of the novel emerges in the little criticism available on it. See Janet Todd, "Introduction," in *Secresy or, the Ruin on the Rock* by Eliza

Fenwick (London: Pandora Press, 1989), viii–ix; and Watson, *Revolution and the Form of the British Novel*, 41.

18 Todd refers to the "shifting views and messages" of the novel, "Introduction," ix; while Watson describes it as a "clash of discourses" in which "no one voice is enabled to elect itself unambiguously as the centre of authority" (*Revolution and the Form of the British Novel*, 42–43). Castle characterizes the novel as a "veritable compendium of the imaginative and stylistic tics deforming so much early English women's fiction," losing sight, perhaps, of the novel's satiric dimension in locating the novel's discursive heterogeneity autobiographically as evidence of "the psychological price that women paid for their swift and subversive entry into the world of English letters" (Review of *Secresy*, 18). Watson suggests that "the tension of the narrative hinges upon the conflict between the letter, identified closely with the heroine, and the plot, associated with Valmont" (*Revolution and the Form of the British Novel*, 42). But while Valmont's plot might have more impact on the plot of the novel than any other – determining the characters of Sibella and Clement as well as a number of the circumstances and crises that take place during the course of the novel – the tangle of embedded plots suggests a systemic problem rather than one specific to Valmont or even the patriarchy to which Watson points.

19 Fenwick here echoes Clara Reeve's definition of "Romantic" as "a particular kind of affectation in speaking and writing" derived from the reading of romances. See *The Progress of Romance through Times, Countries, and Manners*, 2 vols. (London, 1785; rpt. New York: Garland, 1970), I: 66. In the scene on the Rock, Arthur further reveals the effects of romance-reading as described by Reeve: "the passions are awakened, – false expectations are raised. – A young woman is taught to expect adventures and intrigues, – she expects to be addressed in the style of these books, with the language of flattery and adulation. – If a plain man addresses her in rational terms . . . that is not sufficient, her vanity is disappointed, she expects to meet a Hero in Romance," II: 78. Arthur is trying to play the Hero, while his Heroine would, much to his confusion, prefer "a plain man [who] addresse[d] her in rational terms."

20 Ludwig Wittgenstein, *Philosophical Investigations*, trans. G. E. M. Anscombe (Oxford: Basil Blackwell, 1989), 94e (first emphasis mine).

21 Laclos, like Fenwick, begins with the issue of privacy. In the "Editor's Preface," Laclos uses the motif of the recently discovered manuscript and, as Jennifer Birkett notes, draws attention to the editor's transformation of the raw material that he collates and edits: "Laclos' own sense of the tension between 'events' and their representation – the moment where ideology intervenes – is expressed in his fictive editor's conscious expansions or abridgements of an imputedly anterior history." See her "Dangerous Liaisons: Literary and Political Form in

Choderlos de Laclos," *Literature and History* 8 (1982): 87. Laclos, for instance, suggests that he has secured the privacy of the players: "Je dois prévenir aussi que je supprimé ou changé tous les noms des personnes dont il est question dans cet lettres" ("It is my duty to inform you also that I have suppressed or changed all of the names of persons discussed in these letters") (*LD*, 15*n*). The absence of such elisions and editorial intrusions in Fenwick's novel suggests an unfiltered compilation of letters that retains the heterogeneity of multiple authorship.

22 Others of Filmar's age make similar complaints about their elders, suggesting a generational conflict defined by the distinction between the authentic and the proper. Caroline is required to call her mother "Mrs. Ashburn" and laments that "the endearing name of mother is banished for the cold title of ceremony" (*S*, 46). Sibella similarly complains, "Mr. Valmont calls himself my father; and *calling* himself such, he there rests satisfied" (*S*, 73).

CHAPTER 8

'Frankenstein' as neo-gothic: from the ghost of the counterfeit to the monster of abjection

Jerrold E. Hogle

It was already one in the morning . . . when, by the glimmer of
the half-extinguished light, I saw the dull yellow eye of the
creature open; it breathed hard, and a convulsive motion
agitated its limbs . . . Great God! His yellow skin scarcely
covered the work of muscles and arteries beneath; his hair was
of a lustrous black, and flowing; his teeth of a pearly whiteness;
but these luxuriances only formed a more horrid contrast with
his watery eyes, that seemed almost of the same colour as the
dun white sockets in which they were set, his shrivelled
complexion, [and] straight black lips . . . [B]y the dim and
yellow light of the moon, as it forced its way through the
window-shutters, I beheld the wretch – the miserable monster
whom I had created . . . His jaws opened and he muttered
some inarticulate sounds, while a grin wrinkled his cheeks. He
might have spoken, but I did not hear; one hand was stretched
out, seemingly to detain me, but I escaped . . .

Mary Wollstonecraft Shelley, *Frankenstein* (1818), 52–53[1]

[Manfred, Prince of Otranto,] seized the cold hand of Isabella,
who was half-dead with fright and horror. She shrieked, and
started from him. Manfred rose to pursue her; when the moon,
which was now up, and gleamed at the opposite casement,
presented to his sight the plumes of the fatal helmet, which rose
to the height of the windows, waving backwards and forwards
in a tempestuous manner, and accompanied with a hollow and
a rustling sound . . . Heaven nor hell shall impede my designs,
said Manfred, advancing again to sieze the princess. At that
instant the portrait of his grandfather, which hung over the
bench where they had been sitting, uttered a deep sigh and
heaved its breast . . . Manfred, distracted by the flight of
Isabella, who had now reached the stairs, and his inability to
keep his eyes from the picture, which began to move, had
however advanced some steps after her, still looking backwards
on the portrait, when he saw it quit its pannel, and descend on

the floor with a grave and melancholy air . . .[T]he vision sighed and made a sign to Manfred to follow him. Lead on! cried Manfred; I will follow thee to the gulph of perdition. The spectre marched sedately, but dejected, to the end of the gallery, and turned into a chamber on the right hand . . . As [Manfred] would have entered the chamber, the door was clapped-to with violence by an invisible hand.

Horace Walpole, The Castle of Otranto (1764), 23–24

Hamlet Angels and ministers of grace defend us!
Be thou a spirit of health or goblin damn'd,
Bring with thee airs from heaven or blasts from hell,
Be thy intents wicked or charitable,
Thou com'st in such a questionable shape
That I will speak to thee. I'll call thee Hamlet,
King, father, royal Dane. O answer me.
Let me not burst in ignorance, but tell
Why thy canoniz'd bones, hearsed in death,
Have burst their cerements, why the sepulchre
Wherein we saw thee quietly inurn'd
Hath op'd his ponderous and marble jaws
To cast thee up again. What may this mean,
That thou, dead corse, again in complete steel
Revisits thus the glimpses of the moon,
Making night hideous and we fools of nature
So horridly to shake our dispositions
With thoughts beyond the reaches of our souls?
Say why is this? Wherefore? What should we do?
Ghost beckons.

William Shakespeare, Hamlet (1600), 1.4.39–57

I GOTHIC/ANTI-GOTHIC?

There has been at least a mild debate about how "Gothic" *Frankenstein* is. "Despite [certain] affinities," it has been said, "*Frankenstein* departs from the Gothic tradition as obviously as it follows it."[2] Indeed, for some, Mary Shelley goes so far as to write an "anti-Gothic novel . . . within her Gothic tale."[3] But does there have to be an "anti-Gothic" versus "mainly Gothic" dichotomy? Why can't one ultimately be the same as the other for Mary Shelley? What if *Frankenstein* transformed the earlier Gothic by intensifying and complicating what was most basic to it? Might we not agree with Frederick S. Frank when he suggests that Mary Shelley's "novel registers deep traces of the Gothic" and yet its author should "be seen as a revisionist of that tradition" precisely in her continuation of those traces?[4] And couldn't we provide reasons for that view beyond just saying, with Frank and so many others, that *Frankenstein* changes "the Gothic fable of identity" by placing it in "the world of theoretical science" or reconnecting it to "Romantic" versions of "the tragedy of the misspent intellect" (Frank, *First Gothics*, 346)?

I want to argue that *Frankenstein* "registers traces of the [earlier] Gothic" that go very "deep" indeed. For me what seems "counter-Gothic" in *Frankenstein* is made possible by how extremely Gothic it is and by how the Godwin-Shelley circle, particularly in Mary Shelley's novel, redeployed the Gothic mode on the basis of the most basic presuppositions underlying the Gothic itself. I think that *Frankenstein* quite precisely echoes key aspects – the ghosts – in the "Gothic Story" as Horace Walpole first presented it in *The Castle of Otranto*; that the natures of these ghosts reveal the highly conflicted assumptions behind "Gothic" reworkings of past symbolic modes, especially Shakespearean drama; that those assumptions reflect an eighteenth-century transition between states of Western culture in which increasingly waning concepts of signification pull nostalgically backwards while newer, more capitalist alternatives try to make cultural capital out of the older ones; and that this contest between ideological and symbolic tendencies in the Gothic provides a site into which emergent cultural tensions can be transferred, sequestered, disguised, and thus (momentarily) diffused. The creation of this site is based, I find, on a re-counterfeiting (or ghost) of an *earlier* use of signs as counterfeits, and it is this "ghost of the counterfeit" in the Gothic that both works out and embodies – or shows the *dis*embodiment in – the cultural transition underlying *The Castle of Otranto* and much of its progeny.

Moreover, it is this *un*grounded fakery in the "grounding" of the Gothic, its re-presentation of antiquated symbols largely emptied of their older meanings, that opens up a peculiar cultural space into which the horrors generated by early modern cultural changes and their dominant ideologies of the individual can be "thrown off" or "thrown down and under" – "abjected" in the senses emphasized by Julia Kristeva and others in her wake.[5] Such a progression is begun in *The Castle of Otranto* and its immediate successors, but it accelerates most rapidly in English writing when members of the Godwin-Shelley circle, and finally Mary Shelley herself, among others, foreground the ways in which the Gothic ghost of the counterfeit allows us to load the hollowed-out depths in the counterfeits of the past with the least acceptable, most heterogenous aspects of human being in the early industrial era. Abjection becomes a continuously important feature of Gothic and related fictions from around the time of *Frankenstein* on, as several critics have seen already.[6] Yet that occurs because the eighteenth-century Gothic, a regressive-progress-ive genre/counter-genre that is betwixt and between in its recalling and recasting of past forms, provides the symbolic means for that very construction of "self" versus "archaic other." *Frankenstein* turns out to be one major apogee of the Gothic's development from the Walpolean ghosts of older ghosts to the ghost-like representation and sequestering of the abject.

II THE GHOSTS OF THE GOTHIC IN *FRANKENSTEIN*

The depth of *Frankenstein*'s roots in the Walpolean Gothic, which has never been clarified in very specific terms, becomes apparent if we look more closely at the passages quoted above. To begin with, it has long been obvious that *The Castle of Otranto* imitates Shakespeare's *Hamlet*, particularly since Walpole acknowledges the debt in the Preface to his Second Edition (*The Castle*, 8–12). The echoes are especially strong in the scene I have quoted from Walpole: Manfred confronts both a fragment (the "fatal helmet") of the armored ghost of the castle's murdered true owner (Alfonso) and the portrait of his own grandfather (Ricardo) walking out of its picture and "making a sign" to the Prince of Otranto to follow it, much as the Ghost "in complete steel" resembling Hamlet's poisoned father "*beckons*" to Shakespeare's Prince of Denmark on the "platform" at Elsinore. What the description of the creature in *Frankenstein* echoes most, however, from Walpole's "Gothic Story" (his own subtitle for the Second Edition) are changes that *The Castle* makes in the features of the Ghost from *Hamlet*. The several Otranto ghosts, in contrast to Shakespeare's one, are first of all *tearings to pieces* of their predecessor. The *Hamlet* Ghost is split up into multiple specters *and* into gigantic armored portions of one figure that need to be reconnected at the end of the novel for the primal crime to be fully revealed (*The Castle*, 108). In addition, Walpole's second ghost-echo of Shakespeare's "spirit" is the "descending" shade of a *picture*, a moving image of what is already an artificial construct (*within* the story, not just as part of one). Hamlet's attempt to refer his Ghost's "questionable shape" to a deeply material object outside it, his father's "canoniz'd bones," is turned by Walpole into the shade of a two-dimensional signifier. This kind of "vision" is more the ghost of what Hamlet later calls the "counterfeit presentiment" of his father (*Hamlet*, 3.4.54) when he asks his mother to compare portraits of the dead and the usurping King of Denmark in the so-called "closet scene."[7] Frankenstein's creature extends and further develops precisely these "Gothic" transfigurations of Shakespeare. The monster is, like Alfonso's ghost at its fullest, a larger-than-life-size stitching together of dead body-parts torn from their "natural" former owners. It/he also haunts his guilty maker, as Ricardo haunts Manfred, by being an artificial "portrait" of dead life set in motion, the phantasm of an act of counterfeiting.[8]

Once these basic reconstructions of Walpole's recastings become clear for the reader of *Frankenstein*, other "ghostings" of *Otranto*'s uprooted signifiers become quite prominent in Mary Shelley's creation scene. There we find a night-time "light of the moon" that again serves to reveal a large, upright, but fragmentary shape; the "inarticulate sounds" of the monster that recall the mysterious "rustling sound" of the big helmet's plumes; the "breathing" and "convulsive motion" of the awakening creature that echo the way the figure in the portrait "heaved its breast" and "began to move"; and the reaching for communication (the stretched-out hand) that leads in both works to a sudden breaking of contact, to signifers (the "making of signs") seeming yet failing to refer to signifieds or counterparts, as opposed to the revelations in the father-son dialogue that immediately follow Hamlet's first sighting of the Ghost in Shakespeare (*Hamlet*, 1.5.1–91). What all these moments have most in common is a quality basic to the fragmented figures of artificial life at the heart of both scenes: their offering of a representation that at first exposes no signified beyond itself or beyond another signifier, as in the reference of Walpole's huge ghostly fragments only to the armored effigy of Alfonso on his tomb beneath Otranto and its abbey (*The Castle*, 18). In both *Frankenstein* and *The Castle of Otranto*, the initial "horror" of the hero at the emergence of a ghost of counterfeit being is like "the reaction of a reader who finds the letters on a page [losing] their meaning as they lose their ground in a referential depth and order."[9] Communicable signification *must* be initially impossible – the Gothic must be partly *about* "the growing gap between word and thing"[10] – because what Walpolean Gothic heroes and heroines are haunted by most apparently, even in *Frankenstein*, is a pervasively counterfeit existence: the fact of signifiers referring back to signifiers, none of which contain or connect to their own meanings in the ways their users and observers assume they do or wish they would.

Then, too, *Frankenstein* replays *The Castle*, along with some of *Otranto*'s echoes of *Hamlet*, at the level of the basic transgressions to which the ghosts of ghosts refer. Granted, the primal crime for Walpole, the poisoning of Alfonso by Ricardo (his chamberlain) and the shifting of castle ownership from the heirs of the former to the heirs of the latter (*The Castle*, 109), repeats the murder and usurpation of old King Hamlet by his brother Claudius, though Ricardo and his progeny move more completely from one class to another. At the same time, however, Walpole places an emphasis far beyond Shakespeare's on the movements of ghosts as immediate reactions to the attempted misuse of a woman. It is the near-"seizure" of Isabella twice in the above passage from *The Castle* that makes the helmet's plumes "tempestuous" and the portrait heave a sigh. Walpole has turned Claudius' semi-incestuous seduction of Gertrude into Manfred's effort to force sex and marriage on Isabella, the daughter of a rival claimant to the castle, so that Manfred may produce male heirs to shore up the retention of Otranto by Ricardo's line (*The Castle*, 22–23). Manfred's pursuit is never loving and only marginally lustful; Isabella attracts him almost solely as an instrument for his holding on to property, and his own daughter, Matilda, is of use to him only if she is willing to accept a forced marriage, as part of a property alliance, with Frederic, Isabella's father (*The Castle*, 90–92) – a major reason for the (in)famous interchangeability of Isabella and Matilda throughout *The Castle of Otranto*. Compared to Gertrude and Ophelia in *Hamlet*, these women are versions of each other less as names of "frailty" – less as scapegoats for the inconsistency, concupiscence, and deceptive appearances which *men* seek to transfer from themselves *onto* "woman"[11] – and more as commodity objects within a "traffic in women."[12] Foreshadowing some of the heroines in later Gothic novels *by* women, Matilda and Isabella have meaning outside themselves mostly as positioned and exchanged "between men" for the sake of dynastic and property, or other "homosocial," interactions among males alone.[13] Walpole's women are thereby refashioned, since they are really made coins of exchange,[14] into counterfeits of counterfeits (falsified and falsifiable women able to be

substituted one for another) very like the signs of signs that the
ghosts of Alfonso and Ricardo are from the start.

Frankenstein takes this "Gothic" articulation of women as the
merest instruments for men and makes it basic to Victor's primal
crime by giving it another turn of the screw. First Mary Shelley
transforms this instrumentality into Victor's production of a counterfeit person using "instruments of life" that are entirely masculine or
inhuman (*Frankenstein*, 52). Then she compounds that masturbatory
outrage by having her monster request a *man*-made female counterpart for himself, the potential, albeit counterfeit, mother of *his* future
progeny (Victor's view of her on 163); such is the creature's price,
and thus Victor's payment, for settling the dispute between creator
and creation (again "between men"). The usurpation of "true" male
lineage as an original "Gothic sin" bound up with the reduction of
women to instruments now becomes the male "attempt to usurp the
power of women" to give birth,[15] even to become the manufacturer
of future counterfeit women as objects of exchange – a counterfeiting
of pregnancy and delivery by a "sublimated womb."[16] It is this
intensification of Walpole's recoinable female which most directly
breathes life into Mary Shelley's counterfeit being.

The creation scene in *Frankenstein* even extends Manfred's earliest
attempt to turn a living woman into a hollowed out figure: the near-
killing of Isabella in his initial pursuit of her. Her "hand" is "cold"
when it is first "seized" because she is "half-dead with fright and
horror" at a false Prince's attempt to use her as a means to property
and progeny. The most analyzed moment in *Frankenstein* strikingly
echoes this basic "Gothic" potential for transforming a woman into
a dead body. Between the stirring of the creature on Victor's
laboratory table and the looming of the monster's grinning visage at
the foot of his creator's bed, the exhausted Victor falls into a dream:

I thought I saw Elizabeth [Victor's "intended"], in the bloom of health,
walking in the streets of Ingolstadt. Delighted and surprised, I embraced
her; but as I implanted the first kiss on her lips, they became livid with the
hue of death; her features appeared to change, and I thought that I held
the corpse of my dead mother in my arms; a shroud enveloped her form,
and I saw the grave-worms crawling in the folds of the flannel. (*Frankenstein*,
53)

Whatever the many insights that traditional psychoanalytic readings
have drawn from *this* interchangeability of female figures,[17] its status
as pointing to an unconscious root-desire behind the construction

and features of the monster also recalls, even as Victor tries to displace and deny, the Walpolean desire to use a woman sexually-but-instrumentally that turns her from a young lady to a virtual corpse before Manfred's eyes.[18]

After all, the first chase-scene in *The Castle* is but a prelude to Manfred's final and most deadly pursuit of a fleeing girl. Though he takes this young woman in the last chapter to be Isabella still in the act of resisting his suit, she turns out to be his daughter, Matilda (whose "features appear to change"), precisely at the moment he stabs her to death before the underground tomb of Alfonso. At this point (*The Castle*, 104) Manfred instantly becomes a "Savage, inhuman monster" (a pre-creature) in the eyes of young Theodore, the suitor of Matilda and later the "disconsolate" new Prince of Otranto. Theodore, in turn (by now a pre-Victor), finally accepts betrothal to Isabella only as the merest substitute for marriage to the dead Matilda, for whom he still longs in an incurable "melancholy" that entirely possesses him as *The Castle of Otranto* ends (110). Yes, Victor Frankenstein can be psychoanalyzed as a melancholic who has so introjected his dead maternal origin that he must continually seek *and* reject substitutes for it (Elizabeth, the creature) for the sake of still trying to re-embrace, while also working to throw off, the Mother only partly embodied by them (the woman by Elizabeth, her dead body by the creature, and both by the *female* creature whom Victor destroys while creating). But this psychology would not have occurred in the form it assumes in *Frankenstein*, nor would this novel have so strongly helped to inspire the forms of psychoanalysis that now read it this way, if the "materials [had not], in the first place, be[en] afforded" (Mary Shelley, 1831 Preface, *Frankenstein*, 226), if Walpole's neo-Gothic had not provided, partly by recasting Hamlet's sense of his mother in Shakespeare, the interchangeability of women for male desire, the pushing of an instrumentalized woman towards a death-state that becomes the death of another woman, the connection of male "monstrosity" (including an incest-drive) with this transformation, and the young hero in quest of his "true being" and origins who apparently finds them only in a sort of marriage with a substitute, a counterfeit, for a dead love-object. Gothic ghosts of counterfeit existence seem to walk forth, as early as *The Castle of Otranto* and at least as late as *Frankenstein*, as bound up with – indeed, as manifestations of – exchangeable femininity and the turning of *eros* into a death-drive as male desire moves from one counterfeit to another, especially from one counterfeit of woman to another.

III THE ABJECTED "SUBSTANCE" IN *FRANKENSTEIN'S* COUNTERFEIT

At the same time, the "grounding" of *Frankenstein* in falsifying uses of the feminine body also marks a point of divergence where Mary Shelley's novel surpasses the Walpolean Gothic. Isabella and Matilda may become images of death much like the ghosts of Alfonso and Ricardo, but as Victor Frankenstein's dream presses beyond figures of the creature and Elizabeth to the maternal body, the "shroud" that seems to conceal the ultimate love-object reveals "grave-worms crawling in the folds," referring to the gross otherness of bodily decay in ways no symbol in Walpole does. To be sure, Matilda's death is anticipated and Frederic's marriage to her is prevented in *The Castle of Otranto* by the appearance of the ghost of the long-dead Hermit of Joppa, a "figure" with "the fleshless jaws and empty sockets of a skeleton" (*The Castle*, 102). But this third specter of Walpole's, really just a skull in a cowl, is primarily a conventional and quasi-medieval emblem intoning that death is the wages of sin (especially the sin about to be committed by Frederic and Manfred in their proposed exchange of daughters) and serving to remind Frederic of "the behest of heaven engraven" on the large buried sword that led him to Otranto after the dying Hermit helped him dig it up (*The Castle*, 77–79). Like the ghost of the portrait and the fragmented pieces of the effigy on Alfonso's tomb, the skeletal Hermit is a figure of other figures much more than he is a body in decay (indeed, he is *past* decay).[19] Frankenstein's dream-desire *both* keeps maternal decay covered by its signs (the shroud, Elizabeth, the creature, the large and small portraits of Victor's mother [*Frankenstein*, 73, 78, 139]) *and* points to that worm-infested, feminine dissolution, not to mention Victor's necrophilia towards it, as a referent, however hidden, that, like an alien horror, invades the space of some of the signifiers trying to be separate from it.

It seems as if Mary Shelley is returning the Walpolean ghost of the counterfeit of death to the attempted physical references (the "bones" that are mentioned) in Hamlet's first speech to his father's Ghost. As it happens, though, the kind of reference attempted by the "ghostly" symbols in *Frankenstein* is more a combination of brutal concreteness *and* the separation of signifiers from referents. Hamlet's reference to his father's corpse stops well short of mouldering decay. The features of dissolution there are "canoniz'd" and "hearsed" within "cerements," already contained by the cultural management of them in symbolic, religious envelopes. In contrast to this Shakespearean and the Walpolean sign of the dead, the worms in Victor's dream of his mother's corpse are harrowingly immediate and almost fully uncovered – even as the approach to them is mediated by figures, such as the "blooming" Elizabeth and the grinning face of the creature, which keep them at a distance while referring to them as well.

Then, too, the creature's visage, taken by itself, is even more anomolous in its capacities to refer beyond its surface. Unlike the opaque flatness or layers of mere signs in Walpole's ghosts of counterfeits, the skin of Frankenstein's monster "scarcely covered the work of muscles and arteries beneath." These multiple organs and bodily functions manifestly show through, even though they were not supposed to, much as the worms penetrate the shroud of the dead mother or the thin skin of premature infants reveals the complex tangle of body-parts that it covers. Moreover, the racial otherness of the creature, the specific physicality of his "irreconcilable [ethnic] diversity" (Cottom, "Monster of Representation," 61), forces itself on his creator's attention in "his yellow skin," his non-Asian "flowing" hair, and his "straight black lips." True, by the standards that Victor first sets for his representation of life – the construction of a cohesive "being like myself" which will demonstrate the "causation" of existence while being recognizably "human," all with the unified identity of a "new species" (*Frankenstein*, 47–49) – the "inarticulate" creature is a failure of representation, a divorce of the visible signifier(s) from the signifieds and referents originally sought, as are the ghost of Ricardo's portrait and the fragments of Alfonso's effigy in *The Castle of Otranto*. Even so, this monster's half-transparent, "shrivelled" visage composed from fragments of other (and dead) figures does refer, with astonishing precision, to a series of culturally suppressed but very substantial "realities," different ones of which are emphasized by different interpreters of *Frankenstein*.

Indeed, the creature's counterfeit form suggests, while also concealing and *not* being, a host of "othered" levels of existence that are, in the words of David Musselwhite, simultaneously "prescribed and proscribed by the facile categorizings of the [hegemonic] social and cultural order."[20] Especially by embodying the contents of his maker's dream, he/it is and is not the multiplicity of the human body (revealing it to be a *corps morcele* rooted in and susceptible to fragmentation); the incestuous desire for reincorporation with the mother; the attractiveness *and* repulsiveness of the death in that return to the site of birth; the sense of birth as inseparable from a movement towards death; the postpartem horrors of the birth-process, with what was "inside" (including death) now existing "outside" (as living death); the conflation of the masculine with the feminine (a gender-confusion) in the primal relation of son and mother; the placement of a constructed male (the creature) in a female position (that of the love-object/mother), with suggestions of homosexual, as well as incestuous, desire; the condition of existing between and across different races; the state of the gigantic laboring classes uprooted by economic change that are created, colonized, and then (ab)used by the social "science" of the bourgeoisie and capitalist gentry; the attempt both to construct and to deny such a "child" of upper-middle-class aspirations; the transformation of "creation" (supposedly the embodiment of the laborer's work) into "production" (the alienation and wandering of the product from the laborer); the consequent confusion of "sexual reproduction [with] social subject-production" (Spivak, " Three Women's Texts," 259); and the contradictory, even violent energies in individuals and a social order torn between conflicting ideologies over what the "human sciences" do and should reveal about the nature of existence at the start of the nineteenth century.[21] The creature is a "monster" in that it/he embodies *and* distances "all that a society refuses to name" – all the betwixt-and-between, even ambisexual, cross-class, and cross-cultural conditions of life that Western culture "abjects," as Kristeva would put it – "not just because its very heterogeneity, mobility, and power [are] a threat to that society but" because it/he also implies and sequesters "the very flux[es] of energy that made society possible" in ways that hegemonic culture will not recognize (Musselwhite, *Partings Welded Together*, 59).

Frankenstein as "Gothic" thus presents us with an extreme contra-diction that still needs an explanation, despite the many recent interpretations of the novel and its Gothic antecedents. On the one hand, very much like Walpole's figures of older figures, the creature as a specter of counterfeit life is "a sign detached from a visual or verbal grammar" that would immediately explain it/him coherently (Mellor, *Mary Shelley*, 128). He/it enters and is "a construct of signifiers which figures his initial want and lack without fulfilling it"[22] and so can be known, as the primal truth about Alfonso and Ricardo is known from an "authentic writing" (*The Castle*, 110), only as a text referred to many other texts by himself, his creator, and his observers or readers.[23] On the other hand, "the Creature is a figuration . . . more sublimely literal than [most of his] original[s]" (Sherwin, "*Frankenstein*," 901). It/he is "the *absolutely* Other" (Spivak, "Three Women's Texts," 258, my emphasis) pointing immediately, as we have just seen, to intermixed and repressed states of being, the divisibility of the body, "thrown down" social groups, class struggles, gender-confusions, birth-moments, and death-drives (or longings for each of these), as well as to a cacaphony of ideological and intertextual differences. All the while, though, he/it both re-presents each of these alterities *and* keeps them at a great remove by being quasi-human yet strictly artificial. It/he is still a Gothic ghost of a counterfeit, drawn towards yet "protect[ed] from the reality it describes by casting a veil over" it (Montag, " 'Workshop of Filthy Creation'," 309), like the shroud cast over the worm-eaten body of the mother in Victor's dream. *Frankenstein* works to pull readers towards reality's darknesses, but it is equally drawn to, indeed perpetually haunted by, the earlier Gothic signifier and its loss of the increasingly distant past or ground which all such ghosts seem to recall. We now need to decide how the latter led to the former, how the contradiction of the "counterfeit of the abject" came to exist in one of the most influential achievements of Gothic *and* counter-Gothic writing. We need to determine, in other words, in what ways the ghost of the counterfeit enables the abjection it comes to manifest and sequester. We can do that by looking more closely, first, at *Frankenstein*'s point of departure: the Walpolean recasting of Shakespeare and the conflicted assumptions behind it and its most immediate progeny. Then we can examine how the post-Renaissance counterfeit produces a symbolic scheme that allows increasing abjections into its depths *and* how more and more anomalies of pre-industrial being are consequently "thrown off" into Gothic ghosts of counterfeits during the ascendance of English Romanticism, particularly in *Frankenstein*.

IV THE GHOST OF THE COUNTERFEIT IN THE GOTHIC

The Walpolean counterfeit Gothic arises at a time in the European understanding of signs and culture when the notion of symbols as counterfeits since the time of Shakespeare is starting to change into a later assumption. In his intriguing history of how signs have been viewed as relating to their referents in the Anglo-European West since the Middle Ages, Jean Baudrillard finds the tacit sense that signification is and should be "counterfeit" to be the most widely accepted conscious *or* pre-conscious belief about signs from the Renaissance through the dawn of industrial manufacture.[24] Thinking in terms of the counterfeit meant viewing signs the way Hamlet sees the Ghost and its "counterfeit" portrait: as beckoning us towards an image's "determinate links to the world" ("I'll call thee Hamlet, / King, father, royal Dane") yet as finally harboring only a "nostalgia" for (and thus the specter of) a predetermined social or "natural" ground (Baudrillard, "Structural Law of Value," 62). Meaning as counterfeit emerged in the Renaissance of the literate classes, as in that era's promotion of personal "self-fashioning" through a *re*fashioned classical rhetoric,[25] because that period, especially in England by the sixteenth century, saw the first widespread effulgence of a truly mercantile or early-capitalist economy and the assumptions it demanded or allowed. Educated Europeans felt they were leaving behind the eras of what Baudrillard has called the "*bound* sign," the notion of sets of signifiers as referring to an ordained "situation" or "status" where "assignation [was] total, mobility nil" (Baudrillard, "Structural Law of Value," 61). Status and the signs of cultural capital (including the rhetoric) associated with it came to be regarded as more transferable depending on economic success and acquisition. The strict "endogamy of the sign proper to orders of status" now gave way to "the transition of the sign-values of prestige from one class to another" (Baudrillard, "Structural Law of Value," 62). Signs could therefore serve, as they do in *Hamlet*, both as partially empty recollections of former statuses (being still *nostalgic* for absolute grounds for themselves) and as announcements of "natures" that could seem recoined, rhetorically transformed, or simply masked (counterfeited into a "questionable shape") by new displays of social position that reused the signifiers of older ones.

It is this duplicity of drives in the counterfeit that the eighteenth-century British "Gothic," more blatantly than the other kinds of fictional discourse around it, takes to later extremes over a century and a half after *Hamlet* was first staged. At the same time, exploiting the transferability of the *un*bound counterfeit sign, the Gothic's re-counterfeitings make some crucial shifts that further uproot the nostalgic reference in the Renaissance "original." The *image* or *fragment* of that nostalgia takes over the position of the past referent in the neo-Gothic sign; hence the "grounding" of Gothic signifiers mostly in other signs, the pointing of Walpole's ghosts to portraits or divisible effigies, or to earlier authors' ghosts, instead of "natural" persons and their statuses. Indeed, throughout the neo-Gothic "revival" in the eighteenth century, the remnant of "bound-sign" and "natural" meaning is replaced as the "Gothic" sign's point of reference by counterfeits *of* that remnant: pictures of ancestors, restagings of Renaissance plays, words or illustrations in books (such as editions of Shakespeare or pictorial accounts of "Gothic" archi-tecture), falsely "authentic" reproductions (including sham Gothic ruins and Macpherson's "Ossian"), or pieces broken off of archaic structures and reassembled differently, particularly in Walpole's (in)famous toy-Gothic mansion at Strawberry Hill.[26] The supposed medieval "endogamy" of sign and status (or self and "natural" origin) is reduced to a trace of itself, left to be both vaguely longed for and almost entirely, though never quite, thrown away. Walpole's attraction to the Gothic, he tells us in his letters, is to the relics of "centuries that cannot disappoint one," because "the dead" are now so disembodied, so merely imaged, that there is no reason "to quarrel with their emptiness" (*Yale Walpole*, X: 192). Thus, when he writes *The Castle of Otranto*, he feels free to use the Catholic iconography of a "form of Saint Nicholas" watching over and finally "receiving Alfonso's shade" (*The Castle*, 108), even though as an Anglican he flatly rejects such a symbol's claim to truth. His reference to (for him) an antiquated belief-system, as in the reference of his ghosts to portraits, effigies, and outdated emblems of sin, assumes from the start the already broken, empty, and (often) fake nature of the icons he adopts and refashions.

The counterfeit, or more precisely the Renaissance counterfeit of the medieval, has now become the "signified" of the Gothic signifier, so the Gothic is haunted by the ghost of that already spectral past – and thus by its refaking of what is already fake and already an emblem of the nearly empty and dead. Especially in *The Castle of*

Otranto, the Gothic reflects, on the one hand, a longing for the supposed securities of the "bound" medieval sign now fading almost completely behind the surfaces of Renaissance representations and, on the other, the opportunistic manipulation of old symbols for a newer class-climbing acqusitiveness (Ricardo's and Manfred's, not to mention Walpole's own). The "Gothic revival" occurs in a world of increasingly bourgeois "free market" enterprise trying to look like a process sanctioned by more ancient imperatives yet also striving to regard the old icons as empty of meaning whenever they inhibit post-Renaissance Anglican acquisition. Walpole replaces the Preface to his First Edition of *The Castle*, the one where he pretends under a pseudonym to be the translator of an equally non-existent Renaissance manuscript (3–6), with a second Preface (1765) that acknowledges the fakery of the first and then applies the "Gothic" label to his series of counterfeitings, mainly as a consequence of – and a way to further – the success of Walpole's "little piece" in the marketplace (like that of a well-circulated coin; *The Castle*, 7). The new Preface and the "Gothic" designation, in fact, along with Walpole's famous proposal for combining the "ancient and modern" forms of "romance," strive to promote more market success in the name of an even wider free enterprise. The now identified "author" trumpets how "desirous" he is to leave "the great resources" and "powers of the fancy at liberty to expatiate through the boundless realms of invention" on the basis of both established *and* emergent standards in Shakespearean drama and "romantic story" (Preface to the Second Edition, *The Castle*, 7–8).

No wonder Emma J. Clery sees Walpole's second Preface as assuming "infinite vistas of commercial expansion" after its writer had "spotted a gap in the market" and had come to see "fancy" as a form of "wealth" able to be invested and *re*invested in the "commodity" of "fiction."[27] The Renaissance counterfeit's hesitation between nostalgia for the medieval self-and-status link and the transfer of older signs of status from people of one class to people of another has become the "Gothic" aporia between counterfeits of the old nostalgia (signs of what has become empty, even as its remnants still beckon) and recoinings of such bogus archaisms into commodifiable signifiers able to "expatiate" (or "spread out" rootlessly) in a market circulation where "Gothic" fictions can now be reproduced from a mold "grounded" in the refaking of fakes. The several recent analyses of Gothic fiction and theater as oscillating between "conflicting codes of representation or discourses"[28] are all based on this fundamental neo-Gothic interplay of regression towards the counterfeit of a past, on the one hand, and the irreverant use of the counterfeit's images as cultural capital for "free" circulation and profit, on the other.

Here, then, in the anomalous "ghost of the counterfeit," lies the symbolic and ideological mechanism by the which the neo-Gothic mediates between social and cultural orders that are either fading into the past, as they were starting to in the Renaissance (the priestly and the old aristocratic), or rising into dominance (the capitalist and the pre-industrial). In this transition, the Gothic carries the counterfeit's increasing preference for less "bound" signification towards its (il)logical conclusion and so moves towards the more newly emergent sense of the sign, the counterfeit's replacement: the view of the signifier as fundamentally a "simulacrum" (Baudrillard, "Structural Law of Value," 62–64) able to be industrially reproduced on the basis of a pattern or mold that is itself a counterfeit of the counterfeit.[29] Almost all the Gothic fictions written in the wake of *The Castle of Otranto*, as a result, have the same generally Renaissance (and fake) reference point with a jaundiced sense of its nostalgia for an older stability, now gone except for its fragments. At the same time, these "Gothics" also show an awareness that such nostalgia is based on inauthentic signs of already empty forms and is connected to motives of capital acquisition that mechanically reproduce the simulacra of the past to extend the boundaries of the present self's quest for upward mobility. Ann Radcliffe's novels of the 1790s, for example, though they are usually "haunted" by remembered older events, take place before continental backdrops set no earlier than the sixteenth century. These are "grounded" in more recent travel accounts and pictures, never eyewitness observations; as Terry Castle has noted,[30] all aspects of "outside reality" in Radcliffe's Gothic (scenery, edifices, people, memories, documents) are "spectral" – ghostings of the already counterfeit, I would prefer to say – so much so that "every other looks like every other other" in her fiction, to a point where Radcliffe's contemporaries, readers, and successors are inclined to seek "mechanical means [including a flood of Gothic novels] to reduplicate [her and their phantasmic] images of the world" (Castle, "Spectralization of the Other," 238 and 251) Radcliffe's spectral settings, too, are threateningly laden with old Catholic symbols and structures, counterfeit icons for her as much as for Walpole. These have to be exposed as fakes by the ends of her books, even as their attraction is admitted, for social power to be achieved by the heroines and heroes (and readers, vicariously) involved in acquisitive searches for the highest class positions and the most property available to them through the "decent" (as opposed to blatantly manipulative) possession of old counterfeit signs.

Frankenstein certainly continues this "Gothic" ghosting and remarketing of the counterfeit, even to the point of showing the ghost of the counterfeit turning into the simulacrum of industrialized reproduction. The construction of the creature is modelled only somewhat on the Erasmus-Darwin reanimations of dead tissue discussed at the Villa Diodati in 1816. The most immediate "sources" of Victor's artificial man come from his reading (*Frankenstein*, 32–34) in the mostly Renaissance alchemies of Albertus Magnus (d. 1280), Cornelius Agrippa (d. 1535), and Paracelsus (d. 1541). Each of these figures claims or is said to have temporarily generated a mechanical man (Magnus) or a full-bodied demon (Agrippa) or a semi-"transparent" *homunculus* (Paracelsus) to demonstrate or experiment with the genesis of physical life – yet only as these authors have added their own warnings that such efforts are fraudulent and presumptuous attempts to duplicate the power of God,[31] only as such models come to Victor colored by the "modern" condemnation of them as falsities by "the more rational theory of chemistry" (*Frankenstein*, 33), and only as they are reused by the eighteenth-century middle-class scientist to help lift (or *sublimate*) his endeavors from being "realities of little worth" into becoming achievements of "boundless grandeur" (*Frankenstein*, 41). Now we see most clearly why the creature, as an experiment based on incompatible ideologies of "science," is unable to represent the "causes" he is originally supposed to embody. Like English Gothic fiction generally, he/it is a re-counterfeiting of late medieval or Renaissance counterfeits that both desire and deny the reality and accessibility of their references to older or higher grounds of being. It/he also points to how much his remodelling of counterfeits is connected to an acquisitive drive in Frankenstein himself to reconnect fragments of the past in a faked "source of life" so as to achieve a class-leap, or at least a rhetorical advance (an "expatiation"), from bourgeois student to industrial patriarch ("creator and source" of a manufactured "new species"; *Frankenstein*, 49). In addition, as an extension of this self-marketing with counterfeits, Victor's creature is constructed as a prototype (or mold), the basis of a counterfeit becoming an industrial simulacrum. Frankenstein, the pre-industrial scientist-entrepreneur, thereby hopes that a "new race" of figures can be reproduced from his monster's artificial standard, provided that biological reproduction (based on the male monster uniting with a female counterpart) can first be mechanically reproduced by way of a simulacrum of already falsified and instrumentalized womanhood.

The Renaissance counterfeiting and the neo-Gothic recounterfeiting of women, after all, provide especially revealing examples of what it really means in Western signification – and the Gothic – to move from the Renaissance counterfeit to the ghost of the counterfeit to the early industrial simulacrum. In all these and in other modes of producing symbols, as Simone de Beauvoir first saw most completely, woman has been made the "other" of the male "master term" and hence the supposed locus of human multiplicity as opposed to "male unity."[32] "She" is made to embody all the necessary relations of self to other and thus the primordial otherness *within* any construction of a self, in part because biological woman is able to bring forth a different human being out of herself from within herself. During the Renaissance and especially in *Hamlet*, this "othering" is already so "natural" (a culturally established counterfeit "nature of things," to be sure) that the central male figure can displace and scapegoat all of his own differences from himself onto the other that is supposedly woman, not only when he incarnates all "frailty" in her but when he shuffles off his doubts and fears about the impending final duel with "it is such a kind of gainsgiving as would perhaps trouble a woman" (*Hamlet*, 5.2.211–12). This fakery is augmented in Shakespearean drama too, of course, by the fact that the "women" on the stage were played by young men. These "boys of the company" were regarded at the time as enacting a transition away from ambisexual hermaphrodism, the widely accepted androgyny of both sexes in childhood, towards an eventual throwing off of "feminine" elements that was not yet complete, just as Stephen Greenblatt has shown.[33] Establishing woman as inconsistent "other" compared to fully grown, apparently coherent "man" by the time of *Hamlet*, in other words, meant casting the multiplicity of all human youth onto "the feminine" alone, especially in staged representations of women. It was as though the mix in pre-adolescent being were finally an "aberrant" state (Greenblatt's word) which must be sequestered only in woman when adulthood arrives – a supposedly biological destiny that was entirely a social, and again a counterfeit, construction.

The Renaissance counterfeit, then, while claiming to point in part to "natural" status-distinctions once fixed in the past, was also the fabricator and dramatizer of the *fakes* of such distinctions. It helped produce the fiction of "real, eternal" gender differences out of an admitted intermixture of sexual elements in the human being as it developed from birth through adolescence. The ghost of that counterfeit in the eighteenth-century Gothic takes this fictional "othering" of the feminine and turns the resulting difference-from-herself-*in*-herself into an otherness common to every female "other" and thus the exchangeability of one woman for another, now more completely in the service of man-to-man interactions seeking the acquisition of property, capital, and power through the possession of her otherness as common coin, albeit under the cover of a quasi-medieval world. This recounterfeiting, with woman now pulled towards becoming a nearly bodiless, spectral object of exchange (the death of herself as a body independent of masculine property), sets the stage for the mechanical male reproduction of the feminine birth-process and of the body of woman herself, exactly as Mary Shelley reveals in *Frankenstein* at the very time the industrial revolution begins to accelerate. The "otherness" of woman, always counterfeited anyway, comes virtually to epitomize the hidden basis and complex development of the counterfeit symbol. As in Gertrude and Ophelia (and the denied part of Hamlet), Matilda and Isabella, or Elizabeth and Victor's dead mother (and their reincarnations in the creature and his desire for a man-made bride), woman in the Gothic and its sources is *both* an increasingly spectral and manufactured image of the feminine, her dis-embodiment or death, *and* the "other" of the counterfeit and its spectres – certainly the "other" of the creature in Frankenstein's dream – in which the differences of ghosts of the counterfeit from themselves are incarnated and secreted at the same time. Here, in fact, is one way in which the use of women in the Gothic points ultimately to images of mere images *and* to levels of abjected physical and cultural life. Through the spectral counterfeiting of woman and her constantly recreated role as the symbol of multiple otherness, we begin to see how the ghost of the counterfeit so readily becomes the site of the abject in Gothic writing.

V THE GHOST OF THE COUNTERFEIT AS THE LOCUS OF ABJECTION: FROM THE WALPOLEAN TO THE GODWINIAN-SHELLEYAN GOTHIC

In Kristeva's suggestive vision of what "the abject" is (a "thrown off" or "thrown under" form of a dimly recalled and feared multiplicity), there are many betwixt-and-between conditions of life in which it reappears – and behind which it disappears too – as we find in the numerous heterogeneities "othered" into Frankenstein's monster. All of these conditions for Kristeva, though, echo or re-enact the most primordial form of being half-"inside" and half-"outside": the "heterogenous flux" of being partly held inwards and partly pushed outwards by the mother's body at the moment of birth (Kristeva, *Powers of Horror*, 10) *and* the state, at the same time, of emerging *out* of death (pre-natal non-existence) and starting to live *towards* death (the end-point of all the "want" that begins at birth; Kristeva, *Powers of Horror*, 23). This liminal condition of multiple contradictions, where each supposedly distinct state slides over into its "other," is the radical heterogeneity, just barely recalled in the somatic memory, from which a person is never entirely removed yet must work to feel "separated . . . in order to be" a coherent, identifiable being (Kristeva, *Powers of Horror*, 10). Mary Shelley's creature indicates many personal and cultural forms of this "im-possible" between-ness because it/he, first of all, both distances and manifests his creator's (and other people's) return to and avoidance of the emergence from the mother by being the product of a faked birth-process that strives not to be maternal. Moreover, he/it incarnates and disguises Frankenstein's attempt to rise "sublimely" above *and* reembrace "lower" death all at once by recalling both the shrouded body of the worm-eaten mother and the combined body-parts of mostly lower-class people and animals acquired from "charnel houses," "the dissecting room," and "slaughter houses" (*Frankenstein*, 50; see also Marshall, "*Frankenstein*," 59–64). The creature is finally a site of abjec*tion* (the placement, or really *dis*placement, of the abject) because he is an "other" into which these personal anomalies are artificially "jettisoned . . . into an abominable real," one so *absolutely* other as to seem *un*real. It is only such an unreal/real (such an *uncanny* or "unfamiliar familiar") that "keeps the self from foundering" in the abject "by making it repugnant" (Kristeva, *Powers of Horror*, 9). Indeed, it is only in using such a "monster" as a place for the "thrown off" that Victor and others can keep from foundering in *all* the personal or social conditions connected to them which threaten to tear them to pieces in tugs-of-war between incompatible states of being. That is why the creature is the "alien," yet "native" corpus and corpse of the contradictory states in the early nineteenth century of being self-*and*-other, masculine-*and*-feminine, life-affirming *and* death-seeking, whole-*and*-fragmented, high-class *and* low-class, master-*and*-slave, or biologically-*and*-mechanically reproduced, the anomalous conditions he/it was created to deny – or at least to conceal.

The way the ghost of the counterfeit in the Walpolean Gothic has been constructed over time, we can now see, establishes the symbolic parameters for this complex refabrication/concealment of the betwixt-and-betweenness of being that must supposedly be desired and expelled prior to any human attempts to assert an identity. Abjected half-inside/half-outside conditions can be "thrown" into ghosts of counterfeits because the counterfeit and especially its ghost, as processes of signification, are *already* betwixt-and-between interactions of regressions towards and distancings of the past. The counterfeit, at its earliest point, offers a belated nostalgia for a self "bound" to its others (its statuses) that is like the child's "outside" longing for oneness with the "inside" of its primordial mother. Yet there is also the countering drive in the counterfeit, and even more in its ghost, whereby selves or signs, like infants only partly "inside" mother, strive to throw these past bonds away, to break "outside" them (albeit with lingering memories of them) towards a "free market" quest for self-definition by way of the fragments of older, as well as newer, signifiers. In this progression, particularly in the Gothic ghost of the counterfeit, the always already counterfeited past turns increasingly into the locus of its own death. The body of the maternal/historical "origin" becomes the empty sepulchre of itself, and death (behind the vacated sign) thus becomes the origin and the object of nostalgic desire. At the same time, this fragmentation of the supposed original relation between signifier/signified and outside/inside makes the increasingly "floating" signifier or self carry its otherness-from-itself with it, desirous of but torn from a stable past meaning now irretrievably dead. The self or sign remains haunted, however faintly, by a multifarious betwixt-and-betweenness in its nature and a death at the beginning and end of that nature, even as each one moves towards "freer" economic recirculation in early capitalist relationships with other such signs.

The signifier/self in this symbolic scheme wants to increase its mobility towards a status (such as that of the "father" of a new genre or race) vaguely promised by emergent "free market" conditions. It therefore seeks to throw off its othernesses-from-itself and the draw of a lingering relation to death *and* to do so in recastings of the very archaic and fragmented signs in which the multiplicity of the self seems to be both grounded and *un*grounded. The result can seem, on the one hand, a triumphant repossession of remnants of the past in an announcement of new and reproducible recombinations of its uprooted pieces, as in Walpole's creation of his quasi-Catholic "Gothic Story" and Victor Frankenstein's production of his semi-alchemical creature. On the other hand, the same effort involves a displacement of personal and cultural contradictions, including the dread of *and* desire for the past and the death still dimly connected to present life, into the ghost-figures within the new construct that seem at first to be especially empty of older meanings and archaically "other" than the self. The very conception and symbolic enactment of abjection, it turns out, as a process in the post-Walpolean Gothic and in Kristevan analysis, like the Freudian production of the unconscious as a haunted *anderer Schauplatz*,[34] can occur only because the counterfeit and its Gothic ghost first developed as the cultural modes of production we now see them to be. The abject (and its monstrous embodiments) could not have been proposed as a locus for the most basic repressed contradictions – and certainly not for versions of being inside and outside the fading moment of birth and the looming of primordial death in a woman's body – unless there was first the nostalgic/pre-industrial "living death" of the counterfeit shading into the ghost of itself and thereby offering the specter of a hesitation between a primal "bound" meaning, its sepulchral remainders, and the "unbound," but still partly regressive, reproduction of those signs.

Within its constructed "nature," after all, this palimpsest of figures has to deal with the paradox of its every layer being other than itself. It does so by allowing for the placement of that otherness as a "cause" (as an *original* inside/outside death-in-life) in the past situation where the old bound sign supposedly existed, whether or not it had the "nature" that is now retrojected into it. It is in this retrojection that the counterfeit and its specter make particular use of the figure of woman. As we have noted, Shakespeare's Hamlet locates the crime *behind* the primal crime against his father and his status in an "original" fallen human "frailty" that is transferred from males to females (with help, of course, from a long-standing Judeo-Christian tradition about the *first* woman's role in the Fall). That construction is so true for the Prince of Denmark that every kind of male anomaly is primordially caused by women as mothers *or* lovers, "for wise men know . . . what monsters [women] make of them" (*Hamlet*, 3.1.140–41). This fabrication, as we also know, is bound up with the Renaissance counterfeiting of primal human androgyny as finally an "origin" of difference from itself, actually the *counterfeit*'s difference from itself (as when the young men play women), that supposedly belongs to women exclusively and "originally" in the stagings of culture. Hence the Renaissance counterfeit, under male control of course, fashions *its* retrojection of its internal self-division by turning that plurality of being into the original, "natural," "bound" relation of woman to her supposed inconsistency, her greater otherness from herself which is really the counterfeit's alterity projected onto her.

By the time the counterfeit's ghost in Walpole's neo-Gothic, moreover, looks back to such a positioning of woman as signified body, the sequestering of this body into "original" otherness – that early step towards "abjecting" the maternal as the place of inside/outside – has become, in a more spectral form of it, the license for the turning of female forms into exchangable signifiers that also signify the threatened cultural effacement of the individual physical woman. "Natural" woman, already thrown into the primal past *as* an otherness by the counterfeit, now exists in the "Gothic Story" as the referent of a memorial discourse about the between-ness she once embodied that still threatens man, and even later women, with a backsliding fall away from steadiness of purpose. Walpole's Theodore is left with his desire for the dead Matilda whom Isabella ghosts and counterfeits only after confessions about the murder of Alfonso and the descent from him to Theodore solve the greatest mystery in *The Castle of Otranto*: not so much the killing of the original Prince, already hinted earlier (*The Castle*, 24), but the existence and nature of the Sicilian woman who secretly married Alfonso and bore him a daughter, Theodore's eventual mother. The long secrecy about this hidden cause documented in a supposedly "authentic writing" stems from Alfonso's decison "to conceal [his island] nuptials" because he "deem[ed] this amour incongruous with the holy vow of arms to which he was bound" on his way to the Holy Land, the site of his poisoning and the crafting of the "fictitious will" in his name (*The Castle*, 109–10). The original dead woman is covered by a series of counterfeitings about her (and *of* her) primarily as a result of her apparently placing the original dead man in an "incongruous" love-versus-duty oscillation between different codified positions, one island and domestic and the other mainland, martial, and religious. It is thus even less surprising than it has already seemed for *The Castle* to end with Theodore torn between a living counterfeit of his love-object (Isabella as one acquisition of his new property and inheritance status) and the mental image of his formerly "adored," but always inaccesible *and falsely* upper-class, Matilda. The most primal feminine condition in *The Castle*, "known" only through counterfeits, has turned out to be betwixt and between male-oriented codes and stances. To "be woman" in the first "Gothic Story" is to be shifted from one image of her in one context (a counterfeit) to another image of her in a different one (the counterfeit of a counterfeit) – which leaves the "other" one (supposedly the *older* counterfeit) as the locus of the "original" woman's death now recalled, though always as "incongruous," in another woman's image.

Mary Shelley's *Frankenstein*, as I have been suggesting, finally exposes this progression of the counterfeit and its placement of woman for what the whole codifying process has been and become in the Gothic and its ancestry (and elsewhere too). Victor Frankenstein's crafting of a ghost of earlier counterfeits of life "leaves out" the feminine only by casting it quite explicitly where the earlier Gothic ghost of the counterfeit has started to throw both woman and its own otherness from itself: into one figure, the creature, that obscurely refers back to the deep "incongruity" where multiple figures shift between differently coded positions, where love-object becomes dead mother, dead lower-class body fragments become an artifical middle-class science project, and a male visage becomes female features which become love-for-the-mother which becomes her corpse, with each "outside" being a version of its "inside," its buried other and mother. In this way, *Frankenstein* both culminates by exaggerating and critiques by exposing the dynamics of the ghost of the counterfeit in the neo-Gothic, including its way of rooting "monsters" in the "mothers" (the retrojected incongruities of coun-

terfeits) that supposedly "make" monsters of men in *Hamlet*. Mary
Shelley's chief method, as befits the contradictory generic base of
Frankenstein, is to offer counterfeit signs referring only to other
counterfeits, which is all that ghosts of counterfeits can really claim
to do, *and yet* to make those signs point, within and behind the masks
of their fakery, at the many substantial personal and cultural
incongruities which ghosts of counterfeits can be used to sequester in
1816–18 because of their long-standing ways of retrojecting and
burying the betwixt-and-betweenness of femininity, cultural change,
and counterfeiting itself.

For Mary Shelley, of course, to take the potential for this irony in
The Castle of Otranto and turn it into to the more "realized" counterfeit of the abject in *Frankenstein*, there had to be a series of
intervening steps, at least some of which were taken by writers who
were both well known to her and based in Walpole's Gothic. These
will have to be the subject of another study, but I can at least offer
some instances of how the counterfeit develops in the Gothic after
1765 and before 1816. Walpole himself, of course, helps begin the
transition, not just in the ways already suggested, but in using his
ghosts of counterfeits (including his main characters), somewhat as
Mary Shelley will use her creature. He employs them as falsely
antiquated and thus displaced and disguised "conflict zones" of
unresolved class and familial tensions, those multiple states of
between-ness spawned by the cultural transitions of his moment.
Leslie Fiedler and David Punter have shown especially well how
eighteenth-century anxieties about the legitimacy of the emergent
capitalist economic order as it overtook the dominance of the once-
feudal estate and the priesthood were retrojected in Walpole's
Gothic into uprooted icons of the ancestral past, along with some
of the newer inequities of property acquisition; that is why Walpole's Gothic suggests a Freudian Oedipal rivalry between old
aristocratic father-figures and seemingly upstart usurpers, with
women as disputed and even incestuous objects of desire pulled
between the male combatants of different generations and classes.[35]
I would add only that such displacements could not have happened
in the "Gothic" forms they take – and so the neo-Gothic would not
have happened in ways that could be thus read by Marxists *or*
Freudians – had not the symbolic mode of the ghost of the counterfeit, by declaring its own tensions with great force in the neo-
Gothic of the eighteenth century, forced the cultural conflicts of the

time into some of the shapes they assumed in Walpole and his immediate successors.

William Godwin, Mary Shelley's father, for example, fashions a highly Gothic male hero *and* monster all in one by making that figure, even more fully than Walpole makes the shade of Ricardo, the ghost of a counterfeit set in motion across history. In Godwin's most Gothic novel, *St. Leon: A Tale of the Sixteenth Century* (1799), the title character-narrator, supposedly modelled by the author on a portrait of him by Titian (*St. Leon*, I: iv–v),[36] is an acqusitive Renaissance entrepreneur always trying to recreate his waning aristocratic base with non-aristocratic currency. He perpetually "disguis[es even] to himself the real [mercantile] nature of his occupation" (I: 58) in times of transition between "the reign of chivalry" and "that of craft, dissimulation, corruption, and commerce" (I: 67). St. Leon finds he can continue that deception indefinitely only by reusing a now-discredited alchemy and accepting the elixir that will allow him to live forever. Henceforth he exists, undecidably, between the death of his past condition and the survival of its image. He becomes the walking specter of the counterfeit he already was, especially now that he can keep recoining the money by which he keeps deceiving others about his "bonds of alliance" (IV: 112). Increasingly, though, like a coin, he is just a repeated and inwardly empty simulacrum of what he once "drew" as a "character" in his "mind" (I: 75). He comes to regard himself, perpetually shifting across cultural stages and social readings of him, as more and more of "a monster who did not deserve to exist" (IV: 27). The horror of being the ghost of a counterfeit confronts St. Leon most, in fact, when he notes the difference between his pre-elixir love for the maternal, nurturing Marguerite ("Forever thy ghost upbraids me!", I: 100) – a version for some of the Mary Wollstonecraft who died after the birth of the younger Mary in 1797 – and his later way of "throwing off" her and her warnings in an alliance with the vengeful "dun and black" Hungarian Bethlem Gabor, a precursor of the unmothered creature who will, like Gabor, "relieve its secret load [of lost maternity] with curses and execrations" (IV: 123). The perpetuation of counterfeiting for Godwin turns out to be connected entirely to a half-conscious dismissal of, which is also a displaced longing for, the seemingly "uxorious and effeminate" in the male self (II: 37). It is as if womanliness were the difference-from-self that "the spirit of man" must escape to be itself (II: 37), even though that idea only results from Renaissance counterfeiting and can go on to be exchanged for a seemingly different "other" only by the counterfeit's ghost.

Such a realization seems to recur in the most Gothic writing of Percy Bysshe Shelley, not only in his early Gothic novels *Zastrozzi* and *St. Irvyne* (1810), but in his very Gothic lyric/narrative poem *Alastor* (1815–16), where the semi-autobigraphical "Poet" recalled by a Narrator with similar proclivities searches for the basis of his selfhood in sepulchres and ruins while avoiding the feminine and cross-cultural sympathy of the flesh-and-blood "Arab maiden" who dotes on him (*Alastor*, 129).[37] But Shelley, in a self-critique Mary shared, goes further than Godwin in connecting spectral counterfeiting with the ghosting of the feminine. The only connection acceptable to the *Alastor* Poet between the feminine and the symbolic mode of his simultaneously regressive *and* acqusitive search is his onanistic dream-projection of a "veiled maid" in an Indian "dell" (151, 146). She/it turns out to be the ghost of previous counterfeits, of "his own soul" read through an intertextual "web/Of many-coloured woof and shifting hues," that reflects past "Thoughts the most dear to him," the sepulchres of earlier perceptions of the maternal in Nature (156–60, 81–82). This combined refabrication and retrojection of a feminine and multi-cultural "otherness" faces its creator with both its merely constructed nature (telling him "an ineffable tale," 168) and its longing for the inside/outside mother-child relation as always distanced and beneath a veil, all of which keeps the maternal body – and any suggested mingling of bodies and races and classes – forever desired and forever removed (abjected). As Mary Shelley must have seen, this ghosting of existing counterfeits of the feminine *and* of Gothic desire could, as in Manfred's approach to Isabella/Matilda, kill the very "other" it claims to seek and value and thus drain the life out of the seeker's desire, as the life is gradually drained from the never-satisfied Poet (and Victor Frankenstein). She could hardly have missed that potential when she read what she allowed Shelley to write in her journal on October 7, 1814, during their brief residence with Jane Clairmont on Hampstead Heath. Here, while suffering his own debilitating illnesses, he recounts his effectiveness at nearly scaring Jane to death with Gothic stories of the witching hour late at night and thereby refashioning her visage – in an astonishing anticipation of Frankenstein's monster – into "lips and cheeks . . . of one deadly hue" and protruding "eyeballs" seemingly "inserted in ghostly sport in[to] the sockets of a lifeless head" (*The Journals*, I: 33).

Such is the deathly "life" of the Gothic as it confronted Mary Shelley by the time she began *Frankenstein* in 1816. Particularly in the re-Gothicizings of her father and lover, the ghost of the counterfeit had clearly become connected with the "sport" of ab-jecting many alterities: the regression to the maternal-feminine, the fear of the death in that return to birth and womanhood, the possible racial or class (as well as gender) plurality of the self if reconnected to its primordial other, the multiplicity of the acqusitive self seeking to remake itself in the future through the backward looking ghosts of its counterfeited "others" – every one of which could be both affirmed and denied if a Gothic fabricator chose to "throw" it into the recounterfeiting of other counterfeits. Such a construct could always seem to refer only to other signs (such as old tales of the witching hour) and yet could "cast down," even seem to kill, the body of woman and all "otherness" in the process. That is the duplicity extended in *Frankenstein*'s ghost of the counterfeit. Granted, Mary Shelley can place numerous versions of the abject in her creature because of her own experiences with all these abjected dimensions. There was her own involvement as an infant with her mother's death, her father's coldness towards her as a sign of the mother, her first dead child (its birth *as* death), her own class and racial biases, and her sense of the suppression of the feminine (including herself) in culture and scientific discussion, among other matters, just as her most able biographer-critics have shown us.[38] Still, she would have had no fictional place for her representations of the abject, nor could she keep them as veiled as she does by counterfeitings and their ghosts, were it not for the "Gothic" ghost of the Renaissance counterfeit, with all its contradictions, being placed in symbolic motion by Horace Walpole's recasting of Shakespeare *and* for the later intensifications of the counterfeit's "otherness," especially in the Godwin-Shelley circle, that use it to embody and conceal more cultural alterities. *Frankenstein* offers the Gothic ghost of the counterfeit in its most achieved, complex, and influential form up to 1818, using what is most fundamental in the Gothic to alter and deepen (rather than simply reverse) it. There figures that are already ghosts of abjecting, dying counterfeits find their most basic potentials extended in refabrications that finally suggest and conceal even more abjected levels.

NOTES

1 My three principal texts are cited from Mary W. Shelley, *Frankenstein, or the Modern Prometheus: The 1818 Text*, ed. James Rieger, Phoenix Edition (Chicago: University of Chicago Press, 1982); Horace Walpole, *The Castle of Otranto: A Gothic Story* (hereafter abbreviated as *The Castle*), ed. W. S. Lewis and Joseph W. Reed, World's Classics Revised Edition (Oxford: Oxford University Press, 1982); and William Shakespeare, *Hamlet*, Arden Edition, ed. Harold Jenkins (London: Methuen, 1982).

2 Rieger's words in his "Introduction" to *Frankenstein*, xxvi.

3 Paul Sherwin, "*Frankenstein*: Creation as Catastrophe," *PMLA* 96 (1981): 883. See also William Veeder, *Mary Shelley and* Frankenstein: *The Fate of Androgyny* (Chicago: University of Chicago Press, 1986), 143.

4 Frederick S. Frank, *The First Gothics: A Critical Guide to the English Gothic Novel* (New York: Garland, 1987), 346.

5 I cite Kristeva from *Powers of Horror: An Essay on Abjection*, trans. Leon S. Roudiez (New York: Columbia University Press, 1982). Here she draws her key word back to the most literal meanings of *ab-ject*. "Abjection" thus means (a) the "throwing off" of a primordial multiplicity (such as the state of being half-inside/half-outside the mother) that could prevent the emergence of a coherent individual or group "identity" *and* (b) the condition of being "thrown down and under" an external authority (the cultural Law of the Father) that works to socialize the emergent self within a system that denies the multiplicity that has been "thrown off." Abjection is the process in which (a) and (b) occur – and continue to occur half-consciously – and the "abject" is the obscured multiplicity that is "tossed over there" (abject-ed) into a disguised form of it.

6 See Kristeva, *Powers of Horror*, esp. 17–55; Marci M. Gordon, "Kristeva's Abject and Sublime in Brontë's *Wuthering Heights*," *Literature and Psychology* 34 (1988): 44–58; Jerrold E. Hogle, "The Struggle for a Dichotomy: Abjection in Jekyll and His Interpreters," in *Dr Jekyll and Mr Hyde After One Hundred Years*, ed. William Veeder and Gordon Hirsch (Chicago: University of Chicago Press, 1988), 161–207; Diane Long Hoeveler, "The Hidden God and the Abjected Woman in 'The Fall of the House of Usher,'" *Studies in Short Fiction* 29 (1992): 385–95; Tilottama Rajan, "Mary Shelley's *Mathilda*: Melancholy and the Political Economy of Romanticism," *Studies in the Novel* 26 (1994): 43–68; and Anne Williams, *Art of Darkness: A Poetics of Gothic* (Chicago: University of Chicago Press, 1995), 34–37 and 70–79.

7 For a more detailed discussion of how this scene is used in Walpole's reworking of Shakespeare, see Jerrold E. Hogle, "The Ghost of the Counterfeit in the Genesis of the Gothic," in *Gothick Origins and Innovations* (hereafter *Gothick Origins*), ed. Alan Lloyd Smith and Victor Sage (Amsterdam: Rodopi, 1994), 23–33. Note also that eighteenth-

century performances of *Hamlet* were often staged so as to imitiate the vogue for ancestral portraits in British upper-class homes (including Walpole's Strawberry Hill). They frequently presented the "counterfeits" in the closet scene as large, high paintings on the back wall to which Hamlet pointed (as we know from illustrations in eighteenth-century editions of Shakespeare; see T. S. R. Boase, "Illustrations of Shakespeare's Plays in the Seventeenth and Eighteenth Centuries," *Journal of the Warburg and Courtland Institutes*, 10 [1947]: 87 and plate 22c). When the Ghost entered late in that scene during an eighteenth-century rendition, the performer could thus be viewed as a walking image of the great portrait of old Hamlet overhead.

8 We can definitely say that *Frankenstein* was based on perusals of these exact kinds of figures in sources that either included or recalled *The Castle of Otranto* and *Hamlet*. Mary Shelley's *Journals* list her extensive reading in English Gothic fiction prior to *Frankenstein*, including the "Castle of Udolpho" in 1815, which (as her editors suggest) may be a composite listing of *The Castle of Otranto* and Ann Radcliffe's *The Mysteries of Udolpho* – or at least an indication that, for Shelley, the latter is very much rooted in the former. See *The Journals of Mary Shelley, 1814–1844* (hereafter *The Journals*), ed. Paula R. Feldman and Diana Scott-Kilvert (Oxford: Clarendon Press, 1987), 1: 85–92. The author's new Preface to the 1831 edition of *Frankenstein* adds some even stronger indicators of how "Gothic," ghost-like, portrait-like, and quasi-Shakespearean the figure of her creature is. Reconstructing the dream in which she believes she first beheld the central image in her novel, Mary Shelley writes that she "saw the hideous *phantasm* of a man stretched out, and then on the working of some powerful engine, show signs of life, and stir with an uneasy, half vital motion" (*Frankenstein*, 228, my emphasis). This dream-shape, she maintains, recalls more than just the famous Geneva discussions among the Shelleys, Byron, and Dr. Polidori on how "a corpse would be reanimated" with "galvanism" (*Frankenstein*, 227). It also replays this group's oral reading of the Frenchified German ghost stories in Jean Baptiste Eyries' anonymously published *Fantasmagoriana* (1812) and especially one piece from that collection that Mary recalls with great specificity:

There was the tale of the sinful founder of his race, whose miserable doom it was to bestow the kiss of death on all the younger sons of his fated house, just when they reached the age of promise. *His gigantic, shadowy form, clothed like the ghost in Hamlet, in complete armour, but with the beaver up*, was seen at midnight, by the moon's fitful beams, to advance slowly along the gloomy avenue. (*Frankenstein*, 224, my emphases)

Though she modifies this figure in *Frankenstein* so that the "phantasm" of the creature uses much more than a kiss to wreak death on the family of the "sinful founder of [a] race" (now Victor Frankenstein), Mary Shelley's rendition of the original story brings out, not only some

Shakespearean, but several *Otranto* elements in it: the "gigantic, shadowy form"; the "advancing slowly" by moonlight; the silence of the walking specter; the sins of the father being visited on the sons. Moreover, the title of this particular tale in *Fantasmagoriana* is "Les Portraits de Famille." The walking of the ancestral ghost here is the movement of a figure first viewed as a life-size portrait, wherein it seems as if "the artist had copied the terrible features of one risen from the grave" – a passage I quote from "Les Portraits" as it is anglicized by Sarah Elizabeth Utterson in *Tales of the Dead, Principally Translated from the French* (London: White, Cochraine, 1813), 17. There can thus be no question that the literary ancestry of Mary Shelley's creature includes the Walpolean Gothic "ghost of the counterfeit." As we can see in Utterson's translation, "The Family Portraits" is a blatant imitation of several Gothic devices from *The Castle of Otranto*, so much so that the translator identifies that "Gothic Story" by name as the text that "founded" the kind of writing she now renders from German and French originals (Utterson, *Tales of the Dead*, i).

9 Daniel Cottom, "*Frankenstein* and the Monster of Representation," *Sub-Stance* 28 (1980): 60.

10 Robert Miles, *Gothic Writing, 1750–1820: A Genealogy* (London: Macmillan, 1993), 16.

11 See David Leverenz, "The Woman in Hamlet: An Interpersonal View," *Signs* 4 (1978): 291–308; and Jerrold E. Hogle, "Teaching the Politics of Gender in Literature: Two Proposals for Reform, with a Reading of *Hamlet*," in *Changing our Minds: Feminist Transformations of Knowledge*, ed. Susan Hardy Aiken et al. (Albany: State University of New York Press, 1988), 98–133.

12 See Gayle Rubin, "The Traffic in Women: Notes on the 'Political Economy' of Sex," in *Towards an Anthropology of Women*, ed. Rayna Reiter (New York: Monthly Review Press, 1975), 157–210.

13 See Eve Kosofsky Sedgwick, *Between Men: English Literature and Male Homosocial Desire* (New York: Columbia University Press, 1985), esp. 21–27 and 83–96.

14 Walpole was hardly proto-feminist (in fact, he liked younger women of breeding platonically attending to him rather than marrying others), but he was concerned about the reduction of some women he knew to objects of commerce in the marriage market of his era. See his especially strong letter in 1758 about Colonel Yorke's marriage to "one or both of the Miss Crasteyns," each calculated as worth 260,000 pounds, in *The Yale Edition of Horace Walpole's Correspondence* (hereafter the *Yale Walpole*), ed. W. S. Lewis et al. (New Haven: Yale University Press, 1937–83), IX: 230– 31. At the same time, though, Walpole also accepted the linkage of marriage with other modes of "free exchange." In his objections to the Tory-sponsored Marriage Bill of 1753, he sees its aristocratic and church-based restrictions as anachronistically out of

keeping "in a country where liberty gives choice, where trade and money confer equality." See Walpole's *Memoirs of King George II*, ed. John Brooke (New Haven: Yale University Press, 1985), I: 226. For the consequences of such a "free market" orientation in Walpole's Gothic and its immediate progeny, see Andrea Henderson, "'An Embarassing Subject': Use Value and Exchange Value in Early Gothic Characterization," in *At the Limits of Romanticism: Essays in Cultural, Feminist, and Materialist Criticism*, ed. Mary A. Favret and Nicola J. Watson (Bloomington: Indiana University Press, 1994), 225–45.

15 The quoted words here are from Robert Kiely, *The Romantic Novel in England* (Cambridge, Mass.: Harvard University Press, 1972), 169. This "circumlocution of the maternal" in *Frankenstein*, though, is most powerfully discussed in Margaret Homans, *Bearing the Word: Language and Female Experience in Nineteenth-century Women's Writing* (Chicago: University of Chicago Press, 1986), 100–19.

16 Gayatri Chakravorty Spivak, "Three Women's Texts and a Critique of Imperialism," *Critical Inquiry* 12 (1985): 255.

17 See the collation of Freudian readings of this moment in Martin Tropp, *Mary Shelley's Monster: The Story of Frankenstein* (Boston: Houghton Mifflin, 1976), 19–33. See also Marc A. Rubenstein, "'My Accursed Origin': The Search for the Mother in *Frankenstein*," *Studies in Romanticism* 15 (1976): 165–94; Sherwin, "*Frankenstein*," 886–91; James B. Twitchell, "*Frankenstein* and the Anatomy of Horror," *Georgia Review* 37 (1983): esp. 46–60; Veeder, *Mary Shelley and* Frankenstein, 112–17; and Elisabeth Bronfen, *Over Her Dead Body: Death, Femininity and the Aesthetic* (Manchester: Manchester University Press, 1992), 130–39.

18 The echoes of *The Castle of Otranto* at this juncture in *Frankenstein* by no means negate Mary Shelley's other allusions at the same moment, the ones rightly noted by Leonard Wolf in *The Essential Frankenstein*, rev. edn. (New York: Penguin, 1993), 86–87, n. 6. But the Walpolean Gothic echoes link the love-object's and mother's dream-decay directly, as these other allusions do not, to the ghost-like and artificial counterfeiting of birth, life, and lineage – and to the death of woman in and behind that process – so basic to Frankenstein's monstrous fabrication.

19 The extent to which the Hermit of Joppa is a text of other texts, especially from the late Middle Ages and the Renaissance, can be seen in a comparison between Walpole's *The Castle*, 77–79 and 102, and many of the works discussed in Charles P. Weaver, *The Hermit in English Literature from the Beginnings to 1600* (Nashville: Peabody College of Teachers, 1924).

20 I cite David Musselwhite from *Partings Welded Together: Politics and Desire in the Nineteenth-century English Novel* (London: Methuen, 1987), 43–74 (and here from 59).

21 In addition to the work of Rubenstein, Cottom, Spivak, Bronfen, and Musselwhite cited already, see Ellen Moers, "Female Gothic," in *The*

Endurance of Frankenstein: *Essays on Mary Shelley's Novel* (hereafter *The Endurance*), ed. George Levine and U. C. Knoepfelmacher (Berkeley: University of California Press, 1979), 77–87; Gordon D. Hirsch, "The Monster Was a Lady: On the Psychology of Mary Shelley's *Frankenstein*," *Hartford Studies in Literature* 7 (1978): 116–53; Sandra M. Gilbert and Susan Gubar, *The Madwoman in the Attic: The Woman Writer and the Nineteenth-century Literary Imagination* (New Haven: Yale University Press, 1979), 230–46; Barbara Johnson, "My Monster/My Self," *Diacritics* 12 (1982): esp. 6–8; H. L. Malchow, "Frankenstein's Monster and Images of Race in Nineteenth-Century Britain," *Past and Present* 139 (1993): 90–130; Franco Moretti, *Signs Taken for Wonders: Essays in the Sociology of Literary Forms*, trans. Susan Fischer et al. (London: Verso, 1983), 85–90 and 104–08; Paul O'Flinn, "Production and Reproduction: The Case of *Frankenstein*," *Literature and History* 9 (1983): 194–213; Anca Vlasopolos, "*Frankenstein*'s Hidden Skeleton: The Psycho-Politics of Oppression," *Science Fiction Studies* 10 (1983): 125–36; Elsie B. Michie, "Production Replaces Creation: Market Forces and *Frankenstein* as Critique of Romanticism," *Nineteenth-Century Contexts* 12 (1988): 27–33; Warren Montag, " 'The Workshop of Filthy Creation': A Marxist Reading of *Frankenstein*," in *Case Studies in Contemporary Criticism: Mary Shelley/Frankenstein*, ed. Johanna M. Smith (Boston: St. Martin's Press, 1992), 300–11; Timothy Marshall, "*Frankenstein* and the 1832 Anatomy Act," in *Gothick Origins*, 57–64; and Anne K. Mellor, *Mary Shelley: Her Life, Her Fictions, Her Monsters* (New York: Methuen, 1988), 70–126.

22 Peter Brooks, " 'Godlike Science/Unhallowed Arts': Language, Nature, and Monstrosity," in *The Endurance*, 212.

23 See Jerrold E. Hogle, "Otherness in *Frankenstein*: The Confinement/ Autonomy of Fabrication," *Structuralist Review* 2 (1980): 20–48.

24 I cite Baudrillard from "The Structural Law of Value and the Order of Simulacra," trans. Charles Leven, in *The Structural Allegory: Reconstructive Encounters with the New French Thought*, ed. John Fekete (Minneapolis: University of Minnesota Press, 1984), 54–73.

25 Abundant confirmation of Baudrillard's sense that self-construction by signs in the Renaissance was an act of "counterfeiting" can be found in Lawrence Stone, *The Crisis of the Aristocracy, 1558–1641* (Oxford: Clarendon Press, 1965); Stephen Greenblatt, *Renaissance Self-Fashioning: From More to Shakespeare* (Chicago: University of Chicago Press, 1980); and David Quint, *Origin and Originality in Renaissance Literature: Versions of the Source* (New Haven: Yale University Press, 1983), esp. 1–31.

26 For accounts of how basic fakery and play were – along with the illusion of authentication – in mid eighteenth-century neo-Gothic architecture, see Michael McCarthy, *The Origins of the Gothic Revival* (New Haven: Yale University Press, 1982), 48–91; and Dianne S. Ames, "Strawberry Hill: Architecture of the 'As If,' " in *Studies in Eighteenth-Century Culture* 8, ed. Roseann Runte (Madison: University of Wisconsin Press, 1979), 351–63.

Actually, it should hardly be surprising that the "Gothic" of this time refers so fundamentally to the Renaissance counterfeit. After all, the original use of "Gothic" (*gotiche*) as a label for religious and other architecture of the Middle Ages *was* a Renaissance counterfeit. It was an invention of Italian artist-scholars in the early 1400s that pejoratively misnamed, as too low-class or "rustic" compared to Greco-Roman architecture, several older building styles as through they were connected with non-Roman tribes – the Goths or Visigoths – who actually had little to do with what was attributed to them. See Paul Frankl, *The Gothic: Literary Sources and Interpretations Through Eight Centuries* (Princeton: Princeton University Press, 1960), 259–60. The term "Gothic" by the time Walpole borrowed it for *The Castle* and other purposes, then, was very much the shifty recounterfeiting of a Renaissance counterfeit, and it therefore became a moveable simulacrum prone to many reproductions for the sake of locating "cultural capital" in a wide variety of politically useful reference points from the vaguely medieval past. See Mark Madoff, "The Useful Myth of Gothic Ancestry," also in *Studies in Eighteenth-Century Culture* 8, ed. Runte, this time on 337–50.

27 See Emma J. Clery in "Against Gothic" in *Gothick Origins*, 34–43 (from which I quote here), and in *The Rise of Supernatural Fiction, 1762–1800* (Cambridge: Cambridge University Press, 1995).

28 These are Robert Miles' Foucauldian words in *Gothic Writing*, 11, but see also Elizabeth Napier, *The Failure of Gothic: Problems of Disjunction in an Eighteenth-Century Literary Form* (Oxford: Clarendon Press, 1987); Jeffrey Cox, "Introduction," in *Seven Gothic Dramas, 1789–1825*, ed. Jeffrey Cox (Athens: Ohio University Press, 1992), 1–77; and Jacqueline Howard, *Reading Gothic Fiction: A Bakhtinian Approach* (Oxford: Clarendon Press, 1994).

29 My uses of "simulacrum" from here on will refer to Baudrillard's sense of that term, which points primarily at the mechanically reproduced "copy" in the industrial age, which itself refers back to another kind of copy (the mold in the machine, a ghost of that earlier form of the sign: the counterfeit).

30 I cite Terry Castle from "The Spectralization of the Other in *The Mysteries of Udolpho*" in *The New Eighteenth Century: Theory, Politics, English Literature*, ed. Felicity Nussbaum and Laura Brown (London: Methuen, 1987), 231–53.

31 See Radu Florescu, *In Search of Frankenstein* (Boston: New York Graphic Society), 215–22, and William Godwin, *Lives of the Necromancers* (London: Mason, 1834), 261–63 and 325–27.

32 See Simone de Beauvoir in *The Second Sex*, trans. H. M. Parshley (New York: Knopf, 1952), xvi–xxix.

33 See Stephen Greenblatt in *Shakespearean Negotiations: The Circulation of Social Energy in Renaissance England* (Berkeley: University of California Press, 1988), 73–86.

34 The argument that the spacialization and nature of Freud's unconscious was not just anticipated, but substantially formed, by Gothic fiction has been made in older *and* more recent studies of the Gothic ranging from Lowry Nelson, Jr., "Night Thoughts on the Gothic Novel," *Yale Review* 52 (1962): 236–57, to Hogle, "The Ghost," esp. 23–25, and Williams, *Art of Darkness*, 239–48.

35 See Leslie Fiedler in *Love and Death in the American Novel*, rev. edn. (New York: Dell, 1966), 126–41; and David Punter in *The Literature of Terror: A History of Gothic Fictions from 1765 to the Present Day* (London: Longman, 1980), 413–26.

36 *St. Leon* is cited here from the four-volume Third Edition (London: Simpkin and Marshall, 1816).

37 I cite *Alastor* by line numbers from *Shelley's Poetry and Prose: A Norton Critical Edition*, ed. Donald Reiman and Sharon B. Powers (New York: Norton, 1977). Ways in which the Poet of *Alastor* forecasts the hero of *Frankenstein* have been noted for years, most suggestively by Veeder, *Mary Shelley and* Frankenstein, 93–99, and Homans, *Bearing the Word*, 103–11.

38 See Moers, Veeder, Mellor, and Emily Sunstein, *Mary Shelley: Romance and Reality* (Boston: Little, Brown, 1989), esp. 121–32.

Genre, gender, and the private sphere

CHAPTER 9

Autonarration and genotext in Mary Hays' 'Memoirs of Emma Courtney'

Tilottama Rajan

I

Mary Wollstonecraft's The *Wrongs of Woman*, long written out of the canon by being used as a source-book for her life, has recently become an object of serious attention. Mary Hays' *Memoirs of Emma Courtney* (1796),[1] however, remains the victim of a reduction of text to biography that fails to recognize its complex interimplication of textuality and reality. Hays' novel is based on the story of her unreturned passion for the Cambridge radical William Frend. Its autobiographical nature led contemporaries to see it as a scandalous disrobing in public, and the novel is still dismissed as a monologic transfer of "life" into "text." *Memoirs*, however, self-consciously draws upon personal experience as part of its rhetoric, so as to position experience within textuality and relate textuality to experience. From the distinctions by Schiller and the Schlegels onwards, between classicism as impersonal and Romanticism as the revelation of personality, the inscription of the author in the text has been a characteristically Romantic move: expressive not of the egotistical sublime, but of the text as the unfinished transcription of a subject still in process. Hays' text can be seen as part of a larger (post)-Romantic *intergenre* that I shall call autonarration, which is also used (though differently) by male writers such as Rousseau and Wordsworth. Far from collapsing the boundary between life and text, autonarration effects a series of "trans-positions" (to borrow Kristeva's term)[2] among ideology, life, and fiction. The transposition of personal experience into fiction recognizes "experience" as discursively constructed. That Hays draws on her own experience is a way of authorizing what she does, and of reciprocally implicating the reader in the text. But it is also a way of putting the finality of the text under erasure, by suggesting that what it "does" or where it ends is limited by its genesis in the life of a conflicted historical subject.

This paper argues for the importance of Hays' novel to both the feminist and Romantic traditions, and in the process works out a phenomenology of autonarration. But because the novel is relatively unknown, it is necessary to begin by describing it and by saying something about Hays herself. Mary Hays was born in 1760 into a middle-class family of Rational Dissenters near London.[3] Her early engagement to a fellow Dissenter John Eccles ended in tragedy when he died shortly before their marriage. Through the preacher Robert Robinson she met some of the leading intellectuals of the day, and eventually became a member of Joseph Johnson's radical circle. Thereafter Hays made a tenuous living by writing and reviewing, and produced essays, other novels, her own vindication of women's rights entitled *An Appeal to the Men of Great Britain in Behalf of Women* (1798), as well as a six-volume attempt to construct a gynocentric tradition under the title *Female Biography* (1805). Although her relationship with Robinson and William Godwin was purely intellectual, Hays became notorious among her contemporaries for throwing herself at men who apparently did not return her affections. Through Frend she met Godwin, whom she introduced to his future wife Wollstonecraft, and with whom she carried on a long correspondence. Her letters were not only about her (non)relationship with Frend but also about its ramifications: a sexual economy that constructed women only for marriage, and the resulting predicament of single women untrained for a profession. It was Godwin who encouraged her to write a fictionalized version of her experiences. She wrote the novel, she implied to him, for reasons that were neither purely literary nor kathartic but political: "My Manuscript was not written *merely* for the public eye – another latent, and perhaps stronger, motive lurked beneath – . . . my story is *too real*."[4]

Hays is best remembered as the author of Wollstonecraft's obituary and the person who was at her bedside when she died. But though she has consequently been identified with or dismissed as a more outrageous version of Wollstonecraft,[5] there are significant differences between the two. Hays' attitude to passion and to the tradition of romance and sentiment was more positive than Wollstonecraft's.[6] Moreover, *Memoirs* is the work of a woman who could not or did not enter the marriage circuit. For although Wollstonecraft felt it would have been more appropriate for the novel to end with the death of the male protagonist and thus the unavoidable termination of Emma's love,[7] Hays has her heroine outlive the conventional ending of novels about women in death or marriage. Curiously enough, while *The Wrongs of Woman* is about much more than its love interest, Wollstonecraft seems unable to see her way beyond Darnford's possible treachery. But although *Memoirs* seems to be about nothing *but* romantic love, the terms of Emma's life are not really defined by that love. In fact the novel is concerned less with Emma reenacting or even remembering her love than with her writing and potentially reading it, so as to understand women's representation in the symbolic order.[8]

Drawing on Hays' own letters to Frend and Godwin (who appears in the novel as Francis), the novel focuses on the one-sided correspondence between its title character and the man she chooses to love, Augustus Harley. Emma, like so many nineteenth-century characters for whom the family is an imposed structure, has lost her mother and her aunt early in life, has been brought up by an absent father, and has been transferred after his death to the care of an uncle. It is in her uncle's house that she meets the destructively passionate Montague, as well as the highly rational Francis, with whom she exchanges ideas and to whose not entirely sympathetic eyes she later confides the story of her love. Augustus enters Emma's story by way of a violent coach accident to which I shall return, and in which he saves her and Montague from death but is badly injured. Seeming to encourage her friendship at first, he later becomes evasive and refuses to answer her letters. His ostensible reason is his uncle's will, which stipulates that he will forfeit his legacy if he marries. Emma is never entirely convinced by the purely pecuniary motive but her declarations of love and pleas for frankness are met by injunctions to be less selfish and more restrained. Eventually it emerges that Augustus is actually married, to a foreign woman he no longer loves, and whose existence he has concealed for fear of losing the legacy.

This disclosure ends their (non)relationship and Emma, now under financial pressure, marries Montague. She is a faithful wife and mother until a second coach accident outside her home brings Augustus back into her life. She learns that Augustus, having been reduced to poverty, has lost his wife and two of his children to illness. Emma nurses him until he dies, and inherits the guardianship of his remaining son, Augustus Jr. From then on her marriage deteriorates, culminating in Montague's murder of his child by a servant girl and his subsequent suicide. Emma tells her story partly through a series of letters: passionately rational letters to Augustus, and rationally passionate ones to Francis, to whom she writes about the economic predicament of single women and the relationship between reason and passion. The letters are interspersed with narrative to make up the memoirs of the title. But the memoirs are also framed by two letters to the now adult son of Augustus, who is himself involved in a passionate relationship. Ostensibly Emma conveys her (hi)story as a cautionary exemplum to her adopted son. But the epistolary form is potentially transgressive, crossing the bounds of private space so as to say what cannot be said in public, and claiming a certain immediacy and presence. In putting her letters within her memoirs, Emma had allowed their radicalism to be contained within the mode of pastness. But the framing of the memoirs themselves within a return to the epistolary form suspends this cautionary closure, by once again transposing the question of passion from the past to the unresolved present.

Crucial to Hays' novel is the concept of Desire. Desire is part of the text's functioning in ways to which I shall return. But it is also thematically central to a novel that questions the opposition between reason and passion, so as to reposition female subjectivity within the psychosocial economy. Felicity Nussbaum has described how women's sexuality posed a threat to this economy in specifically material ways having to do with the inheritance of property and thus the maintenance of the class system.[9] Emma's aspirations are also subversive because of the social implications of a woman taking the initiative in love. But her desire has to do with more than sexuality. Thus I use the word partly as it is used by Lacan, for whom desire is always in excess of its object, the object being only a partial representation of something beyond it, and thus implicated in a chain of deferrals and transferences. *Memoirs* is not about Emma's desire for Augustus but about something else that is signified by that desire. Moreover, because it suggests the substitutive and still "symbolic" character of the object(s) of desire, the Lacanian term avoids the positivism sometimes associated with political reading. For marriage to Augustus remains a signifier within the symbolic order, while the further transference of Emma's desire to his son is still what Fredric Jameson calls a symbolic resolution: one that allows her to be Augustus' mother, the mother who teaches but also the mother of his desire, and yet as mother in a paradoxical position of origination and subordination. Hays herself recognizes the nature of her project when she points in *An Appeal* to the difficulty of positing women's identity, given that men have so constructed them that "they have lost even the idea of what they might have been, or what they still might be":

We must therefore endeavour, to describe them [women] by negatives. As, perhaps, the only thing that can be advanced with certainty on the subject, is, – what they are *not*. For it is very clear, that they are not what they ought to be, that they are not what men would have them to be, and to finish the portrait, that they are not what they appear to be.[10]

But if the currently Lacanian connotations of "desire" allow us to approach *Memoirs* in terms of the "negativity" of the signifier, there are limitations in his version of the concept. In tracing the history of desire from Jean Hyppolite's influential rereading of Hegel, through Sartre, to Lacan, Judith Butler comments on the attenuation that occurs as desire is transposed from a dialectical to a psychoanalytic and structural framework.[11] Not only does Lacan dissociate desire from any sense of subjective agency, he also denies that desire can be "materialised or concretised through language," whether directly or negatively.[12] Moreover, because he sees desire as endlessly metonymic and unsatisfiable, he dispossesses the means by which it signifies itself of historical specificity or facilitating value, making the signifier no more than a position in an empty series.

In using the word desire, then, I continue to have in mind Hyppolite's rereading of Hegel as part of a negative dialectic that is particularly (post)Romantic. Desire is the "very existence of man, 'who never is what he is,' who always exceeds himself," and who in that sense "has a future."[13] As such, it is the power of the negative in experience, as well as the reflexivity of a consciousness that must know itself partly as an other and as existing for another.[14] Put differently, Emma's love is an articulation of the imaginary within the symbolic, or in Hegelian terms of the subjective within the objective. Beginning as the idealism of a highly romantic subject who resists being confined by things as they are, Emma's desire can express itself only in the socially prescribed form of heterosexual love. Her desire is doubly negative, in the sense that it resists the symbolic order through an identification with the masculine that sets it at odds with itself. Yet this negativity is dialectical and not deconstructive, because desire makes the negative into "something to be labored upon and worked through."[15] For Emma this working through occurs through the epistolary format of the novel, which makes of self-consciousness an intersubjective process. For Hays herself it occurs through the act of writing, in which she must become other than herself in the text in order to know herself.

That Emma articulates herself through romantic love has to do with the way women have been constructed in the social text. She herself makes this point when she refuses to abandon her love of Augustus, referring to it as the mind's necessary "object" and "pursuit," and arguing, "I feel that I am neither a philosopher, nor a heroine, – but a *woman, to whom education has given a sexual character*" (*M*, 120). Thus although Hays' critics found Emma's epistolary pursuit of Augustus unseemly and her concern with her feelings narcissistic, to see the novel as fetishising desire is to miss its pathos. *Memoirs* is strategically rather than essentially about female sexuality. From the beginning Emma's desire is excessive: it exceeds the objective correlative it tries to find in Augustus Harley, and even at the end it survives the dismantling of its object. At first Augustus encourages Emma "in the pursuit of learning and science" (*M*, 71), so that her need for a relationship with him is also a desire for access to knowledge (*M*, 79). Given women's exclusion from all but the domestic sphere, this love is also a desire for the enunciative position within the social order that a woman could have only in relation to a man. But as the convenient vagueness of the word "desire" suggests, it would be wrong to give it a precise referent. For when Emma does acquire the status afforded by marriage to Montague, domesticity becomes an empty signifier that does not satisfy her.

Emma's desire is all the more difficult to characterize because it is not even initially sexual: as she says, it involves a transference of her affection for his mother (*M*, 59), in which she loves in *him* what he must inherit from *her*. What begins as a desire for everything effaced from her own patriarchal upbringing is thus androgynously transcoded onto the masculine as the only sanctioned object of adult female love. Thus it is significant that Emma's specifically sexual desire is set in motion before she actually meets him by Augustus' portrait (*M*, 59). This mobilizing of desire by an image that precedes its re-presentation in a real person anticipates texts such as Shelley's *Alastor*, where the protagonist unites in an image "all of wonderful, or wise, or beautiful, which the poet, the philosopher, or the lover could depicture," before he actually goes in search of his epi-psyche.[16] Figuring the precedence of the signifier over the signified, the portrait marks the fundamentally Romantic structure of desire, not simply as lack, but also as a form of Imagination subversively knotted into the symbolic structures of representation and the family.[17]

If the word desire suggests a non-coincidence of the subject with its object, we also need to set it beside Hays' own more positive term "passion," and to read them as intertextual glosses on each other. The frequent discussions of "passion" in *Memoirs* involve Emma's struggle to rethink the position of women by examining the identifi-cation of emotion as the site of feminine weakness. Hays' views on this subject are highly conflicted. On the one hand, in representing her memoirs as a warning against error, Emma accepts the domi-nant devaluation of passion and related terms such as "romanti-cism" and "imagination." On the other hand, Hays differs from Wollstonecraft in arguing for passion as a form of strength. Writing to Francis, Emma asks, "What are passions, but another name for powers?" (*M*, 86).

The questioning of the hierarchy between reason and passion links Hays to a re-examination of this opposition in Romantic thinking from Blake to Schopenhauer. But whereas Schopenhauer will argue that the representations produced by reason are no more than disguised expressions of the will, Hays' protagonist suggests that passion can be deeply rational. Writing to Francis, she argues that reason and passion are not necessarily opposed, and indeed that reason begins in passion: "do you not perceive, that my reason was the auxiliary of my passion, or rather my passion the generative principle of my reason?" (*M*, 145). This statement significantly revises her earlier condemnation of herself on the grounds that "my reason was but an auxiliary to my passion" (*M*, 61). If reason is originally the elaboration of passion in a series of general principles, the outward circumference of energy as Blake would say, then passion remains vitally necessary to the reconsideration of what would otherwise congeal into law. For Emma's passion causes her to rethink the social structures that condemn that passion as out-rageous, and thus her desire also becomes the site of her emergence as a political subject. Or as she tells Francis, "Had not these contradictions, these oppositions, roused the energy of my mind, I might have domesticated, tamely, in the lap of indolence and apathy" (*M*, 145).

Hays' use of the term passion remains highly conflicted, for the active thrust of the word is continually negated by Emma's acceptance of its patriarchal encoding as something that one suffers and by which one is infected. However, a reading of the term purely in terms of lack does not convey the force of Hays' project. If desire does more than eroticize female powerlessness, that is because the *discourse* of desire in the tradition to which Hays' text belongs is allied with the modes of autonarration and epistolarity. These forms, which will be the concern of the remaining two sections, implicate author and reader respectively in the process of desire. Linda Kauffman has provided a valuable account of how amorous discourse is elaborated through epistolarity, so that the text becomes a letter to the reader,[18] thus putting desire in circulation. But a further untheorized element in her discussion is the "auto-graphing" of many of the texts she describes, either by the author or by the reader. *Jane Eyre* is curiously subtitled an autobiography, and Kauffman's discussion focuses on its correspondence with Brontë's letters to Constantin Heger, the Belgian schoolmaster with whom she fell in love as a young woman. As interesting is the reception history of *The Letters of a Portuguese Nun*, which testifies to a compelling desire to make the nun into a historical person.[19] As Ruth Perry points out, eighteenth-century readers liked to see fictional characters as "real,"[20] in striking contrast to readers nursed on contemporary theory. The blurring of the line between fiction and reality potentially allowed readers to write themselves, or to pursue the trace of their desire, through the text. This conflation of the fictional and the real becomes in the Romantic period a powerfully dialectical use of the subjective as a sub-version of the objective world.

II

Memoirs of Emma Courtney can be seen as an example of autonarration, an intergenre characterized by its mixing of private and public spaces. Autonarration is part of a larger discursive formation characteristic of Romanticism, in which writers bring details from their personal lives into their texts, speaking in a voice that is recognizably their own or through a persona whose relation to the biographical author is obvious. Thus Coleridge's conversation poems are situated within his life through specific references to the time and place of their composition, to friends such as Wordsworth and Charles Lamb, and to incidents from his domestic life. Somewhat differently Shelley in *The Triumph of Life* and Keats in *The Fall of Hyperion* inscribe in their texts what are best described as subversions of themselves referred to by the pronoun "I." Subjectivity, however, is not always indicated by the use of the first person or of local and topographical markers. Thus the Byronic hero is a third person character, but is nevertheless a figure for a public persona that is recognizably a projection of the author himself.

Criticism from Eliot to the present has taught us to exile the author from a supposedly ironic or decentered text, and insofar as the Romantics deviate from this standard of impersonality, the author's presence in the text has been seen as a form of egotistical sublimity. But the author's self-representation through a textual figure is quite different from her presence. On the one hand, subjectivity offers the writer an enunciative position within the social syntax that she is precluded from occupying by the aesthetic grammar of (neo)classicism and (post)modernism. As a subject who is not quite inside the space of the public, she can articulate desires that are different from (or that defer) the received genres of experience. On the other hand, these desires are textualized rather than literalized, so that the writer, in leaving life for text, ceases to be a transcendental ego and confesses her situatedness as a historical subject. Nor is it simply the case that "life" is made into a text. For the historical (as distinct from the fictitious) first-person position also inscribes the textual within the Real, by marking its genesis in and its continued importance for a historical subject.

As a specific form of this larger discourse, autonarration involves not simply the author's entry into the text through the first-person pronoun, but a sustained rewriting in fictional form of events from the author's life. Autonarrations are not fictions but they are also not autobiographies. Thus Hays' text is a highly fictionalized version of her life in which the main character is neverthless writing her memoirs, thus inscribing the text itself as a sub-version of the autobiographical project. I use the term autonarration rather than autobiography or self-writing quite deliberately. As a subset of biography, autobiography assumes a straightforward relationship between representation and experience that allows the subject to tell her life-story either in the form of constative or of performative utterance: either as it was, or as it becomes through the act of rewriting. By contrast the term self-writing refers to a textual articulation of the self that is already not the real self, but the self as it is produced within existing discourses. Self-writing, however, includes diaries, journals, and letters as well as narratives. Autonarration is thus a form of self-writing in which the author writes her life as a fictional narrative, and thus *consciously* raises the question of the relationship between experience and its narrativization. It is not exclusively a women's genre, because some of Kierkegaard's writings fall within this category. Its use, however, tends to put the writer in a female subject-position.

In this sense, Wollstonecraft's first novel *Mary* is not a fully fledged autonarration, because it does no more than evoke the interimplication of life and texts through the titular reference to the author's name. *The Wrongs of Woman*, by contrast, contains sustained parallels between Maria's life and Wollstonecraft's relationship with Gilbert Imlay. These parallels, moreover, are deliberately imperfect in that Maria's lover Darnford occupies the positions of both Imlay and Godwin. He resembles Imlay in being Maria's first real lover, but in the fragmentary endings he also resembles Godwin in being the father of her second child.

The fact that the author is and is not represented by her textual surrogate has significant consequences for the reading process. For instead of generating a series of identifications in which the author recognizes her alter ego in the mirror of the text, and thus enables the reader to find and identify with the autobiographical subject within the text, the reading process involves a series of (mis)recognitions in which we cannot be quite sure of the relationship between textuality and reality. These misrecognitions generate a series of complex intertextual relationships between what is and what could be. For instance, one of the pivotal events in Wollstonecraft's life was Imlay's betrayal of the desires that she symbolically invested in him: desires that were social and political as well as romantic. That Darnford is both Imlay and Godwin narrates the possibility of a repetition that did not happen in quite that way in Wollstonecraft's life. At the same time the transposition of this betrayal into the text is effected through its displacement into an ending that she did not integrate into her novel. This displacement suspends the inevitability of betrayal, both in the text and in life: it removes the betrayal from a climactic position in the text, and by repeating it within a text, it also exposes betrayal as part of a discourse into which women are written and therefore write themselves.

As these preliminary comments indicate, autonarration puts under erasure the assumption made in autobiography that the subject can tell her own story. It is not autobiography because it is still fiction, but it is not just fiction because of its genesis in the life of a real individual. Crucial to the genre is the movement that occurs between the zones of life and fiction. We should not, however, think of the relationship between these zones as being similar to that between story and discourse. "Story" is a foundationalist concept which implies that certain events really happened in a certain order. By transposing her life into fiction, Hays recognizes that her life itself takes shape within a social text. Autonarration therefore involves a double textualization of both the narrative and the life on which it is based. At the same time its genesis in experience is crucial in complicating this textualization by inscribing the Real as what Jameson would call the absent cause of the narrative process.[21] In gesturing beyond the text to the author's "experience," it points us to something that cannot quite be represented in either the text or the public life of the author. This something is what impels her to articulate herself in the two different media of life and text, as if each requires the supplement of the other. Indeed both Hays and Wollstonecraft use a third medium, that of the political tract, although it is the mixed genre of autonarration that sensitizes us to the intertextual and supplementary position of seemingly simpler signifying materials such as "life" and political prose.

But the term life itself needs to be further broken down: into Hays' public history, and the autobiographical pre-text that precedes her interpellation into a social script. The pre-text is a provisional articulation of drives at the level of what Kristeva calls the "semiotic" (*R*, 25). As such it finds no adequate objective correlative in the history of Mary Hays or her fictional counterpart, but can only be sensed through a symptomatic reading of the differences between Hays' history and its further narrativization in Emma's memoirs. Insofar as we can describe it this provisional articulation involves desire: a desire that is at once metaphysical, political and sexual. However, any expression of this desire is already a narrativization of the pre-text produced within the psychosocial structures of the family. In this narrative desire attaches itself to an *animus* or more properly a masculine equivalent to what Shelley calls the epipsyche.

We can note Hays' tendency to idealize men with radical political commitments: whether as mentors like Godwin, or as potential lovers like Frend. Although Johnson eventually published her *Appeal*, Emma Courtney recapitulates the position of a younger Mary Hays in having to express her views on the construction of gender in late eighteenth-century society in a series of private letters to a male correspondent. Hays sought relationships with men because they were her means of access to knowledge, and because the discourse of emotional relationships gave her a way of locating for herself an admittedly ambiguous enunciative position within the social text. Where her relationships with male mentors preserved the gender hierarchy that Emma struggles against in her correspondence with Francis, her more passionate relationships promised (at least ideally) a union with the male that would lead to a transcendence of hierarchy and difference.[22]

If Hays' public history already writes her desire in certain pre-set social forms, *Memoirs of Emma Courtney* tries to displace and defamiliarize this anterior social text. Crucial to this process are the differences between the novel and the "events" that it symbolically transforms. These *differences*, rather than the events themselves or their fictional counterparts, are what allow us to sense the autobiographical pre-text misrepresented in Hays' public life. For it is not that Hays rewrites things as they are in her life into things as they should be in her novel: indeed Emma's life is not resolved with any more outward success than Hays' affair with Frend. Rather, by enacting her relationship with Frend in two different signifying materials, Hays dislodges the mimetic authority of either version and allows the reading process to operate in primarily negative ways that impede its premature closure. That the text does not exactly repeat Mary Hays' history opens up the possibility of a history that could have been different. On the other hand the novel, as a deflected repetition of the life, is both a deferral of that hi(story) which continues to haunt it and to reinscribe its utopian project in the structures of eighteenth-century society, and it is also a difference from its own ending, which could be written differently if transposed into an alternative set of circumstances.

We shall focus only on the most significant of the divergences between life and text: Hays' representation of Augustus. Unlike Frend, he is apolitical. Indeed his concealed passion for his foreign wife marks him as much closer to Emma than he admits, but utterly different from her in his hypocritical attitude to the feelings. Most significant of all is his secret marriage, given that Frend himself married only much later. This change is important not simply because it makes him unworthy of Emma's love, and not because it hints that she could have had Augustus if the plot of her life had been different, but because that possibility destigmatizes her desire and frees the reader from having to judge it in terms of the failure which may well be our only reason for condemning it. At the same time it is crucial that we not rewrite the plot as it is worked out in the symbolic order of Hays' history or that of Emma Courtney, by substituting for it an imaginary ending which discloses the marriage of Emma and Augustus as the text's hermeneutic secret. For this re-positing of the subject within the existing social order is negated both by the displacement of the secret marriage onto a wife who is effaced from the text, and by the (dis)appearance of Emma's name-sake daughter, whose early death prevents the marriage of Emma and Augustus from being consummated in the second generation. The possibility of a marriage exists as no more than a trace, which defers the outcome of Hays' life so as to make us think about it differently. But it is important that Emma's desire should not succeed, because the nature of that desire is that it exceeds its articulation as sexual desire. Augustus' unavailability renders Emma's desire pure excess, a desire that cannot have an object. It also renders this desire innocent, both of the failure that leads us to dismiss it and of the sexuality that cuts off the political radicalism of women's desire in the scandalous memoirs of writers like Charlotte Charke and Laetitia Pilkington alluded to in Hays' title.[23]

Insofar as the pre-text is accessible only through the zone of possibilities generated by the differences between Hays' and Emma's histories, we have been tacitly assuming two further areas of signification in the interaction between text and life, namely the phenotext and the genotext of the novel itself. I borrow these terms from Kristeva, who defines the phenotext as that which communicates "univocal information between two full-fledged subjects." The genotext, by contrast, is a "process" or "*path*" that articulates ephemeral structures and that can be "seen in language" but "is not linguistic" (*R*, 86–87). The phenotext, though quite different from Hays' public history, is its intratextual equivalent because both are produced within the symbolic order. It includes the mimetic and pragmatic (as opposed to expressive) dimensions of the novel: its plot, and its use of the letter as a way of forwarding the memoirs to their addressee as a cautionary tale. The genotext, according to Kristeva, is the unformulated part of the text, evident for instance in rhythm as that which exceeds statement.

Kristeva elaborates the notion of a genotext through writers such as Mallarmé and thus with reference to lyric. Moreover, her association of the semiotic with lyric and of narrative with the symbolic $(R, 90)^{24}$ constitutes a privatizing of the semiotic that can sometimes come across as a failure to retrieve its political potential. Yet in spite of the connection between plot and the symbolic order, writers such as Hays and Wollstonecraft choose subjective narrative rather than lyric because it provides them with a way of entering history. Where lyric allows for the expression of subjectivity, narrative positions this subjectivity in relation to the other, so as to open the genotext to political reading and so as to put it into history. One of my concerns here is therefore to explore what constitutes the genotext of *narrative*, and more specifically of autonarration. As we have seen, the genotext exists partly as an intertext or connective zone between the biographical and diegetic worlds, which is to say that it consists of the possibilities released by the negation of the various scripts into which the subject has been or could be written. But in addition the genotext is also *intra*textual. If the phenotext includes the plot and its characters as positive terms in a narrative syntax, the genotext is something the reader senses in the *form* taken by content: in the rhythms or processes of emplotment and the spaces between characters and generic components. It is also important to remember that the drives produced in the semiotic *chora* and reproduced in the genotext already bear the imprint of cultural structures. The genotext, as something which is not linguistic but is seen in language, is the overdetermined site of an entanglement between residual, dominant, and emergent discourses. Insofar as it generates the gaps in which desire can emerge, this desire is produced *within the symbolic order* as a transgression of this order.

Where the phenotext is positive in the sense of communicating information or positing identity, the genotext can be conceived only as a negativity. As negativity (which is a process) rather than negation (which is thetic) $(R, 109-13)$, the genotext can be located first of all in the diacritical relations between generic components and characters. An obvious example would be the way the affirmative element in

Emma's passion emerges not from what she does, but as something not quite stated and thus never confirmed in the difference between her behavior and the self-destructive passion of Montague.

A far more complex version of the functioning of *différance* and the trace as part of a genotext involves the conspicuous doubling of the first generation protagonists of Hays' novel in the second generation, combined with a simultaneous maintenance *and* reversal of the symmetry that contains the doubling within the boundaries of gender. Emma is repeated as her daughter Emma and Augustus as his son Augustus, with a symmetry that seems at first to perpetuate the gender positions of the first generation. But then Augustus' death becomes little Emma's death, while Augustus Jr. occupies the position in the plot occupied by Emma Sr., in that his own involvement in a passionate love affair provides the pretext for her to send him her memoirs. Or to put it differently, the plot in the second generation does away with the woman and allows the man to survive, but only after the man has come to resemble Emma more than his father. In a metaphoric sense the surviving Emma dies as the woman her child might have been, while her desire survives in the younger man who, by occupying a female subject-position within the social syntax, allows Emma at last to occupy the same subject-position as a man.

This complex rearrangement of the first generation in the second is genotextual, in the sense that we must read it as a psychosocial text (dis)organized by certain rhythms. As important to this text as its characters are the processes by which gender and plot functions are mapped and remapped onto each other. Implicit in my use of the word "processes" is the assumption that narrative (or at least subjective narrative of the sort written by the Romantics) is not simply the plot with its characters. Rather it is an autogenerative mechanism which produces and disposes of events and characters, in such a way that its movements are themselves a symptomatic part of the text's content. In this case the narrative begins by doubling its main characters along familial lines that preserve the separateness of male and female, by giving Emma a daughter and Augustus a son. But then it crosses these lines by partially reversing the roles played by the younger Emma and Augustus in the political economy of the text. The reversal is incomplete, because little Emma resembles Augustus Sr. only in one respect: they both die. It is, however, this incomplete turn, from the maintenance to the rearrangement of gender lines that forms a part of the genotext. The movements of the narrative are traces of something whose provisional articulation in the genotext is itself imprinted by the sexual structures of the symbolic order. In other words, Hays' vicarious self-doubling of Emma as Augustus Jr. narrates her desire for a social order in which the division between reason and passion, male and female, will no longer obtain. This desire, however, is haunted by the possibility that Emma may after all be her daughter, that her desire may die, like so many Romantic projects, before it has lived. It is also haunted by the possibility that Augustus may still be his father's son, that his future may not vindicate the rights of the woman who is no more than his adoptive and metaphoric mother in a family that is an ideal rearrangement of his actual family. Finally this desire is itself produced within the gendered economy that it resists. For the symbolic resolution it projects, provisionally and genotextually, has Emma survive through her masculine counterpart at the cost of killing off the very female self she has sought to vindicate.

At the same time this ambiguous transgression of the social order is connected to a (mis)identification with the role of mother that allows the death of little Emma to function in more than one symbolic register. Emma Sr. survives as (the younger) Augustus' symbolic mother, and can transmit her memoirs to a future reader only by assuming this role, which affords her a position in the social syntax. It seems, moreover, that she can enter the symbolic role only after transiting the literal function of motherhood. At the same time she is not really Augustus' mother, and occupies the role of literal mother only briefly. Even as it marks the loss of what she wants to preserve, little Emma's death is what enables motherhood to be no more than a rite of passage for Emma. It marks her reinscription into the structures of genre and family as the uneasy assumption of a position rather than of an identity, as symbolic rather than imaginary in Lacan's sense.[25] Implicated as it is in more than one signifying path, little Emma's death exemplifies the functioning of the genotext as process rather than thesis, as a conflictual flux that is simplified by any attempt at paraphrase.

If the genotext emerges in the spaces between characters and between characters and their roles, it can also be seen in the structuring of the plot. As distinct from "structure," a concept that codifies a mimetic reading of the plot in terms of what happens in it, what I call "structuring" or "emplotment" are concepts that call for a symptomatic reading of plot in terms of the pathology of its de(form)ation. The most crucial example here is the novel's emplotment through what is itself a highly charged signifier: the mechanism of repetition. Emma and Augustus first meet through an accident in which the coach in which she is travelling with Montague overturns and they are rescued by Augustus, with both men being badly injured. The plot ends with an uncanny recurrence of this accident, in which Augustus is fatally injured, with equally fatal ramifications for Emma's marriage to Montague.

The framing of Emma's passion in terms of violent accidents is a conspicuous departure from Hays' life, for both she and Frend lived on into their eighties. The accident inscribes the end of the affair in highly conflicted ways. In phenotextual terms, the association of passion with violence and ultimately death signifies its destructiveness. But such a conclusion in no way sums up the complexity of the relationships between characters. Throughout the novel Emma's passion has been distinguished from the ultimately murderous passion of Montague. Although she seems destined to meet Augustus, that meeting could just as easily have occurred at his mother's house. That her love for him is associated with scenes of destructiveness is thus accidental. Or to put it differently, at the level of the genotext the accident is itself a figure for the way passion and death are associated in the symbolism of the social text. It comments on the inscription of "passion" within the symbolic order, by marking this association as *accidental*, the result of a metonymic proximity. We can locate the disturbance of the phenotext in the symmetrical neatness of the plot, which deflects our attention from the text as mimesis to the processes that produce figures mimetically as truths whose rigidity is symptomatically registered in this symmetry.

This second reading of the accident is genotextual in focusing on the text as body rather than as mimesis: in focusing not on what the text says, but on what it does not say through its resistance to the rigid skeleton of the plot. As important is the simultaneously structural and psychic mechanism by which the ending is inscribed. For the recurrence of the accident should be read not simply as another stage in the plot but also in terms of what Jameson calls the form of content,[26] or in terms of a de-formation of content that shifts attention from the event itself in the phenotext to its *structuring* as a return or repetition. The event itself, Augustus' death, is not particularly surprising. Indeed if we think of an ending as a text's self-conscious recognition of its unconscious, of what has already happened emotionally, Augustus' death is simply the plot's delayed reaction to his departure from Emma's life some years before. What is shocking is the way the story ends, with an uncanny repetition that foregrounds structure in such a way as to make form take the place of content. In marking its structural mechanisms in this way, the narrative knots the signified within the signfier, so that one must attend not only to what the text says but also to the form in which the abortion of Emma's passion is communicated. This mechanism is all the more conspicuous because it involves a symptomatic rewriting of the novel's pre-text, in which the circumstances of Hays' meeting with Frend and the eventual dissolution of their relationship are much less remarkable.

As a signifier, the mechanism of repetition is highly overdetermined, and can be read in several ways on which we can only touch. On one level, Augustus' departure from Emma's life in the same way he entered it brings the plot full circle. This circularity has the function of purgation as well as closure: the end returns to the beginning to correct it, by disposing of Augustus and thus correcting Emma's initial error. But on another level this confusion of beginnings and endings within the motif of the return undoes the entire project of ending. It is not simply that the second accident reawakens Emma's passion for Augustus, contaminating the present with the past. It also reopens the whole issue of passion as the material site of women's struggles.

At this level the repetition of the accident is connected to other forms of repetition: to the novel itself as memoir or return, and to autonarration as the author's return to her past. Repetition is most obviously a form of obsession: a return to something that cannot be disposed of because it has not yet been worked through. But it is also an occasion for revision, and in this sense it is linked to another instance of repetition in the novel: the repetition of the first generation in the second. This figure, which was to become increasingly common in nineteenth-century narrative, often signifies the taming and attenuation of the past in the present, as in Frankenstein's repetition as Walton or the return of Heathcliff and Cathy as their Victorian children.[27] The repetition of Emma's letters as her memoirs purports on one level to be just such an act of self-taming. But given the curious reversal by which it is the present that functions as a shadowy type of the past in these texts and not vice

versa, the typological drive that mobilizes repetition remains curiously unfulfilled, making the figure the site of a lack. As a moment
of irresolution and unfulfillment, repetition figures the survival of
desire within the asceticism imposed by the symbolic order, infecting
or affecting the reader with this desire, by making reading into
another form of repetition. The link between repetition as a motif in
the plot and the functioning of the figure on a hermeneutic as well as
a diegetic level is explicitly made through Emma's forwarding of her
memoirs to Augustus Jr., who as inscribed reader embodies the
potential for repetition as re-vision, and as Emma's male surrogate
embodies repetition as the possibility of progress.

III

Crucial to autonarration is its implication of the reader in the
continuation of its project. The genre thus participates in what I
have elsewhere described as the major transgeneric form of Romanticism: a transactional text whose significance must be conceived
historically, and must be developed and renegotiated through its
reading.[28] The question of reading is foregrounded in Hays' novel
by its semi-epistolary format. Emma conveys the story of her life
through her letters, and she thus displaces attention from plot to
reflection, from the outside to the inside but also the other side. For
unlike the Portuguese Nun, Emma does not simply write about her
love to her lover: she also writes to Francis and Augustus Jr. Thus the
novel is not simply about desire, but also about the communication
and continuation of desire within an economy in which there is
more than one reader, and thus potentially more than one law.

Much of the recent work on epistolary fiction has approached it
through a vocabulary of presence and absence that emphasizes the
textuality and supplementary status of the letter.[29] Alternatively, the
letter has been seen socioculturally as a site of the alienation that
results from the commodification of language.[30] Either way, epistolarity has been associated with a split between language and
experience, and a consequent loss of power. There is no question
that Emma writes her love because she cannot act it, and that both
her love and her ideas are confined within the space of representation. On the other hand, the very limitations of letters are also
enabling conditions. Because of their marginality in relation to
speech and print, letters were often associated with pietist or

dissenting communities and thus with oppositional culture.[31] Emma herself draws attention to the advantages of the letter when she comments that she can express herself "with more freedom on paper" (M, 39). For her meetings with Francis are generally in the company of others, and even her occasional private walks with him are constrained by an uncertainty about his own relationship to the existing social order. Writing to him without these constraints, she can write to a subject dialectically split between the real and the ideal, between what he is and what he could be.

As the site of a crossing between actual and possible worlds, the intimate letter also blurs the boundary between public and personal space. It says what one is not supposed to say and thus renegotiates the terms of the social contract. Letters were not necessarily read only by the person to whom they were addressed, and for women they occupied a space midway between the private and the public in the information network.[32] Hays herself wrote about her relationship with Frend in letters to William Godwin. Godwin was not only a friend, he was also the author of Political Justice. As such he occupied a position whose ambiguity blurred the boundary between the personal and the public, and thus allowed his correspondent a strategic enunciative position on that boundary. Moreover Hays' letters may also have been read by Mary Wollstonecraft, who certainly read her novel, and who in turn wrote to Godwin and criticized him for his masculine response to Hays.[33] In publishing the novel, Hays formalized what had already happened in her writing of the letters: she placed her situation and her responses to it within a communicative circuit that was not confined to the addressee of the letters or the designated reader(s) of the novel.[34]

A discussion of Memoirs as a letter to the reader must begin with a curious anomaly. The novel in so many ways seems to call for a "female" reader. But whereas Wollstonecraft's Maria addresses her memoirs to her daughter, redirects them to Darnford and Jemima, and then uncertainly brings back her daughter, Emma Courtney's readers are exclusively male. However, the turn to Augustus Jr. should not be read phenotextually as the positing of an actual addressee. In writing to her daughter, Wollstonecraft's protagonist turns towards the future, but also returns to someone whose fate may repeat her own. Hays turns against such doubts by allowing Emma's daughter to die. Yet in so doing she turns not to the male reader addressed in An Appeal, but to the wounded masculine[35] in herself: to that part of herself which cannot survive except by figuring itself as male. The recourse to a male reader must be taken in conjunction with the fact that the novel's male protagonists all die, except for Francis who simply drops out of the narration. These various deaths register the bankruptcy of the patriarchal order, and displace Emma's investment in it to the level of a signifier she is constrained to use. Moreover, the disappearance of Francis, once he has served his purpose as an intersubjective stimulus for Emma's ideas, marks the fact that the male reader is less the designated reader of the text than a facilitating position within a communicative grammar that is still historically situated. In gendering her addressee as male, Emma allows *herself* a position from which she can be heard. Both positions (that of the writer and that of the addressee) shift even within the space of the novel, with the replacement of Francis by Augustus Jr. For Francis is characterized in sufficient detail to limit what Emma can say to him. Although she transgresses those limits by pleading her passion as well as discussing it rationally, Francis, as a representative of the liberal male public of the time, cannot really hear her. Augustus, by contrast, takes no significant part in the novel's action, and we have no way of guessing his responses. His extradiegetic status thus allows him to figure the possibility of a reading not constrained within the present order.

Through the young Augustus, in short, Emma inscribes within the text a space for (re)reading, and associates the reader with a future dialectically connected to her own past. As a figure for the reader, however, the young Augustus is ambiguously within and beyond the novel's diegesis, between the symbolic and imaginary orders. Although the relatively little we know about him leaves us free to imagine his responses to Emma's memoirs, the one thing we do know is the name of his father. Thus what the turn to Augustus allows Emma to do is painfully knotted in to what it disables her from doing. For it requires her to survive in a space that remains symbolic because, in Kristeva's words, it connects "two separated positions" (*R*, 43): that of desire and the means of its signification through an inscribed reader, through a signifier which is still part of the economy of gender.

It is therefore important to remember that Augustus is only the temporary addressee of the memoirs. Through the shift from Francis to the younger Augustus, Hays formalizes what may have been instinctive in the correspondence. She disengages us from identifying with the novel's intratextual readers, using them to create a space within the text which can and will be occupied differently by different readers. This space can be described as the "reading-function," and must be distinguished from concepts such as the "designated reader," the "implied reader," or the "superreader," in that it is a structural position within the text, rather than an ideological position identified with a certain category of person and thus given a specific content. In the writing of the novel the text's communicative grammar is necessarily given such a content in ways that are historically determined. But it is here that the embedding of the novel in the writer's biography becomes important. For by situating her text in the life of a historical subject, Hays asks us to read beyond the ways in which she herself is constrained to write its ending and to inscribe its reading.

The reading-function is implicit in the "temporal polyvalence" which Janet Altman notes as one of the features of epistolarity, but which once again has been associated with the letter as failed communication. Epistolary communication does not occur in a shared space and time like conversation, but instead involves several times: the time of the act, its writing, and its reading.[36] Introducing the notion of time as perspective, epistolarity also introduces the possibility of understanding as historical, and of history as rereading. One of the earlier examples of amorous epistolary discourse is *The Letters of a Portuguese Nun* (1669).[37] In the movement from the nun, who writes only to her uncaring lover and writes only about her passion, to Emma Courtney who writes about social as well as amorous issues, we witness an expansion from the erotics to the politics of desire, effected through a deliberate exploitation of temporal polyvalence. In a sense, however, this expansion had already occurred in the reception history of the *Letters* and analogous texts, and had thus modified the hermeneutics of epistolarity in ways that were crucial to writers such as Hays. For although the nun writes only to her lover, real people write back to the fictional character, culminating in the multiple-authored *Three Marias: New Portuguese Letters* (1972). This process of revision had already begun in the eighteenth century, with an imaginary sequel that supplied the lover's missing responses to the nun, thus rewriting life through fiction.[38]

Crucial to the way the text reaches beyond its inscribed readers to an extratextual reader is the hermeneutics of the autonarrative genre itself. We have demarcated four zones of signification in autonarration: the autobiographical pre-text, which is entirely non-discursive and which constitutes something like what Jameson calls the Real; the public life of the author; the phenotext of the novel; and the genotext, an area of affect and signification that is not so much in the diegesis as it is in a symptomatic *reading* of its psychotropology. Where a purely fictional text could be approached simply in terms of the last two areas, the four zones are part of the more complex dynamic of creation and reception specific to the genre under consideration. By writing their lives as texts that are themselves about women writing their lives, novelists such as Hays and Wollstonecraft register an awareness of their lives as textually constructed. On the other hand, this taking of life into the text is itself taken back into life, because the *Memoirs* have their origins in the experience of a real woman whose life will be affected by their reading. The constant crossings between life and text are represented in the novel by the way characters and functions cross over between the extradiegetic and intradiegetic worlds. As author of the memoirs, Emma is an extradiegetic narrator who is also a character in her own story, and who functions as an intradiegetic narrator in this story when she writes her memoirs for Francis. In the text itself the position of subject is thus shown as moving between the extra- and intradiegetic worlds. Similarly the function of reading is transferred between intradiegetic readers such as Augustus and Francis, who receive Emma's letters, and Augustus Jr., who does not participate in the action of the novel.

These transfers between extra- and intradiegetic worlds analogically interimplicate life and text so as to draw the extratextual reader into the text. But it is the specifically auto(bio)graphic nature of a text such as the *Memoirs* that stops this process from becoming aestheticized as the play of mirrors it becomes in many self-reflexive texts. For in making her personal life public Hays takes certain risks all too evident in the ridicule to which she was subjected, and this "signing" of her text (to borrow a word from Bakhtin)[39] asks us to reciprocate by transposing the text into our own lives. We return here to the importance of desire in this novel. Because autonarration mixes text and life, it also mixes the signifier into the signified in ways for which a purely deconstructive theory of the sign cannot account. The desire which is the subject of the novel transmits itself metonymically to its mode of functioning, so that desire is not simply what the text is about, but is also the means by which its subject is signified. Transposing her desire into the symbolic world of the novel, Hays implicates her text within the desire of a reader for whom reading too is an autonarrative process. It is through this reader that the novel's genotext enters history.

NOTES

1 Mary Hays, *Memoirs of Emma Courtney* (London: Pandora Press, 1987). All references to this text (*M*) will hereafter be in parentheses in the text.

2 Julia Kristeva, *Revolution in Poetic Language*, trans. Margaret Waller (New York: Columbia University Press, 1984), 59–60. References to this work (*R*) will hereafter be in parentheses in the text.

3 My biographical information is drawn from Gina Luria, "Mary Hays' Letters and Manuscripts," *Signs* 3 (1977): 524–30; and from Luria's introduction to her reprint of Hays' *Appeal to the Men of Great Britain in Behalf of Women* (New York: Garland Press, 1974).

4 Hays continues in the same letter by insisting that her aim is to show "the possible effects of the present system of things, & the contradictory principles which have bewilder'd mankind, upon private character, & private happiness" (quoted in Luria, "Mary Hays' Letters," 529–30).

5 See for instance Claire Tomalin, *The Life and Death of Mary Wollstonecraft* (London: Weidenfeld and Nicholson, 1964), 241, 245; James Foster, *History of the Pre-Romantic Novel in England* (New York: Modern Language Association, 1949), 259–60. Another example of the automatic dismissal of Hays is provided by Allene Gregory's *The French Revolution and the English Novel* (London: G. P. Putnam, 1915). Gregory also "deals" with Hays by absorbing her into Godwin, despite her concession that the novel by Godwin to which *Memoirs* bears a "striking resemblance" was published much later (223), and despite the fact that Emma corresponds with Francis on the assumption that opposition is true friendship.

6 While sharing Wollstonecraft's sense that the Rousseauian model of romance wrote women into a male script, Hays may also have found in Rousseau a compelling version of the discourse of desire. Emma Courtney is in the middle of reading *La Nouvelle Héloïse* when her father disapprovingly takes the book away, so that she reads about Julie's passion but not its correction. The resulting misprision shapes her life in ways that are both disastrous and constitutive of her subjectivity. Emma's early interest in romance is sharpened by her father's insistence that she read history, with the result that romance offers her the only available position from which she can express female desire. As such, it is a version of what Lacan calls the imaginary, which attaches the subversiveness of this desire to imagos that are part of the symbolic order.

7 *Collected Letters of Mary Wollstonecraft*, ed. Ralph M. Wardle (Ithaca: Cornell University Press, 1979), 376.

8 I use this term in the sense used by Lacan and Kristeva, to indicate the order in which we are constructed as speaking subjects: the order of syntax, which is also the order of the law and the family. This order is "symbolic" in the sense that the individual's identity within it is always other: a representation of her as something else, for and by someone else.

9 Felicity Nussbaum, *The Autobiographical Subject: Gender and Ideology in Eighteenth-Century England* (Baltimore: Johns Hopkins University Press, 1989), 179–80.

10 Hays, *Appeal*, 70, 67.

11 Judith Butler, *Subjects of Desire: Hegelian Reflections in Twentieth-Century France* (New York: Columbia University Press, 1987), 186.

12 Butler, *Subjects of Desire*, 186–87, 192–98.

13 Jean Hyppolite, *Genesis and Structure of Hegel's Phenomenology of Spirit*, trans. Samuel Cherniak and John Heckman (Evanston: Northwestern University Press, 1974), 166.

14 Hyppolite, *Genesis and Structure*, 162–68.

15 Butler, *Subjects of Desire*, 9.

16 Percy Bysshe Shelley, "Preface" to *Alastor*, in *Shelley's Poetry and Prose*, ed. Donald Reiman and Sharon Powers (New York: Norton, 1977), 69.

17 We might note in passing the frequent use of certain proto-Romantic words and concepts: "image," "imagination," and "portrait" (*M*, 53, 82, 89, 93, 122); "ideal" or "romantic" (*M* 20, 60, 80, 84, 103, 171); and "visionary" (*M*, 46, 84).

18 Linda Kauffman, *Discourses of Desire: Gender, Genre, and Epistolary Fiction* (Ithaca: Cornell University Press, 1986).

19 See Kauffman, *Discourses of Desire*, 160–78 and 92–97. Kauffman seems to endorse the feeling of the authors of the *New Portuguese Letters* that "it is immaterial whether the experience and emotions described in the nun's letters is fictive or real" (283). My argument, that it is rhetorically if not factually material, is slightly different.

20 Ruth Perry, *Women, Letters, and the Novel* (New York: AMS Press, 1980), 74–80.

21 Fredric Jameson, *The Political Unconscious: Narrative as a Socially Symbolic Act* (Ithaca: Cornell University Press, 1981), 35, 81–82.

22 Augustus refers to Emma as his sister (*M*, 71), the role which Mrs. Harley ultimately assigns her (*M*, 156), and which marks the incestuous and forbidden nature of this union within the terms of the symbolic order. Similarly, Emma Jr. and Augustus Jr. are brought up as brother and sister.

23 The scandalous memoirs are discussed by Felicity Nussbaum, who describes them as the first significant form of women's self-writing other than spiritual autobiography (*Autobiographical Subject*, 180). Nussbaum sees the scandalous memoirists as both confirming and contesting the

dominant ideology, and further notes the conflicted position of these writers given the relegation of "unlicensed sexuality to the lower classes" (179). I would further argue that the memoirists' identification of desire with sexuality aborts the emergent radicalism of their texts, and that Hays' representation of a love that is and is not sexual is a way of retaining her right to address a middle-class liberal audience.

24 An exception to this statement is Kristeva's recent article "The Adolescent Novel," in *Abjection, Melancholia and Love: The Work of Julia Kristeva*, ed. John Fletcher and Andrew Benjamin (London: Routledge, 1990), 8–23. Here too she focuses on a series of symbolic positions assumed by the subject of narrative. But inasmuch as these positions are experimental, her concern is (at least potentially) the *engendering* of narrative, the desire that results in the subject assuming different positions in the symbolic order.

25 The imaginary and the symbolic can be seen as different ways of relating to an identity that is always already specular. In the imaginary the subject identifies with the image (or imago) in the mirror. In the symbolic she is uneasily aware of it as a representation.

26 Jameson, *Political Unconscious*, 242.

27 A less well-known example of this motif is Arnold's "Tristan and Iseult," in which the dark passionate Iseult is repeated as Tristan's paler, fairer, and more domestic second love. Arnold's text parallels Victorian novels such as *David Copperfield* in its linking of repetition to the domestication of the Romantic, the conversion of revolutionary energy into evolutionary caution.

28 See Tilottama Rajan, *The Supplement of Reading: Figures of Understanding in Romantic Theory and Practice* (Ithaca: Cornell University Press, 1990); and "The Other Reading: Transactional Epic in Milton, Blake, and Wordsworth," in *Milton, The Metaphysicals and the Romantics*, ed. Lisa Low and Anthony John Harding (Cambridge: Cambridge University Press, 1994), 20–46.

29 Ruth Perry treats the epistolary form thematically, as an expression of separation and isolation (*Women, Letters, and the Novel*, 93–118). Roy Roussel approaches it in terms of presence and absence in "Reflections on the Letter: The Reconception of Presence and Distance in *Pamela*," *ELH* 41 (1974): 375–99. Although her argument becomes increasingly political as the book proceeds, Linda Kauffman's early chapters associate epistolarity with a Lacanian form of desire. Thus she describes desire as "infinitely transcribable, yet ultimately elusive, and . . . therefore reiterated ceaselessly," and she refers to the "metonymic displacement of desire" (*Discourses of Desire*, 24–25).

30 Thus W. Austin Flanders in *Structures of Experience* (Columbus: University of South Carolina Press, 1984), links the letter to "the production of language as a commodity through the use of paper and writing utensils as tools and its consequent distance from primary experience" (79).

31 Katharine Goodman, *Dis/Closures: Women's Autobiography in Germany Between 1790 and 1914* (New York: Peter Lang, 1986), 77.

32 Goodman, *Dis/Closures*, 79.

33 "I think you *wrong* . . . You judge not in your own case as in that of another. You give a softer name to folly and immorality when it flatters – yes, I must say it – your vanity, than to mistaken passion when it was extended to another – you termed Miss Hays' conduct insanity when only her own happiness was involved" (*Collected Letters*, 404).

34 It is further worth noting that epistolary fictions such as the *Letters to a Portuguese Nun* often resulted in revisionary sequels. Not only were fictional letters treated as though they were about real life persons, writers/readers also responded to these novels-as-letters, by creating further fictions in order to rewrite 'life' through fiction (see Perry, *Women, Letters, and the Novel*, 72–84, 111).

35 I owe this term to Ross Woodman.

36 Janet Gurkin Altman, *Epistolarity: Approaches to a Form* (Columbus: Ohio State University Press, 1982), 129–35. Ruth Perry sees "the time lag of long-distance communication" primarily as a cause of misunderstanding (*Women, Letters, and the Novel*, 108).

37 See the account by Kauffman, *Discourses of Desire*, 91–118, 271–312. Kauffman points out that the letters were enormously popular in the eighteenth century, provoking numerous English translations, imitations and sequels (95). It is therefore quite likely that Hays would have read them.

38 See Perry, *Women, Letters, and the Novel*, 111.

39 While recognizing that texts and actions are intersubjectively produced and do not have their origin in a transcendental ego, Bakhtin nevertheless sees the subject as implicated in his or her text. "Signature," according to Morson and Emerson, means "making an act one's own, taking responsibility for it" ("Introduction," in *Rethinking Bakhtin*, ed. Gary Saul Morson and Caryl Emerson [Evanston: Northwestern University Press, 1989], 16).

CHAPTER 10

"The science of herself": scenes of female enlightenment

Mary Jacobus

I want to start by proposing that the scene of female enlightenment is also the scene of sexual difference – or rather, its ideological construction and enforcement. What a woman *knows*, and what a woman *wants*, or must give up, are thoroughly entangled in enlight-enment discourses about women and education. Both knowledge and desire (it goes without saying) are liable to severe restraints. Whether male- or female-authored, Jacobin or conservative, the scene of female enlightenment tends to veer not only towards the question of female sexuality – the dangerous susceptibility that Wollstonecraft's writing encodes as "sensibility" – but also towards the problematic outcome of unconfined feminine desire.[1] For the British women writers who constitute the female enlightenment of the early Romantic period, these restraints often coincide with melancholia, taking the form of melancholic identification with a lost maternal object. When thoughts turn to the education of daughters, the figure of the mother, frequently written out of enlightenment discourse as absent, deficient, or dead (more rarely serving as educator and model), surfaces as a figure of melancholic abjection. What I am here calling "the science of herself" – a science given very different emphases by, for instance, Rousseau (for whom the role of women is to restrain men's desire) or a later prophet of enlight-enment like Freud (for whom the hysterical woman has repressed her own desire) – can be viewed as a form of enlightenment knowledge that occupies, by default, the place of a lost or abjected maternal object. This is a space of negativity, in the sense that a desire or political demand surfaces only in the form of negation or denial. A narrative that says "*no* mother," or "not *that* mother" (or even the heroine's implicit complaint that she is unmothered) becomes a means to admit both melancholia and the mother into the rational discourse from which they have ostensibly been excluded.

In the woman-authored educational fictions of the early Romantic period, the education of the daughter seems not only to demand the reform of the mother, but the installation of sexual difference within the undifferentiated (i.e., masculine) enlightenment subject. Thoughts on the education of daughters typically involve not only maternal abjection, but the unsettling of enlightenment Reason itself – not so much by its sparring partner, passion, or its sometime ally, imagination, as by a melancholia that brings gender implications along with it. A form of knowledge which specifically unmans the father, "the science of herself" involves the feminization of the masculine subject. And as a transposition of genre from educational discourse to the feminine fictions that become a vehicle for both proto-feminist and conservative writing during the 1790s, the scene of female enlightenment also gives rise to another inquiry – an inquiry into the ways in which women were interpellated into what, with hindsight, we call Romanticism. "The science of herself," or knowing (about) women, can even be read as a special form of the negativity that is implicit in the resistance of Romanticism to the imperialism of enlightenment thought. This is not to associate women with incurable irrationality (or, for that matter, to associate Romanticism with resurrecting romance, or celebrating affect). Rather, it suggests that in the novel of female education, the woman who refuses enlightenment, or who insists – however wilfully or wishfully – on what we might now call women's ways of knowing, signals both a representational and a political resistance to the empire of Reason. Flagging the uneasy fit between an enlightenment subjectivity predicated on masculinity and the trope of femininity which is often used to sustain it, she puts in play an alternative narrative and a potentially unsettling model of the gendered subject. If enlightenment itself is a trope, or *topos* (what I am here calling a "scene"), so, by the same token, is femininity; the scene of female enlightenment enacts what might be called its narrative or generic mode – a scene of instruction transposed from educational literature directed at women to the novel, where instruction can be complicated by women writers and refused by female characters. These fictional scenes of female enlightenment might be thought of as enacting what Freud was later to discover, namely, the ways in which the unconscious persistently, if unprogrammatically, resists the imperialism of the understanding (not necessarily, however, in the interests of conservative or reactionary formations). In other words, even negativity can be read as political where women are concerned, and perhaps Romanticism too.

This multi-form narrative of feminine resistance is the one that I want to explore, not only as it gets played out in a variety of late eighteenth-century writings about female education, but also, more particularly, in the plots of novels written by women themselves. "The science of herself," I will argue, inhabits the discourse of enlightenment knowledge as its unacknowledged, unreformed, and potentially destabilizing other – a textual or epistemological unconscious that occupies the ambiguous space where genre and gender collide within the fictional space of the novel. It is tempting to associate this space particularly with "subjectivity," mood, or affect – that is, with a transposition of the social and cultural demarcations of gender into the semiotic markings of the literary text or the counter-eddies of late eighteenth-century literary culture, where melancholia, whether masculine or feminine, occupies a privileged discursive position in aesthetic ideology. The political demand made by this negatively inscribed feminine subjectivity is the measure of the Enlightenment's refusal to accommodate the very discourse of sexual difference that its inquiries into the nature and rights of personhood, bodies, and passions had seemed to initiate. When vindicating the rights of men gives rise to *A Vindication of the Rights of Woman*, femininity turns out to be what complicates the notion on which "rights" themselves are predicated; namely, that of rational (self-)possession by an unalienated enlightenment subject. The estrangement of women from enlightenment discourse marks the limits of that discourse and its ultimate failure to encompass sexual difference, along with the resistance or negativity that complicate relations between psychic life and social or juridical being. "The science of herself," then, might be glossed as knowledge inflected by this negative mode – knowledge situated in the domain where another science, psychoanalysis, poses questions about the limited effects of knowledge when it comes to the enlightenment of women and children, and even men. Femininity, as I propose to read it, becomes a figure for the limits of enlightenment.

I LOVER'S VOWS; OR, AN IMPROPER EDUCATION

I want to open the question of female enlightenment from the margins, where it often takes the form of a baffled pedagogical transaction between the sexes, or an inquiry into the erotics of courtship. In *Mansfield Park* (1814), the proposed in-house performance of Kotzbue's play, *The Child of Love*, translated by Elizabeth Inchbald as *Lover's Vows* (1798), allows Austen to depict the invasion of the English country house by foreign forms of intimacy. In Austen's novel, Inchbald's translation (which is also her domestication) of Kotzbue's play imports literary impropriety into the temporarily unfathered patriarchal family by performing it parenthetically; the scandal is that the bawdy puns (Mary Crawford's) or Jacobin views (Kotzbue's and Inchbald's own) should be permitted to enter the discursive world of Mansfield Park, instead of remaining beyond the pale of relations between the landed gentry whose country houses, vicarages, shrubberies, and parks set the limits for proper intercourse between the sexes while keeping both slavery (the source of wealth) and sexuality (the source of instability) off-stage. *Lover's Vows* features topics that had become associated with the Jacobin women writers of the 1790s – seduction, illegitimacy, and the fallen woman, treated in Inchbald's translation with progressive democratic sentiment. Inchbald herself, in *A Simple Story* (1791), had dealt with the miserable consequences of adultery and seduction that Austen simultaneously identifies and casts out with the throw-away line that announces her final chapter: "Let other pens dwell on guilt and misery." But the figures of the adulterous Maria Rushworth or the improperly brought-up Mary Crawford linger disturbingly in the wings, serving as displaced versions of the enlightened or admonitory Jacobin women who disrupt the domestic sphere by importing the politics of sexuality into the family, reminding us that what the family excludes is also what makes it a space of confinement for women, and that the family always contains within in it the very negativity it attempts to cast out (illegitimacy, adultery, class conflict, the exploitation of bodies, and the expropriation of rights). These negatively exemplary women, whether adulterous wives or unmarried mothers, whether punished or made the victims of tragedy, abjected or progressive (depending on the author's political views), provide what might be called an education in experience. Unassimilable, contradictory, at odds with propriety, such an education reaches beyond the instruction manual to the material and sexual conditions of women's actual lives and knowledge, both inside and outside marriage, within or beyond the confines of the family, to create a disruptive or ambiguous counter-discourse even within ostensibly conservative fictions such as Austen's.

"Lover's Vows" contains a scene of pedagogical courtship that implicitly equates an attempt at female seduction (that is, the seduction of a man by a woman) with female emancipation, as was often the case in both Jacobin fictions and the anti-Jacobin novels that satirized them.[2] In Kotzbue's play, an aristocratic young woman proposes to her tutor, compounding sex-role-reversal with democratic sentiment. Unlike the forward hoyden of the German original ("indelicately blunt" is Inchbald's own characterization), the Amelia of *Lover's Vows* woos her lover in archly educational terms:

> AMELIA . . . [*Hesitating*] perhaps, who can tell, but that I might teach something as pleasant to you, as resolving a problem is to me.
> ANHALT Woman herself is a problem.
> AMELIA And I'll teach you to make her out.
> ANHALT You teach?
> AMELIA Why not? None but a woman can teach the science of herself: and although I own I am very young, a young woman may be as agreeable for a tutoress as an old one.[3]

This last proposition – "None but a woman can teach the science of herself" – proposes woman as the one empowered to give the lesson of love to her male teacher. Her lesson, however, is less that of reversed courtship (women have desires too, and may want to enlighten men about them) than that of the riddle of feminine desire itself. When is it anything else, since "Woman herself is a problem"? The scene between Amelia and Anhalt replays the eroticized and seductive teacher-student relationship of Julie and St-Preux in *La Nouvelle Héloïse* in a more explicitly feminist mode. For the Rousseau of *Emile*, we might also recall, only a man was qualified to teach the science of woman, since the required syllabus is actually the science of man (as opposed to woman); it is women's job to understand men better than they do themselves. If "Woman herself is a problem," as Anhalt glumly opines, Rousseau's solution lay in what Wollstonecraft denounced as the enforced shaping of women to the contours of masculine desire, including men's desire to displace their own sexuality onto women, thereby rendering them responsible for arousing masculine desire, and for making men feel strong instead of weak. By contrast, Anhalt suggests that understanding the enigma of woman – woman constituted as the object of both knowledge and desire – is men's problem. Freud's vexed question, "what does [a] woman want?" hovers anachronistically in the air. When the answer to the oedipal riddle can only be "man," it is hard to know why women should need such extensive education in the first place – a difficulty that Rousseau himself was forced to confront when he drew up his painstaking program for the education of the so-called "natural" woman, in Book v of *Emile*. If the complementary woman can't be found in nature, then she must be educated into artificial compliance with her destined partner.

For a woman, Amelia seems to say, "the science of herself" is the one subject she alone is qualified to teach; hers, after all, is the subjectivity in question. Freud's inquiry – what *do* women want? – allows for a cautious reframing of the question raised by enlightened feminist discourse. This question, "What do women want *to know?*" comes to seem closer to "How is a feminine subject constituted?" (and what has desire to do with this question, anyway?). Wollstone-craft's answer in *A Vindication of the Rights of Woman* – the feminine subject is constituted under conditions of learned weakness, inher-ited debasement, and enforced sexual subordination – emerges from her discussion of the barriers to female education; becoming rational subjects as men become rational subjects is precluded to women by socially imposed deficiencies of understanding (thus Wollstonecraft). Inchbald's novel of improper female education, *A Simple Story*, ends with a sobering verdict on the giddy but attractive, and ultimately tragic heiress, "the unthinking Miss Milner," whose courtship, marriage, adultery, and death shape Inchbald's two-generational novel. Miss Milner's father, writes Inchbald soberly at the close of her novel, had better have given his fortune away than have failed to bestow on his daughter "A PROPER EDUCATION."[4] By contrast, Miss Milner's own daughter, Matilda, is bred in a depressive school of self-restraint and adversity. Not, however, sufficiently schooled in adversity for Mary Wollstonecraft; a review of *A Simple Story* that is generally attributed to her complains that if the unthinking mother's seductive sensibility makes her too attractive, her chastened and debilitated daughter lacks dignity of mind. "Why do all female writers," she complains, "even when they display their abilities, always give a sanction to the libertine reveries of men? Why do they poison the minds of their own sex, by strengthening a male prejudice that makes women systematically weak?"[5] More adversity should equal more strength, not more weakness – not more subjection to masculine fantasy, and hence, more systemic, internalized victim-hood. The libertine reveries of men such as Rousseau should have no place in the "proper education" of women as enlightenment subjects. But, inevitably, these reveries infect the plot of romantic fiction, in part because such fiction draws so heavily on the contra-dictory, collusive materials of romantic and heterosexual love.

Earlier in *A Simple Story*, Inchbald writes: "Education is called second nature"[6] – a second nature that ought to be more powerful than the first, if vows of celibacy or marriage are to be preserved and persons, whether male or female, are to remain inviolate. This "second nature" is at once a supplement to (first) nature and, at the same time, a guarantee of its integrity; the conflict between "nature" and "second nature" is Miss Milner's undoing, and succumbing to her passionate but undisciplined sensibility is what temporarily undoes her noble guardian, Lord Elmwood (Dorriforth), who gives up his own religious discipline – his vows of priesthood – to become the conflicted but eroticized lover who later turns into a betrayed and harshly disciplining husband. This doubleness places a tension at the scene of education, and, I will argue, poses a special problem for enlightenment women. The formation of the natural man – the project of *Emile* – has as its final act the formation of the woman who answers to man's desire that his desire should be at once aroused and regulated. For Rousseau, the contradictory and conflicted ideological labor involved in producing (and internalizing) this perfect feminine complementarity is the mark of second nature. "Amidst our senseless arrangements," he writes, punitively, "a decent woman's life is a perpetual combat against herself. It is just that this sex share the pain of the evils it has caused us."[7] Discipline becomes self-discipline in the Rousseauian system. The acculturation of woman to her melancholy destiny starts early. Here is the specimen catechism which he provides for the girl-child. The first question is: "Do you remember the time when your mother was a girl?" The little girl's instruction goes on to cover pre-existence, youth, age – above all, age – *en route* to its final and sobering destination, death:

> NURSE And what do big girls become?
> LITTLE GIRL They become women.
> NURSE And what do women become?
> LITTLE GIRL They become mothers.
> NURSE And what do mothers become?

LITTLE GIRL They become old.
NURSE Will you, then, become old?
LITTLE GIRL When I am a mother.[8]

And so on. The sticking-point is death: "O nurse, I don't want to die!" exclaims the little girl, interrupting her nurse's litany of obsolescence. What a school of adversity is here. As the nurse's inexorable catechism maps her reproductive career, girl becomes woman, woman becomes mother, mother becomes old and dies. The role of feminine complementarity is merely an episode in this larger scheme of female abjection, whereby women learn that their lives are just a prelude to the afterlife, and that their pleasure is always a hostage to men's need to experience power over themselves in the form of power over women.

For Rousseau, only the sobering lesson of mother-daughter resemblance can instigate the proper female education denied to Inchbald's Miss Milner. In *A Simple Story* a chastened Matilda pays the price for her improperly educated mother's adultery by the enforced humiliations of her own upbringing. By giving education an explicitly melancholic tinge, the women writers of the 1790s provided a central and troubling insight into the Rousseauian model of female enlightenment. Wollstonecraft's term "adversity" names the unavoidable intrusion of female social and sexual subordination into the educational sphere, while melancholia – an understandable by-product of the depressing nursery regimen envisaged in *Emile* – becomes synonymous with the feminine position, and above all with the daughter's problematic maternal identification. Women (especially mothers) are not subjects, not even objects, in an educational process so conceived, but rather its abjects. They are the outcasts or cast-offs of a process in which the constitution of a masculine subject involves making women the locus of both desirable and despicable weakness (hence Wollstonecraft's complaint about *A Simple Story*). The subordination of women gets strategically redefined as the lesson of resignation to a dismal reproductive lot; their only consolation is death – what Wollstonecraft in *A Vindication* calls "the place where there will be neither marrying nor giving in marriage," or Christian after-life. The inquiry into femininity conducted by the women writers of the 1790s can be read as an inquiry into this education in ideologically and socially enforced weakness and melancholia, passed down from mother to daughter in the fictions of the Jacobin and anti-Jacobin female novel. Significantly, however, while the (im)properly educated woman turns out to be a melancholy subject, it is the right to melancholic subjectivity itself that women writers turn out to be claiming on behalf of women. Women learn (like Mary, the miserably unhappy, eponymous heroine of Wollstonecraft's novel about the education of a female Rousseau) that they are deprived even of the right to melancholy subjectivity, since, culturally at least, melancholia is defined as a masculine prerogative. There can be no "proper education" for a subject who is defined from the outset as inherently improper; there can only be a diminished, damaged, or self-destructive subjectivity in which marriage plays an unpredictable part.

The surprise, then, is that where abjection is enforced by the cultural process, the claim to melancholia may in and of itself mark a stage *en route* to vindicating women's rights. Wollstonecraft's objection that *A Simple Story* makes the mother too seductive and the daughter too depressed ("her health undermined by the trials of her patience") points to the troubled subtext of the fictionalized scene of female enlightenment. In this scenario, the heroine is divided against herself, trapped by melancholic identification with a dead mother whose impropriety is a given. Whether adulterous or dead, she leaves her daughter both unmothered and improperly educated; only the father can save her. In *A Simple Story*, the daughter educated in adversity has to be forgiven and accepted by her father in terms that register her psychic equivalence with an erring mother. If an education in second nature is imposed on a second-generation or second-degree fault (the daughter's inherited sensibility, her preprogrammed propensity for victimhood), one might say that here too – for all Inchbald's incipient feminism – it is the woman who pays, and the man who reaps the benefit, which is ultimately that of being able to re-enact the primal love-scene. In *A Simple Story*, Lord Elmwood is at last allowed to reappear in the sympathetic guise of a lover, instead of the unapproachable tyrant he has become, when he momentarily mistakes Matilda for her mother, clutching the body of his daughter to him with the words "'Miss Milner – Dear Miss Milner.'"[9] What "unmans" – the term is Inchbald's – the austere ex-cleric (a former Catholic Father as well as an unbending one) are the words uttered by Matilda: "'Save me.'" Saving the daughter becomes a means of saving the lost mother. But the cost is the mother's casting out, on the one hand, and the daughter's surrender of desire to her father on the other. What we see at work is a version of Freud's proposition in "A Special Type of Choice of Object made by Men" – namely, that the mother is always guilty of sexual relations, always an adulterous or fallen woman, so that the beloved can be rescued in the name of the mother from her own (necessarily errant) sexuality. Although Inchbald nowhere states her conclusion that Lord Elmwood's "unmanning" involves sexual responsiveness to an adulterous or sexualized woman, it is implicit in the double-barrelled structure of her mother-daughter narrative. The daughter is tainted with the inherited legacy of her mother's improper education; only the father can "save" her. By providing the protection of his house and name, he defines the non-negotiable terms of her re-entry into the society from which her spirited and rebellious mother had been summarily ejected as an adulteress (read: a woman of errant and contradictory desires). Those terms include the daughter's passivity in allowing Lord Elmwood to redirect her diminished, simplified, and obedient desires into the approved path of marriage within the now-consolidated extended family. She is permitted to marry, since the alternative is her abduction by another aristocrat, which would represent an offence to Lord Elmwood's property rights (rather than to any supposed rights in her own body); but her partner is Lord Elmwood's nephew and heir, his younger and less doctrinaire self. In effect, she marries, not her conflicted father, but a father-substitute who has no previous religious vows to break when he becomes her lover. Inchbald not only simplifies the plot second time around, but shelves the vexed question of feminine desire altogether.

II THE LUXURY OF GRIEF

As a way to test my proposition – that the scene of enlightenment, when it comes to women, is both pervasively melancholic and maternally inflected – I want to explore another Rousseau-influenced novel that problematizes the relations among mothers, daughters, and melancholia. In Ann Radcliffe's *The Romance of the Forest* (1791), the heroine makes her escape from a Sadeian narrative of harassment and sequestration under the aristocratic *ancien régime* associated with the novel's gothic-romantic French setting.[10] During a well-deserved period of rest and recuperation in the Savoy Alps, she takes refuge in the home of a Rousseauian educator, La Luc, who is modelled on the Savoyard pastor in Book IV of *Emile*. La Luc, who professes "the philosophy of nature, directed by common sense," takes his philosophy (like Rousseau's pastor) from both reason and the works of nature, teaching his parishioners and his family by personal example rather than precept. Radcliffe establishes "the family of La Luc" as an educational scene at the outset, introducing her Rousseauian interlude with an excerpt from James Cawthorne's "Life Unhappy, because We Use It Improperly: A Moral Essay." Cawthorne's lines make the soul – "Nature's finest instrument" – into an organ that can be preserved from the irregular wildness of passion (that is, improper use) by the harmonizing effects of sense: "Till ev'ry virtue, measure'd and refine'd, / As fits the concert of the master mind, / . . . pours along / Th'according music of the moral song."[11] Appropriately, the lesson in Radcliffe's novel, concerning as it does the proper uses of passion, will involve a musical instrument. La Luc offers an interesting contrast to Lord Elmwood in *A Simple Story*. Because he has lost his wife in early youth, his character is tinged "with a soft and interesting melancholy." But calamity has taught him "to feel with peculiar sympathy the distresses of others," while "Philosophy had strengthened, not hardened his heart" (245). Occupied in good works and in educating his children, La Luc has only one "indulgence." As Radcliffe puts it, "the tender melancholy with which affliction had tinctured his mind was by long indulgence, become dear to him" (247). La Luc indulges this "secret luxury" during solitary excursions in which "the deep and silent sorrow of his heart" finds relief in "the deep solitude of the mountains;" it is here, in seclusion from his family, that he can "resign himself to the luxury of grief" (246), a grief whose interior depths are signalled by the doubling of deep and silent sorrow and deep mountain solitude. These depths are reserved within the educational scene for the tender pleasures of melancholy – pleasures, however, that turn out to be reserved for men only. At once a mood and a culture, melancholy functions as a form of covert resistance to the message of Christian sympathy, forbearance, and endurance ostensibly associated with La Luc and with the religious tenor of Radcliffe's fiction more generally. The question in her novels is whether, and on what terms, women may be allowed to participate in a culture of melancholy that is at odds with the sentimental role prescribed for women by domestic ideology. If women belong in the home, while themselves serving as the repositories for familial feeling, melancholia must be located elsewhere. Yet it is in their forays beyond the confines of the home and domesticated ideology that Radcliffe's women typically encounter the obscure pleasures of melancholy.

Defined as "solitary enjoyment," as "luxury" and "indulgence," La Luc's "romantic sadness" (so called) centers erotically on his dead wife, "the idea of her he so faithfully loved." His solitary reveries endlessly replay his failed mourning. Identification with the loved object has prevented her surrender, assuming instead the contours of erotic melancholia (the terms are those of Freud's 1915 essay, "Mourning and Melancholia"). In Radcliffe's story-within-a-story, the Rousseauian father is infected with a malaise for which his daughter is required to provide the cure. It is, in fact, her melancholia that must be cast out, rather than his (which is allowed to remain encrypted in mountain solitude). When La Luc gives a lute to his daughter, Clara, it becomes an absorbing passion for which she neglects her domestic duties, her education, her other artistic pursuits, and her charitable activities among the local peasantry. Clara, who resembles her dead mother, bears the burden of Cawthorne's (and, by implication, Radcliffe's) "moral song." Recalled to duty by a sense of dissatisfaction with herself, she realizes that "This lute is my delight, and my torment!" and in the name of controlling her "inclinations," puts it aside. But, on one of those evenings where Radcliffe enjoys sounding the strain of distantly heard, atmospheric music – strains that often intimate an immanent sexual presence or mystery, as well as the floating signifier of melancholia that is more generally diffused through the Radcliffean landscape into which the errant heroine may stray – Clara succumbs to temptation:

The evening was still and uncommonly beautiful. Nothing was heard but the faint shivering of the leaves, which returned but at intervals, making silence more solemn, and the distant murmurs of the torrents that rolled among the cliffs. As she stood by the lake, and watched the sun slowly sinking below the alps, whose summits were tinged with gold and purple; as she saw the last rays of light gleam upon the waters whose surface was not curled by the lightest air, she sighed, "Oh! how enchanting would be the sound of my lute at this moment, on this spot, and when everything is so still around me!"

The temptation was too powerful for the resolution of Clara: she ran to the chateau, returned with the instrument to her dear acacias,

and beneath their shade continued to play till the surrounding
objects faded in darkness from her sight. But the moon arose, and
shedding a trembling lustre on the lake, made the scene [and
Clara?] more captivating than ever.

It was impossible to quit so delightful a spot; Clara repeated her favourite
airs again and again. The beauty of the hour awakened all her genius; she
never played with such expression before, and she listened with increasing
rapture to the tones as they languished over the waters and died away on
the distant air. She was perfectly enchanted: "No! Nothing was ever so
delightful as to play on the lute beneath her acacias, on the margin of the
lake, by moonlight!" (252)

The imperceptible drift into free-indirect narrative (" 'No! Nothing
was ever so delightful . . . ," ' etc.) signals a moment of ventriloquized
identification on Radcliffe's own part, even as she ostensibly dissociates herself from the daughter's fall into what is patently (to judge by
her father's solitary indulgence) the maternal sublime. "No! Nothing
was ever so delightful" as Radcliffe's, and the (female) reader's
luxurious self-surrender to evocations such as these. Why, then, must
the temptation be so strenuously resisted and finally renounced?

As Radcliffe and her Burkean readers would certainly have
known, not just silence or loud noises, but "a low, tremulous,
intermitting sound" produces sublime effects on the hearer.[12] Radcliffe frequently deploys these effects in her novels as the prelude to
disquieting discoveries – for instance, at the start of *The Mysteries of
Udolpho*, where a mysterious stranger, lingering in the vicinity of the
heroine with obscure intentions and an undeclared identity, is
sufficient both to sexualize the picturesque landscape and render it
vaguely uncanny. Sometimes, however, these musical effects represent a sort of maternal return of the repressed (in Radcliffe's novels,
an ambiguity surrounding the mother's sexuality or her fidelity to
the father often sets the scene for both wanted and unwonted sexual
advances directed at the daughter). In Clara's case, nature is not so
much sublimated as eroticized, haunted as it is by a maternal
remainder, or musical overspill – a semiotics of the alpine sublime
that it is tempting to call the voice of the mother, speaking both
through and in nature. But Radcliffe's extended description of
musical melancholy is the prelude to a didactically enacted ritual of
renunciation. Clara condemns herself for being, in Wollstonecraft's
terms, "weak" (that is, for being both seduced and seductive, captive
and captivating, and perhaps even for harboring libertine reveries of

her own. She has, she confesses, allowed herself to be the subject of uncontrolled inclinations: " 'I have prided myself on controlling my inclinations,' said she, 'and I have weakly yielded to their direction' " (252). Her lute-playing becomes a "temptation" from which she must recoil ("Since I cannot conquer temptation I will fly from it"). She takes the lute to her father and begs him to keep it "till she had taught her inclinations to submit to control" (253), much as Matilda, at the end of *A Simple Story*, puts her "inclinations" in charge of her father, preferring to have none of her own. Deeply moved by Clara's resolve, La Luc restores the instrument to her. But, in this scene of voluntary submission and self-regulated desire, she at first refuses to take it back; in case we missed the point, the ritual is repeated (she proffers the lute again, he hands it back to her once more). Clara's father, Radcliffe tells us, "thought she had never resembled her mother so much as at this instant, and tenderly kissing her, he for some moments, wept in silence." Significantly, it is the father for whom the scene has an overwhelming aftermath: "This scene called back recollections too tender for the heart of La Luc, and giving Clara the instrument, he abruptly quitted the room" (253). Presumably he takes off for the deep solitude of the mountains. What I want to note here is not simply the pleasures of melancholy that are to be found in a landscape associated with the dead mother, or the infusion of pleasurable music-making with female auto-eroticism, or even Clara's obedient surrender of pleasure as she internalizes La Luc's paternal control, giving him the right to enjoy what she must abjure. Rather, it is the way the daughter's disturbing resemblance to her mother once more unmans the father with "recollections too tender," just as Matilda's resemblance to her mother (" 'Miss Milner – Dear Miss Milner' ") had temporarily unmanned Lord Elmwood with recollections of his dead, desirable, adulterous wife.

One might well ask why the daughter must curb her solitary pleasures, while the father is allowed all the secret luxury of grief. Nature's finest instrument seems to require gender-differential tuning – seems, in Clara's case, all too seductively feminine, as if to signal the identity between the erotic potential of mother and daughter that is figured in the pleasurable solitude of the evening landscape. This haunting music at the margins of her novels allows Radcliffe to introduce the irrational, the sexual, the disruptive discourse of female – and often, maternal – sublimity or sublimation (here, the mother who is lost to the daughter through death, as well as to the father). Clara, therefore, is far from being a transparent window onto the Rousseauian scene of education, like the architecturally significant glass door in the La Luc family home that opens on the Savoyard landscape. She makes us see, albeit darkly, not only that feminine "weakness" is a rich source of masculine pleasure; but that feminine self-command is enjoined on the daughter precisely because of the father's permitted (or fatal) "weakness" for her mother. It is this weakness that occupies the novel's secret place, or reserve, of melancholy. La Luc does indeed teach by example; but he teaches that the luxuries of grief and solitude are for men only, and must be controlled by making women more self-abnegating than men are. The scene of this exemplary lesson in control is the family – the domestic enclave to which Clara belongs and from which only her father is permitted to stray (after all, it is the heroine's wanderings in *The Romance of the Forest* that exposes her to abduction and worse). Radcliffe, in fact, has accurately reproduced the scene of female education in *Emile*, where constraints imposed on women become the mode of simultaneously arousing and restraining the desires of men and women's role is to make men strong by surrendering their own desires; it is this that makes possible the domestication of desire. Surrendering her lute, Clara gives back to the father what she has risked claiming for herself, but what should properly belong to him alone – the erotic relation to the mother that haunts the Savoyard landscape. Her music opens the secret reserve within the tranquil domestic sphere ruled over by her father, serving as an unacknowledged point of resistance to its pastoral order. This resistant feminine subjectivity is predicated on a lost or wandering mother whose "shade" not only invades the alpine landscape, but inflects the novel's seductive semiotics, its "voice." Clara's power to captivate, while herself being held captive by the scene, represents the glass through which we are permitted to glimpse a split in feminine subjectivity. Ostensibly alluring to men (especially fathers), such feminine self-division and truancy serve to link Clara to other women, whether her dead mother or the (implied) woman reader whose errant desires she is supposed to moralize through her obedient surrender of desire.

III ABJECT FIGURES

The twist in *The Romance of the Forest* (as so often in Radcliffe's novels) is the introduction of the dead mother as the sign of forbidden pleasure. If the luxury of grief – as much as the licensed enjoyment of sexuality – is the mark of a masculine sensibility, women's claim to melancholia, however tenuous, may take on a transgressive dimension; no wonder Clara's lute has to be surrendered to her father. Significantly, it is Mary Wollstonecraft who makes the most overt claim for melancholia as a transgressive form of subjectivity that is denied to women, quite as much as the enlightenment Reason that is indispensable if women are to be recognized as having souls (capable, that is, of Christian immortality and a meaningful existence in the hereafter). Wollstonecraft's *Thoughts on the Education of Daughters* (1787) devotes an entire chapter to "The Benefits which arise from Disappointments." "Most women," she begins, "and men too, have no character at all." Women (like lutes) are liable to be swayed or consumed by this passion or that; only reflection can strengthen and establish "a character, which will not depend on every accidental impulse."[13] Anticipating her criticism of Inchbald's *A Simple Story*, Wollstonecraft writes that "In the school of adversity we learn knowledge as well as virtue." Disappointment and suffering, sensibility and the virtuous passions, serve to teach the melancholic female that sighing will only cease, and tears be wiped way, "by that Being, in whose presence there is fulness of joy." In an infinitely deferred future, the disappointed daughter can only look to "the better country to which we are going" for the fulfilment denied her in the present. Sublimation enters the scene in the guise of religious resignation: "when a person is disappointed in this world, they turn to the next."[14] The same melancholy education in deferred gratification, disappointment, and sublimation structures Wollstonecraft's closely contemporary novel, *Mary* (1787), whose plot makes failed mothering and failed marriage virtually interchangeable.

Wollstonecraft takes the epigraph of *Mary* from Rousseau ("*L'exercice des plus sublimes vertus élève et nourrit le génie*"). But her preface specifically dissociates her heroine from Sophie. Mary is a feminized genius, "a woman who has thinking powers" – not just elevated by her misery, but in love with it, in fact eroticized by it. As a child, "Her sensibility prompted her to search for an object to love; on earth it was not to be found: her mother had often disappointed her, and the apparent partiality she shewed to [Mary's] brother . . . produced a kind of habitual melancholy, [and] led her into a fondness for reading tales of woe . . ."[15] A disappointing mother leads to habitual melancholy and a taste for lacrimose writing. The

implicit equation – maternal disappointment equals melancholia –
redefines an education in "adversity" as motherlessness (significantly,
the death of her mother as Mary reaches adolescence coincides with
her loveless, arranged marriage to another reluctant adolescent in
order to unite two family estates). Mary's other love-objects are
repetitively disappointing: an ailing female friend and a sickly father-
figure, both nursed into their graves, neither, perhaps, quite as
grateful as they should be (like her mother). No wonder Mary learns
that happiness is only to be found, in the novel's ambiguous closing
words, in "that world *where there is neither marrying*, nor giving in
marriage."[16] In so far as it packs an explicit feminist protest, *Mary*
attacks arranged marriages, fashionably empty-headed mothers, and
the neglect of daughters in favor of sons. But its message is
complicated by Wollstonecraft's emphasis on melancholic sublimation. Both the state of women and a future state are predicated on
disappointment. Maternal deprivation points the way to Mary's
unhappy psychic solution; her resignation involves an identification
with death (hence her unvaryingly dead or dying love-objects), while
nursing her dying mother anticipates the inevitability of her own
death at the end of the novel. The crypto-feminist aspect of *Mary*,
however, is its claim to the melancholic sensibility which is permitted
La Luc while being officially off-limits for Clara. Choosing to
identify her heroine with Rousseau, rather than with Sophie – with
the teacher rather than the pupil – means that Wollstonecraft
vindicates women's rights, not just to Rousseau's "thinking powers,"
but to the erotic sensibility – the problematic susceptibility to sex –
that for Wollstonecraft feminized Rousseau even as it defined his
libertine imagination, making her, in her own words, half in love
with him.[17] Nor could it have been lost on Wollstonecraft that for
the orphaned Rousseau, the lost object *par excellence* was a mother –
the lost object who defines his erotic relations to "maman" while
giving him something in common with a motherless woman.

A *Vindication of the Rights of Woman* (1791) takes a different tack. In
the long chapter on "The Prevailing Opinion of a Sexual Character" which specifically attacks Rousseau's theories about female
education, we find Wollstonecraft now saying that, while gentleness,
forbearance, and long suffering may be Godlike and sublime,

what a different aspect [gentleness] assumes when it is the submissive
demeanour of dependence, the support of weakness that loves, because it

wants protection; and is forebearing, because it must silently endure injures; smiling under the lash at which it dare not snarl. Abject as this picture appears, it is the portrait of an accomplished woman, according to the received opinion of female excellence, separated by specious reasoners from human excellence.[18]

"Abjection" now appears as the companion of resignation and silence – a mere step away from the ideological enforcement of feminine weakness as a necessary precondition for women's dependence, subordination, and survival. Wollstonecraft's portrait of "a thinking woman," prepared by adversity for a future life (*"where there is neither marrying,* nor giving in marriage"), gives way to this abject endurance of social injury – "the portrait of an accomplished woman, according to the received opinion of female excellence." Wollstonecraft's *Vindication* echoes the closing words of *Mary,* pointing to women's inadequate preparation for the after-life; but now it is their subordination that expressly precludes successful sublimation in the hereafter:

How women are to exist in that state where there is neither to be marrying nor giving in marriage, we are not told. For though moralists have agreed that the tenor of life seems to prove that *man* is prepared by various circumstances for a future state, they constantly concur in advising *woman* only to provide for the present. Gentleness, docility, and a spaniel-like affection are, on this ground, consistently recommended as the cardinal virtues of the sex; and, disregarding the arbitrary economy of nature, one writer has declared that it is masculine for a woman to be melancholy. (118)

If indeed "it is masculine for a woman to be melancholy," then there is nowhere to go but backwards – to the regressive abjection of Rousseau's nursery catechism, for instance, with its lesson of women's life-long subordination to their dismal reproductive destiny. Thus it is that religious sublimation, the third term in the Kristevan triad (melancholia, abjection, sublimation), falls into place as Wollstonecraft's first-line-of-defence emancipatory strategy. Whether associated with death, as it is in *Mary,* or placed beyond women's reach by their inferior education, as it is in the *Vindication,* sublimation (as Kristeva reminds us) is always lined with the abject, and the abject is another name for the archaic, pre-objectal maternal "Thing" (the not-yet object of a not-yet-subject). Laying claim to the masculine prerogative of melancholia could thus be read as a means to chart, however precariously, a path towards the emancipation of women on the only grounds available within current sexual ideologies. If women can attain to melancholic subjectivity, they may at least be permitted to enter the symbolic by the back door, the space of affect associated with the mother and hence with Kristeva's archaic, place-holding father.[19] An abject becomes a proto-subject, however improperly, by means of this melancholic identification with the lost mother and her desire. Melancholia constitutes at once a feminine counter-culture – a contestatory position from which to vindicate the rights of woman – while at the same time providing the basis for the (de)formation of Romantic feminine subjectivity in the face of enlightenment sexual indifference. This deformation serves to call in question the implicit gendering of enlightenment Reason as masculine and sensibility as feminine (rather as libido, for Freud, while ostensibly belonging neither to men nor to women, nonetheless belongs on the side of "masculine" activity as opposed to "feminine" passivity).

In the family romance of Wollstonecraft's *Vindication*, Liberty, not melancholy, is the mother of virtue: "Liberty is the mother of virtue, and if women be, by their very constitution, slaves, and not allowed to breathe the sharp invigorating air of freedom, they must ever languish like exotics, and be reckoned beautiful flaws in nature" (121–22). The sign of abjection (as in *Mary*) is this constitutional feminine weakness, both in mind and body: "dependence of body naturally produces dependence of mind . . . Most men are sometimes obliged to bear with bodily inconveniences . . . but genteel women are, literally speaking, slaves to their bodies, and glory in their subjection" (130). Both the languishing exotic – the seraglio-slave of Rousseau's voluptuous fantasy – and the genteel woman who is a slave to her body and glories in her subjection become figures for the confinement of women's minds, and for the defective rationality that springs from lack of education, rights, and liberty. But Wollstonecraft's turn to the body (like her turn to melancholia) allows her to explore the underside of enlightenment Reason. What is at stake for her is not only the gendered body's troubling and irrational connection with feminine sensibility (whether Miss Milner's wayward pursuit of forbidden objects or Clara's romantically "uncontrolled inclinations"), but its susceptibility to seduction, its resistance to Reason and even to enlightenment itself.[20] How easily rationality collapses into the power that "swallow[s] up" all other forms of power (156), the power that resists its sway. Sensibility in *A Vindication* tropes sexuality; we should recall that it was the seductive power of Miss Milner's "sensibility" that Wollstonecraft had complained about in her review of *A Simple Story*. Why, Wollstonecraft demands in the *Vindication*, "females should always be degraded by being subservient to love or lust" (110), she is at a loss to know. As she goes on to argue in a famous passage, Rousseau is himself a type of the victim of sensibility – or rather, the sexual susceptibility to women that feminizes him:

> But all Rousseau's errors in reasoning arose from sensibility, and sensibility to their charms women are very ready to forgive. When he should have reasoned he became impassioned, and reflection inflamed his imagination instead of enlightening his understanding. Even his virtues also led him further astray; for, born with a warm constitution and lively fancy, nature carried him towards the other sex with such eager fondness that he soon became lascivious. (189)

Rousseau, Wollstonecraft asserts, debauched his imagination by practising self-denial ("a romantic kind of delicacy"), and only sought the solitude of nature "merely to indulge his feelings" (189). The resemblance to Radcliffe's La Luc is obvious. Recast as the self-denying, lascivious slave of passion (as opposed to being the slave of the body, like genteel women), Rousseau turns out to be a type of the eroticized, libertine sensibility masquerading as enlightened educator. But, even more important, the process involves his feminization – his unmanning by an inflamed imagination (presumably, an erotic maternal remainder). Rousseauian susceptibility may be one that all women are ready to forgive because it is susceptibility to women. But what Wollstonecraft seems most ready to forgive Rousseau for is the way he comes to resemble a disappointed, susceptible, and unmothered woman – herself.

IV A ROMANTIC PROJECT

Wollstonecraft presses the enlightenment claim for Reason on behalf of women, yet for her the scene of enlightenment is itself mined from within by women's own longing to be seduced. The rake, she writes, haunts their imagination (every woman yearns for a Lovelace). Seduction and self-seduction make "the science of herself" treacherous ground for systematic pedagogy. My final model for such pedagogy is drawn from Maria Edgeworth's novel of rational education, *Belinda* (1801), best-known for its anti-Jacobin caricature of a cross-dressing proto-feminist eccentric, Harriet Freke, who champions the rights of women to duel and to declare their love to men; it is her presence that wreaks gender-havoc throughout *Belinda*'s subplot. But Edgeworth's novel also includes a failed experiment in Rousseauian education on the part of its reluctant, ambivalent, and unmanly hero, Clarence Hervey.[21] Hervey seemingly vacillates in his choice of potential partner between three women: the frantically social, manic-depressive, and terminally ill female libertine, Lady Delacour; the stable, intelligent, and virtuous young heroine, Belinda, who must make her way through the obstacles that society places in the way of a good marriage (eventually, to Hervey himself), and who finally succeeds in curing both marriage and Lady Delacour; and the appealingly uneducated *ingénue*, brought up in seclusion, whom Hervey intends as his wife. Charmed by the picture of Sophie in *Emile*, and repelled by the libertine licentiousness symbolized by the *ancien régime*, Hervey brings back from his pre-Revolutionary travels in France "the romantic project of educating a wife for himself"; he will be both Mentor and Emile, and she will be his Sophie.[22] In quest of an appropriate subject for this wishful Rousseauian experiment, he stumbles on a young woman living in romantic retirement with her grandmother. Rachel (her real name) is the daughter of a sixteen-year-old runaway who died broken hearted when her husband abandoned her; reared in almost total ignorance of men, Rachel is turned over to Hervey after the convenient demise of her grandmother, but not before she extracts a death-bed promise from Hervey not to ruin her. But Rachel is clearly destined for sexual ruin, or, at the very least, for abandonment and betrayal. Everything, from her artless blush to her well-turned arms and the roses she innocently proffers the stranger on their first encounter, marks her out as the innocent victim of a pathetic narrative that will replicate her mother's plight. But Hervey, it turns out, is to be a highminded (if self-deceiving) rather than an immoral teacher, adhering to his romantic project even when he no longer wants to claim his reward:

Her simplicity, sensibility, and, perhaps more than he was aware, her beauty, had pleased and touched him extremely. The idea of attaching a perfectly pure, disinterested, unpractised heart, was delightful to his imagination: the cultivation of her understanding, he thought, would be an easy and a pleasing task: all difficulties vanished before his sanguine hopes.

"Sensibility," said he to himself, "is the parent of great talents, and great virtues; and evidently she possesses natural feeling in an uncommon degree; it shall be developed with skill, patience, and delicacy; and I will deserve, before I claim my reward." (348)

Edgeworth nuances Hervey's account of his plans for Rachel with skepticism ("the cultivation of her understanding, *he thought* . . . "); this is an educational program conceived in the abstract. Rather than deceiving and seducing her, Hervey whisks her off to Windsor under the protection of a genteel widow from whom he, in turn, extracts "a solemn promise, that she would neither receive nor pay any visits. [She] was thus secluded from all intercourse with the world" (351). Nature, however, upsets his plans by implanting contradictory desires in Rachel herself – nature, and books, a form of second nature that installs a prior lover in her virginal heart.

For Edgeworth, Hervey's "romantic project" is subverted from within by his own preposterous fantasy. Renaming his charge "Virginia St. Pierre," after the artless romantic heroine of St. Pierre's *Paul et Virginie* (a natural heroine who dies as a direct consequence of her acculturation), Hervey has her painted as the chastely passionate child of nature, Virginie. But Virginia – although touchingly grateful – proves to be an unexpectedly resistant pupil. Nor is it just that her indolence, docility, and obedient attachment to Hervey are less satisfying to him than he had anticipated (what will they talk about after marriage?). Edgeworth, in fact, uses the story of Virginia to mount a double critique of the Rousseauian scheme of female education. First, Virginia's charming limitations reveal Hervey's experiment as anything but intellectually disinterested. He is "engaged in defence of a favorite system of education" on one hand, while on the other, "All that was amiable or estimable in Virginia had a double charm, from the secret sense of his penetration, in having discovered and appreciated the treasure" (352–53). Hervey's overvaluation of his objects (both his Rousseauian system and his *protégée*) is the immediate target of Edgeworth's satire; as he comes reluctantly to see, Virginia can "merely be his pupil or his plaything" (358–59). But Edgeworth also hints that "penetration" of "the treasure" is indeed the ultimate end he has in view. And he wants to be there alone. In the Rousseauian sexual economy, the more deferred the consummation, and the more virginal the treasure, the greater the erotic pay-off. But secondly, and more interestingly, Edgeworth intimates that Virginia has romantic desires of her own – desires ambiguously implanted by both nature and books – and that

the very books on which Hervey models his romantic project are
what subvert his teaching: "Virginia's mind was . . . *exalted* by
romantic views . . . As she had never seen anything of society, all her
notions were drawn from books" (359). Ironically, it is her own
reading of St. Pierre's *Paul and Virginia* that awakens her to the
meaning of love. The passage in which Virginie, disturbed and
confused by her newly aroused feelings for Paul, goes to her mother
for refuge against them, proves also to be the turning-point for
Edgeworth's Virginia. Here is St. Pierre, read aloud in Edgeworth's
narrative by Virginia's motherly companion, Mrs. Ormond:

"She thought of Paul's friendship, more pure than the waters of the
fountain, stronger than the united palms, and sweeter than the perfume of
flowers; and these images, in night and in solitude, gave double force to the
passion, which she nourished in her heart. She suddenly left the dangerous
shades, and went to her mother, to seek protection against herself. She
wished to reveal her distress to her; she pressed her hands, and the name of
Paul was on her lips; but the oppression of her heart took away all
utterance, and, laying her head upon her mother's bosom, she only wept."
(360–61)

"'And am I not a mother to you, my beloved Virginia?'" asks Mrs.
Ormond, whereupon Edgeworth's Virginia flings her arms round
her, "as if she wished to realise the illusion, and to be the Virginia of
whom she had been reading" (361). Virginia is constituted as a
desiring feminine subject in her own right, not through Hervey's
imagination, but through her own romantic, Rousseauistic reading.
Romance is engendered within the very confines of the educational
space in which Virginia has been enclosed by her mentor.

Mrs. Ormond – obstinately persisting in the fiction that Virginia
unconsciously loves Hervey – tells her "'I know all you think, and all
you feel: I know . . . the name that is on *your* lips.'" But there are
limits to this wishful amorous knowledge, just as there are limits to
Hervey's educational oversight. In the face of Mrs. Ormond's
maternal omniscience, Virginia protests: "how could you possibly
know *all* my thoughts and feelings? I never told them to you; for,
indeed, I have only confused ideas, floating in my imagination, from
the books I have been reading. I do not distinctly know my own
feelings" (361). The impossibility of knowing – whether for Virginia
herself or for her well-intentioned mother-substitute – makes Virginia one of the bearers of the novel's unconscious (the other is a
superstitious, Obeah-haunted West Indian servant). Despite, or

alongside, Edgeworth's commitment to the cause of rational education and social morality for women, Virginia comes to figure
resistance to the fantastic Rousseauian project that is critiqued in
the figure of Hervey – and, in some sense, to the entire enlightenment project of her novel. If, as Virginia protests, she does not
distinctly know her own feelings, the imperialism of enlightenment
is always subject to the limits of knowing. Her story belongs to the
elsewhere of the irrational (whether the passion nourished in
Virginia's heart in St. Pierre's novel, or West Indian Obeah magic).
Virginia's lurking indifference to Hervey surfaces in a confused
dream, compounded of scenes from *Paul and Virginia* and from her
other romantic novel-reading. In her dream, Virginia is seated next
to St. Pierre's Paul, when Hervey appears to accuse her of
ingratitude; later, two knights fight over her, until one of them
(Hervey) is killed by the other (Paul). The *mélange* of St. Pierre's
eroticized Rousseauism and medievalized romance suggests that
Virginia's inner life has already been colonized by the accidents of
representation ("second nature" to the lush colonial "nature" of St.
Pierre's *Paul and Virginia*). Neither her grandmother nor Hervey
have been able to prevent the picture of an ideal lover – "a very
proper picture" (350) – from occupying her supposedly virginal
imagination. The improper residue of this romantic preoccupation
with an ideal lover are alternating "fits of melancholy and of
exertion" – alternating tears (mystifying) and efforts to please
Hervey (gratifying). Troubled by his perception of Virginia as "a
girl of a melancholy temperament," rather than a flattering *tabula
rasa* for his educational project, and fearing for the consequences to
her if he should abandon her, Hervey honorably resolves to marry
his reluctant *protégée*, in spite of the fact that he is himself now in
love with the novel's heroine, Belinda.

Virginia, through her apparent ineducability, educates Edgeworth's readers in the meaning of feminine resistance. While
dutifully and naively trying to please Hervey, she discovers and
articulates for herself that " 'Wishes, and feelings, and sentiments,
are not to be so easily regulated' " (380). In Edgeworth's system of
imperfect regulation, romance comes to the aid of the rational
happiness which Belinda's marriage to Hervey betokens. Virginia
embodies the premise that feeling can't after all be taught – or
rather, as Virginia herself protests, that feeling comes untaught and
unbidden: "do you think I cannot *feel* without having been taught?"

she demands (378). There is always something that eludes education, an unpredictable direction to affective and erotic life which insists on finding its own object. Virginia's escape from Hervey's educational love-nest is contrived but ingenious. Edgeworth wheels onto the already crowded stage a wealthy plantation-owning father, now anxious to recover his long-lost daughter and remorseful about his long-ago abandonment of her "spoiled" novel-reading mother ("a sentimental girl, who had been spoiled by early novel-reading," 386). Predictably, her father exclaims at their reunion, " 'My child! – the image of her mother!' " (389), enforcing the mother-daughter link that had made Virginia such an ambiguously apt subject for Hervey's Rousseauian experiment (always-already seduced and abandoned, so to speak, like her mother before her). But Edgeworth's final *dénouement* unexpectedly confronts Virginia with another picture – not of herself as St. Pierre's Virginia, but of St. Pierre's Paul. Its electrifying effect on her elicits the confession that in her dreams just such a man has played the part of lover. The man she dreams of, and now finds portrayed in Paul, turns out to be based on another picture she had once glimpsed in her former life with her grandmother. The book, the dream, and the picture coalesce in this prior image ("he was the knight of the white plumes," 442). The original for both pictures, it transpires, is a young man who had (unknown to her) fallen in love with the vision of Rachel tending her roses, before ever Hervey came on the scene to rename her in the self-serving interests of his Rousseauian scheme. When the original of the pictured lover appears on stage at last, Virginia "gazed as on an animated picture, and all the ideas of love and romance, associated with this image, rushed upon her mind" (449). A previous lover had occupied her heart all the time – installed there by a yet prior representation, which later comes to occupy the place of St. Pierre's Paul. *Paul and Virginia* turns out to be a place-holder, in which the *mise en abyme* of representation unfolds to remind us that there can never be a virginal woman, nor a heart empty of desire. No virgin, however sequestered, can be defended against cultural seduction; no mind, however unbookish, can be secluded from the lure of reading; no imagination, however innocent, can resist the romance of representation.

All this, of course, is thoroughly contrived on the level of Edgeworth's plot. With the close of the book swiftly approaching, one character complains testily: "I like to hear *how* people become happy in a rational manner" (450). But Edgeworth seems to want to show us the irrationality of happiness, the power of the imagination, not to mention the romance of representation. What she calls "the huddled style of an old fairy tale" turns out to be the subtext of this novel of rationally achieved, socially regulated happiness. "Something," says Edgeworth's spokeswoman, "must be left to the imagination" (450). That something, whether fairy tale or romance, is fiction itself, since Virginia derives her sentimental education from those infallible if seductive aids to the imagination, the novels that ruined her mother before her. The image of the prior lover in her heart suggests, if only by the strength of its association with novel-reading, that romance too is a kind of "second nature," calling in question the very idea of "virginity" or unadulterated nature; there is no such thing as an inviolate treasure – no feminized *tabula rasa* for Hervey's educational experiment. Like education, romance supplements nature to such an extent that in the last resort it is impossible to tell them apart. Edgeworth's harnessing of the Rousseauian plot to her own fiction undoes Hervey's "romantic project," not so much because Virginia turns out to have ideas of her own on the subject of love, but because the supposedly inviolate subject is always penetrated by the "un-conscious" of representation – an unconscious in which romance and the desire of the mother (shaped by prior novel-reading) coincide. At the very end of the novel, Edgeworth turns to her audience in a moment of calculated artifice, announcing that: "Our *tale* contains a *moral*, and, no doubt, / You all have wit enough to find it out" (451). The secret of modern, companionate marriage, she implies, is rational happiness plus romantic love. But the real moral of the novel seems to lie elsewhere, offstage, in the mother's reformation or "cure." The melancholic, diseased and abject Lady Delacour – a *reprise* of the giddy Miss Milner, grown old and seemingly incurable – occupies the maternal position in *Belinda*. But this is a comedy, and even pathology must respond to the marriage plot. A wound to her breast (caused indirectly by her misplaced friendship for the disruptive feminist, Harriet Freke) has been the source of all Lady Delacour's troubles. This is the imagined breast cancer that makes her a secret melancholic, accounting for her failed marriage to a jealous husband, her ambivalent refusal of mothering, and her neglect of her sad young daughter. But at the close of the novel, cured of her cancer, redeemed by Belinda's moral influence, and transformed by the demands of Edgeworth's up-beat plot, the

contradictory and good-natured (as well as melancholic) Lady
Delacour turns out to have a heart after all. It is she who emerges to
play the part of impresario at the final *dénouement*, disposing of the
couples to their happy marriages and serving as the mouthpiece for
Edgeworth's moral. Edgeworth's own romantic project in *Belinda*, we
see with hindsight, was to heal the wounded maternal breast – not
only restoring romance to the scene of female enlightenment, but
simultaneously reforming the abjected mother and recovering her
for the daughter. In Edgeworth's version of the family romance, the
contrivances of fiction permit the lost mother's recovery for a
romantic plot that installs the daughter as the rightful heir to the
novel of education. In the process, new and contestatory forms of
subjectivity emerge to transform the novel into a vehicle for female
emancipation. Belinda, the giddy heiress of Pope's *The Rape of the
Lock*, and the eighteenth-century prototype for Inchbald's contrary
Miss Milner (who likewise rejects a lord without knowing why),
becomes the heroine of a new female plot in which a young woman's
entry into society involves both the reformation of romance and the
recovery of the mother. Edgeworth's *Belinda* permits the novel of
female education to have a heart as well as an enlightened head.

Romanticism can be read not only as one outcome of the Enlightenment, but as a form of resistance to the imperialism of enlightenment thinking. Women, in turn, come to figure that resistance –
identified as a knot within the *dénouement* of enlightenment education.
Rousseau's scheme for the regulation of female desire involved
processes scarcely less arduous than Freud's account of the acquisition of femininity. But it was Rousseau himself who became synonymous with the feminized subject of Romanticism constructed in
Wollstonecraft's fictional and non-fictional works, and Freud for
whom women were made, not born – establishing the tortuous
acquisition of femininity as the model for subjectivity in general. I
want to end by invoking the psychoanalytic scene of female enlightenment to which I alluded at the start. Freud's lecture "On
Femininity" (1933) opens by positioning its imaginary audience in
relation to "the riddle of femininity" along the axis of sexual
difference: "Nor will *you* have escaped worrying over this problem –
those of you who are men; to those of you who are women this will
not apply – you are yourselves the problem." Locating women
themselves as the problem (for men), Freud implies that they can

only ever be the object of psychoanalytic inquiry, never its subject. As I have tried to argue for the women writers of the 1790s, the enlightenment discourse of female education – transposed from educational writing to the realm of feminist vindication or feminine fiction – provided an opportunity to worry the problem of women into a full-blown discourse of feminine subjectivity. As we have seen, enlightenment discourse tended to characterize a specifically feminine subjectivity as the outcast of reason – as abject, weak, depressive, or simply ineducable. On the face of it, this was the model of feminine subjectivity that women writers like Inchbald, Radcliffe, Wollstonecraft, and Edgeworth tried to combat with their emphasis on education and rationality. But by their construction of a maternal genealogy, by their claim to melancholia, and by their attempted restoration of romance, they could be said to have produced the discourse of femininity that is missing both from the enlightenment discourse of Reason and from Romantic privileging of the solitary masculine subject. What I have called "The science of herself" simultaneously dismantles the enlightenment educational project and installs femininity as a potential locus of resistance to enlightenment – a resistance arguably synonymous with Romanticism, redefined as a space where gendered subjectivity subverts the empire of Reason. The rest is psychoanalytic history, since Freud was not only a belated prophet of the Enlightenment but an incurable romantic who found himself, at the end of his life, confronting the irreducible phenomenon of women's unconscious resistance to enlightenment. What eluded the science of psychoanalysis, finally, was a maternal remainder in the archeology of the subject – an unsolved problem or negativity called "Woman." The question of femininity remained for Freud himself the unanswerable question posed by psychoanalytic knowledge. It was no accident, then, that the women analysts should have taken up the challenge of the so-called "Great Debate" over feminine sexuality during the 1920s and 1930s. In this later replay of the scene of female enlightenment, they too were asserting, with Inchbald's Amelia, that "None but a woman can teach the science of herself."

NOTES

1   For the tyranny of an enlightenment education predicated on female subordination, see Alan Richardson, "From *Emile* to *Frankenstein*: The

Education of Monsters," *European Romantic Review* 1 (1991): 147–62. See also Beth Kowaleski-Wallace, "Milton's Daughters: The Education of Eighteenth-Century Women Writers," *Feminist Studies* 12 (1986): 275–93. For the equation of "sensibility" and sexuality, see William Godwin's account of Mary Wollstonecraft in love in *Memoirs of the Author of the Rights of Woman* (1798); and Mary Wollstonecraft and William Godwin, *A Short Residence in Sweden and Memoirs of the Author of 'The Rights of Woman'*, ed. Richard Holmes (Harmondsworth: Penguin, 1987), 243.

2 See, for instance, Mary Hays in *The Memoirs of Emma Courtney* (1796) and Maria Edgeworth's satire on female declarations of love in *Belinda* (1801); cf. also Colin B. Atkinson and Jo Atkinson, "Maria Edgeworth, *Belinda*, and Women's Rights," *Éire-Ireland: A Journal of Irish Studies* 19 (1984): 94–118.

3 Elizabeth Inchbald, *Lover's Vows; A Play* (London: Longman, Hurst, Rees, and Orme, 1798), 38–39.

4 Elizabeth Inchbald, *A Simple Story*, ed. J. M. S. Tompkins and Jane Spencer (Oxford: Oxford University Press, 1988), 338.

5 *Analytical Review*, x (May-August, 1791); see *A Wollstonecraft Anthology*, ed. Janet Todd (New York: Columbia University Press, 1990), 227.

6 Inchbald, *A Simple Story*, 73.

7 Jean-Jacques Rousseau, *Emile: or, On Education*, trans. and ed. Allan Bloom (New York: Basic Books, 1979), 369.

8 Ibid., 379.

9 Inchbald, *A Simple Story*, 274.

10 See Alan Richardson, "From Emile to *Frankenstein*: The Education of Monsters," *European Romantic Review* 1 (1991): 147–48, for the surfacing of educational questions in the context of the Gothic novel in general and *The Romance of the Forest* in particular.

11 See Ann Radcliffe, *The Romance of the Forest*, ed. Cloe Chard (Oxford: Oxford University Press, 1986), 244–45 and *n*. Subsequent page references in the text are to this edition.

12 See Radcliffe, *The Romance of the Forest*, 388*n*.

13 Mary Wollstonecraft, *Thoughts on the Education of Daughters* (London: Joseph Johnson, 1787), 112.

14 Ibid., 116, 117.

15 Mary Wollstonecraft, *Mary, A Fiction and The Wrongs of Woman* (London: Oxford University Press, 1976), 5–6.

16 Ibid., 68.

17 See *Collected Letters of Mary Wollstonecraft*, ed. Ralph M. Wardle (Ithaca and London: Cornell University Press), 263.

18 Mary Wollstonecraft, *A Vindication of the Rights of Woman*, ed. Miriam Brody Kramnick (Harmondsworth: Penguin, 1975), 117. Subsequent page references in the text are to this edition.

19 For a reading of Mary Wollstonecraft Shelley's incest-novel, *Mathilda*, in similar Kristevan terms, see Tilottama Rajan, "Mary Shelley's *Mathilda*:

Melancholy and the Political Economy of Romanticism," *Studies in the Novel* 26 (1994): 43–68.

20 For an interesting challenge to the conventional opposition of reason and passion or imagination in Wollstonecraft's life and work, see Orrin N. C. Wang, "The Other Reasons: Female Alternity and Enlightenment Discourse in Mary Wollstonecraft's *A Vindication of the Rights of Woman*," *The Yale Journal of Criticism* 5 (Fall 1991): 129–49: "rather than seeing Wollstonecraft as being caught between the gender demands of male reason and female imagination, I see her text actively trying to disrupt that duality's assignation of gender, by strategically associating 'woman' with a variety of local, contradictory identities" (131).

21 See Colin B. Atkinson and Jo Atkinson, "Maria Edgeworth, *Belinda*, and Women's Rights," 94–118; Hervey's educational project is modelled on the unsuccessful experiment of Richard Edgeworth's friend, Thomas Day, who brought up two orphan girls for the same purpose (see 115n).

22 Maria Edgeworth, *Belinda* (London: Everyman, 1993), 343. Subsequent page numbers in the text refer to this edition.

CHAPTER II

The failures of romanticism

Jerome McGann

> I found it hard, it was hard to find,
> Oh well, whatever, never mind.
> > Nirvana, "Smells Like Teen Spirit"

The failures of romanticism involve some of its most famous, or infamous, moments.

1 Plate 3 of Blake's *Jerusalem*, with major parts of its text gouged away.

2 The climactic passage of Shelley's *Epipsychidion*, so ludicrous to the priests of modernism like Eliot and Leavis:

> One hope within two wills, one will beneath
> Two overshadowing minds, one life, one death,
> One Heaven, one Hell, one immortality,
> And one annihilation. Woe is me!
> The winged words on which my soul would pierce
> Into the height of love's rare Universe,
> Are chains of lead around its flight of fire. –
> I pant, I sink, I tremble, I expire!

3 Equivalent moments in Byron, for instance *Childe Harold* III stanza 97, when a grandiose move toward absolute expressiveness stumbles and fragments to the tortured incompetence of his "voice-less thought":

> Could I embody and unbosom now
> That which is most within me, – could I wreak
> My thoughts upon expression, and thus throw
> Soul, heart, mind, passions, feelings, strong or weak,
> All that I would have sought, and all I seek,
> Bear, know, feel, and yet breathe – into *one* word,
> And that one word were Lightning, I would speak;
> But as it is, I live and die unheard,
> With a most voiceless thought, sheathing it as a sword.

4 Or any number of passages where Keats seems to lose his head – for instance, stanza 3 of the "Ode on a Grecian Urn," whose much-ridiculed mantra on the word "happy" can still leave many with "a heart high sorrowful and cloyed."

> Ah, happy, happy boughs! that cannot shed
> Your leaves, nor ever bid the spring adieu;
> And happy melodist, unwearied,
> For ever piping songs for ever new;
> More happy love, more happy, happy love!
> For ever warm and still to be enjoyed . . .

As I shall try to indicate later, all of these passages ultimately draw their stylistic authority from conventions of sensibility and sentimentality. Polluted in the classicist texts of modernism, those cultural forms should be recovered not only for themselves, but for the sake of their descendant romantic texts as well.

We are dealing here with a mode of poetry Blake called the "Buildings of Los(s)." Poetry as the expression and even the embodiment of loss and failure. The usual undertaking of these matters follows a Wordsworthian/Coleridgean line: "For such loss . . . abundant recompence" ("Tintern Abbey," 88–89). According to this view, there is – there must be – a faith that looks through death. The philosophic mind of romanticism works to redeem the harrowing logic of ultimate loss: perhaps even, as in certain Christian and Marxian schemas, to transform it into splendor.

But a serious problem lurks beneath these elegant compensatory formulas. We know this from Wordsworth's own poetry, whose best moments regularly betray their conscious commitments. The difficulty can even be glimpsed in chapter 14 of *Biographia Literaria* when Coleridge is laying out his (now normative) definition of romantic imagination as "the balance and reconcilement of opposite or discordant qualities." The text gives Coleridge's version of Wordsworth's "abundant . . . recompence." In doing so, however, the syntax releases an odd, and certainly an unwilled, ambiguity. The entire context shows that Coleridge intends the preposition "of" to mean "made from" or "composed of," but the phrasing briefly opens itself to one of the word's other primary meanings: "belonging to." The one logic asks us to imagine a harmony reigning over discordant materials, the other to wonder if states of discord and contradiction might themselves possess or generate (otherwise un-recognized) harmonic conditions.

Compensatory elegy and an aesthetics of balance: their equivalent logics were specifically raised against the threat of what Wordsworth elsewhere calls "Getting and spending," a dynamic that "lays waste our powers," according to the poet. All the romantics perceive and suffer this dynamic of evacuation.

> We wither from our youth, we gasp away,
> Sick, sick, unfound the boon, unslaked the thirst . . .

Such a text focuses not on reconciling harmonies but on tumult and waste. A sonnet like "The world is too much with us" defines the romantic fear of that dismembering and disempowerment. But other strains of romanticism were less timid, if not more reckless. This is the poetry written in astonished sympathy with the storm clouds of the nineteenth century, first announced by Blake: "Rintrah roars and shakes his fires in the burdend air." The correspondent poetry is what Byron famously called "a storm whereon [they] ride, to sink at last." Consumed within its ravishing economies, Shelley speaks the simplest truth when he says: "I pant, I sink, I tremble, I expire."

This storm of extremist passion does not blow from a nature that never betrayed a loving heart. On the contrary, it is a kind of Lucretian forcefield, a perpetual flood of energy. Among canonical English romantic poets, Blake articulates its dynamic as a cosmic mythos of "Eternal Death" and complete expenditure. So he imagines the Last Judgment as a dionysian feast in which all things are literally "consumed": eaten up, drunk up, burned up, annihilated. *All* things, including the Buildings of Los themselves, the enginery that sustains this "eternal" apocalypse. This *is* the great eucharist: "Timbrels & violins sport round the winepresses" to accompany a dance of death, Agape visioned as the *Liebestod* of "Luvah's daughters" and "Luvah's sons":

> They dance around the dying, & they drink the howl and groan;
> They catch the shrieks in cups of gold, they hand them to one another,
> These are the sports of love, & these the sweet delights of amorous play –
> *(Milton* Plate 25[27]: 37–39)

Redemption comes in and as ecstasy, something quite different from the redemption pursued through logics of compensation. It is the redemption that earlier crucified Clarissa Harlowe. Translated into a formally elegiac structure, it appears often in Shelley's work, and most famously in *Epipsychidion* and *Adonais*. The injunction of the latter – consummated in the overwhelming last four stanzas – is simple yet catastrophic.

> The One remains, the many change and pass;
> Heaven's light forever shines, earth's shadows fly;
> Life, like a dome of many-coloured glass,
> Stains the white radiance of Eternity,
> Until death tramples it to fragments. – Die,
> If thou would be with that which thou dost seek!
>
> (stanza LII)

The imperative verb establishes the mission of Shelley's verse. This is not the poetry of epitaphs, where the experience of loss is replaced by the memorial tribute of a shrine of loving language. Shelley goes to Keats's grave in Rome, to the grave that is Rome herself, only to "pause" briefly (stanza LI) before "The bones of Desolation's naked-ness/Pass" utterly away from his higher purpose (stanza XLIX). The point is not to fix a memory of loss forever but to establish all things on a basis of present and immediate life.

A new figural alphabet was drawn up for such a life in the aftermath of Locke's philosophic revolution. Its characters spell the language of the heart, with all its volatile intensities of feeling and sensibility. "Man is a sensational animal": this Lockean vision of the age's new "inlets of Soul," as Blake called them, will reverberate through all levels of culture. So far as poetry is concerned, the new philosophy brought a root and branch revaluation along gender lines. This happens because of the traditional association of women, children, and otherwise primitive creatures with the languages of the body.

The most efficient way to pursue this important subject is through the myth Byron created for his despair. In seeking the kindred or tutelary spirit of his cosmic gloom, he invariably turns to female figures – or to feminized male figures disguised with female names. The implicit argument in Byronic elegy is that his acquaintance with grief comes not from a man but from a woman of sorrows – indeed, comes from woman as the model of sorrow and suffering. Byron's greatest declaration of this view comes in Canto I of *Don Juan*, when Julie plays Diotima to Juan's Socrates in her letter of farewell.

Indurated Byronic sorrow signifies a loss from which there is no redemption. The traditional figure for such a loss is Satan, to whom, of course, Byron will turn often enough. But the contemporary equivalent of Satan, in Byron's imagination, is an archangel fallen

not through an excess of knowledge but through an excess of love.
To Byron such a figure is a woman – more particularly, any woman
who acquires human lineaments by discovering (to herself and to the
world alike) her imperfection, as well as the (ironically virtuous)
source of that imperfectness: love (more especially, erotic love).
When the Corsair leaves a name "linked with one virtue, and a
thousand crimes" (*The Corsair* III: 695–96), he fulfills a mythic
structure whose prototype Byron clearly imagines to be feminine. As
Julia tells Juan, while the disasters suffered by men may be mitigated
by various resources, women are (as it were fatally) determined
simply "To love again, and be again undone" (*Don Juan* I st. 194). In
a fallen world, love is not wisdom, it is catastrophe.

Byron's imagination therefore sees woman as a figure of exquisite
contradiction: at once emblem of perfection and byword of faithless-
ness. This mythos of Woman gets established very early – in *The
Giaour*, for example, it is already completely elaborated. In accepting
the total structure of this ideological formation, Byron discovers the
model of his own despair. For according to this myth, "the woman
once fallen forever must fall" ("[To Lady Caroline Lamb]" 14), like
Satan hurled from heaven. In Byron's rendering, a cosmic myth
yields up its social ground: no woman can ever recover her reputation once it has been lost. With that loss she henceforth stands
beyond redemption. Entering this mythos, however, Byron discovers
a new (other)world where the rhythms of redemption no longer
function. It is a region of perfect loss, a place where one may see that
"not in vain/Even for its own sake do we purchase pain" ("[Epistle
to Augusta]," 40): where one may see not necessarily *why*, but
certainly *that*.

This Byronic reading of women's cultural experience has its
immediate source, I believe, in eighteenth-century elegy. As the case
of Byron suggests, many of the most impressive practitioners of such
writing were in fact women – writers like Charlotte Smith and Mary
Robinson. The latter's collection of sonnets *Sappho and Phaon* (1796) is
important not merely for some of its excellent poems, but also
because it clearly defines an elegiac tradition (sapphic) that veers from
the more traditional and well-known line. Smith's work is interesting,
on the other hand, just because she doesn't write out of the (bisexual)
erotic myth that will prove so fruitful for so many women poets for
the next two centuries. In the historical framework of English
romanticism, Smith is to Robinson as Hemans will be to Landon.

The peculiar force of Smith's *Elegiac Sonnets* (first published in 1784) comes from the fact that they are *not* elegies for some particular person or persons. *Lacrymae rerum*, they mediate a general condition. Smith then deepens the gloom by arguing, as Plath would do much later, that poets serve a savage god. The opening sonnet of Smith's popular and influential book brings a cool report on the visible darknesses of a poetical vocation. It is no comfort that "The partial Muse" has "smil'd" on her chosen ones ("Sonnet 1," 1–2). Poetry brings the consciousness of suffering, and the sympathy that follows only exacerbates the situation:

> For still she bids soft Pity's melting eye
> Stream o'er the ills she knows not to remove,
> Points every pang, and deepens every sigh . . .   (9–11)

As so often in Smith's verse, wordplay generates corrosive ironies: "knows not to remove" suggests both "knows better than to remove" and "knows not how to remove." So a knowledge comes through this poetry that is worse, in its way, than no knowledge at all, since it is (in Manfred's words) "the knowledge of its own desert" (*Manfred* 3.4.136). A dismal conclusion is foregone:

> Ah! then, how dear the Muse's favors cost,
> *If those paint sorrow best – who feel it most!*

Echoing *Eloisa to Abelard* (366), the final line introduces a disturbing possibility into Pope's argument that "well sung woes shall soothe" the suffering soul. What if it were otherwise, what if poets must be "cradled into poetry by wrong," as Shelley's Maddalo (i.e., Byron) will soon argue ("Julian and Maddalo," 545)? Smith's verse is all the stronger, all the more disturbing, for its hypothetical rhetoric. The poem ends with no clear resort – not even the resort of those desperate last stands that Byron would shortly make famous.

The *Elegiac Sonnets* relentlessly pursue that dreary vision. Near the conclusion of the sequence, for example, Smith continues to discover new ways to fail. When she rededicates herself to "Fancy" in sonnet 47, she has no illusions about the machinery of illusion:

> Thro' thy false medium then, no longer view'd,
> May fancied pain and fancied pleasure fly,
> And I, as from me all thy dreams depart,
> Be to my wayward destiny subdu'd;
> Nor seek perfection with a poet's eye,
> Nor suffer anguish with a poet's heart.

Uncannily adept at subtle wordplay – which is why she makes such good sonnets – Smith rebuilds the labyrinth she "knows not to remove." The key words are "Thro'" and "fly": the former carrying both a spatial and a causal/intellectual sense, the latter meaning both "flee" and "move through" or "hover in." Depending on how one takes those words, the sestet manages to find itself lost on both sides, that is, lost whether Smith, like Sappho, practices poetry or abandons it. A generation later, when Keats stumbled into this same "purgatory blind," he wrote the "Ode to a Nightingale" and dramatized the pathos of his disillusion. Beginning where Keats left off, Smith dramatizes the perfection of hers.

There is no doubt that Byron followed Smith's sentimental tradition, rather than Wordsworth's romantic one, when he began to explore his waste places. But neither is there any doubt that he raised her dark measures to a spectacular level – briefly, that he made them romantic. If the gloom of the forever failing and falling woman provides the model for Byron's satanism, he charges the model with grandeur. Sentimentalism turns meteoric in his hands:

> The hour arrived – and it became
> A wandering mass of shapeless flame,
> A pathless comet, and a curse,
> The menace of the universe;
> Still rolling on with innate force,
> Without a sphere, without a course,
> A bright deformity on high,
> The monster of the upper sky! （*Manfred* 1.1.116–23)

This is the figure Byron and his poetry made. Again and again he seems struggling to break wholly free from his sentimental sufferings – ultimately, to break wholly free from the doomed poetry that expresses and discovers those sufferings. Starry fables repeatedly call to him as promises of resurrection and better rewards:

> Ye stars, which are the poetry of heaven . . .
> That fortune, fame, power, life, have named themselves a star.
> The starry fable of the milky way. . .
> She saw her glories star by star expire . . .
> (*Childe Harold* III, st. 88; IV, sts. 151, 80)

Figures all of an ultimate perfection, they stand for a sentimental ideal, as we see quite clearly in the famous stanza 14 of *Beppo*:

One of those forms which flit by us, when we
Are young, and fix our eyes on every face;
And oh! the loveliness at times we see
In momentary gliding, the soft grace,
The youth, the bloom, the beauty which agree,
In many a nameless being we retrace,
Whose course and home we knew not, nor shall know,
Like the lost Pleiad seen no more below.

Here the thought is strictly sentimental: to make feeling, and in particular human love, the ground of an experience of perfection: to "Blend a celestial with a human heart" (*Childe Harold* IV, st. 119). Numa and Egeria, Venus and Anchises, Manfred and Astarte: all consummate in "the lost Pleiad," who suffered her eclipse from the starry heavens because she fell in love with a mortal man. But if the thought is sentimental, the attitude in the poem is romantic throughout. The whole point of *Beppo* is to rewrite and redeem the disaster threatened by Byron's own imagination. In *Beppo* romantic irony comes to the rescue, much as the spot of time would come in Wordsworth's poetry.

How different is the road taken by Felicia Hemans in "The Lost Pleiad," whose memory fixates on loss and whose ironies do not flaunt or celebrate themselves. That the poem has been so long forgotten turns it to an index of its own key thoughts, and of the sentimental tradition it so splendidly represents. The point and force of the work depend upon its sympathetic recovery of the Byronic inheritance announced in the title.[1] And the date of the poem is crucial. Though she wrote it the year before he died, in 1823, its initial book publication came a year later, in 1825. That is to say, the poem's association with Byron's death was established very early. In fact, however, the poem isn't an elegy for his death but an elegiac meditation on the meaning of his life, and specifically on the diminishment his fame underwent in the last few years of his life. As such the poem is, like *Adonais* and the *Elegiac Sonnets*, a poem about the poetry of loss.

The historical context of the poem – the realities that feed lines like "Though thou art exil'd thence" (8) – is the period from 1816, the year Byron left his homeland in a cloud of scandal, never to return. His own poetry of 1816–24 made much of his exilic situation, and Hemans – whose work's thematic center is the ideology of home and country – strongly sympathized with Byron's imagination, as

this poem among many others clearly demonstrates.[2] "The Lost
Pleiad" focuses specifically on another known feature of those years
– the gradual decline in England of Byron's immense fame as a poet
and cultural icon.[3]

Perhaps the most arresting feature of the poem is the ease with
which Hemans genders her textual signs female. The move is all the
more notable because the subject is Byron, whose symbolic status
could not be more erotic or more male (whether in a homo- or a
heterosexual frame of reference). In this poem the world, including
the universe of poetry, is unequivocally feminine. The importance of
Hemans's approach has nothing to do with sexual issues but
everything to do with cultural ideals of poetry and art. From the
opening stanza the subjects are fame and poetry:

> And is there glory from the heavens departed?
> – Oh! void unmark'd! – thy sisters of the sky
> Still hold their place on high,
> Though from its rank thine orb so long hath started,
> Thou, that no more art seen of mortal eye.

Conflating "the lost Pleiad" Merope with the exiled poet Byron,
Hemans establishes poetical terms for an inquiry into the relation of
poetry and the world. In this respect the poem distinctly anticipates
Tennyson's "The Lady of Shalott," although its view of the relation
is more Byronic than Tennysonian – more bleak than oblique.[4]

In the center of the poem (stanzas 2–4), Hemans seems to fix her
gaze on the stellar universe to ponder obsessively one simple but
terrible fact: that the loss of the Pleiad appears to make no difference
whatsoever to the order of the stars or to their watchers. The night
still "wears her crown of old magnificence" (7), mariners still chart
their voyages by the Pleiades, all "the starry myriads burning" (11)
continue in their courses: "Unchang'd they rise, they have not
mourn'd for thee" (15). Hemans is careful to preserve the Byronic
character of this situation – for example, in lines like these:

> No desert seems to part those urns of light,
> 'Midst the far depth of purple gloom intense.   (9–10)

Byron's poetry had fairly mapped, for the romantic age, the psychic
territory of the desert, and of course he had become, like his famous
heroes, a byword of "gloom intense." Furthermore, perhaps no
living poet had ever acquired a fame like Byron's, nor does Hemans's
poem doubt the splendor of his work. Indeed, that splendor under-

scores her new astonishment at his fall and the disappearance of his glory. Recollecting Act 1 of *Manfred*, where Byron/Manfred is represented as an erratic and destroyed star, Hemans wonders in stanza 4 how such a figure could have been "shaken from thy radiant place" (16).

The eclipse of Byron thus becomes a lesson on a familiar theme: *sic transit gloria mundi*. That is the moral of the final stanza.

> Why, who shall talk of thrones, of sceptres riven?
> – Bow'd be our hearts to think of what *we* are,
> When from its height afar
> A world sinks thus – and yon majestic heaven
> Shines not the less for that one vanish'd star.   (21–25)

Although in one sense nothing could be more conventional, the stanza gains a special force by exploiting the female perspective the poem has adopted from the outset. These lines, Hemans's entire poem, speak with a double consciousness. Hemans knows very well that the heaven of poetry, like the world of thrones and scepters, is a place (and emblem) of male power. The figure of Merope stands for Byron, and in this frame of reference – as in Shelley's *Adonais* – all the signs stand for men. But because here the sign is resolutely feminized, a fresh set of views work themselves into the texture of the poem.

So Hemans is able to exploit Byron's notoriety, the scandal of his erotic life, to underscore the meaning of Merope as yet another figure of the fallen woman. More important, by placing her in a context where the central subject is poetic fame, "the lost Pleiad" becomes a sign of the poet – including the male poet – as woman. As Hemans's poem suggests, this feminine lightsource has never *not* been part of the "starry myriads" even though it has long been eclipsed, indeed mythically (eternally, ideologically) eclipsed.

We turn briefly to Mary Robinson to clarify what Hemans is insinuating here. Robinson's *Sappho and Phaon* is a crucial work of the period because its central points are so openly declared: that Homer need not be taken as the symbolic origin of western poetry, that another source – Sappho – might be assumed; and furthermore, that Sappho's fate, her eclipsed glory, should be read literally – as a betrayal (in every sense). Betrayed by love (the gods, Aphrodite), by her own passion, and finally by her male lover Phaon, Sappho and her mythic history become in Robinson's verse a modern myth of women's cultural inheritance.

From 1780 or so that myth becomes widespread in women's writing. The most modest and retiring of poets, Hemans writes out of its cultural perspective. But "The Lost Pleiad" shows how the sapphic myth need not be treated with the kind of passionate extravagance that Robinson cultivated in her verse. The strength of Hemans's poem lies in its reserve. Recalling the cool indifference of Byron's aggressively measured lyrics, Hemans softens Byron's edges. Indeed, she explicitly displaces that coldness to the realm of the "starry myriads," the familiar heavens of poetic tradition. In this sense Merope's is a fortunate fall since it removes her from that imaginative universe. Hemans's poem thereby fashions an alternative (feminine) aesthetic out of what now comes before us as an illusive spectacle of art. Her poem gives its allegiance to a sympathetic consciousness that is deliberately eclipsed when art commits itself to fame.

In this respect "The Lost Pleiad" is a reading of Byron – literally, a *sympathetic* reading, one that points to what she takes to be its true genius and lost soul. Furthermore, insofar as Byron appears in her poem as the very symbol and index of "the poetical," the reading amounts to a reading of the entire tradition of poetry as it descends to her age. What she comes to argue is no more and no less than this: "he who would save his life must lose it." Nursed in a long and deep experience of loss, "The Lost Pleiad" proposes an aesthetic of absolute contradiction. Canonized saints inhabit the heavens of poetry, by which the world sets its course and measures magnificence. Those are the saints of culture, the figures known through great traditions. To Hemans's view, however, there is another world "no more seen . . . of mortal eye." It is a world of absolute loss whose motto, in no Dantean sense, is simply: lasciate ogni speranza. Hemans writes that sign not above the entrance to hell, but over this world, its culture, its poetry.

In this kind of work, as in Charlotte Smith's, poetic failure ceases to be simply an available subject or theme; it becomes a textual event, a new foundational feature of imaginative work. Our customary framework for understanding this mordant turn in the history of poetry has been the emergence of enlightenment and the authority of science, which appeared to announce the supercession of poetry as a norm of culture. In that context, poets and their defenders were soon drawn into various rearguard actions, skirmishing to maintain whatever shreds of authority they could. Hemans's imagination of disaster, however, like the Russians before Napoleon, simply abandons all those traditional positions in order to follow the central insight of the sapphic myth of poetry as that myth gets developed through the emergent history of women's sentimental writing. The myth – a historical construction of the eighteenth century – is simple, eloquent, impossible: poetry is the discourse of failure. That is to say, it is the only discourse to preserve the theoretical power of absolute truth-telling. Through this poetry we become citizens of a scandalized world ("which is the world / Of all of us": *The Prelude* [1850] XI. 142–43): a kingdom divided against itself, a house built on sand.

It is no wonder, then, that high modernism set a face of flint against such endeavors. Thrones, principalities, powers, and dominions, religious as well as secular, build myths of perdurance and enlist figures of imagination to shore up their ruins and fragments. Sentimental writing tends to flee such projects, including – perhaps especially including – the projects that are most dear to itself. Hemans's work may be fairly defined in precisely those terms: witness, for example, a poem like "The Homes of England."

Landon's poetry executes the sapphic program even more clearly. This happens for two principal reasons, I think. First, her predominant subject is erotic love. Second, she foregrounds the commercial context of poetry and art. Much more traditional in this respect, Hemans displaces the latter subject into the discourse of fame, as one sees in a poem like "The Lost Pleiad." By contrast, Landon's poetry rarely forgets the Distinction now being critically re-explored by Pierre Bourdieu:[5] the symbiotic relation of cultural fame and marketing, poetic creation and the social production of texts. From that vision comes a peculiar and telling erosion of the romantic "I" and its historical substrate, the integral self.[6]

Like Smith and Hemans, Landon's writing is always tied to financial needs. If it is too much to say that all three "wrote for money," they all did need the money that their writing produced and they were forced to measure their work in commercial terms. Far more than Wordsworth, Laetitia Landon understood what it meant to live in the city of the Buildings of Loss, with its intense economies of getting and spending.

That knowledge determines the special character of her work, which always becomes what it beholds. And when her explicit subject is Art or Beauty, Landon delivers some shocking revelations to the ideologies of romanticism. As an instance I ask you to consider the piece she wrote for the 1829 *Keepsake*:[7] the untitled lines written after Landseer's portrait of *Georgiana, the Duchess of Bedford* ("Lady, thy face is very beautiful"). The central theme of this work is what the poem itself calls "vague imagination" (21). The phrase – at once threadbare and selfconscious – is tellingly chosen to rust through that bright new machine invented to turn out the pure products of romanticism.

As with so much of Landon's best writing, this work unfolds a kind of antipoem. The work selfconsciously exploits its own factitiousness. Much could be said about its mannered poeticality, the work's false elegancies, so reminiscent of Keats, that startle and disturb the reader from the outset – as the word "very" in the first line emphasizes. Here it is sufficient to see, and to say, that the poem properly exists in the closest kind of relation to the original picture, as Landon's socio-economic treatment of her subject emphasizes. Furthermore, in this case art's relation to the economics of class, so central to Landseer's painting, receives a full bourgeois reinscription.

The textual situation is subtle and complex. Proceeding from the semantic wordplay in line 19 ("But thou art of the Present"), we observe the relationship the work is fashioning, in every sense, between text and picture. For instance, at the semantic level the poem simultaneously reflects upon its nominal subject, the Duchess, and addresses its real subject, the "art of the Present."[8] For Landon's poem is not written on the Duchess or the painting so much as on the relation of the two. In this case the relation is signalled through two correlative forms: on one hand Landon's own verses, and on the other the visible language in which her poetry gets articulated – *The Keepsake* and its (reproduced) engraving.

Here one wants to recall the fact that Landseer's fame as an artist was largely secured through engravings that broadcast his work rather than through his original oils. The "Georgiana, the Duchess of Bedford" is "of the Present" in several senses, all of which are important to Landon. But most important are the contemporary artistic representations of the Duchess – the painting, the engraving, and now Landon's poem, the last two being framed and represented in *The Keepsake for* MDCCCXXIX, which is how the title page reads. Signifiers of Beauty, each comes forward here in a selfconscious, perhaps even a shameless, state of artistic exhaustion. Completely integrated, the engraving, the poem, and the book correspond to what Marx would shortly explore as "the commodity form," that is, value abstracted into a fetishized condition.[9] In Landon, the exponent of that structure of illusions is the work of art, which her poetry works to demystify.

In contrast to Marx, however, for whom critical analysis is a form of intellectual mastery, Landon demystifies through a process of sympathetic identification. As a rule, romantic writing tries to resist or escape the (shameful) condition that Landon's poem solicits. Wordsworth's reluctant and finally repudiated engagement with the same volume of *The Keepsake* measures a crucial difference between two otherwise closely related styles of poetry.[10] It equally measures the differential that romanticism sought to establish between itself and its feeding source, the discourse of sensibility and sentiment. Landon returns to that source via her immediate romantic inheritance. But her writing makes no effort to transcend its commercial circumstances. On the contrary, it becomes what it beholds, mortifying itself through its sympathetic involvement. Romanticism's faith in beauty and art – imagination as a means of grace – gets recovered by a paradoxical move. Through her writing romantic poetry regains authenticity by a profoundly sentimental act. Identifying itself as a commodified form, her poetry forecloses that final (romantic) illusion of art: that it lives in a world elsewhere.

Sentimental writing begins as a selfconscious appropriation of the wisdom of the body, the knowledge that comes through sympathetic understanding. It articulates "the true voice of feeling." Recall the differences between sentimental and romantic traditions of love poetry and their *stil novisti* and petrarchan precursors. The latter pursue a poetry of vision, an art tied to this world through an intimate relation with the highest and most spiritual of the senses (or so it was believed). Love is a vision of the beautiful. In sentimental writing, by contrast, the emblem of love is the kiss, where the authority of feeling and the lowest order of the senses asserts itself.

That assertion, however, involves no diminution of the powers of human intelligence. On the contrary, it argues for a deeper order of intelligence. For Charlotte Dacre, a kiss is the pre-eminent sign of what the age called Intellectual Beauty.

> The greatest bliss
> Is in a kiss –
> A kiss by love refin'd,
> When springs the soul

> Without controul,
> And blends the bliss with mind.
>
> For if desire
> Alone inspire,
> The kiss not *me* can charm;
> The eye must beam
> With *chasten'd* gleam
> That would my soul disarm.

This poem turns kissing to a philosophical event. An all but explicit argument is being made against the authority of genital erotics, with its dominantly instinctual dynamisms. Not that Dacre aims for an experience of order and control. Rather, what she imagines is a kind of deliberated ecstacy. For her, the kiss, and not sexual congress, becomes the sign of a love emanating from the willing soul, which moves to the rhythms of a conscious desire. In such a case, kissing determines the structure of the sexual experience, not vice versa.

From the 1780s the Paolo and Francesca episode comes to obsess the poets exactly because of the ethical and philosophical questions raised by the story and its images. In the *Commedia* the pilgrim Dante collapses in sympathy for the damned lovers, but the poet Dante means us to see that such sympathy involves a failure of vision and understanding. Indeed, it is a sympathy that fails precisely because it operates like the kiss of Paolo and Francesca – that is to say, instinctually. In Dante's imagination, a genital erotics determines this fatal kiss and hence seals the lovers' damnation. God's sympathy and love are more surely founded, just as His view of these acts is different from the untutored pilgrim's view. The *Commedia* is Dante's way of seeking to approach that higher view.

How different are the ways of sentimental and romantic poets. Not that they fail to grasp the ethical problems involved; but the lover's kiss now operates through a tradition complicated by the arguments and experiences of Rousseau, of Sterne, of Goethe. Once again we encounter a failure of love, only in this situation the failure is not a spiritual falling-off. Now, in a wholly secular sense, "the spirit is willing, but the flesh is weak":

> For the sword outwears its sheath,
> And the soul wears out the breast,
> And the heart must pause to breathe,
> And love itself have rest.
>
> (Byron, "So We'll Go No More A-roving," 5–8)

In this famous passage the word "soul" stands closer to our late twentieth-century meaning than to Dante's. It is a meaning Byron appropriated from writers like Smith and Robinson.

In sentimental writing sympathy is both of and with the body. The *Songs of Innocence* take Jesus as a model of love just because he appears so mortal and even helpless – in the figures Blake took from sentimentalism itself, like a child or a woman. Much romantic verse will seek to reimagine this fragility as triumphant strength – witness *Prometheus Unbound*. What I am pointing to here, however, is a contrary spirit altogether, one committed to disempowerment, to the order of the losers and the death-devoted.

This way of writing finds poetry an inevitable resort from the grand illusions entered through enlightenment and science. In this respect it is a poetical theory and practice firmly located in history – indeed, its theory and practice make historicality, with all its nontranscendental features, a defining quality of the poetical. Romanticism feeds upon this theory, but only to raise up cries of resistance, or to build temples in excremental places. Sentimental poetry, by contrast, brings all of its illusions, including its lost illusions, down to earth.

One encounters this work most surely through the developing line of women's writing, in Great Britain particularly: beyond Hemans and Landon to Christina Rossetti, Charlotte Mew, Veronica Forrest-Thomson. But their names are legion. The continuity of sentimental verse, whether in its secular or its Christian modes, is unmistakeable to anyone who has thought about it. One can scarcely *not* see the similarities between a postmodern writer like Forrest-Thomson, for example, and a postromantic writer like Landon. Forrest-Thomson teases us into thought of these parallels throughout her work: her poem "Strike," for example (which comes written "*for Bonnie, my first horse*"):

> Hail to thee, blithe horse, bird thou never wert!
> And breaking into a canter, I set off on the long road south
> Which was to take me to so many strange places,
> That room in Cambridge, that room in Cambridge, that room
> in Cambridge,
> That room in Cambridge, this room in Cambridge . . .[11]

Like Landon, Forrest-Thomson sets out for poetry by going to the proper cultural places. Where Landon went to Byron and Keats, this Scots writer "canters" south to England and university – again like

Landon, playing fast and loose with the master language (canting, chanting):

> I was on some sort of quest.
> There was an I-have-been-here-before kind of feeling about it.
> That hateful cripple with the twisted grin. But
> Dauntless the slughorn to my ear I set.

The poem travesties the entire British tradition, travesties – like Landon yet once more – the deadly (so far as poetry is concerned) concept of "tradition" itself. What remains from such grim and comical emptyings? Nothing but the poetry and the human life it signs:

> What there is now to celebrate:
> The only art where failure is reknowned.

NOTES

1 My reading differs slightly, I think, from one intimated to me by Nan Sweet, in a correspondence we have had. Sweet emphasizes both Shelley and Byron as important presences in the poem. I am grateful to her for sharing her knowledge of the poem with me, and in particular for important facts about its publication history. See also Sweet's essay "History, Imperialism, and the Aesthetics of the Beautiful: Hemans and the Post-Napoleonic Moment," in *At the Limits of Romanticism: Essays in Cultural, Feminist, and Materialist Criticism*, ed. Mary A. Favret and Nicola J. Watson (Bloomington and Indianapolis: Indiana University Press, 1994), 170–84.

2 See Tricia Lootens, "Hemans and Home: Victorianism, Feminine 'Internal Enemies,' and the Domestication of National Identity," *PMLA* 109 (March 1994): 238–53.

3 The decline in Byron's reputation was explicitly commented upon at the time, and Byron himself was quite aware of it, as many scholars have noted. See for example Samuel C. Chew's *Byron in England* (John Murray: London, 1924): "The Anti-Byronism that so quickly overtook the poet's posthumous reknown is here [in 1823] definitely beginning in his lifetime" (117). See also Herman M. Ward, *Byron and the Magazines, 1806–1824*, Salzburg Studies in English Literature: Romantic Reassessment 19 (Universitat Salzburg: Salzburg, 1973), esp. chapter v.

4 In a letter to me Anne Mellor suggests that one ought to read "Byron" as Merope's beloved, Cyrus, with the implication that Merope is Hemans's self-projection. And of course that structure of reading is also operating in the text. My point is that Hemans's identification with Merope comes "through" a mythic structure that has been gendered from the outset in masculinist terms, and that she understands that structure and exploits it in her poem.

5 Bourdieu's project has been elaborated through a whole series of books and essays; see in particular his decisive *Distinction: A Social Critique of the Judgement of Taste*, trans. Richard Nice (Cambridge, Mass.: Harvard University Press, 1984).

6 For useful discussions of Landon in this general frame of reference, see Mellor, *Romanticism and Gender* (New York: Routledge, 1993), 110–23; Glennis Stephenson's essay "Poet Construction: Mrs Hemans, L.E.L., and the Image of the Nineteenth-Century Woman Poet," in Shirley Neuman and Glennis Stephenson, eds., *Reimagining Women: Representations of Women and Culture* (Toronto: University of Toronto Press, 1993), 61–73; and see also Sonia Hofkosh's "Disfiguring Economies: Mary Shelley's Short Stories," in Audrey A. Fisch, Anne K. Mellor, and Esther H. Schor, eds., *The Other Mary Shelley: Beyond Frankenstein* (New York: Oxford University Press, 1993), esp. 204–08, for a good succinct treatment of the aesthetic economies of the Gift Book.

7 This is the volume of the *Keepsake* in which Wordsworth, Coleridge, Southey, and Moore, among other notables, were induced to publish by its editor (and friend of Wordsworth) Frederick Mansel Reynolds. Peter Manning's essay on Wordsworth's involvement with the 1829 volume is thorough and important, showing as it does the sharp difference between Landon's and Wordsworth's involvement in the book (see "Wordsworth in the *Keepsake* of 1829," in *Literature in the Marketplace*, ed. John O. Jordan and Robert L. Patten [Cambridge: Cambridge University Press, 1995], 44–73). Whereas Landon's work is thoroughly integrated into the conventions of the annual, Wordsworth's is not – indeed, he had to be coaxed to participate (although he did so, like everyone else, for clear commercial motives). Unlike Landon, however, Wordsworth could not make the commercialization of his work a thematic part of his writing. But this is exactly what Landon does. The aftermath of his involvement left Wordsworth with a sense that he had done something sordid by letting his work appear in the pages of the *Keepsake*. Interestingly, I think Coleridge's contributions to the annual are much more integrated to its conventions – especially that strange and neglected piece "The Garden of Boccaccio," which Coleridge wrote to "illustrate" an engraving given him by Reynolds.

8 That kind of cross-grammatical aural wordplay is quite common in Landon's work. The most dramatic example I suppose is her characteristic triple pun "eye/I/aye," which recurs in her verse (see for example "A Child Screening a Dove from a Hawk").

9 See the first volume of *Capital*, chapters I–III, and esp. chapter I, Section 3, parts C and D, and Section 4.

10 See above, note 7.

11 Veronica Forrest Thomson, *Collected Poems and Translations*, Agneau 2 (London, Lewes, Berkeley: Allardyce, Barnett, 1990), 84.

Index